POLYCENTRIC
MONARCHIES

POLYCENTRIC MONARCHIES

How did Early Modern Spain and
Portugal Achieve and Maintain
a Global Hegemony?

Edited by Pedro Cardim, Tamar Herzog,
José Javier Ruiz Ibáñez and Gaetano Sabatini

REGIÓN DE MURCIA
fundación**séneca**
AGENCIA REGIONAL DE CIENCIA Y TECNOLOGÍA

Centro de História de Além-Mar
CHAM
Universidade Nova de Lisboa
Faculdade de Ciências Sociais e Humanas
Universidade dos Açores

sussex
ACADEMIC
PRESS

Brighton • Portland • Toronto

RED COLUMNARIA

Individual chapter contributions copyright © Sussex Academic Press, 2012. Introduction and editorial organization of this volume copyright © Pedro Cardim, Tamar Herzog, José Javier Ruiz Ibáñez and Gaetano Sabatini, 2012.

The right of Pedro Cardim, Tamar Herzog, José Javier Ruiz Ibáñez and Gaetano Sabatini to be identified as Editors of this work has been asserted in accordance with the Copyright, Designs and Patents Act 1988.

2 4 6 8 10 9 7 5 3 1

First published in 2012 in Great Britain by
SUSSEX ACADEMIC PRESS
P.O. Box 139
Eastbourne BN24 9BP

and in the United States of America by
SUSSEX ACADEMIC PRESS
920 NE 58th Ave.   Suite 300
Portland, Oregon 97213–3786

and in Canada by
SUSSEX ACADEMIC PRESS (CANADA)
8000 Bathurst Street, Unit 1, PO Box 30010, Vaughan, Ontario L4J 0C6

British Library Cataloguing in Publication Data
A CIP catalogue record for this book is available from the British Library.

Library of Congress Cataloging-in-Publication Data
Polycentric monarchies : how did early modern Spain and Portugal achieve and maintain a global hegemony? / edited by Pedro Cardim . . . [et al.].
    p. cm.
Includes bibliographical references and index.
ISBN 978-1-84519-544-1 (h/b : acid-free paper)
    1. Spain—History—House of Austria, 1516–1700. 2. Portugal—History—Spanish dynasty, 1580–1640. 3. Imperialism—History—16th century. 4. Imperialism—History—17th century. I. Cardim, Pedro.
DP171.P65 2012
325'.346009031—dc23
                                                                2012010932

Typeset and designed by Sussex Academic Press, Brighton & Eastbourne.
Printed by TJ International, Padstow, Cornwall.
This book is printed on acid-free paper.

Contents

Red Columnaria

Columnaria (www.redcolumnaria.com) is a scholarly network, created in 2004 in order to facilitate communication and collaboration among researchers interested in the Iberian worlds in Europe, the Americas, Asia and Africa. Built of several independent groups that are organized thematically or regionally, it nevertheless ensures constant contact and exchange between members. Its principal aim is to overcome national and nationalistic historiographies as well as language barriers by facilitating international collaboration. It also wishes to mobilize a sufficient number of historians so to allow a global analysis of the past. Because of its particular structure, Columaria is both local and global, allowing for an analysis that — like the network itself — is focused on specific locations, as well as on a wider history on a global scale.

At the present, Columnaria includes historians from some fourteen countries. It has organized and sponsored over one hundred colloquiums, conferences, seminars, and expositions, and had been involved in publishing some thirty books, its activities mainly taking place in Spain, Portugal, Italy, Mexico and Brazil. It has annual meetings that were celebrated in Spain (2005, 2006, 2010 and 2012), Mexico (2007), Italy (2008), Portugal (2009), and Brazil (2011). The 2012 meeting is scheduled for Spain and the 2013 for Peru. The activities of Columnaria were generously supported by the Séneca Foundation, and the autonomous region of Murcia, Spain, as well as local universities, entities and municipalities where activities took place. It is currently coordinated by the four editors of this volume, whose aim is to showcase what Columnaria is and what it wishes to achieve.

Editors'
Acknowledgments

The editors of this volume would like to thank the Fundación Séneca (Agencia de Ciencia y Tecnología — Región de Murcia) and, most particularly, its director Antonio González Valverde, for their continuous support, as well as for the financial aid for the translation and editing of this book. Pedro Cardim's contribution is part of a research carried out within the following two projects "A comunicação política na monarquia pluricontinental portuguesa (1580–1808): Reino, Atlântico e Brasil," a research project directed by Nuno Gonçalo Monteiro in the Instituto de Ciências Sociais da Universidade de Lisboa, Lisbon and funded by Fundação para a Ciência e a Tecnologia (PTDC/HHIS-HIS/098928/2008) and "*Propaganda y Representación. Lucha Política, Cultura de Corte y Aristocracia en el Siglo de Oro Ibérico,*" a research project directed by Fernando Bouza Álvarez at the Universidad Complutense, Madrid, funded by the Ministerio de Ciencia e Innovación, Spain (HAR2008-03678/HIST). Gaetano Sabatini's contribution was supported by two research projects: "La corte virreinal de Nápoles en la Monarquía de los Austrias: recursos materiales y representación del poder" (HUM2004-04062), Ministerio de Educación y Ciencia, Spain and "Mercanti portoghesi e circuiti finanziari nella Monarchia spagnola, 1580-1640," (DSSGA, 2008-2010), Università degli Studi Roma TRE, Italy.

Deserving special thanks are Ana Díaz Serrano and Daneo Flores Aranciva who, over the years, dedicated time, energy, and patience to see Columnaria born, grow and flourish. Gratitude is also due to Paul Kersey, who translated many of the chapters of this book. Last but not least, we would like to acknowledge the help, assistance, and guidance of Anthony Grahame, Editorial Director at Sussex Academic Press.

Introduction

Polycentric Monarchies
How Did Early Modern Spain and Portugal Achieve and Maintain a Global Hegemony?

Pedro Cardim, Tamar Herzog,
José Javier Ruiz Ibáñez, and
Gaetano Sabatini

Having succeeded in establishing their presence throughout Europe, Asia, Africa and the Americas, in the early sixteenth century Spain and Portugal became the first imperial powers on a worldwide scale. Between 1580 and 1640, the period in which these two entities formed a union, they achieved an almost global hegemony. Though they lost their political primacy in the seventeenth century, the two monarchies survived and continued to enjoy relative success until the early 1800s; indeed, their cultural and political legacies persist in many countries around the world even today. The aim of this collection is to answer two essential questions: how and why was this possible?

Historians who have studied the Spanish and Portuguese monarchy in the past have done one of two things. They have either written the history of Spain, Portugal, Italy, the Americas (and so forth) separately, or they envisioned a "composite monarchy" with clearly defined domineering centers (Madrid and Lisbon) and a series of subjected, subaltern kingdoms, entities or cities. The first limited their analysis to tracing the histories of present-day states. Applying anachronistic reading to a past that was different from our present, they adopted a national narrative to describe a period, in which most historians would deny the existence of nations. While for the first group of historians the history of the Spanish and Portuguese monarchies became the sum of many separate national histories, for the integrants of the second group it could be reproduced by using as a model the modern state. The composite monarchy they imagined was, on most accounts, an entity, which depended on dynamic relations between a center and periphery and which, whether openly confessing it or not, could also be assimilated to some degree to nineteenth- and twentieth-century colonialism. Under this guise, the history of both monarchies became the narrative of a relationship between the king on the one hand, local elites on the other. This history stressed the role of clientelism, the fierce defense of local autonomy, and the importance of constant negotiations. According to this portrait, "true" politics only occurred in Madrid and Lisbon, while the periphery (i.e., everywhere else) was a mere receptor that could accept or reject what the center had to offer, but in no way actively participated in the making of politics on a global scale. Because colonialism was involved, either the Monarchies' territories in Africa, Asia and the Americas were studied separately from the European domains, or European domains were integrated into the whole by an analysis that argued for the existence of an "internal colonialism," somewhat similar to the "external" one. Because most historians have envisioned the historical experience of the Spanish and Portuguese monarchies in this way, they rarely questioned what their structure was, how European, African, Asian and American territories were held together and which were the mechanisms that allowed them to expand so quickly and so widely, and to maintain their hegemony over time.

The editors and contributors of this book propose a radically different model. Rather than portraying the Iberian Monarchies as the accumulation of many bilateral relations arranged in a radial pattern, they argue that these political entities were polycentric, that is, that they allowed for the existence of many different interlinked centers that interacted not only with the king but also among themselves, thus actively participating in forging the polity. Rather than national, proto-national, or "colonial," they were multi-territorial. Because they included such distinct units as the different kingdoms of Spain, the Low Countries, the Holy Roman Empire, several city-states in Italy and Portugal, as well as many overseas territories in Asia, Africa and the Americas, they were both stable and unstable. The constant negotiation, contacts and competition between their different sub-units and the continuous change in the political weight of each territory, guaranteed that, despite permanence, the internal structure of both monarchies was highly mobile. Constantly shifting, this complex geometry created a political structure that was simultaneously both solid and durable on the one hand, malleable and changing on the other. Internal unity was not maintained by coercion alone. It mostly depended on a general adhesion to a discourse of loyalty to King and religion. By maintaining doctrinal loyalty to Rome, incorporating many of the traditional functions of the Church and much of its personnel, and absorbing the principal of active religious militancy (with its corollaries, such as intolerance of dissidence), Iberian kings thus endowed their crowns with a new meaning. The ensuing period of extreme violence that was unleashed in the sixteenth century created a context that propitiated the appropriation of these conceptions not only by elites in Europe and Americas, but also by entire populations. While the kings developed mechanisms of territorial incorporation, ecclesiasts working for them elaborated on the universalism of their power.

If religion and loyalty to king were important, also extremely essential to success was the promise (and often the granting) of greater social, economic, cultural and political opportunities to local populations, now inserted into a larger, almost global, structure. Social and spatial mobility was considerable, and so were the possible rewards. The incorporation of territories to the Monarchy, in short, offered individuals, families, groups, corporations and entities multiple opportunities. And, although differences existed between every and each domain, the territories of the monarchy could not be easily classified into a dichotomy of center versus periphery, colonies versus non-colonies, European versus African, Asian and American domains.

In order to present this polyhedral vision of the Iberian Monarchies, this collection of essays includes several case studies of concrete territorial entities, interpreted and understood *within* the wider context of the Monarchy. A principal argument is that although it is impossible to understand the whole without analyzing the specifics of place and time, no region of the Monarchy can be studied without considering the other regions. Thus, although the authors of individual essays are all experts of a region or a place, they all engage in a global reading of local history in order to both historicize and de-nationalize (as well as de-essentialize) their particular histories. Together, they argue that, beyond differences — which were often important — all units of the Monarchy considered themselves (and indeed were to some degree) centers, and all adhered to common practices and guidelines as they watched and emulated (or not), one another. Nontwithstanding our wish to advance our concrete knowledge of early modern Spanish and Portuguese monarchies, our ultimate goal is to demonstrate how histories focused on current nation-states and current conceptions of colonialism have obscured our understanding of the past.

Avoiding anachronistic reading, collectively, the authors of this volume also argue for the need to decipher what "success" and "failure" meant during the early modern period. Rather than comparing the Iberian Monarchies to other European models (mainly Britain) or judging their performance according to modern criteria such as the degree by which they achieved the formation of a rational, bureaucratic administration, they insist that historians need to reconstruct the way contemporaries understood and judged events. That today we think that the structures of the past were inadequate is much less important than understanding how individuals, groups, and political entities belonging to the Iberian monarchies framed their goals, sought out to accomplish them, and whether they achived their aims. Such an analysis would reveal that certain aspects that were traditionally considered signs of poor functioning or even failure were, in reality, elements of strength that allowed the governing of such far-flung domains. Under this guise, jurisdictional conflicts were not exceptions but instead the norm. They were means assuring both the inclusion of local interests and the neutralization of centripetal tensions.

At stake, therefore, is the need to study concrete practices that would allow identifying the elements upon which the Iberian Monarchies based their expansion and success or, said differently, understanding what the diverse territories stood to win or lose, change or conserve, by being included in these larger hegemonic structures. A comprehensive history of the Iberian Monarchies, in short, should not outline what was happening in the court, but how an imperial reality was built on an everyday and local level. Having debated these issues in several meetings (sponsored by *Red Columnaria*, a research network based in Murcia, Spain, but covering — like the Monarchies it studies — the globe), the authors now wish to share their conclusions with a larger audience.

The book is organized in three parts that observe the Iberian Monarchies as territorial constructions: **Part I — Spaces of Integration; Part II — Spaces of Circulation**; and **Part III — External Projections**. The first four chapters that make up Part I (Schaub, Mazín, Cardim and Bentes Monteiro) examine the integration of different territories into the monarchical network. Schaub demonstrates the profound overlapping between Spanish, Portuguese and local institutions in the Azores. There, he argues, polycentrism was reproduced because purportedly a Portuguese territory, its incorporation within the Hispanic monarchy allowed different powers obeying diverse interests to compete locally, making local society truly hybrid. Experiencing both moments of convergence and instances of separation and conflict, the Azores both belonged to the Monarchy and defended its individuality at the same time. Mazín demonstrates how different centers belonging to the Spanish monarchy competed with one another regarding their respective prominence. Hoping for royal approval, they also observed the situation of other centers, ensuring that they were not preferred to them without a just cause. Preference depended on multiple factors, but it was ultimately sanctioned by the king. It could vary over time, as witnessed by the gradual rise of the Americas within the Spanish structures and the parallel demise of the Low Countries. If Mazín cares for polycentrism in Madrid, Cardim speaks about these issues in Lisbon. The Portuguese parliament (*Cortes*), he argues, was an assembly of cities that together may have represented the kingdom, but that individually sought to defend each its own interest. Competing with one another on seating and allocation, these cities depended on the king to grant them what they considered their proper place in the hierarchy that made these disparate units into a kingdom and a monarchy. And, although initially the place of overseas territories in the assembly was not guaranteed, eventually it included representatives, albeit only a few, from Asia and Brazil. Bentes Monteiro also describes the multicentric body politic of the Portuguese monarchy by focusing on both royal efforts to reconstruct it in the aftermaths of the independence of Portugal (1640) and local reaction (in Bahia, Brazil). Bahia, he argues, found its place in this complex political structure by both ties of affection and making important and painful (economic) sacrifices.

All four cases demonstrate the degree by which insertion in the larger polity allowed on the one hand the emergence of both the monarchy as a whole, and, on the other, greatly modified local society. Collaboration, in short, may well have been consubstantial to the existence and development of the Monarchy, but it was also central to the political culture and practices that emerged locally. Tensions between a global discourse of allegiance and local needs were continuous but rather than weakening the Monarchies, they fortified them.

The Iberian monarchies were also spaces for circulation of people, money, institutions, and ideas (see the next five contributions by Soria, Sabatini, De Luca, Zúñiga, Herzog and Pardo that form **Part II**). Soria examines intermarriage between individuals of different localities across Spain. He demonstrates that the circulation of administrators, soldiers, and ecclesiastics, named by the king to serve in posts located outside their region of birth, brought about a gradual consolidation of transregional and transnational groups, which were tied to one another by family and friendship ties, but were also linked to the court. Sabatini studies how Portuguese bankers in Naples were able to connect the different centers of the monarchy through their economic activities. Dependent on the king in Madrid, but also on development in other parts of the Iberian peninsula, as well as in Naples and elsewhere in Italy and Europe, they constructed a network that depended on their individual capabilities, their contacts with high officials, their local position, as well as the enormous political space to which they now belonged. The absence of any of these factors, Sabatini argues, would make their position frail. Indeed, an unwelcoming viceroy, or the uprising in Portugal — that was sought to compromise their loyalty— could easily bring them down, as indeed it did. Studying the local economy in Milan, De Luca demonstrates that debt created relations not only between individual creditors and debtors but also between a large public of creditors and the state, which lent money through the issuing of public debt. Explaining that the economic blossoming of the city during the sixteenth and the seventeenth century was at least partially due to its insertion in the Spanish Monarchy, he analyzes how local society reacted to the monarchy's need of income by adopting innovative economic instruments and methods. Becoming creditor of the king ensured its loyalty. After all, it could not rebel against a Monarchy that owed its institutions and particulars so much money in such advantageous terms. Yet, in the process of lending, local society was greatly modified:

new social stratification emerged, collaboration between the different units and localities of the dutchy was assured, new economic activities took place, and a new understanding of money and credit slowly appeared. The emergence of new groups that circulated widely within the Monarchy while sustaining it was thus central to the survival of both the locality and the whole. Yet the fate of such individuals was also tied to that of their particular territory: when Portugal separated from Spain, the Vaz of Naples were doomed (Sabatini). In order to avoid such bad fortune, the creditors of Milan remained loyal (De Luca).

Moving to the realm of ideas, Zúñiga demonstrates how notions of social and racial classification travelled in space, creating a homogeneizing affect, yet also allowing for local interpretations. The movement of people between different centers of the Monarchy thus spread certain shared preoccupations, but it did not guarantee that all responses would be identical. Herzog demonstrates how, in the process of being projected on a global scale, the meaning of Spanishness (and foreignness) has universalized. Rather than being dependent on place of origin or descent as has been the case before, it now designated adherence to a common religion and a culture that, theoretically, all those included in the Monarchy shared. Pardo demonstrates that also shared among the inhabitants of the Monarchy was a political culture and a political discourse that tied the different units to the ensemble.

Together, these six essays in **Part II** argue that, parallel to the persistence of frontiers between the different units of the Monarchies, an articulated, polycentric network also existed, supporting the diffusion and exchange of people, goods and ideas. An important element in guaranteeing the success of these political bodies, this circulation allowed the day-to-day construction of shared (as well as differentiated) practices and gave the king the political, ideological and economic support he needed. It also ensured the existence of a wide variety of individuals and groups who tied their fate and fortune to the continuation and success of the Monarchy, and it allowed contemporaries to view the territory as a whole, rather than as the simple accumulation of units.

Finally, the last two chapters (Herrero and Ruiz Ibáñez — making up **Part III**) question the outer limits of the Iberian monarchies by demonstrating both their porous nature as well as the importance of exterior projection to their success or failure. Herrero demonstrates that the integration of local elites in the Monarchy could extend beyond its political borders and include the leading sectors of the so-called mercantile republics that, despite current day appreciations, were not radically different in their orientation or structures than the Monarchy itself. Not only Milan and Naples (as De Luca and Sabatini demonstrate) but also Genoa and the United Provinces were tied to and thus dramatically affected by the Monarchy, as a result both belonging and not belonging to it at the same time. According to Ruiz Ibáñez, because of its commitment to defend Catholicism, the Spanish king could send soldiers to Paris and take part in what was essentially a local political and religious power struggle. That French historiography has portrayed this episode as a foreign conquest is one thing. That it truly was is another. Indeed, seen from the perspective of contemporaries, the presence of Spanish troops in Paris was not an external occupation, but the affirmation of a world hegemony that could aid locals (or be rejected by them) according to the case.

Instead of framing their analysis in terms of "the (heavy) cost of empire," as historians have done in the past, both Herrero and Ruiz Ibáñez thus suggest that the reputation of the king and monarchical commitment to certain policies, as well as the cooptation of territories which were not quite under his control, were vital to the survival of the Monarchy. This projection to the exterior included longstanding alliances that supported rebellious populations (as in Paris) or consolidated economic networks (as in the mercantile republics) through both dependence and symbiosis.

Polycentric Monarchies is more than just a chosen title. It represents a proposal to interpret the past differently, calling into question many of the assumptions historians until now have taken for granted. Insisting on the differences between present and past, it proposes a post-national history that rejects both a center — periphery analysis as well as a preliminary separation between a metropolis and colonies. It suggests instead that if we wish to understand the expansion and success (as well as eventual failure) of Iberian Monarchies, we must inquire on the relations between local and global dynamics by constructing a truly internationalized historiography that, without scarifying the particularities of place and time, also cares about what is common and repetitive. The history of the Iberian Monarchies, we sustain, is above all the history of the protagonists who lived in it and, often, suffered the consequences.

PART I

Spaces of Integration

Maritime Archipelago, Political Archipelago

The Azores under the Habsburgs (1581–1640)

1

Jean-Frédéric Schaub

If both the Spanish and Portuguese monarchies began as polycentric political-institutional systems, this character became even more pronounced during the period of their union, from 1581 to 1640.[1] From the moment Philip II was sworn in as King of Portugal and until the Lisbon uprising of December 1640, the two monarchies constituted together the most extensive empire that history had known up to that moment. The rules governing their merger were defined by the chapters elaborated at the Cortes of Tomar.[2] In all fields of jurisdictional, governmental and commercial activity, the Portuguese monarchy enjoyed complete autonomy from its Spanish partner. Though Lisbon had lost its status as a courtly city, it never ceased to function as a capital and as the seat of the Portuguese highest tribunals and Councils and it continued to act as one of the centers of the empire. Indeed, some locals even thought that it would be plausible to convince the kings of Spain and Portugal to move their capital from El Escorial near Madrid to the city of the Tajo (Lisbon).[3]

Because of this constitutional structure, all matters concerning the colonies — i.e., anything and everything that had to do with Portugal's overseas settlements — were managed by Portuguese jurisdictional organs. Among them were the tribunals in Lisbon and the Council of Portugal, which assisted the king wherever he went.[4] In the Azores, a Portuguese Atlantic archipelago, the union between Spain and Portugal nevertheless implied the presence of Castile in the form of a military garrison (*presidio*). In principal, the institutional relations between the officers of the garrison and the local authorities on the islands were based on the same principles as the accords of Tomar. Nevertheless, the Spanish soldiers deployed on the island of Terceira answered exclusively to the military jurisdiction, and all governmental and economic matters regarding the island were the responsibility of the Council of War in Madrid and the Captain-General of Portugal in Lisbon. The local Portuguese militia was disbanded at an early date (1583–1589), leaving the Spanish contingent as the only military presence until 1589, when the Crown decided to reestablish native militias as a means of strengthening the island's defenses.

In the late sixteenth and early seventeenth century, Portuguese imperial policy did not yet follow one unique and coherent political and institutional pattern or model.[5] No specific overseas tribunal existed, because the *Conselho da Índia* in Lisbon, formed under the authority of the Habsburgs in 1607, only operated until 1614.[6] As a result, the Lusitanian character of the Portuguese empire (and its distinction from the Spanish empire) was preserved through other means, including, for example, the diffusion of a distinct written culture and a broad web of commercial interests.[7]

This chapter deals with a case that may seem rather marginal: the Azores Islands during the union of the crowns. In the early seventeenth century, this Atlantic archipelago was a minor element in the fabric of the empire, especially when compared to the declining *Estado da Índia* and a flourishing Brazil. Yet, thanks to the ocean currents and the strong winds, during the Early Modern period the Azores played a strategic role in protecting sea routes for ships that returned to the continent from America, Asia and Africa.[8] What happened in the islands during the union of the crowns and, more particularly, between 1590 and 1642, has so far won no scholarly attention. The objective of this chapter is to present a few key elements for the elaboration of such a history.

The focus will be the island of Terceira, which performed the most important strategic function because of its sheltered port of Angra. Terceira is also the best described island in historical documentation from the Habsburg period. Following a description of the sources available for historical research and a general analysis of the main features of the Habsburg period, we will identify how the union played out in that space, mainly by observing the sources of authority and arbitrage through the analysis of a few local disputes.

Sources for the History of Azores during the Union

Until the present, no systematic account of the political processes taking place in Azores' society during the union has been published. Referring exclusively to the case of the island of Terceira, its two most known chroniclers or compilers, the late seventeenth century Father Manuel Luís Maldonado (1644–1711), and the erudite Francisco Ferreira Drummond (1796–1858), barely scraped together two marginally coherent accounts, both of which are plagued with significant gaps.[9] Between 1878 and 1892, Ernesto do Canto (1831–1900) published a collection of sources for the history of the archipelago in twelve volumes under the title *Arquivo dos Açores*.[10] Given the patriotic fervor of those years, the Habsburg period is mentioned primarily in documents related to the resistance movement against Philip II that emerged on Terceira in 1581–1583, and the *Bragancista* Restoration (1641–1642), with only very few documents pertaining to the intervening years. If published sources are scarce, even more so original documents. By the seventeenth century, the documentation that should have been preserved on the archipelago, especially on Terceira, had largely disappeared. Undoubtedly, the best sources salvaged are found in the island's parish registries, which provide an impressive amount of information on the local society.[11] These circumstances explain why Maldonado, the island's first chronicler, felt so much more at ease when tracing the genealogies of the principal families than in his attempt to elucidate Terceira's political-institutional evolution.[12] Thanks to another scholar and genealogist, Friar Diogo das Chagas, however, we do have accurate lists of the Castilian field marshals and Portuguese *corregidores* of the period, though they provide little more than a broad outline.[13]

The writing of Terceira's history began when Avelino de Freitas de Meneses systematically explored the *Guerra Antigua y Moderna* ("Old and Modern War") and *Estado* ("State") sections at the General Archives of Simancas in Spain.[14] It than became clear that because of the fundamental importance of the Castilian garrisons established at Angra do Heroísmo, San Sebastião and Praia da Vitória, the administrative correspondence that this presence generated could shed light on the history of the islands in ways that neither local sources, not even the documentation of royal tribunals in Portugal, could.[15] Freitas de Meneses' work covers the first ten years of the union, but leaves the other fifty years untouched. It was not until 2008 that a collective study of the history of the Azores finally included a chapter based on the records in Simancas, which had been digitalized by the *Instituto Açoriano de Cultura*.[16] These records, taken from the sections labeled *Guerra Antigua* ("Old War") and *Contadurías Mayores de Cuentas* ("Principal Accounting Offices"), cover the final two decades of the sixteenth century and the period between 1600 and 1616, with some references that extend beyond this timeline.[17] Yet, although research on the *Guerra* series at Simancas has been systematic, it has tended to emphasize the island's fortifications. Nonetheless, digitalized documents and summaries of others related to the Azores not yet digitalized also deal with the crises and conflicts that occurred on the islands during these years. Furthermore, while most municipal documentation from Angra has disappeared, including both the *vereações* (municipal council acts) and the *registos* (letters received),[18] these types of documents were preserved much better at the villas of San Sebastião and Praia da Vitória, the city of Horta on the island of Fayal, and Ponta Delgada on São Miguel.[19] These records, and especially letters sent to cities on the archipelago from the Court or Lisbon, contain important information.

The Essential Characteristics of the Period

At the present stage of research, it is impossible to give a detailed account of the political events that had occurred on the islands during the Habsburg period. As mentioned above, such an account would depend on documentation that becomes abundant only during moments of tension or open crisis. Rather than reproducing normality, it reflects the alarms that were set off in the jurisdictional and governmental systems of both Madrid and Lisbon when peace and harmony on the Azores were in peril. For these reasons, caution must be exercised when attempting to elaborate a global narrative of the period from the sources we currently have. Prudence, however, should not impede us from extracting some information from the archival materials that were produced during times of conflict, and use them in order to observe what hid beyond the disputes themselves.

Terceira was the Portuguese territory that fought most fiercely against the ascension of Philip II, and was the last one to recognize him as its legitimate monarch.[20] The island was virtually divided into two sections: one that followed the project of dom António prior do Crato, Philip II's chief rival; and another that from the very outset placed its destiny in the hands of the Spanish king who took his oath at the *Cortes* of Tomar in 1581.[21] Not only was the island divided but the entire Europe witnessed António's attempt to undertake the reconquest of Portugal from his base on Terceira, with the support of Portuguese fleets that were hostile to the Spanish Monarchy. Spain's takeover of the island was met with a wave of condemnations that left an

indelible mark throughout the period.[22] Nonetheless, it is clear that the memory of
dom António was still very alive in the decade of 1620–1630 when his son, dom
Manuel, attempted to equip a fleet and return to the Azores.[23] Whatever the case was,
in the mid-1580s, the governors of the Castilian garrison on the Terceira were only
able to establish peaceful relations with the local society after they issued a general
amnesty for all those involved in the recent rebellion.[24]

With the granting of power to the first military governor of the Azores don Juan
de Urbina in 1583, Spain began to erect a political system, in which military commanders intervened in elections to the municipal councils (*cabildos*). Not much is known
about how this happened. Systematic research into the administrative documentation
of the period and review of the historiography available on the topic demonstrate that
no definitive institutional scheme — or even one minimally consolidated — ever
prevailed during the reign of the Habsburgs. As a result, until the present, not even
the best historians have succeeded in their efforts to sketch a simple, but solid, framework that would allow to delineate the exact boundaries of different authorities
working locally, such as the Chambers of Angra and Ponta Delgada, the *donatário*
captain, the judge (*ouvidor*) of the said captain, the *corregidor* of the Azores, the armys'
suppliers, the bishop, and the Castilian military governor, to name just the most
important ones.[25] Nor is it entirely clear what competencies the tribunals in Lisbon,
the Captain General of Portugal, the Viceroys or governors of Lisbon, and the
Councils of War in Madrid and Portugal enjoyed with respect to the Azores. Though
this ignorance may be a reflection of the nature of the documentation we have (and
we lack), a much more probable hypothesis is that an overlapping of boundaries was
in reality the political-institutional norm of Ancient Regime societies. But what stands
out in the case of the Azores was the speed with which an overseas society that had
existed for fewer than one hundred and fifty years had developed — by the early seventeenth century — such a complex institutional stratigraphy. The archipelago's
administrative system was, in fact, the product of a succession of institutional layers
that accumulated over the years without the later strata ever completely abolishing the
earlier ones.

The different powers on the island of Terceira rested in the hands of its most
important families: the Cantos, Castros, Bethencourts, Ferreria de Melos and
Pamplonas, among others. Avelino de Freitas de Meneses described that system in the
following terms, right on the eve of the arrival of the Spanish authorities:

> The holders of power in towns were the people in the government, that is, local nobility. The
> law usually restricted the exercise of politics to a limited number of noblemen that could
> transmit this privilege to their descendants. In municipal chambers, power belonged to a fixed
> and limited oligarchy whose cohesion depended on family links and certain perpetuation
> strategies such as blood alliances and celibacy. On councils of higher importance, the desire
> to reach certain positions prompted terrible quarrels which derived in the creation of
> opposing parties. In the most delicate situations, conflicts provoked the intervention of magis-
> trates at the Court who kept extreme zeal to control political competence over other social
> groups.[26]

There was no reason to reform this oligarchic scheme during the reign of Philip II.
Rather, the union of the crowns introduced new variants onto the same chessboard.
During this period, the jurisdictional separation between Portugal and Spain was

respected in the Azores just as it was in the other Portuguese territories. In theory, at least, cases brought to the king from the city of Angra were heard by Portuguese tribunals. As was the case on the Iberian Peninsula at the same time, local authorities did not recognize the validity of any instrument or letter that was not written in Portuguese.[27] When the magistrates of Terceira wished to defend a cause before the court, they sent an attorney to present the matter to the members of the Council of Portugal in Madrid.[28] When he learned that the island's authorities had used the court's attorney, Field Marshal Pedro Esteban de Ávila expressed his grievance in the following terms: "they send a person to this court to accuse me as has been their custom with almost all my antecessors since Juan de Urbina."[29]

A second phenomenon that merits attention is the longstanding presence of Spanish troops on the island. Payroll lists from 1583 suggest that they numbered some two thousand fighting men, though in the early seventeenth century the military justice of the Council of War cited lower figures (only five hundred soldiers from Castile and Aragon, plus a few more from Flanders and Italy). Reports also document a surprisingly large number of mixed marriages between soldiers born in Spain and native islander women. In her examination of the island's parish registries between 1583 and 1640, María Hermínia Morais Mesquita counted approximately 485 such unions between Spanish citizens and women born on Terceira or in other Portuguese dominions.[30] This means that the percentage of marriages involving Spaniards, decade by decade, during the period of the union were: 1584–1589 = 37.7%; 1590–1599 = 36.1%; 1600–1609 = 15%; 1610–1619 = 9.3%; 1620–1629 = 14.3%; and 1630–1639 = 8.5%.[31] These figures do not take into account the marriage of the children born of these mixed couples who wed in the first two or three decades, as their condition as offspring of Spanish fathers was not recorded in parish lists because they were born to Portuguese mothers on Terceira. The impact of mixing is particularly extraordinary if we compare marriages of women from Terceira with Spanish *vs.* with Portuguese men from the Iberian Peninsula. During this same six decades the former attained a mean of 20%, while the latter constituted only 9%.

The numerous marital unions of Spanish soldiers with Portuguese women makes it difficult to trace any clear dividing line between a group of foreign soldiers with separate jurisdiction, and a wider Portuguese society on the isle. This reality produced numerous complaints by many field marshals, especially those who, recently disembarked from the Iberian Peninsula, discovered that half of the soldiers awaiting them had married locally or were living in common-law unions with native women, and had sired children.[32] Could the fact that the information in church records so seldom mentions the half-Spanish origin of many of its parishioners be a reflection of a process through which these foreign subjects became intimately integrated into Portuguese society?[33] Whether such was the case or not, the physical presence of Spanish soldiers in the urban space (i.e., outside the gates of the garrison) during times of heightened tensions may well have been seen as anomalous and abusive, as it became evident, for example, when Castilian governors entered into negotiations with municipal authorities to rent houses as living quarters for Spanish soldiers.[34]

Marital unions, however, involved not only low-ranking soldiers and women from the island's lower classes. Extending their age-old custom of choosing marriage partners from among the politically well-positioned sectors of the population, the leading families of Terceira's oligarchy had no qualms about marrying their daughters to high ranking Spanish military officials. One case that stands out was that of Estevão Ferreira de Melo, who in the late sixteenth century functioned as the "supplier of the army and navy of the Indies."[35] Of his five daughters, two married members of local, affinal families, while the other three wed Spanish officials: Maria de Mendon a Ferreira became the wife of one Pedro de Castro do Canto; Ines Ferreira de Melo married Vital de Bettencourt, a jurist in the Chamber of Angra; Luiza Ferreira de Melo wed Hernando Ortiz del Río, the Castilian garrison's accountant; Joana Ferreira de Melo married Diego de Miranda y Quirós, a field marshal, general and governor of the garrison (1599?–1602?); and, Filippa Ferreira de Melo wed Filipe Espínola de Quirós, Diego's nephew.[36] By the 1620s, we find mixed marriages involving the daughters of the local oligarchy and men born of mixed unions. For example, Manuel do Canto e Castro — the leader of the local section that opposed Spain in the upheavals of 1625 (see below) — married his daughter Maria da Luz Pires do Canto to Ignacio Castil-Blanco, the son of Pedro Muñoz de Castil-Blanco, a Spaniard.

A third characteristic of the period is that in the final years of the sixteenth century, Philip II issued instructions for the construction of a Spanish fort at Monte de Brasil, overlooking the Bay of Angra do Heroísmo. The primary objective was to provide a vantage point from which to watch over the city, yet a secondary but not less important task was to protect the fleets. Because the Azores in general, Terceira in particular, served as refuge for fleets returning from America, Asia and even Africa, they attracted European and Mediterranean pirates. Thereafter it became vital to protect the fleets that made stopovers on the archipelago during periods when attacks by English, Dutch, French, Berber and Turkish corsairs intensified.[37] The first stone of the fort was laid in 1593 by field marshal Antonio de la Puebla.[38] The construction of the fort, the constant repairs that it required, and its staffing with the Spanish troops that lived behind its thick walls, could be the guiding thread for a monographic study of the relations between the garrison and the Portuguese city up to the end of the Habsburg era. For example, while it took Terceira three years to recognize Philip II, the castle of San Felipe at Monte de Brasil resisted more than a year before surrendering to the new *Bragancista* authorities in March 1642.

The fourth element that characterized the period were the tensions generated by exports of wheat and other staples (potable water, firewood, cloth) from the islands to the Iberian Peninsula, Madeira, and the Portuguese garrisons in Morocco.[39] Both the wheat producers and its merchants were assiduous in assuring supplies for those far-off places, even at the cost of producing scarcity of grain on the islands and, in particular, shortages when it came to supplying the Spanish troops. The garrison's field marshals complained constantly that the Portuguese traders sold their buyers wheat and other necessary supplies at inflated prices, compared to those native islanders and commercial ship captains had to pay.[40]

How many Spanish Soldiers were Stationed on Terceira?

In 1583, after the victory of Álvaro de Bazán, Marquis of Santa Cruz, over dom António's last remaining supporters, theory has it that two thousand Spanish soldiers were assigned to the garrison on Terceira, a number similar to those deployed at Spanish garrisons on the Iberian Peninsula.[41] However, reports filed by Miguel Ponce, the accountant who arrived from Castile in March 1595 charged with the task of putting the regiment's accounts in order, raise many questions as to the real dimensions of the Spanish military presence on the island.[42] Twelve years after the initial deployment of Spanish troops, it was difficult to determine with certainty, which individuals were really soldiers and which had become integrated into local society:

> . . . [the officers] have assented to, and permitted, that many positions in the Infantry remain empty [and] that soldiers would not fulfill their obligations [but] still receive pay, because of the private needs of the officers, as if the majority of those young men were their assistants or servants in their houses.[43]

The administrative documentation available to the accountant Ponce revealed a situation that was quite distinct from the reality that met his eyes:

> . . . [they] have granted other kinds of established positions to persons who in truth are not so named, [and] do not have the appearance and distinguishing marks indicated on the lists. Some of whom have died.

Like in Gogol's famous novel, *Dead Souls*, officials distributed positions vacated by the deaths of soldiers according to their own convenience:

> . . . most of the soldiers in those companies are very poorly described (. . .) Also, many positions in the military continue to exist and are maintained though their holders have vacated them without permission, and some have died many days after such absences. In theory, the lists of the twelve companies of soldiers of Castilian jurisdiction included one thousand four hundred places at the end of the 16th century, but in reality, the castle of San Felipe at Monte de Brazil, where most of the troops are stationed, held no more than four hundred and nineteen soldiers in 1611.[44]

The inspection by Miguel Ponce is a clear warning to historians interested in estimating the Spanish military presence on the basis of lists elaborated *in situ* by field marshals and a succession of military inspectors and accountants. It also illustrates the degree of autonomy that Spanish officers had attained from the Council of War in Madrid in the space of a few short years.[45] Inspectors went through trials and tribulations. Several months elapsed before they were finally assigned accommodations, received permission to examine the books kept by suppliers and accountants, and question witnesses on the conditions on the island. To make matters worse, once they were installed, there was no shortage of individuals ready to denounce the luxuries and abuses of their lodgings.[46] Unfortunately, we have no way of knowing who was lying and who was telling the truth, but perhaps this is not the salient point. What *is* significant is that such episodes give clear indication of the stubborn opposition that emerged among the Castilian troops to the inspections, to which they were subjected.

Spanish Soldiers and Portuguese Society: Separate Jurisdictions?

Upon the death in 1595 of Antonio de Puebla, the Spanish field marshal in Terceira, several letters were sent from Angra to Madrid. The bishop of the Azores, the *corregidor* and the local Council all addressed shrill missives to the king through the Council of War. According to the bishop Manuel de Gouveia, when the deceased field marshal felt death approaching he left a last will and testament naming Captain Juan de Amilibia as his successor.[47] However, that letter never found its way into the hands of the bishop, as it was delivered to the *corregidor*, who proceeded to open it in the presence of the captains and officers of the regiment. What's more, the *corregidor* Diogo Monteiro de Carvalho added a striking commentary: "His designation was well received by the Spaniards and by the people . . . ".[48] The Chamber also informed the Spanish metropolis, though their observations were rather surprising:

> The notification was rather well received by the Portuguese and the infantry due to the experience they had while he was on this island . . . We believe he will always comply to his duties because of his personal qualities and by the knowledge he possess of these islands and the positions he held in such a praiseworthy manner . . .

The municipal council expressed their desire for the return of Juan de Urbina: "It would be of great mercy to all these islands, and especially to this one, that Johan de Orbina would again take command, since his return would prove of great benefit in times so hard."[49] It voiced not only its opinion on the choice of the interim field marshal for the Spanish garrison, but also advanced the proposal to have Juan de Urbina, the architect of the military government on the island after the victory in 1583, restored to that position in order to fight piracy. Cleary, there was a disagreement between Spaniards and Portuguese and inside each group as to how to proceed.

But the Spanish Crown was not the only entity responsible for the military defense of Angra. The Portuguese local militia was still active under the traditional leadership of the "supplier of arms," an office held at that time by the large Canto e Castro family.[50] There were also remnants of Juan de Urbina's early regiment, with reserved positions for "Portuguese gunners" who, though by 1595 were considered anomalous, remained in place until 1610.[51] Field marshal Pedro Sarmiento implored the Spanish Crown to send new men to restore the garrison's full potential because the vacancies that had opened were being filled temporarily by "foreigners":

> I also see that there are in this [regiment] twenty-one foreign, Flemish, French, Portuguese and Moorish soldiers that are included on the said list, thus my desire that [Your Majesty] supply me with [troops] so that I can discharge them.[52]

Conflicts: Where Were the Dividing Lines?

The terrible violence that characterized the confrontations taking place between 1581 and 1583 would suggest that in the future the main dividing line in Terceira's society would be between native islanders and Spaniards. However, as we have already seen, the real situation on the island was much more nuanced because the two societies had mixed together both at the level of interpersonal bonds and that of institutional overlaps. Conflicts involving Spanish soldiers, give additional proof for this lack of separation on the one hand, internal conflicts inside the Spanish group on the other. As had happened in Antwerp in 1576, the mismanagement of the consignments of funds sent to pay salaries and buy supplies and equipment triggered riots and desertions. On more than a few occasions, soldiers fed up with their living conditions fled to the mountains or to the other islands of the archipelago, aided by both natives living inland and Azorean sailors.

Beginning with an uprising that broke out in May 1602 within the very walls of the castle, field marshal and governor don Diego de Miranda y Quirós, was forced to deal with constant uprisings by soldiers unhappy with their economic plight. When the secret plot to protest was discovered by one of his confidants, he had no choice but to sentence nine of his soldiers to execution by garrote.[53] Another riot erupted two years later, but on that occasion the conspirators made no attempt at discretion. To the contrary, they made their dire predicament public by protesting against the payroll officer:

> . . . this past month of July the five hundred soldiers who have remained in the Castle posted placards saying that if Pedro de Eredia does not pay them, then they will take payment into their own hands; as I have in letters from the lieutenant at whose door the placards were placed.[54]

Letters sent by the governor, Pedro Esteban de Ávila, to the Council of War between 1622 and 1625 reveal this daily reality during a period of heightened tensions among various groups within Terceira's society.[55] The first missives detail how the new governor attempted to deal with the age-old problems that all of his predecessors had faced. Because he did not succeed in convincing the government in Lisbon to send the funds required for the maintenance of the castle at San Felipe,[56] he attempted to increase vigilance on the activities of the archipelago's Portuguese customs officials (*alfândega*) and, at the same time, refused to send soldiers to the island of São Miguel to pick up the wheat stored there for his troops.[57] But it was at this stage that Ávila began to comprehend the complexity of the system that supplied and financed the garrison he commanded. This was particularly true when he discovered that some of the funds he required had to come from that same island's customs office:

> . . . most of the money in this consignment is from the duties yielded by the *alfândega* on San Miguel, 28 leagues distant, and though the [lawyer] Antonio Ferreira de Vetancor, the supplier on these Islands, issues strict instructions to the customs agents on San Miguel to comply (. . .) they have no effect as he remains [here] on this Island and, though he visits those [ones] from time to time to admonish the customs agents to hand over what they owe to the Royal Treasury, upon his return here the accountant of that customs house lets them off the hook or they obtain [permissions] from the kingdom that allow them to delay making payment.[58]

The recently arrived and rather ingenuous captain announced his intention to accompany the Portuguese supplier the next time he went to pressure the customs agents on São Miguel. However, within a few months, he came to understand that a large number of individuals had a hand in provisioning the castle: agents in far-off customs houses, the municipal councils of Angra and Ponta Delgada, various suppliers and accountants, most of them in the Portuguese jurisdiction, the Realm — i.e., the Crown's tribunals in Portugal — the Council of War, and the Treasury of the Court.

At that point, de Ávila, greatly disillusioned but no longer as naive, entered into open conflicts with various local institutions.[59] The governor of the castle did not trust the Portuguese supplier of the army Manuel do Canto e Castro, who was responsible for organizing part of the city's defense in the event of an attack by foreign fleets, to mobilize the militias if this were to happen. To test him, he decided to sound a false alarm but, as the entire city soon learned of his pretentions, the Portuguese attacked the Castilian garrison instead of going out to defend the piers that were assigned to them. The situation soon took on the dimensions of a riot and forced the governor to shoot the castle's cannons right over the roof of the house of Manuel do Canto e Castro. But that authentic act of war of which he was victim, led the supplier to appeal to the memory of the resistance movement that had mobilized against Philip II in 1581–1583, in which his famous aunt Violante do Canto e Castro, Pedro Eanes do Canto (his father?), and his cousin Estevão Ferreira de Melo, had all been key figures:

> The people who were in Y(our) M(ajesty's) service during the uprisings that occurred on this island have not taken Manuel do C(ant)o's side, nor do they think it right that he raise his person so high and try to become owner of everything, as this is not convenient for Y(our) M(ajesty's) interests.[60]

The intentions of the rebel group organized by the supplier and the *corregidor* were to mobilize the city's public space and demonstrate their rejection of all things Castilian:

> . . . those [people] have taken it upon themselves to make the term Castilian opprobrious to the Portuguese and to transform their discontent into mortal hated and abhorrence; and their audacity goes so far as to persecute with rabid fervor all those who show affinity for the Crown of Castile, leaving them beaten and threatened.[61]

This rejection had repercussions on the composition of the fraternity of the *Santa Misericórdia* of Angra (hospital) whose members included several Castilians, among them Pedro Esteban de Ávila himself, and Felipe de Spínola (nephew and brother-in-law of the former governor, Diego de Miranda y Quirós), both of whom were married to important Portuguese women. Other soldiers, of lower rank, had also joined this fraternity, which carried great weight in the city's political life. However, at one juncture the *corregidor*, Vaz Freire, decided to expel all Castilians from the confraternity:

> . . . I affirm that I have also treated the Portuguese in every way possible with friendship and familiarity in Y(our) M(ajesty's) service, [but] they are highly offended by this and complain to Y(our) M(ajest)y at the Supreme Council of Portugal (. . .) I stepped aside to demonstrate my sentiments, as it is most convenient to Y(our) M(ajest)y's service that such persons remain in that confraternity and even become involved in the government of the city.[62]

To prevent the situation from deteriorating further, in 1625 the Council of War in Madrid decided to recall the Castilian governor from the garrison. Nonetheless, the confrontations that took place in the 1620s demonstrate that the memory of the 1581–1583 period was still very much alive. An anti-Castilian sentiment was used to obtain a clamorous local victory to which the central institutions seem to remain indifferent. Neither the donator captain the Marquis of Alenquer — a man highly esteemed at the Court of Madrid — nor the governor of Lisbon, nor the Council of War, nor even the Count-Duke of Olivares himself, was capable of demanding the return to order. It is ironic that none of the Monarchy's agents and institutions had sufficient authority to impose solidarity in organizing local defenses, precisely when Philip IV's right-hand man had just drawn up the document for the union of arms.

Conclusion: A Physical or Political Archipelago?

During the period of the union of the two crowns, the Azores were governed by both traditional Portuguese jurisdictional authorities and Spanish military institutions. The case of the island of Terceira and its capital city present important features that are revealing of the political dynamics of the Portuguese and Spanish empires in the late sixteenth and early seventeenth centuries. Terceira was the last Portuguese territory to recognize the legitimacy of Philip II's election as King of Portugal, and the one that challenged it most doggedly. After its conquest by sea and land (led by Marquis de Santa Cruz in 1583), local authorities and Spanish officials stationed at the garrison, had to find some working basis amidst several areas of institutional overlap. In certain situations the governors of the garrison applied heavy pressure on the local chambers of government, though with a marked lack of success. They wished to intervene in the formation of the Portuguese militias and the election of their leaders. However, local authorities were able to resist such invasive initiatives by resorting to the traditional tools of jurisdictional protection, such as filing numerous appeals with their *corregidor* and the tribunals in Lisbon, and even sending attorneys to defend their autonomy at the court. During those years, the presence of soldiers stationed at the garrison left an indelible mark on Terceira's society, as is reflected in the large number of mixed marriages that took place between Spanish soldiers and native Azorean women. This interweaving confounded the criteria that would usually separate military life from a city's civilian population. However, during times of extreme tension this mixing did not impede leaders from mobilizing public opinion by using explicitly anti-Castilian arguments. The relations that the natives of Terceira established with the institutions of the Monarchy and their Spanish compatriots were thus never univocal or simple. Furthermore, there is no doubt that when the wellbeing, safety or influence of certain families in the local oligarchy was threatened, anti-Spanish epithets never failed to prove efficacious.

Abbreviations

AGS   Archivo General de Simancas.
GM   Guerra y Marina.
BL   British Library.
BPAAH   Biblioteca Pública e Arquivo Regional de Angra do Heroísmo.

Notes

1 Cardim, 2004, 355–383.
2 Bouza Álvarez, 1987.
3 Bouza Álvarez, 1994, 71–94.
4 Marques, 2005; Cardim, 2004, and 2008, 349–388.
5 Hespanha and Madeira Santos, 1994, 449–478.
6 Mendes da Luz, 1952.
7 Curto, 1998; Costa, 2002.
8 Matos, 1985 and 1983.
9 Maldonado, 1989–1998. Two studies on the method of Maldonado: Rodrigues, 1983; Sousa, 2005. Francisco Ferreira Drummond, 1850–1864. Consult online at: http://pt.wikisource.org/wiki/Anais_da_Ilha_Terceira

10 Damião Rodrigues, 2002. Consult the digital edition of the first series of fifteen volumes (1878–1959) by the Universidade dos Açores online at: http://arquivodigital.uac.pt/aa/index.html

11 Damião Rodrigues, 2001; Mesquita, 2005–2006. Mesquita defended her doctoral dissertation, *As gentes de Angra no século XVII*, at the Universidade do Minho in 2004. It is the most complete study yet conducted of Terceira's society in the 17th century. Consult the digital version at: http://www.neps.ics.uminho.pt/citcem/ficheiros/Teses%20 Doutoramento/Hermínia%20Mesquita/As%20Gentes%20de%20Angra%20no% 20Séc%20XVII.pdf.

12 Maldonado, 2007.

13 Chagas, 1989. The list of Castilians at the Castle of San Felipe del Monte Brasil has been established by the Portuguese army. Consult it at: http://www.exercito.pt/portal/exercito/ _specific/public/allbrowsers/asp/acessibilidade/comandantes.asp?ueo_id=143.

14 Casas de Bustos, 1997; Meneses, 1987.

15 On the situation of sources for the administrative history of the Habsburg Portugal, see Luxán Meléndez, 1988; Schaub, 2001a and 1998.

16 Drumond Braga, 2008, vol. 1, 235–268.

17 The digitalized series can be consulted on the Internet at:
http://www.iac-azores.org/biblioteca-virtual/simancas1/index.html (*Guerra Antigua*, 1590–1605).
http://www.iac-azores.org/biblioteca-virtual/simancas2/index.html (*Guerra Antigua*, 1605–1616).
http://www.iac-azores.org/biblioteca-virtual/simancas3/index.html (*Contaduría mayor de cuentas*, 1ª época, 1580–1628).
http://www.iac-azores.org/biblioteca-virtual/ simancas4/index.html (*Contaduría mayor de cuentas*, 2ª época, 1599–1616).
The cataloguing has been very systematic, though the selection of documents is biased in favor of those related to the construction of the fortifications and the artillery at Terceira.

18 Some information has been conserved in two manuscript volumes that include part of the records from Angra. They are held at the BPAAH, entitled: *Tombo das coisas mais importantes da Câmara de Angra* and *Livro 2 do tombo e regimento da Camara de Angra*.

19 The documentation from the *Câmara de Horta* can be consulted on the Internet. The first three books of *registos* cover only the period of the Habsburgs: http://arquivo.digital.uac.pt/dah/index.html.

20 Meneses, 1985.

21 Marques, 2003.

22 Frutuoso, 1963, chapters 20, 147–153, and 29, 207–212.

23 AGS, GM, leg. 897, letter from field marshal don Pedro Esteban de Ávila to the king, Angra, April 4, 1623; *ibid.*, letter from field marshal don Pedro Esteban de Ávila to the king, Angra, September 6, 1623.

24 Treslado do perdão geral que sua Mag(esta)de concedeu as Ilhas por ter outra opinião e não a sua, BPAAH, Tombo das coisas mais importantes da Câmara de Angra, ff. 22r–25r.

25 For two studies of the period prior to the union of the crowns with elements that help understand the institutional fabric, see: Gregório, 1999 and Rodrigues, 2004.

26 Meneses, 1995, 587.

27 AGS, GM, leg. 601, doc. 137, Diego de Miranda Quirós, May 7, 1602.

28 BPAAH, Tombo das coisas mais importantes da Câmara de Angra, between 168r and 198r.

29 AGS, GM, leg. 897, letter from field marshal Pedro Esteban de Ávila to the king, Angra, June 16, 1623: "invian a persona a esa corte a quejarse de mi como lo han acostumbrado hacer con casi todos mis antecesores desde Juan de Urbina".

30 Mesquita, 2004, 99–103.

31 *Ibid.*, 193.

32 AGS, GM, leg. 452, doc. 93A, letter from field marshal Antonio Centeno to the king on the inconvenience of marriages of Spanish soldiers in Terceira with native women, Angra, February 16, 1596.

33 *Ibid.*, 102–103.

34 BPAAH, Tombo das coisas mais importantes da Câmara de Angra, ff. 35r–40v.

35 Santos, 1989, vol. II, 622.

36 Padre Manuel Luis Maldonado, Fenix Angrence. Parte genealógica, (CD-Rom), Presidencia do Governo Regional dos Açores, Terceira, 2007.

37 For example: BPAAH, Livro 2 do Tombo e regimento da Câmara de Angra, ff. 386r–387r, letter from the Marquis de Alenquer to the supplier of the army of Terceira, Manuel do Castro e Canto, to warn of the possible arrival at the islands of a fleet from Algiers, sent from Lisbon, March 25, 1617; AGS, GM, leg. 601, doc. 142, letter from field marshal Diego de Miranda Quirós to the king to report the arrival of ships from the north, Angra, May 14, 1602; AGS, GM, leg. 897, letter from field marshal Pedro Esteban de Ávila to the king to report the arrival of a fleet from Algiers, Angra, May 16, 1623.

38 Araújo, 1963, 38–116; Valdemar Mota, 1993–1994.

39 BPAAH, Livro 2 do Tombo e regimento da Camara de Angra, ff. 42v–43v.

40 AGS, GM, leg. 601, doc. 138, copy of information collected on the request of the governor, Diego de Miranda Quirós, on the price of wheat on Terceira, Angra, June 3, 1602; and AGS, GM, leg. 601, doc. 139, copy of information collected on the request of the governor, Diego de Miranda Quirós, on the price of meat on Terceira, Angra, June 3, 1602.

41 Schaub, 2001a.

42 AGS, GM, leg. 425, doc. 130, letter from Pedro de Paz Salas and Miguel Ponce to the king, reporting their arrival at Terceira on March 12, 1595.

43 AGS, GM, leg. 426, doc. 222, report by Miguel Ponce, Angra, April 24, 1595; AGS, GM, leg. 429, doc. 54 d, Angra, June 23, 1595.

44 AGS, GM, leg. 760, letter from Francisco de Aduna to the king, Terceira, October 12, 1611.

45 AGS, GM, leg. 427, doc. 213. Copy of a letter from Miguel Ponce and Pedro de Paz Salas to the king, Angra, May 25, 1595.

46 AGS, GM, leg. 453, docs. 141 and 142 (copy), memorial by Anton Coll on the outlays made to condition the houses of the *visitadores*, Angra, March 17, 1596.

47 AGS, GM, leg. 429, doc. 58, letter from the bishop of Angra to the king, Angra, July 13, 1595.

48 AGS, GM, leg. 429, doc. 56, letter from the *corregidor*, Diogo Monteiro de Carvalho, July 11, 1595.

49 AGS, GM, leg. 429, doc. 63, letter from the Chamber of Angra to the king, Angra, July 15, 1595, on Juan de Urbina's high reputation among the local people, see: Frutuoso, 1963, 227.

50 BPAAH, Tombo das coisas mais importantes da Câmara de Angra, ff. 25r–29v.

51 AGS, GM, leg. 431, doc. 64, letter from Miguel Ponce and Pedro de Paz Salas to the king, Angra, September 15, 1595; AGS, GM, leg. 743, letter from field marshal D. Pedro Sarmiento, to the king, Terceira, June 18, 1610.

52 AGS, GM, leg. 743, letter from D. Pedro Sarmiento to the king on the situation at the Castle of San Felipe, Terceira, March 15, 1610.

53 AGS, GM, leg. 601, doc. 140, letter from Diego de Miranda Quirós to the king, reporting on the riot that occurred at the Castle, Angra, May 13, 1602.

54 AGS, GM, leg. 632, doc. 356, memorial by field marshal Diego de Miranda Quirós, to the king s.l., 1604.

55 The originals of this correspondence are stored in various bundles in the section *Guerra y Marina* of the Archivo General de Simancas, especially numbers 897 and 952. The British Library holds some copies that were ordered by Pedro Esteban de Ávila himself, in case the

originals were to fall into the hands of the corsairs, BL, Add. 28439, but the two sets are not identical.

56 Letter dated July 3, 1622, BL, Add. 28439, f.2.
57 Letter dated August 24, 1622, BL, Add. 28439, ff. 5–9.
58 Letter dated January 15, 1623, BL, Add. 28439, ff. 15–17.
59 Schaub, 2001b.
60 AGS, GM, leg. 897, letter from field marshal Pedro Esteban de Ávila to the king, Angra, June 16, 1623.
61 AGS, GM, leg. 897, letter from field marshal Pedro Esteban de Ávila to the king, Angra, July 17, 1623.
62 AGS, GM, leg. 897, letter from field marshal Pedro Esteban de Ávila to the king, with the list of Castilians who were excluded from the confraternity of *Misericórdia*, Angra, November 10, 1623.

Bibliography

Araújo, Miguel Cristóvão de, "A Restauração da Ilha Terceira (1641–1642): cerco e tomada do Castelo de São Filipe do Monte Brasil pelos Terceirenses", *Boletim do Instituto Histórico da Ilha Terceira*, XVIII, 1963, pp. 38–116.

Bouza Álvarez, Fernando, "Lisboa sózinha, quase viúva: a cidade e a mudança da corte no Portugal dos Filipes", *Penélope. Fazer e desfazer a história*, n. 13, 1994, pp. 71–94.

——, *Portugal en la Monarquía Hispánica (1580–1640). Felipe II, las Cortes de Tomar y la génesis del Portugal Católico*, Madrid, Universidad Complutense, 1987.

Cardim, Pedro, "La jurisdicción real y su afirmación en la corona portuguesa y sus territorios ultramarinos (siglos XVI–XVIII): reflexiones sobre la historiografía", in Francisco Aranda Pérez and José Damião Rodrigues (eds.), *De Re Publica Hispaniae. Una vindicación de la cultura política en los reinos ibéricos en la primera modernidad*, Madrid, Sílex, 2008, pp, 349–388.

——, "Los portugueses frente a la Monarquía Hispánica", in Bernardo García and Antonio Álvarez Ossorio (eds.), *La Monarquía de las Naciones. Patria, nación y naturaleza en la Monarquía de España*, Madrid, Fundación Carlos de Amberes, Universidad Autónoma de Madrid, 2004, pp. 355–383.

——, "O governo e a administração do Brasil sob os Habsburgo e os primeiros Bragança", *Hispania*, LXIV/1, 216, 2004, pp. 117–156.

Casas de Bustos, Rocío, "Las Azores en la política de Felipe II. Su documentación en el Archivo de Simancas", in Alberto Vieira (ed.) *Os arquivos insulares (Atlântica e Caraíbas): Actas do IV Colóquio internacional de história das ilhas atlânticas*, Funchal, Centro des estudos da história do Atlântico, 1997.

Chagas, frei Diogo das, *Espelho cristalino em jardim de várias flores*, ed. Artur Teodoro de Matos, Avelino de Freitas de Meneses, Vítor Luís Gaspar Rodrigues, Ponta Delgada, Universidade dos Açores, Centro de Estudos Doutor Gaspar Frutuoso, 1989.

Costa, Leonor Freire, *Império e grupos mercantis. Entre o Oriente e o Atlântico (séc. XVII)*, Lisbon, Livros Horizonte, 2002.

Curto, Diogo Ramada, "Cultura Escrita e Práticas de Identidade", in Francisco Bethencourt and Kirti Chaudhuri (eds.), *História da Expansão Portuguesa. Do Índico ao Atlântico (1570–1697)*, Lisbon, Temas e Debates, 1998, pp. 469–477.

Drumond Braga, Paulo, "Espanhóis, continentais e açorianos. Um espaço para a libertação", in Artur Teodoro de Matos, Avelino de Freitas de Meneses and José Guilherme Reis Leite (eds.), *História dos Açores. Dos descobrimentos ao século XX*, Angra do Heroísmo, Instituto Açoriano de Cultura, 2008, vol. 1, pp. 235–268.

Ferreira Drummond, Francisco, *Anais da Ilha Terceira*, Angra do Heroísmo, Câmara Muncipal, 4 vols., 1850–1864.

Frutuoso, Gaspar, *Livro sexto das saudades da terra*, Ponta Delgada, Instituto Cultural de Ponta Delgada, 1963.

Gregório, Rute Dias, "Configurações do patrocínio religioso de um ilustre açoriano do século XVI: o 1° Provedor das Armadas, Pero Anes do Canto", *Arquipélago. História*, 2nd series, vol. 3, 1999, pp. 29–44.

Hespanha, António Manuel and Catarina Madeira Santos, "Le forme di potere di un impero oceánico", in R. Zorzi (ed.), *L'epopea delle scoperte*, Florence, Leo S. Olschki, 1994, pp. 449–478.

Luxán Meléndez, Santiago de, *La Revolución de 1640 en Portugal, sus fundamentos sociales e sus caracteres nacionales. El Consejo de Portugal (1580–1640)*, Madrid, Universidad Complutense, 1988.

Maldonado, Manuel Luís, *Fénix Angrense. Parte Genealógica*, (electronic document, CD-Rom), ed. José Damião Rodrigues, Angra do Heroísmo, Presidência do Governo Regional dos Açores, 2007.

——, *Fénix Angrense*, ed. Hélder Parreira de Sousa Lima, Angra do Heroísmo, Instituto Histórico da Ilha Terceira, 3 vols., 1989–1998.

Marques, Guida, "L'invention du Brésil entre deux monarchies (1580–1640). Etat d'une question", *Anais de história de Além-mar*, VI, 2005, pp. 109–137.

——, "La dimension atlantique de l'opposition antonienne et l'enjeu brésilien (1580–1640)", *Anais de história de Além-mar*, IV, 2003, pp. 213–246.

Matos, Artur Teodoro de, "A Provedoria das Armadas da ilha Terceira e a Carreira da Índia no século XVI", in *Actas do II Seminário Internacional de História Indo-Portuguesa*, Lisbon, Instituto de Investigação Científica Tropical, 1985, pp. 63–72.

——, "Os Açores e a Carreira das Índias no século XVI", in *Estudos de História de Portugal. Homenagem a A. H. de Oliveira Marques*, vol. II, sections XVI–XX, Imprensa Universitária, Lisbon, Editorial Estampa, 1983, pp. 93–110.

Mendes da Luz, Francisco Paulo, *O Conselho da Índia. Contributo ao Estudo da História da Administração e do Comércio do Ultramar Português nos Princípios do Século XVII*, Lisbon, Agência Geral do Ultramar/Divisão de Publicações e Biblioteca, 1952.

Meneses, Avelino de Freitas de, *Os Açores e o domínio filipino (1580–1590). A resistência terceirense e as implicações da conquista espanhola*, Angra do Heroísmo, Instituto Histórico da Ilha Terceira, 1987, 2 vols.

——, "Os ensaios de organização política e seus resultados: as ilhas como modelo experimental para governo à distância", *Boletim do Instituto Histórico da Ilha Terceira*, vol. LIII, 1995, pp. 577–592.

Mesquita, Maria Hermínia Morais, *As gentes de Angra no século XVII*, doctoral dissertation, Universidade do Minho, 2004.

——, "Escravos em Angra no século XVII: uma abordagem a partir dos registos paroquiais", *Arquipélago. História*, 2nd series, IX–X, 2005–2006, pp. 209–233.

Mota, Valdemar, "Fortificação da Ilha Terceira", *Boletim do Instituto Histórico da Ilha Terceira*, LI-LII, 1993–1994, pp. 129–327.

Rodrigues, Graça Almeida, "Três visões históricas da colonização portuguesa no Atlântico: Góis, Cadornega e Maldonado", *Boletim do Instituto Histórico da Ilha Terceira*, vol. XLI, 1983, pp. 378–396.

Rodrigues, José Damião, "Ernesto do Canto e a Historiografia Oitocentista dos Descobrimentos", in *Ernesto do Canto — retratos do homem e do tempo*. Actas do Colóquio, Universidade dos Açores, October 25–27, 2000, Ponta Delgada, Centro de Estudos Gaspar Frutuoso/Universidade dos Açores-Câmara Municipal de Ponta Delgada, 2002, pp. 387–401.

——, "Modelos e práticas da justiça régia: a corregedoria dos Açores ao tempo de D. João III", in Roberto Carneiro e Artur Teodoro de Matos (eds.), *D. João III e o império. Actas do Congresso Internacional comemorativo do seu nascimento*, Lisbon, Centro de História de Além-

Mar-Centro de Estudos dos Povos e Culturas de Expressão Portuguesa, 2004, pp. 513–528.

——, "Problemas da investigação histórica nos Açores: o estado dos arquivos paroquiais", *Arquipélago-história*, Ponta Delgada, 2nd Series, vol. V, 2001, pp. 733–742.

Santos, João Marinho dos, *Os Açores nos sécs. XV e XVI. Fontes para a história dos Açores*, Ponta Delgada, 1989, vol. II.

Schaub, Jean-Frédéric, *Le Portugal au temps du comte-duc d'Olivares (1621–1640). Le conflit de jurisdiction comme exercice de la politique*, Madrid, Casa de Velázquez, 2001a.

——, "Conflitos na Ilha Terceira no Tempo do Conde-Duque de Olivares: Poder Militar Castelhano e Autoridades Portuguesas", in *Actas do Congresso Internacional Comemorativo do Regresso de Vasco da Gama a Portugal*, Avelino de Freitas de Meneses (ed.), Ilhas Terceira e S. Miguel (Açores), Universidade dos Açores/Comissão Nacional para as Comemorações dos Descobrimentos Portugueses, 2001b, pp. 21–31.

——, "Dinámicas políticas en el Portugal de Felipe III (1598–1621)", *Relaciones*, 73, 1998, pp. 169–211.

Sousa, Ana Madalena Trigo de, "A Fénix Angrense do padre Manuel Luís Maldonado: Estudo da parte histórica", *Islenha*, 36, 2005, pp. 4–41.

2 | Architect of the New World
Juan de Solórzano Pereyra and the Status of the Americas
Óscar Mazín Gómez

To David A. Brading

I

Were the Americas kingdoms or colonies? Because of its complexity, as well as importance, this question has been, is, and will continue to be a topic of debate.[1] Recent research regarding the Iberian Monarchies and their legal structures have only complicated matter further,[2] creating a tangled web of explanations that were heavily influenced by the modernist perspective of the nation-state. Among other things, this could happen because the question itself was anachronistic. While important to the proponents of the nation-states that were instituted after the demise of the Monarchy in the nineteenth and twentieth centuries, it was completely irrelevant in the first half of the seventeenth century, when the identity and status of the Crown's American possessions was mainly understood as a juridical, not a political, issue. As Carlos Garriga has elucidated convincingly, because they were incorporated into the Crown of Castile as "accessories", the New World was bereft of a political constitution of its own.[3] Nevertheless, as time passed, the Indies went through a process of territorialization, at the end of which, and following the Castilian juridical order, its distinct parts attained a sufficiently developed structure meriting the title "Kingdoms and Seigniories" [*Reinos y Señoríos* . . .], used, for example, in the *Recopilación de leyes de los reinos de las Indias* ("Compilation of the Laws of the Kingdoms of the Indies"), published in 1681. Provided with jurisdictions, local power-groups claimed rights under the king's protection. In the process, they forged an authentic local personality.

How did the incorporation of the New World differ from that of other territories in the Spanish Monarchy? This question is important because it allows us to understand how local power groups vindicated the particular identity of their territory. From the late fifteenth century, incorporation into the Monarchy could follow different routes. Territories could be incorporated by dynastic union or succession, annexation or conquest. Each method produced a distinct status mediated by two additional categories: aggregation and integration.[4] Incorporation by aggregation conserved the pre-existing laws and privileges of the aggregated unit, creating the fiction that the king was lord only of that unit (*aeque principaliter*). Incorporation by integration, on the contrary, made certain possessions like the West Indies, "accessory" entities to an existing crown, in this case, the Crown of Castile to which they thereafter belonged. Although clear in theory, in practice, the implementation of both aggregation and integration produced many difficulties, most clearly expressed during the fiscal and military urgencies that characterized the sixteenth and seventeenth centuries.[5] Furthermore, Madrid's efforts to achieve an expeditious and centralized control placed restrictions on the maneuvering and the negotiating capacity of power groups in each territory. It led these groups to defend their relative autonomy by appealing to traditional juridical resources of a contractual nature and pointing out commonalities in judicial and political structure with the other parts of the Monarchy. The range of expressions and responses these elites used requires that historians proceed with caution and evaluate their meaning according to context of territory and time.

Furthermore, within the Spanish Monarchy, "aggregation" came to be identified with a different and superior type of social organization. Everywhere, that is even in territories incorporated by conquest and made accessories of Castile, as was the case of the Americas, the preservation of the laws and customs (incorporation by aggregation) enjoyed a greater prestige and favor than incorporation by integration. As a result of the wish to match other territories in terms of prerogatives and privileges, by the late seventeenth century in both New Spain and Peru arguments were made insisting that, in continuance of the supposed "cession of sovereignty" by the autochthonous rulers of Mexico and Cuzco, these two territories had "aggregated" themselves to the Crown of their own volition. These claims were made in order to obtain a substantial degree of autonomy that would support local groups' efforts to reaffirm their power, belonging and social influence. They would also hopefully make it possible to consolidate the place that these kingdoms occupied in the Monarchy as a whole.[6]

The motherland, or *patria*, whether this was the place where one was born, grew up, or lived, emerged as the primary referent of loyalty with respect to the Monarchy,[7] almost always connoting a sense of duty and religious devotion. In the Indies, as in other royal domains, obedience to the Crown was thus founded upon the sentiments and creed that individuals professed to their motherland, their saints, their Virgin, their king, and their God. One feature of Spanish policy was to re-orient local life without modifying it substantially, which is the equivalent of saying that royal power was based on consensus.[8] This enabled the Creole elites to maximize the possibilities of relative self-government that the Monarchy's conventional structure granted them.[9]

The key moment in the construction of the juridical personality of the Americas was the period between 1620 and 1650, when both the Creole power groups in the Indies and the king's own Councils in Madrid, launched a series of claims. The American possessions were not an isolated case in this regard. Although more violently, in the mid-seventeenth century European elites also expressed their frustrations to the Crown with the secession of Portugal (December 1640) and the uprisings in Catalonia (June 1640), Naples and Sicily (1647).[10] The Councils were the royal organs most keenly aware of the need to grant a minimum of benefits to the leading groups in the different dominions under their charge, but they also defended their own honor and dignity within the Monarchy's polysynodal system. In part, the claims that appeared in mid-century were a response to the reform initiatives of the Count-Duke de Olivares, acting for King Philip IV. The announcement and implementation of these measures, especially the Union of Arms (*Unión de Armas*, 1626–1627), rarefied the atmosphere and hindered dialogue between Madrid and territorial elites in Castile and other parts of the realm. Reactions emerged against any measure that might affect the contractual character of the relationship with the Crown, and even against the slightest hint of a predatory Monarchy incapable of comprehending local problems and unwilling to compensate the elites sufficiently to justify their loyalty.[11]

As part of this global picture, in 1624, the *Ayuntamiento* (municipal council) of Lima sent a strongly-worded protest to the king, stating that instead of adopting the conventions of etiquette established for the nobility of each Viceroyalty, the Viceroys of Peru and Mexico conducted themselves according to their sentiments of affection or disaffection. This affront was greater in Lima because, according to the complainant, of all the king's possessions in the Indies, Peru was the place where more nobles resided. In response, in 1629, the Viceroy Marquis of Guadalcázar left his successor, the Count of Chinchón, a detailed list of the styles and treatment to be used at the Court of Lima, a list that passed from one Viceroy to the next until the end of the eighteenth century.[12] Notwithstanding his consent in this matter, at the end of his term in office Guadalcázar boastfully defended the Vicerregal faculty to appoint all military posts in the kingdom without the intervention of the Monarch.[13]

The situation in Peru, however, pales in comparison to that of New Spain, where things took a dramatic turn in the 1620s and continued to degenerate into the 1650s. Leaving aside the destitution, in 1642, of the Viceroy Duke of Escalona, a close relative of the Duke of Braganza who had been placed on the throne by the Portuguese rebellion, the crisis had several other momentous expressions. First, riots that repudiated reforms that violated local customs and interests and unseated the government of the Viceroy Marquis of Gelves in 1624.[14] These riots were inspired by the confrontation between that Viceroy and Juan Pérez de la Serna, the Archbishop of Mexico, who enjoyed the solid support of the *Ayuntamiento* of the capital and the partial support of the local *Real Audiencia* (high court). Second, a somewhat similar conflict in 1645–1647 between don Juan de Palafox, the bishop of Puebla (in his role as an inspector (*visitador*) of New Spain) and the Viceroy Count de Salvatierra. The prelate, who had benefited from the protection of the favorite Count-Duke de Olivares, tended to favor increasingly the interests of Creole groups. Ever since before the fall of the favorite (1643), Palafox had conducted his inspection with an attitude little inclined to patronize the dictates of Madrid, and much more in tune with the contractual framework in mind. Among other things, he attempted to strengthen the *Ayuntamientos* of New Spain by empowering their *alcaldes ordinarios* (councilor-judges) despite the vociferous opposition of the Count of Salvatierra.[15] Yet, what really set off the crisis in New Spain was the conflict between the practices of local power groups, defended in the name of "justice", and the autocratic exercise of power by most of the Viceroys during the Monarchy's most pressing moments.

The authority of the Viceroy in Peru, apparently more consolidated than in New Spain, had its principal detractors in the heirs of *conquistadors* and *encomenderos*, a group thirsty for honors and ennoblement. The situation in Mexico was more complex: there, instigated by the Episcopate, social actors like merchants, some members of the royal court (*Real Audiencia*), and the *Ayuntamientos* of the capital city and Puebla de los Ángeles vindicated their importance and joined forces to topple viceregal regimes or make it extremely difficult for viceroys to govern.

The hypersensitivity of local groups had repercussions that were felt all the way to the King's Councils in Madrid. From the beginning of Philip IV's reign, the eagerness of the councils to recover their medullar role in governing the Monarchy had been frustrated because the Count-Duke de Olivares thwarted them by resorting to *ad hoc* meetings attended by his dependents and clients. Complaints about the Councils' obstructionism were a recurring theme in the correspondence.[16] By 1626, claims accumulated. They included those of the Councils themselves as collegial entities,[17] those related to rights of priority and to the number of councilors born in the dominions they governed,[18] and those concerned with the territories under their charge.[19] There were also several disputes over precedence among the Councils themselves: Portugal's against that of Aragón and the Two Sicilies in 1627;[20] the Indies against Flanders in 1628;[21] and Italy against the Council of Portugal in 1634.[22] The relative importance of each Council was important. Those granted more dignity and prestige than others enjoyed greater power of representation and individuals found belonging to them more attractive. In any case, disputes over precedence reminded the Crown that the Councils were the supreme instances of the political structure and, therefore, the most legitimate entities for governing and imparting justice in the concert of the Monarchy.

II

This context explains the interest in analyzing the *Memorial y discurso histórico de las razones que se ofrecen para que el Real y Supremo Consejo de las Indias deba preceder en todos los actos públicos al que llaman de Flandres* [*sic*], published in 1629 by don Juan de Solórzano Pereyra, at that time, the defendor of royal interests (*fiscal*) of the Council of Indies.[23] The declared purpose of the essay was to defend the Council against the Council of Flanders through a summation of precepts. But, in reality, the ambition and scope were much wider. In this text, Solórzano classified the Indies from the juridical and historical points of view by discussing the insertion, place and transcendence of these territories in the wider context of the Iberian Monarchies by using a highly erudite and critical apparatus marked by a hundreds of digressions, not mere annotations, most of which were in Latin. This was not his first publication, as in that same year, his celebrated *Indiarum Iure* (*On the Laws of the Indies*), a synthesis of the Crown of Castile's titles of dominion over the New World and a description of the American social order, was published in Madrid.[24] Solórzano must have been pleased with his *Memorial,* because years later, in his *Política Indiana* (1647) he renounced his earlier intention to include its arguments in that new publication.[25] Until the present, the *Memorial* has been the focus of only one pioneering study — by Feliciano Barrios[26] and a few brief annotations.[27] In this chapter, I will only highlight its most important topics and especially its critical apparatus, heretofore ignored. I will base my analysis on a critical edition of the *Memorial . . .* that I am currently in the process of elaborating. This critical edition compares both the Madrid edition of 1776, found in the author's *Obras sueltas,*[28] and the 1629 *princeps* edition, published, as was the case with his *Indiarum Iure,* in Madrid by Francisco Martínez.[29]

Like other writings by Solórzano, the *Memorial* pertains to the classic tradition of ancient republicanism, according to which identity and law are intertwined and the essential defining political factor is the relationship individuals and social bodies have with their native land. From the early decades of the seventeenth century, especially in Peru, many published pamphlets defended the right of Spanish-Americans to occupy ecclesiastical benefices and public offices in the Indies and even the Council of State discussed the possibility of reserving one permanent seat in the Council of Indies for an individual native of the Americas.[30] This tradition, which was characterized by an argumentative unity and was rich with doctrinal content, allowed the residents of the West Indies both to claim and to stress the full continuity between the two sides of the Atlantic. That is, to argue that New Spain was a natural prolongation of the Old.[31] Rhetorically, this argument sought to anchor the legitimacy of present on the past, and on the accumulation of distinct pieces of a "common law" and of privileges granted by the kings over many centuries. It adopted the lines of a republican logic sustaining that the reception of honors rewards and promotes the virtues of citizens as well as those of the social bodies and institutions.

The occasion for writing the *Memorial* was the pretension of the Council of Flanders and Burgundy — approved by the Monarch — to precede the Council of Indies in the royal hand-kissing ceremony held on Christmas 1628. This event was of particular transcendence because it displayed Spain's polysynodical structure. While hand-kissing ceremonies could be celebrated on special occasions, such as the succession of a new sovereign, the arrival at court of a new consort queen, the birth of a royal heir (*infante*), or a victory of royal arms, they were also held annually on the afternoon of the second day of the Feast of Nativity. The question of what would happen at Christmas was of a particular importance because due to its repetitive nature, it constituted a model for royal hand-kissing ceremonies. Unlike processions, such as that of *Corpus Christi*, the Christmas ceremony entailed direct contact between each Council and its individual members and the Royal person. Consequently, all Councils showed great concern over the order of precedence.[32]

The particular act in question took place on the afternoon of December 26, in the chamber of the "ordinary audiences," at the royal fortress (*alcázar*) in Madrid. After the different Councils were "called-to-order" by the Chief Steward, the king entered the hall and took his seat beneath a curtained canopy. Then came the turn of the Councils. The first to enter were the attorneys of the first Council, followed by the palace and court judges (*alcaldes*). Then came the councilors of that specific Council and, at the end, its president, who was first to kiss the king's hand. After doing so, the president took his place to the right of the Monarch and proceeded to announce the names of each councilor, judge and attorney as they approached the king to kiss his royal hand in silence before returning to their assigned seats. The hall was then emptied to make way for the following Council.[33]

The order of precedence between the different Councils at court ceremonies was established apparently in 1570, during the reign of Philip II, upon the arrival of Queen Anne of Austria.[34] At that time, the Council of Castile, which always presided, was followed by that of Aragon, the Inquisition and Italy. Next in line were the Council of Indies and the Council of the Orders, while the last to appear were the tribunals of Finance (*Contaduría de Hacienda*) and the Chief Accounting Office (*Contaduría Mayor de Cuentas*). The Councils of State and of War were excluded from the ceremony because they did not attend in the form of a collective body. However, by the reign of Philip IV, three significant changes had been introduced. The first was made in 1581 as a result of the union of the two Iberian crowns, thereafter instituting the rule that the Council of Italy would be followed by that of Portugal. The second change mandated that the Council of Crusade would be included in the ceremony and would come after the Tribunal of Finance, at the very end. The third change, and most relevant to our story, was that in the autumn of 1628 orders were given for the recently restored Council of Flanders to precede the Council of Indies and to occupy, thereafter, a place right behind the Council of Portugal. Clearly, it was this third change that moved Solórzano to pen his pamphlet.

Disagreements over precedence at court were common in the period from 1620 to 1650. It is precisely for that reason that the abovementioned dispute between Councils should not be dismissed as a mere anecdote.[35] What provoked Solórzano to write his text was the reconstitution of the Council of Flanders in 1627, ordered after the death of Archduke Albert of Austria in 1621. The passing away of the Archduke had put an end to the regime that emerged when Spain ceded its sovereignty over the Low Countries in 1598. Although the Archduke's widow — the *infanta* Isabella Clara Eugenia — continued to serve as the governor of the dominion, in order to ensure its sovereignty, the Crown was forced to make a series of concessions, one of which entailed recreating for Flanders a Council similar to the other Councils that existed at court. Before that date, a Ministry responsible for the Low Countries existed in Madrid, with a state councilor who was also a seal keeper assisted by a secretary, and charged with handling the business of Flanders and Burgundy. In 1588, when a second councilor was named and instructions and ordinances were elaborated stipulating its composition and competency, this ministry became a "collateral college." When sovereignty was ceded to the Archduke in 1598, the ministry lost much of its power, and, after the death of the second councilor in 1595, it was further marginalized. Because no one was named to succeed the deceased second councilor, the collateral college ceased to exist, and this was also accompanied by the designation of a "secretary of State for the House of Burgundy," who attended to certain matters, but never enjoyed a total control over the correspondence with Brussels, a responsibility that fell to the Council of State.[36]

Solórzano was not the only member of the Council of the Indies to react against the decision of giving preference to the Council of Flanders at the royal hand-kissing ceremony. The council itself sent a representation (*consulta*) to the king, dated December 22, 1628, whose authorship Feliciano Barrios attributes to don Rodrigo de Aguiar y Acuña, dean of councilors of the Indies. Together with this representation, the *British Library* holds the copy of another *Memorial*, sent by the Council of the Indies to the king, which presents eleven reasons as to why the Council of the Indies should not be preceded by the Council of Flanders and Burgundy.[37]

III

Solórzano begins his representation by analyzing the relations between the king, his court and his Councils. Using arguments that draw on Roman law and classical authors such as Ovid, Seneca, Lactancius and Symmachus but, above all, Cassiodorus and other more recent writers, like Baldo de Ubaldi (*ca.* 1320–1400), Solórzano posits the Roman Byzantine court as a paradigm for imitation. Following the example of Theodosius or Justinian, he describes the wisdom of the prince and considers him as the greatest expert on law. He also takes pains to emphasize the generosity with which the monarch grants favor, such as appointments to offices, among which the office of councilor was of the highest stature. The visual aspect is important to him. As each councilor bows before the monarch, his gaze meets that of the king. This annual demonstration of reverence to the sovereign at Christmas rewards both the Councils as a whole and each of its individual members in particular, because it ties them not only to the monarch but also to the grace linked to the birth of the Redeemer. In addition to this Christian connotation, Solórzano also compares the annual royal hand-kissing ceremony at Christmas to the adoration of the sacred purple toga of the Roman emperors. According to him, Spain was the only place that had continued this ceremony through the centuries. If the king's gaze confirmed the honor and dignity of the ministers object of his grace, at the same time it also exalted the sovereign himself.

For Solórzano, because imparting justice through the Councils raised Spain's sovereign above every other monarchs in terms of authority, letters and prudence, among all the other instances of the Spanish Monarchy, only they, the Councils, could grant the royal hall its full splendor. In accordance with the Roman paradigm and the belief in ancient nobility as a moral and social category, Solórzano argues that the kings of Spain rewarded the virtue and efforts of their councilors in three areas: the performance of their ministries, the exercise of arms, and the exercise of knowledge. Rewards came by way of granting titles of nobility and stipends from the Royal Exchequer.[38]

The Council of the Indies merited the king's favor, Solórzano argued, because of its history of services rendered and its willingness to respond to the needs of the Monarchy and those of the sovereign himself. The harm inflicted upon this body by changing the order of precedence was more deeply felt because the effects of royal gaze at the Christmas hand-kissing ceremony accumulated over time. In contrast to what had happened with the Council of Flanders, the Council of the Indies had felt these effects year after year during four successive reigns.[39] Since there was no cause to punish the Council of Indies, Solórzano considered the changes introduced in the ceremony a grievous injustice. The law, he said, did not allow transgressing what had been observed since ancient times. Novelties could only be admitted when they were indispensable or when they were of great and unquestioned utility. Citing the dispute between the cities of Burgos and Toledo, which fought doggedly over precedent in antiquity, vote and seat at the Cortes of Castile, he concluded that precedence was almost a possession and that altering it implied dispossession.[40]

Having established the importance of the Councils in the wider context of the Monarchy, Solórzano went on to argue that, as happened with the precedence of kings and princes that were judged according to the quality of their realm and vassals, the quality and preeminence of the Councils should be proportional to the kingdoms and states they governed and represented. Already in his *Indiarum Iure* (book 1, chapter, 16, no. 45) Solórzano made a similar point. He demonstrated that at that particular moment the king of Spain was first among all the world's monarchs. To illustrate this point, he cited a recent text by the German jurist Christopher Besoldus (1577–1638), in which the author ridiculed the king of England's pretensions to preeminence.[41] He also insisted that, although in the past Besoldus had recognized the French monarch's place above the king of Castile, by the 1620s he no longer did. Turning to the New World, Solórzano thus argued that the Council of the Indies was responsible for the government of not only a territory or a kingdom, but instead of an empire that embraced several realms and provinces, a view he reinforced by citing numerous authors who had referred to the Indies as an "empire."[42] Even Jean Bodin, a writer rather unsympathetic to Spain, he said, had recognized that the Indies perhaps made the Spanish Monarchy ten times greater than the Turkish Ottoman Empire. The most extended monarchy that the world had ever seen included a whole other universe, one "many times larger" than the Old World. For Solórzano, nothing could be more revealing of this grandeur than the Christian implementation and conversion of the Indies, where God was praised at all hours and latitudes.

Taking yet another route, Solórzano noted that by law the nobility and importance of a kingdom was measured and contemplated also on the basis of the profits and riches extracted from its fruits. According to him, virtually all kingdoms on earth were now sustained by the wealth of the Americas, they all envied and esteemed the Spanish Monarchy for that reason.[43] Indeed, even Flanders would admit that its sustenance depended on the support afforded by the riches of the Indies.[44]

Precedence was also regulated by the relative antiquity of the Councils. Both Roman and common law, in addition to authors like Juan de Platea, Casaneo and Tiraquel (1480–1558), taught that whoever came first enjoyed a greater importance in law and no one who was newer should be allowed to precede the older. They thus agreed that a double order resided within the court: one which granted priority to time and another that measured greatness in terms of honor. The first was of special interest to Solórzano, who held that it was comparable to primogeniture and, therefore, was rooted in divine, natural and positive law. Antiquity could also be assimilated to the veneration of age in the Roman *urbs*. The Council of Flanders that did not exist earlier as a body could not, therefore, aspire to a greater authority than the Council of the Indies. Furthermore, antiquity should be measured also from the moment in which the territories were united with, added to, or incorporated in, the Monarchy. That is, the antiquity of kingdoms in terms of their origins and foundation was less important than the date of their union with, or incorporation into, the Crown.[45] The Indies (understood as "all the islands and mainland discovered so far and [those] yet to be found"), had been incorporated by the Catholic Kings at the time of Columbus' original discovery (1492) and, in 1493, upon their recognition as a Castilian territory, they received the title of "empire" from the Pope. By contrast, the territory of Flanders was first inherited by Charles V (in 1506) and only later was incorporated in the Monarchy (1515). It was also unclear whether the kings had established or sworn that they would never transfer or des-incorporate Flanders from the Crown. Indeed, Philip II's donation of those lands to the archduke Albert of Austria in 1598 as dowry of the *infanta* Isabella Clara Eugenia proved the contrary, thus leading to the conclusion that Flanders was only (re)incorporated to the Crown in 1621. The incorporation of the Indies to Castile and the prohibition of ever alienating it[46] led Solórzano to suggest that the Americas may even have the same preeminence and antiquity as Castile itself. This was radically different than the cases of Aragon, Naples, Sicily, Portugal, Milan, Flanders and all other royal domains, which had been incorporated into the Monarchy through unification or aggregation, thus "maintaining their prior status". Because the Indies and Castile constituted one single kingdom and crown, the former could be governed directly by the Council of the latter, as happened until 1524, when the Council of the Indies was at last constituted.

In order to accredit its early incorporation (1492) to the crown, Solórzano referred to the Americas as a single entity, rather than a territory divided by Viceroyalties, kingdoms or provinces. Yet, the immensity and diversity of the New World eventually imposed themselves. Because patriotism was the primary referent, both in Madrid and in the Americas, such issues as these kingdoms' and provinces' accessory character with respect to Castile, their wealth, and the antiquity of their incorporation into the Crown, took on local hues and expressions. For example, the members of the Council of Indies refuted the claim that in the respective case of the Indies and Flanders, conquest was of less importance than inheritance. As far as the councilors were concerned, there was no natural or legal cause that could surpass in importance the criterion of antiquity of incorporation.[47] Furthermore and as mentioned above, in the late seventeenth century in both Mexico and Peru both Indians and Creoles argued that both entities had been *aggregated* to the Crown voluntarily. This of itself, weakened any claim diminishing the importance of the Americas because of conquest.[48]

Thus, while the Indies were a kingdom, perhaps an empire, Flanders was but a mere earldom that had been a completely feudalized entity of the Holy Germanic Empire and under the authority of French kings from its origins to 1526.[49] This was the reason why Flanders appeared almost last in the list of the sovereign's titles. Certainly, Flanders was the largest of the earldoms and had the best and most numerous cities, towns and lands; it was perhaps the most important of royal possessions in Europe but was not more important than the New World.

But, if by law the nobility and estimation of a kingdom was measured on the basis of the benefits extracted from its fruits and wealth, then there was no doubt but that within the Indies in 1629, when the *Memorial* was published, Peru held the most preeminent position. This was well illustrated by the promotions that several Viceroys received to serve in Peru after governing Mexico. On the other hand, according to antiquity Mexico came first. If Solórzano were aware of it, he certainly made a point of not mentioning it.[50]

Solórzano was unable to influence the royal mind. Neither his *Memorial*, nor the representation and *memorial* sent by the Council of Indies, met with success. No testimony survives as to why this was the case. Perhaps what carried the greatest weight was the deference Philip IV felt towards the royal family, and mainly to his aunt, *doña* Isabella Clara Eugenia, governor of the Low Countries. Her ability and her permanence in that position were beyond discussion and merited the strongest support at this strategic moment, in which Flanders was reincorporated into the Crown. Solórzano himself may have referred to deference when he mentioned in his *Memorial* that the modified order of precedence that placed the Council of Flanders above that of the Indies had to be "of maximum and evident utility" and when he argued that the king's decision was based, instead, on "reasons of state that often trample those based solely on rigorous justice".[51]

IV

The accessory character of the Indies in relation to Castile, the immensity of its territories, and the claims for a monopoly on office holding by natives (*naturales*), among others, supported the preeminence of the New World within the Spanish Monarchy. Yet, there were constant affirmations to the contrary, relegating the Indies to a subordinate, secondary position.[52] This subordination fuelled a local hypersensitivity. In their claims to the Crown, local power groups invoked justice and demonstrated a patriotic fervor, often characterized by a powerful vision of the past. Although somewhat analogous developments also happened on the Peninsula – In the midst of the worst crisis in Spain's hegemonic aspirations, writing in Castile, Diego de Saavedra

Fajardo similarly bore witness to developments that encouraged all to hold on to what was theirs, to rediscover antiquity and to cling to what has withstood the test of time[53]– in the Indies such claims were more numerous, tenacious and archaic. It was there that conservation as justice was brandished as the fundamental concern. Instead of adopting a "reason of state," as the channel through which theoretical anxieties were expressed, as José Luis Villacañas argues, a process of confessionalization began.[54] This process allowed the Spanish crown both to rely upon, and encourage reliance upon, religious mysteries, devotions and symbols such as the Immaculate Conception of Mary, as foundations of its legitimacy.

The idea that the New World was integrated rather than aggregated to the Crown of Castile led authors such as Juan de Solórzano, Juan de Palafox and Lorenzo Ramírez de Prado, among others, to extrapolate a series of privileges of a consensual nature that could favor Creole groups and their interests. The debate as to whether the Americas were or were not *accessory* in nature thus gave rise in the second half of the seventeenth century to an ambiguous identity as well as an imperfect system of self-government. Enjoying, until the reign of Charles III (1759–1788) of a relative autonomy in the context of the Catholic Monarchy, the Indies, in short, may have never been neither true "kingdoms" nor genuine "colonies".

Abbreviations

ACCMM   Archivo del cabildo catedral metropolitano de México, *Correspondencia*, libro 20.

AGS   Archivo General de Simancas.
Expediente sobre dotar una plaza del Consejo de Indias en criollos, 1635, *Estado*, 2655.37.

BL   British Library.
Dr. Juan Bautista Valençuela Velázquez, *Discurso que hizo el señor doctor don . . . , de el Consejo de su Majestad en el Supremo de Castilla, i su Governador Presidente de la Real Chancillería de Granada, siendo Regente del Consejo Supremo de Italia, sobre precedencia del dicho Consejo, i Regentes del, al Consejo y Consejeros de Portugal*, Granada, 1634, Eg. 348.
Consulta del Consejo de Indias al rey, *Ca.*1628 Eg. Ms. 348.

Notes

1 Lempérière, 2005.
2 To cite but a few examples, and with no pretension to exhaustiveness, see Ruiz and Vincent, 2008, p. 400; Gil, 2006, and the pioneering works of Hespanha, 1989a and 1989b, 445–455. Many other historiographical references from the past twenty years are found in Mazín, 2007.
3 Garriga, 2006, 35–130.
4 Mazín, 2007b.
5 As Sir George Clark wrote in 1929, the 17th century never saw seven full years without a war between some European states: 1610, 1669–1671, 1680–1682. Thus, in the European context war could be considered a vital condition that was much more normal than peace; Clark, 1945, 98, cited by Parker, 1986, 82.
6 Gil, 2007.
7 Rucquoi, 2007.
8 Hausberger and Mazín, 2009.
9 Garriga, 2006, 25.
10 Parker, 2006.

11 Ruiz Ibáñez, 2007, 240.

12 Torres, 2006, 96–98.

13 Relación de gobierno del marqués de Guadalcázar, 1629, in Hanke, 1978–1980, vol. II, 249–273.

14 The events of the riot of January 15, 1624 were the subject of detailed reports and analyses. "Relación del levantamiento que hubo en México contra el virrey", in García, 1982, 265–273. See also the documents relating to the Marquis of Gelves in Hanke, 1977, vol. III, 111–248; and Israel, 1975, 135–160. Finally, see Cañeque, 2004, 79–80, 96, 100–102.

15 Álvarez de Toledo, 2004.

16 Elliott, 1986, 37.

17 Thus, for example, in 1627 the Council of the Indies succeeded in having the king designate one of its councilors as Archbishop of Mexico. That prelate, don Francisco Manzo y Zúñiga, restricted quite considerably the power of the Viceroy Marquis de Cerralvo, successor of the vilified Marquis de Gelves.

18 In April 1635, the Council of State discussed whether one of the positions of councilor of the Council of the Indies should be granted in perpetuity to a Creole from those provinces, AGS (Archivo General de Simancas), *Estado*, 2655.37. I thank Fernando Bouza for providing a photocopy of this consultation and the resulting deliberations.

19 The New World dominions were the object of a reconnoitering by the Council in the decades 1630–1650, to demonstrate what the efforts to Christianize the Indians had achieved there, and the resulting density of Spanish colonization. Also described were the chain of cities, the inhabitants and the mineral and botanical resources found in its territories. Gil González Dávila, the royal chronicler, and Juan Díez de la Calle, a Council official, collected part of the information; the first in his *Theatro de las Indias Occidentales* (1649), that gave an account of the history of the dioceses and many of its cities; the second in an inventory of almost 5,000 functionaries in the Indies. Another claim by the American realms consisted in elaborating the final stages of an ample code of laws, an old project that was completed in 1636 by functionaries of the Council such as Antonio de León Pinelo and Juan de Solórzano Pereyra. Their collection was mediated by earlier collections of local decrees and by the juridical treatise that Solórzano Pereyra elaborated during his time as judge (*oidor*) in Lima. His *Indiarum Iure* (1629) was later translated by the author as *Política Indiana* (Madrid, 1647), a synthetic work that presented systematically the New World's social order. As is well known, the publication of the great legal code in Madrid did not take place until 1681. It appeared under the aforementioned title: *Recopilación de leyes de los reinos de las Indias*.

20 Barbosa de Luna, 1627. I thank Pedro Cardim for this reference.

21 Solórzano, 1629.

22 Valençuela, 1634. A print copy is in the British Library, Eg. 348.

23 Upon his return to the court of Madrid after many years as a judge in the *Audiencia* of Lima (1610–1627), Juan de Solórzano Pereyra first served as the attorney of the Council of Finance (*Hacienda*) (named February 26, 1628). He only served in this capacity for four months, as the King then named him attorney of the Council of the Indies. Though promoted to councilor on October 18, 1629, he continued to serve as attorney because his replacement, don Juan de Palafox y Mendoza, did not arrive until 1632. García, 2007.

24 Solórzano, 1629b.

25 He admitted, however, that he had not done so due to lack of space, Solórzano, 1996, book 5, ch. 15, no. 49.

26 Barrios, 2002, vol. I, 265–283.

27 The most important and recent mention is García, 2007, 193. David Brading (1991, 239–254) had previously characterized Solórzano's *Memorial*. . . as a "document of State". Though he does not refer explicitly to the *Memorial* . . . John H. Elliott, 1992, 53, evokes the teachings that Solórzano imparted there.

28 This is the second edition of the complete works of Solórzano, Zaragoza, 1676. The 1776 edition has numerous typographical errors due to the repositioning of the annotations and digressions which were placed as footnotes. This fact has diminished its importance and appreciation by scholars.

29 I use the copy of the first edition (1629) from the José Toribio Medina Collection at Chile's *Biblioteca Nacional*. Typical of the times, its 100 annotations and digressions are arranged around the main text, and thus reflect the same importance and hierarchy. Fernando Corona and Sara Gabriela Baz are collaborating with me on a critical edition of this text.

30 For example, in Cervantes, 1619; later works are cited in Garriga, 2006, 29, note 80. On the Council of State's discussion of a permanent seat for a Creole in the Council of the Indies, see above, note 18.

31 So it was expressed in 1611 by don Jerónimo de Cárcamo, canon of the Cathedral of Mexico who was sent to the Court of Madrid as the procurator of his Church: "I elaborated an *información en derecho* [information on law] that while brief is respected for its erudition, in which I show that the customs that the Churches in the Indies have received from those in Spain must not be reputed or measured by the time passed since their founding and observance in the Indies, but by the antiquity and legitimate and immemorial prescription they carried from Spain, and that are thus customs of legitimate unmemorable [*sic*] prescription", Jerónimo de Cárcamo to the Dean and chapter of Mexico, Madrid, May 30, 1611, ACCMM (Archivo del Cabildo Catedral Metropolitano de México), *Correspondencia*, vol. 20.

32 This order of precedence was tied to the royal decree of November 24, 1570, "Sobre las precedencias que a de aver entre los consejos y tribunales que residen en la corte", Barrios, 2002, 267.

33 Barrios, 1996, 48–49.

34 Barrios, 2002, 268.

35 Barrios, 2002, 269, refers to two examples: King Philip II's rejection of the Council of the Inquisition's pretension to follow that of Castile, which meant preceding the Council of Aragón; and the events of October 18, 1598, when the Council of Portugal excused itself from the funeral honors paid to that sovereign because it expected to receive a better place than the one assigned to it for the occasion. The first finds support in Rodríguez, 1980, 61–65; the second in Cabrera, 1877, t. IV, 297–333.

36 Esteban, 2005, 25–26.

37 Barrios, 2002, 270–271. Like Solórzano, don Rodrigo de Aguiar y Acuña had been a judge in the southern Viceroyalty, but in the *Audiencia* of Quito. In 1604 he was appointed to a seat as a councilor of the Indies. He took possession in 1607 and remained there until his death on October 5, 1629. He was replaced in that post by don Juan de Solórzano Pereyra, Schäfer, 2003.

38 Rucquoi, 1997, 273–298.

39 As set down in the Council's consultation with the king, presumably written by don Rodrigo de Aguiar y Acuña. Barrios, 2002, 271.

40 Until the Cortes of Alcalá de Henares in 1348, the city of Burgos held first place and spoke for all the other cities. But on that occasion, Toledo was thirsting for the first vote and the best seat, adducing its greater antiquity and nobility and the fact that it had been the court of the Visigoth kings. Given that Burgos occupied the first bench — the one reserved for the procurators — the King assigned another to those from Toledo, in front of the royal throne and in the middle of the hall. But the dispute continued. The matter was settled temporarily by conserving Burgos' rights, though when the Monarch spoke he did so in the name of Toledo. Because this issue was left pending, every time that their procurators came together, the controversy flared up anew. As late as the Cortes of Madrid in 1566 and 1570 when the proposition was read, those from Burgos and Toledo stood up simultaneously, both with the intention of responding to the king. Philip II calmed them by pronouncing

these words: "Toledo shall do as I command: let Burgos speak". López, 1861–1882, vol. I, 32, and vol. III, 24.

41 Here, I refer to the *Disertatione iuridico-politico de praecedentiae et sessionis praerogativa*, ch. 2.

42 Abraham Ortelio, Antonio de Herrera y Tordesillas, Juan Botero, Tomás Porcacho, Juan Magino, Diego de Valdés, Camilo Borrelo, Gregorio López Madera, José de Acosta, fray Alonso Fernández, fray Juan de Torquemada, Rodrigo Zamorano and Jacobo Maynoldo.

43 In his annotation number 48, Solórzano included a note from Camilo Borrel. According to this author, Queen Elizabeth of England had been obliged in parliament to recognize that his possession of the Indies made Philip II the most powerful king in the world.

44 The author makes an approximate calculation of the mineral wealth extracted at Potosí and other mines in the Indies. Up to the year 1628 he estimates a figure of 1,500 million pesos, counting only the metal for which the "royal fifth" had been paid (*lo quintado*); based on José de Acosta, Gil González Dávila and Simón Mayolo, annotation number 44.

45 Here, Solórzano bases his arguments on the aforementioned Besoldo, Aloisio Riccio and Eneas Silvio (1405–1464), who was appointed Pope in 1458 under the name of Pius II. In his history of the Council of Constance, the latter explains how that Synod considered the antiquity of the different realms only in relation to the date of their conversion to Christianity.

46 He cites four provisions: 1st: don Carlos and doña Juana, his mother, for the Island of Hispaniola, Barcelona, September 14, 1519; 2nd: by the same sovereigns, in general for all the islands discovered and yet to be discovered, Valladolid, July 9, 1520; 3rd: don Carlos, for New Spain, Pamplona, October 22, 1523; 4th: don Carlos, for the province of Tlaxcala, Madrid, March 13, 1535.

47 Consulta del Consejo al rey, BL, Eg. Ms. 348, ff. 74r y v.

48 In his book *Felicidad de México* (Mexico, 1666), dedicated to Santa María de Guadalupe, Luis Becerra Tanco claimed that New Spain had been incorporated into the Monarchy by aggregation. Between 1693 and 1750, the Indians of Peru, as a group, succeeded in obtaining from the Crown the most significant concessions in terms of social recognition in the entire history of the Viceroyalty. The autochthonous elites were able to push back social frontiers and prove that the Indians should enjoy the same privileges as old Christians. Thus, in 1699 in Spain an Incan cacique asked the Council of the Indies to establish an order of cavalry for Indian nobles with Santa Rosa de Lima as its patron saint, Estenssoro, 2003, 451–459.

49 Jean Bodin suggests that with respect to the Indies the King of Spain was the Pope's feudatory, having received his investiture from the pontiff. But this is refuted by Gregorio López Madera, fray Juan Márquez and Solórzano himself. These authors show that the bull stipulated no such clause and establish that it contains a clear and absolute concession and donation on the part of the papacy.

50 We know that New Spain was incorporated in 1523. It is unclear whether a similar official document was ever sent to Peru. Nevertheless, the antiquity of the former is evident from the dates in which their respective *Real Audiencia* were established: Mexico in 1527 and Lima in 1542. Real cédula por la cual se incorpora la Nueva España a la Corona . . . , Pamplona, October 22, 1523, in *Cedulario*, 1960, 11–15.

51 Solórzano, 1996, book V, ch. XV, no. 4.

52 By analogy with the Councils of Aragon, Italy and Portugal, Philip IV was inclined to accept that there be a permanent seat for a Creole councilor in the Council of the Indies. However, the Council of State brought to his attention the following reasons why no established rule obliged him to concede a place to a Creole: first, the distance and time required to recruit a deserving candidate, and then to replace him upon his death; second, because the territories of the Indies were so numerous and widespread that if he awarded a seat to one Creole all the rest of provinces would feel demeaned and irritated; third, that the example of the

Councils of Aragon and Italy did not apply, because their respective kingdoms had joined *"aeque principaliter*, which was not the case of the Indies, as [they] are ruled by the laws of Castile"; fourth, that naming a Creole would not necessarily result in obtaining general news from the Indies, as rarely was one person so well informed; in contrast, they could be obtained by appointing the most able subjects in the *Audiencias* of Lima or Mexico, whether Creoles or not. Gerónimo de Villanueva to the king, April 29, 1635, AGS, *Estado* 2655.37.

53 Saavedra, 1640. The edition of the *Idea de un príncipe católico* . . . most often used is that of Juan Bautista Verdussen, Antwerp, 1676, a work better known as *Empresas políticas*.

54 Villacañas, 2008, 75–103.

Bibliography

Actas de las Cortes de Castilla, Madrid, Real Academia de la Historia, 1861–1882.

Álvarez de Toledo, Cayetana, *Politics and Reform in Spain and Vice-Regal Mexico, The Life and Thought of Juan de Palafox 1600–1659*, Oxford, The Clarendon Press, 2004.

Barbosa de Luna, Pedro, *Memorial de la preferencia que haze el Reyno de Portugal, y su Consejo, al de Aragón, y de las dos Sicilias* . . ., Lisbon, Geraldo de Vinha, 1627.

Barrios, Feliciano, "Solórzano, la Monarquía y un conflicto entre Consejos", in Feliciano Barrios Pintado, coord., *Derecho y administración pública en las Indias Hispánicas. Actas del XII Congreso Internacional de Historia del Derecho Indiano (Toledo, 19 a 21 de octubre de 1998)*, Cuenca, Ediciones de la Universidad de Castilla-La Mancha, 2002, vol. I, pp. 265–283.

Barrios, Feliciano, "Los consejos de la monarquía hispánica en las *Etiquetas Generales* de 1651", in *Homenaje al profesor Alfonso García-Gallo*, Madrid, Universidad Complutense, 1996, vol. 3, pp. 43–62.

Brading David A., *Orbe indiano, de la Monarquía católica a la república criolla*, Mexico, Fondo de Cultura Económica, 1991.

Cabrera de Córdoba, L., *Felipe Segundo, Rey de España*, Madrid, 1877.

Cañeque, Alejandro, *The King's Living Image: The culture and politics of viceregal power in seventeenth century Colonial Mexico*, New York, London, Routledge, 2004.

Cedulario de la metrópoli mexicana, Mexico, Departamento del Distrito Federal, Dirección de Acción Social, VII Feria Mexicana del libro, 1960.

Clark G. N., *The Seventeenth Century*, London, 1929; 2nd edition, London, 1945.

Elliott, John H., *The Count-Duke of Olivares, A Statesman in an Age of Decline*, New Haven and London, Yale University Press, 1986.

Elliott, John H., "A Europe of Composite Monarchies", *Past and Present*, no. 137, november 1992, pp. 48–71.

Esteban Estríngana, Alicia, *Madrid y Bruselas, Relaciones de gobierno en la etapa postarchiducal, 1621–1634*, Leuven, Leuven University Press, 2005.

Estenssoro Fuchs, Juan Carlos, *Del paganismo a la santidad*, Lima, Instituto Francés de Estudios Andinos, Pontificia Universidad Católica del Perú, Instituto Riva-Agüero, 2003.

García, Genaro, *Colección de documentos inéditos y muy raros para la historia de México*, 3rd edition, Mexico, Editorial Porrúa, 1982, pp. 265–273 (Biblioteca Porrúa, 58).

García Hernán, Enrique, *Consejero de ambos mundos. Vida y obra de Juan de Solórzano Pereyra (1575–1655)*, Madrid, Fundación Mapfre Instituto de Cultura, 2007.

Garriga, Carlos, "Patrias criollas, plazas militares: sobre la América de Carlos IV", in Eduardo Matiré, coord., "La América de Carlos IV" (Cuadernos de Investigaciones y Documentos, I), Buenos Aires, Instituto de Investigaciones de Historia del Derecho, 2006, pp. 35–130.

Gil Pujol, Xavier, "La generación que leyó a Botero", in Mario Rizzo, Gaetano Sabatini and José Javier Ruiz Ibáñez eds., *Le forze del príncipe. Recursos, instrumentos y límites en la práctica del poder soberano en los territorios de la Monarquía hispánica*, Actas del seminario Internacional, Pavía, 22–24 de septiembre del 2000, Murcia, Universidad de Murcia, 2005, pp. 971–1022.

Gil Pujol, Xavier, *Tiempo de política, perspectivas historiográficas sobre la Europa Moderna*, Barcelona, Publicacions i Edicions, Universitat de Barcelona, 2006.

Gil Pujol, Xavier, "Integrar un mundo. Política y territorio en la Monarquía española de los siglos XVI y XVII", in Óscar Mazín ed., *III Jornadas de Historia de las Monarquías Ibéricas: Las Indias Occidentales, procesos de integración territorial (siglos XVI–XIX)*, (25–27 de septiembre de 2007), Mexico, El Colegio de México, (forthcoming).

Hausberger, Bernd and Óscar Mazín, "La Nueva España, los años de autonomía", in *Nueva Historia general de México*, Mexico, El Colegio de México, (2009), (forthcoming).

Hanke, Lewis, *Los virreyes españoles de la Casa de Austria, Perú*, Madrid, Ediciones Atlas, 1978–1980, vol. II.

Hanke, Lewis, *Los virreyes españoles de la Casa de Austria, México*, 1977, vol. III , pp. 111–248 (Biblioteca de Autores Españoles, vol. CCLXXV).

Hespanha, Antonio Manuel, *Vísperas del Leviatá. Instituciones y poder político (Portugal, siglo XVII)*, Madrid, Taurus, 1989.

Hespanha, Antonio Manuel, "'*Dignitas numquam moritur*' on a durabilidade do poder no Antigo Regime", in A. Iglesia Ferreiro ed., *Centralismo y autonomismo en los siglos XVI y XVII. Homenaje al profesor Jesús Lalinde Abadía*, Barcelona, Universitat de Barcelona, 1989, pp. 445–455.

Israel, Jonathan, *Race, Class and Politics in Colonial Mexico (1610–1670)*, Oxford, Oxford University Press, 1975.

Lempérière, Annick, "La 'cuestión colonial'", *Nuevo Mundo Mundos Nuevos*, Debates, 2005, online in february 8 2005. URL: http://nuevomundo.revues.org/index437.html.

López de Ayala, Pedro, *Crónica del rey don Pedro*, Madrid, Ibero-Americana, s/f.

Mazín, Óscar, in collaboration with Carmen Saucedo, *Una ventana al mundo hispánico, ensayo bibliográfico*, Mexico, El Colegio de México, 2007.

Mazín, Oscar ed., *III Jornadas de Historia de las Monarquías Ibéricas: Las Indias Occidentales, procesos de integración territorial (siglos XVI–XIX)*, Actas (September 25–27 2007) México, El Colegio de México. (Forthcoming).

Mendoza, Lourenço de, *Suplicacion a su Magestad Catolica del rey nuestro señor, que Dios guarde. Ante sus Reales Consejos de Portugal y de las Indias, en defensa de los Portugueses . . .* , Madrid, 1630.

Ortiz de Cervantes, Juan, *Información a favor del derecho que tienen los nacidos en las Indias a ser preferidos en las Prelacias, Dignidades y Canongías y otros Beneficios Eclesiásticos y Oficios Seculares de ellas*, año de 1619. [Probably printed in Madrid by the widow of Alonso Martin around 1619–1620].

Parker, Geoffrey, *España y los Países Bajos, 1559–1659*, Madrid, Rialp, 1986.

Parker, Geoffrey Parker, coord., *La crisis de la Monarquía de Felipe IV*, Barcelona, Crítica, Instituto Universitario de Historia Simancas, 2006.

Rodríguez Besne, J. R., "Notas sobre la estructura y funcionamiento del Consejo de la Santa y Suprema Inquisición", in J. Pérez Villanueva, *La inquisición española, nueva visión, nuevos horizontes*, Madrid, Siglo XXI, 1980, pp. 61–65.

Rucquoi, Adeline, "Être noble en Espagne aux XIVᵉ–XVIᵉ siècles" in Otto Gerhard Oexle y Werner Paravicini, eds., *Nobilitas. Funktion und Repräsentation des Adels in Alteuropa*, Göttingen, Vandenhoeck & Ruprecht, 1997, pp. 273–298.

Rucquoi, Adeline, "Reyes y reinos en la Península ibérica medieval", in *III Jornadas de Historia de las Monarquías Ibéricas: Las Indias Occidentales, procesos de integración territorial (siglos XVI–XIX)*, (september 25–27 2007), Mexico, El Colegio de México (Forthcoming).

Ruiz Ibáñez, José Javier and Bernard Vincent, *Los siglos XVI–XVII, política y sociedad* en *Historia de España 3er milenio*, Madrid, Editorial Síntesis, 2008.

Saavedra Fajardo, Diego de, *Idea de un príncipe político christiano representada en cien empresas*, 1ˢᵗ ed., Munich, 1640; 2ⁿᵈ ed., Milan, 1642.

Schäfer Ernesto, *El Consejo Real y Supremo de las Indias: su historia, organización y labor administrativa hasta la terminación de la Casa de Austria*, Madrid, Junta de Castilla y León, Marcial Pons, 2003.

Solórzano Pereyra, Juan de, *Memorial y discurso histórico de las razones que se ofrecen para que el Real y Supremo Consejo de las Indias deba preceder en todos los actos públicos al que llaman de Flandres*, Madrid, Francisco Martínez, 1629.

Solórzano Pereyra, Juan de, *Disputationem de Indiarum iure sive de iusta Indiarum Occidentalium inquisitione, acquisitione et retentione: tribus libris comprehensam*, Madrid, Francisco Martínez, 1629.

Solórzano Pereyra, Juan de, *Política indiana*, Madrid, Fundación José Antonio de Castro, 1996, 4 vols.

Torres Arancivia, Eduardo, *Corte de virreyes. El entorno del poder en el Perú del siglo XVII*, Lima, Fondo editorial de la Pontificia Universidad Católica del Perú, 2006.

Villacañas Berlanga, José Luis, "El final de la Edad Media", *Res publica revista de filosofía política*, no. 19, año II, 2008, pp. 75–103.

3

The Representatives of Asian and American Cities at the Cortes of Portugal

Pedro Cardim

In the early modern period, the crowns of Portugal and Castile incorporated a series of territories located in the Atlantic, the Indian Ocean and the Pacific. In the aftermaths of this process, both monarchies became body politics that, in the words of Bernardo Vieira Ravasco secretary of state of the Estado do Brazil in 1687, were "scattered in the four corners of the world and composed by several kingdoms, states and provinces . . . ".[1] Divided into two main groups, their territories included "ancient kingdoms" captured from Muslims during the so-called "Reconquista" of the Iberian Peninsula (Portugal; Castile-Leon; Aragon; Navarre) and "newly acquired territories", among them former Muslim kingdoms conquered at the end of the Christian re-conquest, as well as lands obtained by overseas expansion. Whereby the first were assimilated as Castilian or Portuguese territories, their political apparatus was substituted by that of their Christian rulers, and their main cities were granted a seat at the Representative Assemblies (*Cortes*) of Portugal and Castile, the faith of the newly acquired territories was radically distinct. Although similarly to what happened in Iberia, overseas territories were also incorporated into the Portuguese and Castilian crown, contrary to what happened in Europe, their right to have representation in the Cortes of Portugal and Castile became a vexed question. Why and how this happened is the subject of this chapter. I will first analyze the issue with regard to the extra-European municipalities of Portugal and then proceed to compare it with what happened in Castile. In the conclusion I will explore the implications of these findings to the debate on the status of these extra-European territories.

Representatives of Overseas Cities in the Portuguese Assembly

During the sixteenth century the Cortes of Portugal, summoned nine times, only included representatives from municipalities located on the Iberian Peninsula.[2]

Information provided by José Damião Rodrigues, Pedro Puntoni, Rafael Chambouleyron, Guida Marques and Letícia Ferreira was fundamental to the elaboration of this chapter. I sincerely thank all of you.

During this period the level of participation was generally poor. At the assembly summoned in 1562,[3] for example, only 38 out of the 91 localities with a seat at the Cortes sent a representative, and only 13 of those that took part in the meeting sent petitions to the king. Overseas representation, including the islands of Azores and Madeira (which were not strictly "overseas territories") and despite otherwise assiduous participation by European municipalities was lacking even at the highly important meeting of the Cortes of 1581 when Portugal was officially incorporated into the Habsburg Monarchy.[4] The same thing happened in the meeting that followed (in 1583).

During the call for the Cortes of 1619 and because Philip II announced that he would be visiting Portugal to attend the meeting, several municipalities from Luso-America requested authorization to send representatives to Lisbon. Among them was São Luís do Maranhão, located in the northern part of contemporary Brazil. In their letter to the king, the local elites stressed their continuing struggle against the French who attempted to invade the region, also highlighting the role played by them in obtaining victory over these European rivals. Representing themselves as the true conquerors of these lands, and based on that claim, they requested additional political rights.[5] Yet, when the cortes met, no representatives from overseas municipalities were present.[6] The issue whether overseas territories could send representatives fell into oblivion thereafter, as no Cortes were summoned in the 1620s and 1630s. After 1640, when Portugal obtained its independence, the duke of Braganza, now king, hoping to rally support, summoned frequent Cortes. He also attempted to expand participation in the assembly in order to demonstrate that the Braganza dynasty would rule in a completely different manner than the Habsburgs, which, by that stage, were often portrayed in the Braganza's propaganda as tyrants. Yet, despite these promises, and the importance of the 1641 meeting — in which the different units of the kingdom swore allegiance to the new dynasty — no representatives from overseas city councils were present.[7] The same happened in 1642. Nevertheless, as José Damião Rodrigues has pointed out, 1642 marked the first attendance by representatives of a city from the Azores (Angra), who were granted a seat in the second row of the room where the opening session took place.[8]

In 1645, however, representatives from a non-European city, Goa in India, participated for the first time in the Cortes. João Baptista de Chaves (scribe of the court of Goa, the Casa da Suplicação) and Manoel de Lis (accountant of the Mesa da Consciência, another court in Goa) who were sent to the meeting were granted a seat in the first row of the opening session, right behind Lisbon, Oporto, Évora, Coimbra and Santarém. Said otherwise, they were included in the most prominent section of the assembly and were seated in the first of the eighteen rows facing the king. Nevertheless, the monarch was very clear in defining the place that ought to be occupied by the representatives of Goa. Although in the first row, they were the last to be included in it, explicitly behind the representatives of the most ancient and prominent cities of "European" Portugal.[9] The representatives from Goa not only took part in the opening ceremony. They were also among the so-called "definidores", that is to say, a small group of deputies that was selected to take part in all the sessions and thus play a major role in the making of the most important decisions. Indeed, they even met with the king himself![10] One of the criteria to choose the "definidores" was to pick councils that were heads of judicial counties. In other words, those who represented not only the local community, but also the region in which they were located.

The decision to grant Goa with this very honorable place in the assembly and to distinguish it with the rank of "definidor" was probably due to the fact that it was the head of the "Estado da Índia". It therefore could be considered to represent the ensemble of its municipalities. As for Angra in the Azores, in this meeting of the Cortes of 1645 it was represented by Tomé Correia da Costa and Feliciano da Silva de Almeida, both seated at the second row. Other cities in the Azores and Madeira were not represented.

In 1653, for the first time, a representative from Portuguese America took part in the meeting. Jerónimo Serrão de Paiva came directly from Salvador for that end and he was classified as "procurador do Brazil".[11] Although Serrão de Paiva was relegated to a secondary section of the assembly, similarly to the representatives of Goa, he succeeded in being appointed "definidor". The following year, the city council of Funchal (on the island of Madeira) was granted a seat at the Cortes.

From this moment onward, these municipalities regularly participated in the Portuguese parliament. In 1668, when the Cortes was summoned to swear prince Peter as regent, representatives from Goa (D. Francisco de Lima) and from Salvador (Joseph Moreira de Azevedo) took part in the assembly. In January of 1674, the regent granted seat in the fifth row at the opening session to a representative from São Luís do Maranhão (Northern Brazil). Manuel Campelo de Andrade who was chosen was already at the court, representing the region.[12]

That Goa, Salvador and São Luís do Maranhão had been chosen as representatives of overseas domains was probably related to their role as heads of judicial circumscriptions. In addition, Goa, Salvador and São Luís were the capital cities of the main Portuguese overseas dominions: the "Estado da Índia", the "Estado do Brasil" and the "Estado do Maranhão". It was thus strategic for the recently enthroned dynasty to count with their presence and perhaps support. Furthermore, from the late sixteenth century, Goa and Salvador acted as representatives in fiscal negotiations of the several city councils included in their jurisdiction.[13] They may have even sponsored local assemblies that gathered representatives of other municipalities. But perhaps at a time when rivalries with other European powers were increasingly intense, equally important was royal wish to tie these territories as closely as possible to metropolitan authorities.

Although the individuals chosen to represent Goa, Salvador, and São Luís de Maranhão were of extremely diverse trajectories, they were all experienced in matters of local government. José Moreira de Azevedo who represented Salvador in 1668, for example, was municipal judge. Manuel Campelo de Andrade, of São Luís, was judge of orphans and *Procurador* of that municipality in Lisbon. Some representatives could boast their military service record. Such was the case with Manuel de Lis, representative of Goa in 1645, and Jerónimo Serrão de Paiva, *Procurador* of Salvador in 1653. Others had an important involvement in commercial activities, for example Francisco de Lima, representative of Goa in 1668. Although with strong roots in the local or regional political scene, and with a proved capacity to establish relations with the crown and the central administrative bodies, not all these men were born in the territories they represented.

The American Cities in the Cortes of Castile

As happened in Portugal, American and Asian territories conquered by Spain were incorporated into Castile. In principle, therefore, there was nothing preventing them from sending representation to the Cortes of Castile. Furthermore, since the early sixteenth century, Castilian law allowed the American municipalities to gather together in local assemblies, aimed at discussing common affairs. Yet, not having been invited to participate, as early as 1518, the town councils of Santo Domingo expressed their wish to send a "general representative of the island" to the meeting. Their petition was denied, the king arguing that only he could decide who would be invited to the Cortes.

In the 1520s, hoping to obtain a seat at the parliament, the town council of Mexico sent an alderman to Spain. Several southern Castilian cities such as Jaen, Seville, Granada and Murcia, it claimed, have recently obtained such a seat because they were "heads of the kingdom" (*cabeza del reino*). Because Mexico was "the head of New Spain" it should be given the same treatment.[14] King Charles I denied the petition, arguing it may set an unwelcomed precedent that may lead other Spanish American cities to pursue the same end. However, in 1530 the crown changed its decision, granting the city of Mexico the rank of "first vote among the cities and villages of New Spain, similarly to what happened in Castile with the city of Murcia". Several years later Philip II granted Lima the same privilege. Yet, although the participation of American cities was now theoretically allowed, apparently, neither Mexico not Lima ever took part in the assembly. This may have been due to the fact that, until the reign of Philip II, the inhabitants of Spanish America were exempt from paying most taxes levied in Spain and, instead, paid taxes particular to the New World. This fiscal particularity may explain why the participation of American cities in the Cortes was not an urgent or an important matter for neither the crown nor the cities. Furthermore, the cities may have feared that their participation may result in the application of new taxes in their jurisdiction.

One way or the other, in their decisions, the kings specified that although invited to the Cortes of Castile, American cities could not organize their own assemblies. Or said otherwise, the summoning of meetings to solve specific issues was allowed, but these were explicitly forbidden to bear the name of "Cortes". Instead, they were to be called "congresses" (*congresos*). In other words, the term "Cortes" was to be exclusively used to name the assemblies summoned by the king and in which he would be present. In the following years this policy remained fixed and meetings that took place in both the viceroyalty of New Spain and in Peru indeed took the designation of "congresses." The same thing happened in Portuguese India and Brazil, where several "juntas de cidades" took place that, although called by the viceroy or the governor were never considered "cortes".[15]

Facing financial hardship and hoping for financial gains, mainly, the extension of several levies already existing in Europe to the Americas, at the end of the sixteenth century and the beginning of the seventeenth century, Castilian authorities considered the possibility of instituting representative assemblies one in each of the two American viceroyalties. Even though the aim was to impose a tax burden similar to the one that was being negotiated at the Cortes of Castile, these assemblies would maintain their designation as "congreses," not Cortes.

Under Philip IV and the ministry of count-duke of Olivares, the Spanish crown took measures to bring four representatives of each American viceroyalty to the Castilian Cortes. The aim was mostly fiscal: Olivares wanted to extend the Castilian tax burden to the American territories.[16] In Olivares's view (in his famous "Gran

Memorial" of 1624), the viceroyalty of New Spain was "almost in Castile" ("casi uno en Castilla"). Yet, at the same time, a new understanding of the relationship between king and the Americas emerged. According to it, American cities were not allowed to call their meetings "Cortes" because the king's authority in the New World was more absolute than in Europe. Count of Chinchón, viceroy of Peru, expressed this opinion in 1628 arguing that "I recognize that in the Indies there are no meetings of the Cortes, branches or estates, or parliaments, and therefore the royal power of his majesty is free and absolute" (*Si bien reconozco que en las Indias no hay Junta de Cortes, Brazos, Estamentos ni Parlamentos, y que así la potestad real de Su Magestad es libre y absoluta*).[17]

The Council of Indies seemed to agree. Answering Chinchón it stated that:

> The Indies are very different than the other kingdoms, not only in the power that vassals have in these cases, but in their quality. There may be gentlemen of quality there, who may be worthy of all types of grants, but these tend to be those who have less influence in helping to obtain such (financial) measures. And it is more possible to find help in the merchant guild and other men of commerce. And there is no vote in the Cortes nor in a meeting of city council, except meetings of ministers that viceroys call with a few citizens that they chose and with these agreements, that are communicated to the royal delegates (corregidor) and ecclesiastics, these issues are easily introduced in the municipal councils and cathedral chapters when it is convenient.[18]

While debate on the status of American municipalities continued, it is clear that, although contrary to Americans of European descent that were extent of paying taxes, the Indians did pay taxes, the authorities did not envisage the possible participation at the Cortes of representatives of the native populations. Only on exceptional occasions was this population included as happened in 1584, with the symbolic presence at the Cortes of representatives from the Indian community of Tlaxcala (Mexico).[19]

Overseas Territories and Political Status

In order to understand what was at stake in debates regarding the presence of overseas municipalities at the Cortes, several issues needs addressing. First: in the Portuguese context, the exact meaning of the expression "overseas lands" was not clear. It reflected the perspective of those who regarded the "rest of the world" from a European point of view. Yet, although in theory it included all territories located outside Europe, in reality such territories could have highly differentiated status. The Azores and Madeira, for example, were not considered overseas lands and therefore were not under the jurisdiction of the Portuguese Overseas Council (created 1642). This may have happened because these two archipelagos were not inhabited and thus their incorporation could not be portrayed as a "conquest". Furthermore, they were incorporated into the Portuguese empire in a very early stage of its maritime expansion and, because they lacked native population, the authorities were able to reproduce in them the Portuguese political and social structures. Other territories were just as varied. They consisted of lands with very different political status and very diverse range of rights and duties. This was true in both Europe and overseas. Thus, although in general the status of lands located in Europe was automatically higher than those located elsewhere, admitting deputies of non-European municipals to the Cortes could generate conflict with ancient towns located on the Iberian Peninsula, which had no representation in the assembly or, on the contrary, who were represented and wanted to keep representation to a minimum in order to ensure their exclusivity and privileges.

Second: in the early stages of colonization, municipal councils were very precarious. It usually took several years before the administration of these cities acquired the capacity to establish a more or less systematic political communication with the crown and to deal with the complexity of courtly politics. When the overseas urban centers of the two Iberian crowns began expressing the wish to interact with the crown more intensely, they were forced to cope with the asymmetric character of these political ensembles, which discriminated against them, preferring the Peninsular domains.

Contemporary political culture included several criteria to evaluate the rank of a territory. It considered its "age" and the age of its institutions. In principle, the older a land or an institution was, the higher its rank. Geography was also taken into account: to be located outside Europe was automatically considered a negative feature, usually associated with inferiority and lack of civilization. The way a territory entered into the body politic was also an important element with political implications. For those that were incorporated, the fact that they were "conquered" meant that their jurisdictional identity could be erased. In addition, lands classified as "conquests" shared a secondary status because their institutions and inhabitants were often deprived of some of the most basic political rights. One of those rights was precisely the capacity to send representatives to a parliamentary assembly. Another factor was the question who had taken the initiative to establish a political link between two territories. In principle, the "author" of such a union was in a position of superiority vis à vis the land that was subject to incorporation. One other important criterion to assess the rank of a territory was the date of incorporation. In principle, lands that entered earlier had more preeminence than those who were incorporated later. Other criteria were the existence of political institutions shaped by European patterns, the contribution of the inhabitants to the ensemble of the body politic, the dignity of the noble families living in the territory, its political and economic relevance, the distance from the court and so forth.

Taking all these criteria into account, it is easy to understand why, in the early stages of expansion, overseas dominions were relegated to a secondary position within the ensemble of territories that were part of the Iberian monarchies. This downgrading was justified by the following reasons: their entry into the Iberian crowns was relatively recent, most of them were "conquests", which meant that they were assimilated and not aggregated (i.e., they did not preserve their original jurisdictional specificity), they had been incorporated rather than had chose to incorporate, they were located outside Europe and (even) outside Christianity, and were often considered uncivilized. Furthermore, at their early stages of existence, most such territories had no institutions capable of interacting with the crown at the same level as Iberian territories. It took some time before their local elites developed the capacity to fight for their rights and privileges. Finally, no king ever visited the overseas territories or envisaged the possibility of establishing a royal court there.

This ensemble of factors explains why, at the beginning of colonization, the overseas territories shared a secondary rank within both Iberian monarchies. They may also explain why the municipalities of Goa and Salvador integrated late into the Cortes and why representatives from African municipalities were never admitted.

Nevertheless, far from being static, the political status of each territory could be modi-fied. That belief led several Spanish America municipalities to request representation in the Cortes. It also explained why local elite from Goa and Salvador were so eager to maintain and if possible improve their status. Following this logic, in 1673 the ruling elite of Salvador, already represented in the Cortes, requested the regent of Portugal a seat in the first row of the assembly, equaling them to the rank of Goa (in India). According to them, there were plenty of reasons why their petition was justified. By that time, the *Estado do Brazil* (of which Salvador was capital) was becoming increas-ingly important to the Portuguese body politic. It has given plenty of proof of its loyalty to the Portuguese crown, for example, in its immediate support of the Braganza dynasty. It had played a major role in the war against the Dutch and against the natives. It had contributed greatly to the fiscal obligations included in the peace treaty with the United Provinces and in the dowry of Catherine of Braganza. Finally, the crown recently created the title of "Prince of Brazil".[20] In 1674, Peter, the regent, agreed. From that year onward, the representatives of Salvador held a rank equal to Goa in the parliament.

Concluding Remarks

Several decades ago, Charles Boxer astutely remarked that, in the second half of the seventeenth century, Goa and Bahia were placed on a level with the cities of metro-politan Portugal, over a century before the principle of "no taxation without representation" became one of the reasons for the political break between Great Britain and the Thirteen Colonies.[21] Boxer's remark is, indeed, very pertinent. From the mid-seventeenth century onwards, three (and not two) overseas Portuguese cities — Goa, Salvador and São Luís do Maranhão — were represented at the Portuguese parliament. Delegates from these cities participated in the opening sessions and played a very active role in negotiations with the crown.

Things in Castile worked differently. Although the town councils of Mexico and Lima were granted the right to send their representatives to the parliament, they did not. The reasons were multiple: the costs of sending representatives and the time that was needed to make the voyage, the reluctance of several older Iberian municipalities to share their rank with the recently created American enclaves and, finally, but perhaps most importantly, the fear of being required to adopt new fiscal measures negotiated at the Castilian parliament.

As a result, the Portuguese Representative Assembly became a unique case: it was comprised of representatives of one hundred Portuguese Iberian cities and towns, as well as delegates from three extra-European territories. True, this was an exiguous number: three overseas representatives as opposed to about one hundred representa-tives from within Europe. Nonetheless, three was more than other empires were willing to do. These developments perhaps explained how the Portuguese monarchy was able to maintain its multi-continental character.

There is no doubt that a comprehensive analysis of the political representation of overseas cities demands a further study. Such a study would include the social profile of delegates, the connections between them and the ruling elites of the three cities, the actual participation of overseas representatives in each one of the meetings, the contents of petitions sent by overseas municipalities and the response they received and, finally, the study of other means of representation overseas cities may have used, such as a permanent representation at the court. These representations that American, African, and Asian municipalities sent to Lisbon throughout the entire colonial period embodied their hope of making their rights respected and ensuring their prerogatives in regard to the crown's central administrative bodies. It is probably that despite the importance of the Cortes, having a permanent representative was a much more efficient method to protect and promote their various interests.

One way or the other, a study of the Cortes highlights the inner structure of the Portuguese (and Spanish) Monarchy, which was based on hierarchy and asymmetry, the way political rights were distributed and "used" by the local elites through processes of inclusion and exclusion, the capacity of overseas municipalities to communicate and negotiate with the political centre, as well as testifies that these municipalities felt as members of an imperial organization and committed to imperial goals. Representation in the Cortes also allowed them to join in the decision-making process, it linked the political centre and the territories that were part of the Monarchy, it identified and gave place to both European and non-European vassals and, finally, it clarified that the nature of royal power was different in Europe and elsewhere. Rather than based only on political domination and economic exploitation, the early modern Iberian monarchies were also moral and political spaces of inclusion and exclusion, in which hierarchy and differentiation were the fundamental principles.

Abbreviations

AN-TdT   Arquivos Nacionais — Torre do Tombo, Lisbon.
BNP   Biblioteca Nacional de Portugal (Lisbon).
BPA   Biblioteca do Palácio da Ajuda (Lisbon).

Notes

1 " . . . o corpo de uma Monarquia dividida por todas as quatro partes do Mundo e composta de tão diversos Reinos Estados e Províncias como a de Portugal . . . " — quoted by Puntoni, 2010, 189.
2 "Planta das Cortes de Torres Novas, 1525" — BNP, Mss. 201, nº 131; about the Cortes of Portugal, Cardim, 1998 and 2005.
3 "Gráfico das cortes reunidas em Lisboa em 1562". BPA, 44-XIII-42 fl. 68–68v.; Cruz, 1992, 18; Barbosa Machado, 1736, 162 ss.
4 Bouza Álvarez,1987, 279 ss. and 411–414. See also "Notícia das cortes de 1579 com o nome dos procuradores", BPA, 50-V-23 fl. 48–50v.; "Notícia das cortes de 1580 com o nome dos procuradores", BPA, 50-V-23 fl. 53–54.
5 Marques, 2002, 7–35. See also Marques, 2009, 285 ss.
6 Auto do Juramento que El Rey Dom Phelippe Nosso Senhor, Segundo deste nome, fez aos três Estados deste Reyno, & do que elles fizerão a sua Magestade, do reconhecimento, & aceitação do Príncipe Dom Phelippe nosso Senhor, seu filho, Primogénito. Em Lisboa a 14 dias do mês de Julho de 1619. E assi o acto das Cortes que a 18 dias do mesmo mês se celebrou nella . . . , Lisboa, Pedro Crasbeeck, 1619.
7 "Gráfico da sala de Cortes de 1641" — AN-TdT. Maço 8 de Cortes, nº 1.
8 Rodrigues, 1994, 235.
9 "Procuradores de Cortes de Goa: Alvará do Lugar que hão de ter nellas" — AN-TdT. Chancelaria de D. João IV, Liv. 25, fol. 83, 25 November 1643.
10 "Cortes de 1645 — Braço do Povo. Livro dos termos e assentos". BNP, cod. 3722, fl. 25 ss.
11 "Procuradores que estão por definidores com voto e declaração dos que estão com alter-

nativa em as cortes que se começaram em 22 de Outubro de 1653". BPA, 51–VI-19, fl. 345–347.

12 "Alvará para que o Procurador do Maranhão possa ir a Cortes" — AN-TdT. Chancelaria de D. Afonso VI, Liv. 46 f. 95v. — "por sua petição me reprezentou Manoel Campello de Andrada procurador do estado do Maranhão que asiste em esta cidade para effeito de lhe conceder que em nome do mesmo estado tivesse Luguar nas cortes que de presente he de selebrar e tendo comsideração a se ter comsedido esta graça a outras conquistas e não duvidar a este requerimento o procurador da coroa, hey por bem e me praz que o supplicante tenha luguar nas cotes como procurador do ditto estado como pede e visto o que allega de sua procuração não especificar que era de Cortes se obrigara por termo na forma do estillo para que no tempo que se lhe remetão fazer vir procuração para este particullar e para auer memoria da mercê que faço a este estado se tomará por lembrança na secretaria do Estado e se cumprira este Alvará como nelle se contem e uallera posto que haja de durar mais de hum anno sem cmbargo da ordenação Livro Segundo titulo quarenta em contrario . . . ", 28 November 1673.

13 See Miranda's work on the fiscal policy of the *Estado da Índia* during the first two decades of the 17th century (2010); see also Santos, 2010.

14 Ramos Pérez, 1967; Borah, 1956, 246–257; Bronner, 1967. See also Lohmann Villena, 1989, 33–40; Martínez Cardos, 1956.

15 Magalhães, 2009, 137 ss.

16 Díaz Rementeria, 1992, 184.

17 Lima, 14th March 1628 — cfr. Bronner, 1967, 1138.

18 "Las Indias son muy diferentes de los otros reinos, no sólo en el poder que los vasallos tienen en estos casos, sino en la calidad dellos. Que aunque hay caballeros de calidad, en quien caben todo este género de mercedes, suelen ser los que tienen menos mano en ayudar a estos arbitrios. Y se suele hallar más ayuda en el consulado de los mercaderes y en otros hombres de trato. Y no hay votos en Cortes ni junta de ayuntamiento, sino que hacen los virreyes juntas de ministros y llaman algunos vecinos, cuales les parece, y con aquellos acuerdos, y comunicándolo con los corregidores y los prelados, fácilmente se introduce la materia en los cabildos eclesiásticos y seglares, cuando conviene y se halla dispuesta" Bronner, 1967, 1139.

19 Díaz Serrano, 2009.

20 Since the mid-16th century the heir of the Portuguese crown held the title of "Prince of Brazil"; "Registo de Huma Carta para a Sua Alteza sobre o lugar de o lugar no banco de Cortes nessa cidade e nas cortes que Vossa Alteza mandar celebrar em janeiro de seiscentos e sessenta e oito e se deu assento a esta cidade da Bahia no segundo banco e nos achamos obrigados a pedir a Vossa Alteza seja servido fazer lhes mercê de que tenha seu lugar no primeiro e nos mais actos que celebram pois concorrem nella todas as razoens de merecimento para esta honra que podem pedir se e não serem maiores as da cidade de Goa a quem se concedeu porque este Estado do Brazil he da grandeza e importância ao serviço de Vossa Alteza e esta cidade cabeça delles e lealdade tão nascida de seu amor como serviço na promptidão e alegria com que aceitou e celebrava a felice aclamação do Rey Dom João quarto digníssimo Pai de Vossa Alteza os serviços que com vidas e fazendas fizeram nas guerras dos Olandezes por tempo de quarenta annos e actualmente se estão fazendo de vinte a esta parte no gentio bárbaro desta capitania quaze toda a sua custa deste povo [. . .] e sobretudo esta despeza, contribue com hum milhão e duzentos e oitenta mil cruzados a quarenta por anno para a paz de Olanda e dote da Sereníssima Rainha da Gram Bretanha e o que he mais achavanos todos com fidelissimo animo para tudo quanto Vossa Alteza mandar de seu serviço com pessoas vidas e fazendas como servião nossos passados demais de todas estas razoens e que so persistem todo o merecimento he a de Vossa Alteza se immortular Principe do Brazil que parece obriga a Vossa a que honre com maior lugar que aqui pedimos e mais tento esta cidade do Porto que nas cortes tem o primeiro banco Deos

Guarde a Vossa Alteza esperamos esta mercê que aos reaes pez de Vossa Alteza pedimos com toda a devida omição. Guarde Deos a Real pessoa de Vossa Alteza como seus vassalos havemos mister. Bahia Nove de março de Mil seiscentos setenta e três anos" Documentos Históricos do Arquivo Municipal de Salvador — Cartas do Senado — vol. 1, 118–119. I wholeheartedly thank Letícia Ferreira of the Universidade Federal Fluminense for calling my attention to such an important document.
21 Boxer, 1965, 109.

Bibliography

Auto do Juramento que El Rey Dom Phelippe Nosso Senhor, Segundo deste nome, fez aos três Estados deste Reyno, & do que elles fizerão a sua Magestade, do reconhecimento, & aceitação do Príncipe Dom Phelippe nosso Senhor, seu filho, Primogénito. Em Lisboa a 14 dias do mês de Julho de 1619. E assi o acto das Cortes que a 18 dias do mesmo mês se celebrou nella . . . , Lisbon, Pedro Crasbeeck, 1619.

Barbosa Machado, Diogo, *Memorias para a Historia de Portugal, que comprehendem o Governo del rey D. Sebastião . . .* , Lisbon, Joseph Antonio da Sylva, 1736.

Borah, Woodrow, "Representative institutions in the Spanish Empire in the New World", *The Americas*, 13, 1956, pp. 246–257.

Bouza Álvarez, Fernando, *Portugal en la Monarquía Hispánica (1580–1640). Felipe II, las Cortes de Tomar y la génesis del Portugal Católico*, Madrid, Universidad Complutense, 1987.

Boxer, Charles R., *Portuguese Society in the Tropics. The Municipal Councils of Goa, Macao, Bahia, and Luanda, 1510–1800*, Madison, The University of Wisconsin Press, 1965.

Bronner, Fred, "La Unión de las Armas en el Perú. Aspectos político-legales", *Anuario de Estudios Americanos*, 24, 1967, pp. 1133–1176.

Cardim, Pedro, *Cortes e Cultura Política no Portugal do Antigo Regime*, Lisbon, Edições Cosmos, 1998.

——, "Entre o centro e as periferias. A assembleia de Cortes e a dinâmica política da época moderna" *in* Mafalda Soares da Cunha and Teresa Fonseca (eds.), *Os Municípios no Portugal Moderno. Dos Forais Manuelinos às Reformas Liberais*, Évora, Colibri-CIDEHUS-Universidade de Évora, 2005, pp. 167–242.

Cruz, Maria do Rosário Themudo Barata Azevedo, *As Regências na Menoridade de D. Sebastião. Elementos para uma história estrutural*, Lisbon, I.N.-C.M., 1992.

Díaz Rementeria, Carlos, "La Constitución de la sociedad política" *in* Ismael Sánchez Bella, Alberto de la Hera and Carlos Diaz Rementeria, *Historia del Derecho Indiano*, Madrid, Mapfre, 1992, pp. 167–190.

Díaz Serrano, Ana, *El modelo político de la Monarquía Hispánica desde una perspectiva comparada. Las repúblicas de Murcia y Tlaxcala en el siglo XVI*, Doctoral Dissertation, Universidad de Murcia, 2009.

Lohmann Villena, Guillermo, "Notas sobre la presencia de la Nueva España en las cortes metropolitanas y de cortes en la Nueva España en los siglos XVI y XVII", *Historia Mexicana*, vol. 39, No. 1, *Homenaje a Silvio Zavala* II, Jul.–Sep., 1989, pp. 33–40.

Marques, Guida, "O Estado do Brasil na União Ibérica: dinâmicas políticas no Brasil no tempo de Filipe II de Portugal", *Penélope. Revista de História e Ciências Sociais*, nº 27 2002, pp. 7–35.

——, *L'Invention du Brésil entre deux mondes. Gouvernement et pratiques politiques de l'Amérique portugaise dans l'union ibérique (1580–1640)*, Doctoral Dissertation, EHESS, Paris, 2009.

Martínez Cardos, J., *Las Indias y las Cortes de Castilla durante los siglos XVI y XVII*, Madrid, 1956.

Magalhães, Joaquim Romero, "A cobrança do ouro do rei nas Minas Gerais: o fim da capitação — 1741–1750", *Tempo*, 27, December 2009, pp. 135–150.

Miranda, Susana, "O financiamento do Estado da Índia (c. 1580–1640): fiscalidade e crédito", in *Portugal na Confluência das Rotas Ultramarinas*, Faculdade de Ciências Sociais e Humanas da UNL, Lisbon, CHAM (workshop held on December 3 and 4, 2010).

Puntoni, Pedro, *O Estado do Brasil. Poder e política na Bahia colonial (1548–1700)*, dissertation to get the *Título de Livre-Docência em História do Brasil*, Universidade de São Paulo, Brasil, 2010.

Ramos Pérez, Demetrio, "Las ciudades de Indias y su asiento en Cortes de Castilla", *Revista del Instituto de Historia del Derecho Ricardo Levene*, Buenos Aires, 18, 1967, pp. 170–185.

Rodrigues, José Damião, *Poder Municipal e Oligarquias Urbanas. Ponta Delgada no Século XVII*, Ponta Delgada, Instituto Cultural de Ponta Delgada, 1994.

Santos, Letícia Ferreira dos, *Amor, sacrifício e lealdade. O donativo para o casamento de Catarina de Bragança e para a paz de Holanda (Bahia, 1661–1725)*, Master Dissertation, Universidade Federal Fluminense — Niterói (Rio de Janeiro), 2010.

Overseas Alliances

4

The English Marriage and the Peace with Holland in Bahia (1661–1725)

Rodrigo Bentes Monteiro

In the 1650s and 1660s, the new Braganza monarch of Portugal entered into a series of treaties with both England and the Low Countries. Historians who studied these episodes tended to focus on their geo-political and diplomatic consequences. But what happened if we study them as observatories for the way the various units and groups within a composite monarchy both integrated in as well as created the whole? I propose to do so by analyzing the treaties and the difficulties of implementing them as a dialogue between the king and his subjects in Bahia regarding the constitution of the body politic of Portugal.

I. Negotiating Peace, Negotiating a Dowry

The constitution of a British Republic in 1649 and the arrival of Prince Rupert's royalist fleet in Lisbon in the midst of a war between Portugal and Spain generated a complicated political situation. The following year, as an armada sent by the English parliament anchored in Cascais, the Republic's ambassador asked King John IV to hand the Prince over to the British. Because the Portuguese Monarch refused, advocating his neutrality, the English fleet closed off the mouth of the Tagus river, thus practically blockading Lisbon. This was the beginning of an undeclared war between the two countries with the English, among other things, attacking the fleet of Brazil. Shortly afterwards, Madrid recognized the Republic. In 1652, Portugal agreed to restore English merchandise confiscated in 1650 and pay until 1654 annually 50 thousand pounds in reparations. These arrangements were not mutual: the Portuguese kingdom was not compensated for the seven-month blockade, the embargo on Portuguese merchants in England and the attack on Brazil Company's fleet.[1]

At the end of 1655, the government of the British Republic claimed the first

Translated by Roger Arthur Gough. This essay has benefitted from the research of Letícia dos Santos Ferreira, of the Post-Graduate Programme in History of the Federal Fluminense University. I wish to thank her for cataloguing the primary sources and for our exchange of ideas.

thirty thousand pounds owed by Portugal. In June 1656, with yet another English fleet within sight of Lisbon, Portugal ratified the 1652 treaty. In 1657, Castile conquered the town Olivença, Portugal failed to do the same with Badajoz and the Dutch blockaded the mouth of the Tagus. In 1659, Spain and France signed the Peace of the Pyrenees in which, among other things, the Spanish Monarchy offered Marie-Thérèse of Austria as wife for Louis XIV. By not including Portugal in the treaty, France weakened Spain, perpetuating the war in the Peninsula. But the possible restoration of Charles II, present at the congress, to the English Crown ended by catalyzing the whole conference.[2]

During this period Portugal and England were also negotiating a settlement. Although earlier attempts to convince Cromwell to form an alliance against Madrid were rejected, the Portuguese ambassador in London presented a memorandum on the Anglo-Portuguese relationship since 1640. He emphasized the support given to Royalists by the Braganzas in the English civil war and convinced English merchants to request Charles to back their pretentions for the maintenance of trade privileges in Portugal. But the most important offer the ambassador could make was to marry the English king to Catherine of Braganza, who would come with a dowry of two million cruzados. Tangier was also offered as a reward, as was an offensive alliance against the Dutch in Asia, which would enable England to possess the former Portuguese outposts if taken from the Dutch, except for Muscat and half of Ceylon. The Earl of Clarendon, Charles' right-hand man, also requested the concession of Bassein, Mozambique and Recife or Rio de Janeiro (the choice between these two would be Portugal's), and the right to sail to Brazil without the obligation to pass through Lisbon. On February 1661 the Portuguese ambassador to London returned to the English capital with a new suggestion: the handing over of Bombay. The offer was accepted by Clarendon and, on 23 June, a treaty between England and Portugal was agreed upon, to be followed by Portuguese and British ratifications.

For historian Rafael Valladares, the Tagus crisis of 1650 allowed London to measure forces with Portugal and Spain, eventually increasing its power over a divided peninsula. Similarly, although the Braganzas had obtained military and diplomatic assistance against Madrid, the 1661 treaty was nonetheless a British triumph. Lisbon delivered Tangier and Bombay to London, and allowed it to keep its former possessions in Asia. Furthermore, according to the treaty, if the Portuguese would re-conquer Ceylon, it would deliver up the port of Galle to England and share the trade in cinnamon with English merchants. Another concession was to allow the residence of four English families in Goa, Cochin and Diu, and in Bahia, Pernambuco and Rio de Janeiro, where they could trade under the same regime as the Portuguese. For his part, Charles II was to send to Portugal a thousand horses and two thousand infantrymen, replaced if necessary. He was also to guarantee the presence of ten warships during eight months, and promise that English ships in the Mediterranean would assist Portugal if necessary, that is, if Lisbon or Oporto were in danger of a siege. Diplomatically, England would not sign peace with Spain that would be to Portugal's disadvantage. It would also not deliver Dunkirk and Jamaica to Philip IV. Finally, in a secret article, the British king would serve as mediator between Lisbon and The Hague in the Luso–Dutch confrontation in the East.[3] The dowry of two million cruzados were to paid in one year, the first half coming over with the future Queen in the English fleet escorting her to London, a quarter after six months, and the last quarter after a year. In the Court, the Queen consort would be free to practice Roman Catholicism and, should she be widowed, could return to Portugal with her belongings, except the dowry. The *infanta* would further retain her dynastic claims to the Portuguese throne for herself and her descendants.[4]

The 1661 treaty clearly threatened Madrid. It signaled the acceptance of the house of Braganza among European royal families and, in addition to military and diplomatic assistance, it implied the possibility of a union between England and Portugal. After all, should D. Afonso VI and D. Pedro die, D. Catarina would become Queen of Portugal, and her heir would unite both crowns. Given the gravity of these prospects, Philip IV tried to undo this marriage arrangement by offering to the English king other princesses as consorts, although none with Catherine's dowry. Fearing a joint Anglo-Luso attack, he also took steps to protect the Spanish fleets. Philip also consulted the Council of Portugal — resurrected in 1658 — how to proceed and arranged for pamphlets to be sent to Portugal and its provinces overseas, inciting its inhabitants to oppose the handing over of Tangier and Bombay. Last but not least, he requested the Pope to refuse dispensation for Catherine to marry the Anglican king, and he encouraged privateering off the Portuguese coast to prevent payment of the dowry.[5]

Contemporaneous were also diplomatic negotiations between Portugal and The Hague. After a first phase, in which negotiations led by Ambassador Francisco de Sousa Coutinho and Antonio Vieira was over, from 1658 the so-called "Brazil affair" — the demand that Portugal indemnify the Low Countries for the loss of Pernambuco and neighbouring captaincies — was entrusted to Fernando Teles de Faro, Luís Álvares Ribeiro and the Count of Miranda. For historian Evaldo Cabral de Mello, the Anglo-Portuguese treaty almost annihilated the possibility of reaching an agreement with The Hague. Faced with the dilemma of breaking with the States General, or jeopardizing the chances of the London treaty, the signing of the Luso–Dutch agreement was delayed. But not knowing of the existence of the secret clause of the Anglo-Portuguese alliance and fearing hostilities with Holland, eventually the Count of Miranda accepted to sign the treaty, conditioning it with the inclusion of a secret article allowing Portugal to negotiate compensation for the losses the Netherlands had incurred because of the refusal of the Portuguese to put Dutch trade on a par with the English one.[6]

The Portuguese Council of State concluded that Miranda had obtained a favorable agreement, and in June 1662 the English monarch stated that in spite of the possible damage to British trade, he did not oppose the Luso–Dutch treaty. But the Portuguese crown could not satisfy the money owned to both Great Britain and the States General. In November 1662, when the States General also ratified the treaty, albeit requesting a longer period to capture Cranganore, Cochin and Cananor, Lisbon may have used this delay a pretext to distance itself from the treaty, whose trading conditions and financial commitments were beyond its possibilities.[7]

2. Celebrating a Marriage and Remembering a Debt

If "peace with Holland" was regulated by diplomatic and commercial arrangements, for Portugal and some of its overseas domains, the marriage of Catherine of Braganza to Charles Stuart was symbolically charged. The Holy See and other European states had not yet recognized the new dynasty. With the death of their two eldest brothers,

D. Catarina, D. Afonso and D. Pedro were the only remaining descendents of John IV, who could be used to foment marriage alliances. Formerly considered as a possible spouse for the Duke of Aveiro or for Don John of Austria, the Portuguese *infanta* Catarina was also offered to Louis XIV, D. John IV's preferred option. A Luso–French marriage would entail the recognition of a royal status to D. John IV by a most important continental Catholic power, hopefully making the acceptance of him as a monarch by the other kingdoms easier. But Mazarin's request for a dowry of two million cruzados was above what was planned and in 1658, with the signature of the Peace of the Pyrenees between Spain and Portugal, this option was closed. Thereafter, and with the restoration of Monarchy in England, the Portuguese hoped for an English alliance.[8]

The importance of the alliance with England is clear from festivities in Lisbon upon the *infanta*'s departure. Since 1552, there had been no princely wedding in the city. Furthermore, this was the first marriage of a member of the Braganza dynasty and the first public festivities since the Hapsburg period. On 5 August 1661, the news of the alliance was made public, and was celebrated with lights, fireworks and three day long festivities. The ceremony ratifying the marriage agreement was graced by the presence of notables and was preceded by a *Te Deum* in the royal chapel, attended by D. Afonso VI, D. Luisa de Guzmán and D. Catarina. The councils, tribunals and ministers of the court kissed the hands of the new British consort queen in her chamber, flanked by the regent. This was followed by a thanksgiving procession and bull fights lasting three days and celebrated in the decorated Rossio square, all making for a brilliant spectacle. On the first day of the festivities, D. Catarina watched from the veranda of the palace with D. Afonso VI at her side. Also present on another veranda were D. Pedro, accompanied by the officials of the royal household, ladies in waiting and ladies of the court, the English Ambassador and the Commissioner of the States General. The ceremony ended with a parade.[9]

On 22 March 1662, the Earl of Sandwich arrived to Lisbon with the English fleet that would take D. Catarina with it. He entered town preceded by the English ambassador and was welcomed by the inspector of the royal household and members of the most important noble families that had supported the restoration (the coming of power of John IV). After meeting with D. Afonso VI, Sandwich was received by the regent D. Luisa and by D. Catarina, and delivered to them letters from Charles II. A banquet in the house of the *infante* D. Pedro followed. The departure of D. Catarina was planned for Sunday, 23 April. Preceded by D. Afonso VI and D. Pedro, Catarina left the Chamber with D. Luisa and arrived to the throne room, where she was met by officials, grandees and noblemen. The committee than passed to the German room and to the chapel yard, where mother and daughter separated. The streets were decorated with arches, and fountains. Kissing a relic of the cross, Catarina proceeded to the Cathedral, accompanied by magistrates and principal ministers of the justice on horseback, followed by the court notables on open litters, and coaches with ladies in waiting in the end of the procession. She was in the back of a coach next to D. Afonso, with D. Pedro sitting facing both. In the front was the Duke of Cadaval, preceding the Master of the Horse. Behind came the British Ambassador, followed by the Captains of the Guard forming a mounted escort, and the titled nobility. After the celebration in the Cathedral was over, D. Catarina returned to the *Terreiro do Paço* to board the ships waiting for her at the Tagus. Along the ornamented course, she was saluted by the cannons of the forts, castles, vessels and infantry, and the bells of churches and convents, in addition to dances, merrymaking, lights, trumpets, woodwind and minstrels. A Triumphal Arch was set up in the *terreiro do Paço*, courtesy of the Lisbon City Council.[10]

As she was passing under the arch, Catarina was again saluted by soldiers. The river itself was full of boats and gondolas, with people merrymaking, dancing and sounding music. A third artillery *salvo* sounded as D. Catarina was boarding the ship. A veranda was constructed to link the *Casa de India* to the quay. Along it the titled nobility and others, followed by the officials of the *Casa de India* stood, each kissing the hands of the *Infanta*. Those who went on to kiss the king's hands were told by the monarch that they should only kiss her, not his hand. D. Catarina then entered the cutter helped by D. Afonso VI, followed by D. Pedro, ladies, the Earl of Sandwich and Portuguese nobles, the officials of the royal household and the members of the city council last.

The making of this ceremony involved quarrels about precedence, it expressed underlying conflicts, and could be studied for the meaning of the allegories and symbols used. Nonetheless, perhaps most important is to stress how the event was used to demonstrate the insertion of its participants in the new body politic that the Braganza created in Portugal in 1640 and was now reinforced by the alliance with Stuart Great Britain. Indeed, this moment communicated the ritual participation of the Portuguese vassals in the destiny of their monarchy.[11] This pedagogy of power foresaw festivities in the entire kingdom and in its overseas domains. As happened in Lisbon, in Brazil's capital, Bahia de Salvador, the city council, operating under the orders of the Governor-General Francisco Barreto de Meneses, appointed a treasurer and an adjutant to buy what was necessary for the festivities, the local procurator taking note of the money withdrawn, the people who received it, and the expenses incurred. In a letter to the officials of the council, the Governor explained that he imagined the festivities including three days of bull fights, parades, street comedies, street lightening and artillery salvos. Although his text sounded somewhat laconic when compared to festivities in Lisbon and England, it nevertheless reproduced a statement of political unity. The celebration was to unite the community by virtue of the marriage of the infanta to the British king. Perhaps for that reason the governor's letter also evidenced the compulsory character of participation. Commemorations, he ordered, would have the presence of "people of all conditions that may be gathered, so that as long as the festivities last they will impart happiness to the city and rejoicing shall be shared in common as its cause is held in common".[12]

The description of the funeral of the Governor-General Afonso Furtado de Mendonça in Bahia in 1676, give yet another proof of the importance of the English marriage. Recorded at the request of the Governor's nephew living in the Court of Prince D. Pedro and aimed at glorifying the life of the deceased, the author, a Spaniard settled in Brazil, nevertheless mentioned the difficult situation of the city in the following terms: "But my Lord, as this is well known, so also are, Your Lordship, the many calls upon it with which today this city is encumbered, with 60.000 ducats for maintaining the infantry, 40 for the dowry of the most serene Queen of Great Britain and the peace with Holland, which is always delayed".[13] That is, fourteen years after the marriage, the dowry of Catherine of Braganza and the Peace with Holland still reverberated in Bahia. The body politic perhaps continued to exist, but it was now governed by another logic. Rather than participation in festivities, it now involved economic difficulties due to the city's contribution to the *infanta*'s dowry.

---

3. From Dowry to Donation: Portugal and its Territories Overseas

According to Troni, dowry giving had Germanic roots and was present in the Roman judicial tradition, in which it designated the assets a bride gave her husband to meet the matrimonial expenses. Dowry was a matter of honor. It implied status and prestige for bride, and marked her value as an object of exchange. In the Iberian Peninsula, the custom of daughters endowed by their fathers and wives by the husbands — the *arras* — was consolidated in the thirteenth century. In royal weddings, dowry and *arras* represented the relations between the contracting dynasties. Because of this feature and as Troni has rightly observed, dowry and peace treaties were often related. One could thus argue that the voluminous dowry of D. Catarina expressed Portugal's gratitude in exchange for the considerable aid requested from Great Britain. Including a certain amount in money, this monetary concession by way of dowry was linked to the territorial and mercantile concessions (the freedom to trade), which were part of the peace treaty. Because Charles II only agreed to help Portugal in exchange for the marriage, the dowry had no meaning without the treaty, and vice-versa.[14]

Although the agreement envisaged the dispatch of the first million cruzados with the new Queen, most of the payment was delayed for at least a year. In June 1661, the English monarch sent the Earl of Sandwich to patrol the seas against Portugal's enemies. Before proceeding to take possession of Tangier, the Earl arrived to Lisbon. There he found to his displeasure that because of increasing difficulties to gather the dowry, a large part of it (some 930.000 cruzados) would be paid in securities and the likes. Efforts by the Procurator of the dowry (Duarte da Silva) to exchange merchandise for cash, won him an annual revenue (a *tença*) and a title of nobility.[15]

In reality, efforts to gather the dowry began in Lisbon even before the marriage contract was signed in 1662. As early as February 1661, D. Luisa de Guzmán, Catarina's mother and the widowed queen, ordered the Council of the Treasury to double the *sisas* (local tax) everywhere in the kingdom for two years. She had hoped that this measure and the sale of royal property would be sufficient to cover the amount without calling for a meeting of parliament (*Cortes*). Yet, decrees, letters and royal orders sent to the Council of the Treasury and to the Lisbon City Council in 1661 and 1662 demonstrate that funds were lacking. As early as May 1661, a royal resolution ordered the Lisbon City Council and the House of the Twenty-Four to propose alternative taxes needed "for a great business, which is currently being negotiated with England".[16] In July that year, it became known that the "business" was Catarina's marriage, and that the Council has agreed to a new tax, because it was quicker and easier to collect. News of the tax caused mutiny in Oporto. In May 1663, Mello e Torres — now the Marquis de Sande — sent a letter to the kingdom communicating the liquidation of the first million of the dowry. The other half still needed to be paid.[17]

Eventually, developments in Portugal (the *coup* that put Afonso VI in power, the lack of sufficient funds and popular opposition to tax increase, the ascent of Prince D. Pedro in 1668, the devaluation of Portuguese currency, the lowering prices of sugar and tobacco, and finally the War of Spanish Succession) led to renewed pressure on Portugal's overseas domains. Already in February 1662, in a letter to the Governor-General of Brazil, the monarch requested from Bahia and its annexed captaincies (Pernambuco and Rio de Janeiro) "a very considerable sum amounting to six hundred thousand cruzados to complete the second payment of the dowry".[18] He also requested that these territories pay part of the indemnity to the Dutch States General.

These contributions ended up being permanently connected under the recurring title *donation of the dowry for England and peace with Holland*.[19]

A donation was in principle a voluntary act. On 24 April 1662, two royal letters requesting this help were presented to the Salvador City Council, "nobility and people". The Governor-General reminded them all of the importance of complying with these requests, "and the obligation that so principally touched the vassals of this state that they contribute with what was lacking for the dowry and necessary for the peace".[20] He ordered the election of six men who, together with the officials of the Council, within two days, would evaluate the capacity of the state of Brazil to contribute, establishing values and means of contribution, and indicating the part that would correspond to each captaincy. This single effort nevertheless covered what were theoretically two different contributions. Concerning the dowry, the king requested his vassals to "make an effort to do this service with the greatest amount possible",[21] informing them that 600 thousand cruzados were lacking for the second payment of the dowry and allowing them to define the amount of their donation as they wished. Concerning the reparations to be paid to the Dutch, the king directed the "captaincies interested in the peace", to pay an annual fee fixed at 120 thousand cruzados. On 27 April, 1662 in the presence of the Governor and the Council, the *junta* proposed —in addition to the payment of indemnities to Holland— to contribute to the dowry with 20 thousand cruzados annually for sixteen years. As a result, the annual donation of the state of Brazil to both causes would be 140 thousand cruzados, a sum accepted by the Governor. The *junta* and the officials of the Council than divided this sum among the captaincies: Bahia would pay 50 thousand cruzados, Pernambuco 47 thousand, and Rio de Janeiro 36 thousand. Although initially the Council of Bahia played a major role in obtaining this arrangement, also controlling what other capitancies and capital cities would do, the Governor-General eventually modified the agreement, levying participation also on localities such as São Paulo, Itamaracá and Paraíba, and changing the relative weight of each capitancies. Thereafter Bahia were to pay 80 thousand cruzados, Rio de Janeiro 26 thousand and Pernambuco 25 thousand.[22]

In October 1663, the Viceroy Count of Óbidos, launched a campaign for a "donation for the dowry". He insisted that Bahia contributed in relation to the earnings and property of its inhabitants including slaves, cattle, businesses, salaries, public offices, interests and real estate. He then proceeded to nominate officials in charge of the inventory of the goods existing in the colony, without exempting owners "of any quality, right, preeminence, or condition."[23] The treasurer general of the donation campaign was to inform the Council of any deficiencies, accepting the amounts owed in money, sugar, Brazil wood or tobacco. New lists would be drawn up annually to ensure the regular running of the campaign. Although the clergy was exempt from the donation, "their freely given contribution" was expected. The Governor warned of grave penalties to those who would hid their properties or goods. In 1664, the officials of the Bahia Council drew up a series of rules to implement these measures. They determined that the traders of the city would pay one *vintém* per *arroba* of white and raw sugar, and two *vinténs* per *arroba* of tobacco, which would be loaded in the port of Salvador. The goods donated by the city would be branded with the letter B, "so that in the kingdom [of Portugal] it would be known that they were from Bahia".[24] The measures elaborated by the council also included the instruction that non-married vagrants and freed slaves could be arrested and taken to the sugar or saw mills to work for up to 20 days and that products in the waterfront warehouses would not be taxed. All the inhabitants of Bahia were to contribute in accordance with this standard. The council of Bahia recognized that the inhabitants of Sergipe have already collaborated with a thousand *arrobas* of tobacco, those of Porto Seguro and Ilhéus with 200 thousand *réis* in Brazil wood each, the towns of Boipeba, Cairu and Camamu together with 600 thousand *réis* in flour and the captaincy of the Espírito Santo with four thousand *réis* in cotton cloth. Should the 80 thousand cruzados be exceeded, the council ruled that the excess would be shared by the people of Salvador and its back country.[25]

In 1678 D. Pedro sent instructions to the city ordering the *Mestre de Campo General* to continue with the donation for his "much loved and esteemed sister". Worried that the sources of income may be dying out "as those vassals according to news that I have contribute with everything they have"[26] and denouncing a fall in the amounts collected since 1671 in Bahia, Rio de Janeiro, Pernambuco and Angola — which would henceforth be included in the collection—the prince reminded his vassals that since 1674 the "peoples of the state of Brazil and the kingdoms of Angola" had committed themselves to contributing 92 thousand cruzados annually. According to a resolution of 1665, these sums were to be divided in the following manner: 42,666 from the city of Bahia and its territories, 20 thousand from Pernambuco, Itamaracá and annexed captaincies, 19,333 cruzados from Rio de Janeiro and its captaincies, and ten thousand cruzados from Angola. The Prince then appointed the *Mestre de Campo General* responsible for the collection and ordered him to supervise the work of the city councils. The Prince also determined that debtors would be sentenced in the *Relação* (royal court) of Bahia, or by the superior judges (*Ouvidor*) in Rio and Pernambuco. The City Council would make annual remittances coincide with the departure of the fleets. The donations originating in Angola that would arrive in bills of exchange would be used to pay the merchandise sent for Lisbon.[27]

The criteria used for the regional division and the method of collection are outside the scope of this chapter. But the rules and resolutions produced over time suggest the constant need to adjust the donation of Bahia, than capital of the state of Brazil. During the first decades of the seventeenth century, when sugar production had expanded because of growing demand by the international market, the captaincy of Bahia experienced a transfer from Indian labor to the use of African slaves. The city of Salvador dominated the imposing Bay of Todos os Santos, but it depended on the adjacent land — the *Recôncavo* — for the food, provisions and agricultural products that made its port an important centre for the transatlantic trade. Seat of the Governor General, the Court of *Relação* and the Bishopric — from 1676, Archbishopric — religious life in the capital was enriched by the presence of the religious orders, with a Jesuit school and Franciscan, Benedictine and Carmelite monasteries. The *Misericórdia* provided help for the poor and sick, and members of the principal families, royal administrators, mill owners and merchants supported its activities. The City Council was in charge of local government. In 1681, Salvador had some three thousand houses, organized according to parishes. Since the end of the sixteen hundreds, new towns were created in nearby localities, but in most of them government was mainly informal, the pre-eminence of Salvador over them prevailing.[28]

According to census, in 1676 there were some 130 sugar mills in the area, reaching 146 in 1710 when Bahia became the most important sugar producing region of Portuguese America, overtaking Pernambuco after its occupation by the Dutch. Other crops, especially tobacco, also flourished in the Capitancy, although none ever outweighed sugar. Bahia's mill owners were divided into groups depending on their antiquity: the members of the first group acquired land after the foundation of Salvador; the members of the second arrived in 1580, when sugar production started to expand rapidly; between 1620 and 1660 another wave of new owners appeared, as veterans of the wars against the Dutch purchased properties at low prices. Owners, fleeing with slaves and capital before the Dutch occupation, also came from Pernambuco. It is estimated that a third of the owners born in Brazil were descendents of sugar cane workers, a clear sign of upward social mobility. The owners who originated in immigrant families entered sugar production assisted by their parents, in their majority sugar cane workers or mill owners. Immigrants who acquired sugar mills had exercised before trading offices or professions, such as lawyers or judges.[29]

By the seventeenth century sugar mill owners came to constitute a well established group, tightly united by marriage. "White," or at least so considered, its members, who called themselves "noble", exercised power locally. Although endogenous marriages reinforced the preponderance of certain families, royal magistrates, government officials, tradesmen from Salvador and sugar cane workers could be incorporated into the group. For mill owners, political activity was both a duty and a privilege, and as good, honored and wealthy men, they occupied positions in the City Council, whose functions covered many areas of interest to the sugar sector: roads, slaves, prices, taxes, as well as defending local interests and petitioning the Governor or directly the crown on important or urgent matters. Until 1698, when Jaguaripe, São Francisco and Cachoeira were elevated to the status of towns, the Salvador City Council was the only local Council in the Capitancy of Bahia. All City Councils were affected by the nomination of *Juiz de Fora* (royal magistrates) in 1696, because thereafter the Juiz, nominated by the crown, presided over the Councils.

The sugar market suffered fluctuations, with periods of low prices or weak demand, which affected the Capitancy. Between 1650 and 1680, the economy in Bahia performed well, with high sugar prices compensating the substitution of Indians by slaves, the main expanse for owners. In 1680 prices fell and costs rose and competition from the West Indies began to affect seriously Brazil. In 1688, due to a general recession and in an attempt to diminish debt, the Portuguese currency was devalued by increasing the nominal value of gold and silver coins by 20%. This measure raised prices and increased monetary flow from America to Portugal, generating scarcity. In 1695, a government mint was created in Bahia, transferred to Rio de Janeiro in 1698, in order to issue coins for the state of Brazil, attributing to them a value of 10% above that of the coins coming from Portugal. But the War of the Spanish Succession rekindled the demand for sugar. Nonetheless, and despite migrations southward due to the discovery of gold in the interior, the Bahia economy performed well until the 1720s, when production difficulties increased.[30]

In 1665 smallpox killed many slaves. In 1667, storms delayed the arrival of the fleet, lowering the price of sugar. There was drought in 1671 and 1673. Between 1686 and 1691 Bahia and Pernambuco were ravaged by yellow fever, decimating the slave population. The harvest of 1688–1689 was excellent, but the expectation of another large harvest in the following year was dashed by heavy rain. Although mill owners blamed their difficulties on these calamities, for historian Stuart Schwartz the real problem was the transformation of the Atlantic world.[31]

4. The Sacrifice of Bahia

In March 1673, the "vassals" of Bahia petitioned Prince D. Pedro that their procurator would occupy like Goa the first bench reserved for participating localities in the next meeting of the parliament (*Cortes*) in Lisbon, and not the second bench, as has been the case before. The reason to "merit this honor"[32] was the greatness of the state of Brazil, the "loyalty born of their love and the prompt service and happiness",[33] with which they had acclaimed D. John IV, the effort, lives and properties consumed in the war against the Dutch and the wild Indians in the remote back country, and the maintenance of an infantry. But, above all, Bahia "contributed with one million and two hundred and eighty thousand cruzados at forty a year for peace with Holland and the dowry of the Most Serene Queen of Great Britain".[34] The petition also alluded to the title "price of Brazil" used by D. Pedro.[35]

As they had already done in 1672, in July 1686 the members of the Salvador City Council sent a letter to D. Pedro II representing the state of the land and the lack of resources of its inhabitants. Overloaded with impositions such as the maintenance of the infantry and the donation, they suggested to increase the period of payment of the dowry to 32 years and proposed adjustments so as "not to overload too much this people". In accordance with the letter, in 1686 resources were few, cultivated land was devalued and "loaded with rights and taxes"[36] that caused ruin, death and destitution. Women donated their earrings and skirts, and the Governor-General, Marquis of Minas, gave charity to the poor and sick "with very liberal hand and expenses from his estate." Because the "state of misery in which these peoples find themselves" was general[37] they requested the king to suspend the donation and extend the term of payment, "as this is to show our loyalty and desire to Your Majesty's Royal Person".[38] Days later in another text, the same officials mentioned a representation made in 1665 reporting on the "discomfort" of the captaincy's inhabitants with the excessive contribution of 80 thousand cruzados, and requesting extension of the term to 32 years "because today the peoples are paying the same that they paid at the beginning"[39]. They complained against the privileges of the clergy, whose buying and selling was exempt from the donation and asked the king to observe that "these his faithful vassals [are] much diminished today through lack of resources, and [are] full of misery."[40] Not only was the story of the earrings and skirts removed from women and widows repeated but also added was the complaint of the need to sell off parts of sugar mills to contribute to the donation. The City Council proposed that all the farms, properties, goods bought or inherited be evaluated by the original value of their entry onto the list, and that the donation would fall on all persons of any quality or condition.[41]

In August the following year, the members of the Council reported to the king about the low esteem in which "our fruits of Brazil, sugar, and tobacco" were held, with few sales to foreigners due to the competitors. Considering the trade lost, it was urgent to "find a remedy" so as not to ruin Brazil and Angola "because if the labor devoted to the fruit of Brazil were to cease, the slave business of Angola would also be lost".[42] The members proposed a reduction in taxes, among them the donation of the "dowry of the lady Queen of England and peace with Holland" and the maintenance of the infantry.

In July 1693, the "nobility of the city of Bahia" prepared a protest to the City Council to be forwarded to the Portuguese king. In it, the lords alluded to the wear and tear that Brazil had sustained because of the wars, the "donation for peace with

Holland",the maintenance of the infantry, and the fall in the prices of sugar. They also mentioned the devaluation of the *moeda serrilhada* (milled-edged coin) and the risk in giving it the same value in Brazil and in Portugal, as it would be more profitable to send it to Portugal than to use it to buy local produce. The nobles urged the king to find a remedy for the "conservation of His Monarchy".[43]

How should we read these complaints? João Adolfo Hansen, a literary theorist, argued that seventeenth-century rhetoric was mainly associated with the maintenance of hierarchies and customs. Reading the minutes and letters of the City Council regarding the donations, Hansen fails to appreciate their empirical referential, which provides evidence of institutional conflicts and popular discontent. Thus, although he is right that in their letters municipal officials insisted that they defended the *common good* of the *mystical* body of the state of Brazil even in cases in which they defended their own interests, which were in conflict with royal orders, nonetheless this did not necessarily mean that their representation were not trustworthy. The letters of the City Council many have been a spectacularly self-referenced performance, but they were not necessarily satires or speeches transformed into poems as Hansen argued[44]. Letters attempted to amplify the problem by mentioning other taxes and disbursements in order to increase the impossibility of payment. The members of the Council also described themselves as "zealous" individuals, who had great desire to serve the Prince and not be remiss in regard to what he has requested, but whose resources could not cover this "love and will." They never questioned royal sovereignty and continuously referred to themselves as vassals. This enabled them to proclaim their fidelity yet to contradict royal wish by non-payment. Letters thus alternated between orders obeyed and disobeyed, requests and demands, and explained these alternations with the need to comply with the *common good*, which was also the officers' own good. Many of the problems mentioned in the letters were real (hunger, disease, drought), yet invoking misery was also a means of arousing benevolence and threatening with rebellion.

Above all, the way Bahia's society dealt with the donation demonstrated how its agents used the occasion to reaffirm existing hierarchies and make the politics of the city visible to the king through the discussion of the most important questions: sugar, privileges, conflicts with the clergy, taxes, and so forth. By doing so, they presented the region as a community of local interests that pleaded before the Portuguese monarchy. Describing events and actions, letters writers thus made the presence of the King palpable, but also reproduced his absence and, most particularly in matters of taxation, alternated between negotiation and opposition by creating a distance. Rather than simple hierarchical records as Hansen has maintained, the letters of the Council to the king were expressions of what has been lived through as well as reflected a practice. Hierarchy was a key factor. In the mystical body, members recognized their obligations, guided themselves by these rules and considered themselves a "wholly unified one" in as Francisco Suárez has argued.[45]

This Bahian discourse of both integration and distancing from the larger Portuguese body politic reflected both what was requested and what was given, or perhaps exchanged, because the *donation of the dowry* was not rigorously an imposition, but implied gratitude, benefit and recognition between overseas vassals and the monarchy, terms patent in the language contemporaries used. In his study of the gift, Marcel Mauss argued that in archaic societies exchanges and contracts were accompanied by presents, which were voluntary, but obligatorily given. Mauss underlined the dual character free but interested, of payments. He insisted that in these economies groups contracted mutually, exchanging affability, rites and honors as a way to pact with one another and under the permanent threat of war. For Mauss, these exchanges between men and between men and gods clarified one aspect of his theory of sacrifice, namely, that it was necessary to exchange, and dangerous not to. But the offerings made to men and gods also had peace as their objective. Mauss interpreted the coins thrown into a marriage procession, the purchase price of a bride, or the giving of alms and offerings as elements of this exchange. They linked together credit and honor, because gift implied both credit, and prestige for the one making the gift, as well as the obligation of the receiver to retribute.

These elements may have subsisted beyond the Archaic societies described by Mauss.[46] They could certainly have influenced *Ancien Régime* societies such as seventeenth-century Bahia.[47] There, the situation expounded — an event symbolizing aggregation to the monarchy, invested with a vocabulary of sentiments, requests and contributions to an ancestral custom such as dowry giving — can be analyzed in terms of the international treaties and the economic issues they entailed, as it often was. But it can equally be interpreted in accordance with the contractual values of reciprocity and the common cultural reference that included political participation in parliament, ritual spectacles, and dialogue with the crown.

Thus, if Schwartz and Hansen attenuate in different ways the lamentations of the officials of the Salvador City Council — because according to them these may be explained by the fluctuations in the international market or rhetorical requirements — the study of the marriage of Catherine of Braganza, of the peace with Holland and of the donation to both reveals a much more complex situation. In the delicate political climate of the restoration, alliance making was a means to preserve the kingdom and its important overseas possessions. In Portugal and in Bahia, Catarina's marriage was celebrated as a rite of integration of the vassals into the new Braganza monarchy. Nevertheless, celebrating festivities was not enough in order to belong to this body politic. Belonging also depended on the payment of taxes. The doubled *sisas* and multiple donations and the many thousands of cruzados requested from the state of Brazil were paid sacrificially, or so, at least, they were presented. In this setting, the exact figures and destination of the donation were of little importance, as was the fact that it was suspended in 1725 and then substituted by another donation, this time for the marriage between Portuguese and Spanish princes. What is fundamental is to understand the exchange between the new dynasty and its American vassals, one involving both aid and recognition. As the poet Gregório de Mattos once wrote "Through natural reason / no-one gives, what he does not have, / and for the same reason / no-one asks, for what he does not want."[48]

Abbreviations

DHAMAC   *Documentos históricos do arquivo municipal de Salvador. Atas da câmara.* Salvador, Prefeitura de Salvador, 1949, v. 4.

DHAMCS   *Documentos históricos do arquivo municipal de Salvador. Cartas do senado.* Salvador, Prefeitura de Salvador, 1951, 1952, 1953 and 1959, vs. 1, 2, 3 and 4.

DHBN   *Documentos históricos da Biblioteca Nacional.* Rio de Janeiro, Biblioteca Nacional do Brasil, 1928, 1944, 1948, 1949 e 1950, vs. 4, 66, 79, 86 and 89.

Notes

1 Valladares, 1998, 123–124.
2 Kishlansky, 1997, 213–239.
3 The "myth" of the diplomatic success of the Restoration would have been created by the Englishman Edgar Prestage, concerned to mitigate the criticisms of Great Britain by a Portugal traumatized by the effect of the ultimatum of 1890, which terminated Portuguese expansionism in Africa. Valladares, 1998, 290.
4 The treaty stipulated the renunciation by the *infanta* of her paternal inheritance, but maintaining the right of succession to the crown for herself and her heirs. The discrepancy with the forged *atas* of the Cortes of Lamego, important in the Restoration of Portugal, which removed from the Portuguese succession those Portuguese princesses married to foreign princes, will be noted. What applied to Isabel of Portugal, wife of Charles V and mother of Philip II of Spain, no longer applied to Catherine of Braganza. Political opportunity dictated the rules of the agreement.
5 Valladares, 1998, 176–177.
6 Mello, 1998; Machado, *Tratados* . . . , I, 111–137.
7 In the Low Countries, Portugal would be accused of not paying the indemnity. As regards the part amortizable in salt, the export rate was not substantial, and the requests for Dutch ships in Brazil were ignored. Also, articles on navigation in Africa were not observed, nor was the exemption of taxes on merchandise brought by Dutch ships to Lisbon or Oporto. There were new negotiations under threat of the use of force, and in July 1669 the second Hague treaty, by which Portugal gave up Cochin and Cananor, in the possession of the East India Company, as guarantee of the late payments and of the expenses incurred, was signed until, the financial commitments of the treaty of 1661 having been discharged, the dispute was settled by diplomacy. The indemnity was over 2,500,000 cruzados, through tax on exportation of salt from Setúbal. The period for payment was extended to 20 years and the payments fixed at 150 thousand cruzados. Should Portugal not fulfill the agreement, the Low Countries maintained their rights in Brazil. The regent D. Pedro ratified the treaty in November under threat of the Dutch navy in the Tagus. For Cabral de Mello the treaty of 1669 substituted the indemnity scheme: in place of Brazilian products, Portugal bought the North-East with Indian possessions and salt from Setúbal. Payment was to stretch out until 1711, in the War of the Spanish Succession, after the Portuguese option for the Anglo-Dutch alliance. Mello, 1998, 247–249.
8 Troni, 2008, 37–79.
9 Troni, 2008, 113–131; Santarém, 1859, 236–256; Machado, *Epitalâmios* . . . , I, 91–105.
10 Freire, 1893, 102.
11 There are reports that tell of the landing of Catherine and the celebration of her marriage in England, far from the stigma of non-recognition of Portugal's independence by Rome. Machado, *Epitalâmios* . . . , I, 63–342; Kantorowicz, 1978.
12 "todos os estados de gente que a costumam fazer se puderem formar, para que enquanto as festas durem alegrem a cidade e seja comum o regozijo quando é tão comum a causa dele". DHBN, 1949, 86, 151; Monteiro, 2002, 130–131.
13 "Mas Senhor, como isto é notório, também o são, Vossa Senhoria, os muitos empenhos com que hoje se acha esta cidade, com 60 U ducados para sustento da infantaria, 40 para o Dote da sereníssima Rainha da Grã-Bretanha e paz da Holanda, de que anda sempre atrasada". Schwartz & Pécora, 2002, 132; Monteiro, 2002, 320; Schwartz, 2004, V, 7–26.
14 D. John IV had endowed D. Catarina in 1656, with the island of Madeira and the bishopric of Funchal without jurisdiction over the land, the city of Lamego and its bishopric, the town of Moura, with jurisdiction and prerogatives of the house of Braganza, with the exception of customs duties and *sisas*. Marrying outside the kingdom, the princess sold this property to the infante D. Pedro. As *arras*, Charles would give 30 thousand pounds annually to his consort after one year of marriage, and a palace. Should D. Catarina outlive her husband,

she could take her goods with her, the return journey paid for by Great Britain, maintaining the annual pension, even not being resident on English soil. In the event of dissolution of the marriage, the *arras* would guarantee the return of the dowry to the infanta, with or without children. Troni, 2008, 101–113.

15 The treasurer of the dowry donated more than 396 thousand cruzados, and also silver marks. The Lisbon Chamber contributed with money and sugar to the value of 40 thousand cruzados, and Duarte da Silva donated 175 thousand. The "gifts" totalled approximately 967 thousand cruzados, with jewels, bills of exchange and silver, and the new Marquis of Sande intervened to consider this part of the dowry valid, without exchanging it for money. There were exchange problems in England, leading the procurator of the dowry to advance 1,200 cruzados of his own money. Troni, 2008, 101–113.

16 "para um negócio grande, que de presente se está tratando com Inglaterra".

17 Created in 1387, the *sisa* was a tenth part of what was bought or sold, with the exception of gold, silver and bread. Ecclesiastics and Commanders of the order of Christ were exempt from the tax. In the first half of the 17th century, the organization of the *sisas* established a fixed amount (the "*cabeção*") paid by each municipal chamber to the royal treasury, the modes of collection being chosen by each municipality, diminishing their importance for the crown. But in Lisbon the *sisas* were not organized in this way, but collected by specialized departments. Silva, 2005, 241–244. In addition to the *sisas*, the means used in the kingdom were various: sale of income from chamber and chapters of various dioceses, of interest on royal consignments, compulsory loans, the Queen's jewels, money owed by the English to the Lisbon customs.

18 "uma soma muito considerável que importa a seiscentos mil cruzados para se ajustar o segundo pagamento do dote".

19 DHBN, 1944, 66, 190–193. Donations were a common means of obtaining resources in the 17th century, providing immediate income to the royal treasury, outside the court sphere. For Fortea Pérez they signified thanks, an honour of customers to their patrons, a benefit justified in the acts of mutual recognition between vassals and their lord. In seventeenth century Spain the donations were offered by private lay folk, corporations such as the chambers, some clerics and religious institutions. Fortea Pérez, 2000, 31–76.

20 "e a obrigação que tão principalmente tocava aos vassalos deste Estado contribuírem com o que faltava ao dote e era necessário para a paz".

21 "se esforçarem a concorrer a este serviço com a maior soma que fosse possível".

22 DHAMAC, 1949, 4, 136–140.

23 "de qualquer qualidade, foro, preeminência, ou condição".

24 "para que no Reino se conheçam são da Bahia".

25 DHBN, 1928, 4, 125–130; DHAMAC, 1949, 4, 190–202.

26 "sendo que aqueles vassalos segundo notícias que tenho contribuem inteiramente com o que lhes toca".

27 Part of the document deals with charity for widows and orphans of the war dead in Portugal. DHBN, 1948, 79, 233– 244.

28 Schwartz, 2005.

29 On the heterogeneous group of the sugar cane workers, Schwartz, 2005, 253.

30 Schwartz, 2005, 147 and 163; Hanson, 1986.

31 Schwartz, 2005, 163 and 174.

32 "razões de merecimento para esta honra".

33 "lealdade tão nascida de seu amor como serviço na prontidão e alegria".

34 "contribui com um milhão e duzentos e oitenta mil cruzados a quarenta por ano para a paz de Holanda e dote da Sereníssima Rainha da Grã-Bretanha".

35 DHAMCS, 1951, 1, 118–119; Machado, *Legal proceedings of the courts* . . . , II, 209–276; Cardim, 1998. Since 1673 the owners paid 380 *réis* per box of sugar sent for maintenance of the local infantry. Schwartz, 2005, 164–165.

36 "por não carregar tão demasiadamente este povo". "carregadas de direitos e tributos".

37 "com mão mui liberal e despesa de sua fazenda"; "miserável estado em que se acham estes povos".

38 "que isto é insinuar nossa lealdade e vontade a Real Pessoa de Vossa Majestade".

39 "porque hoje vêm a pagar os povos o mesmo que pagavam ao princípio".

40 "nestes seus fiéis vassalos muito atenuados hoje por falta de cabedais, e cheios de misérias".

41 DHAMCS, 1953, 3, 28–30 e 33–36; DHBN, 1950, 89, 57.

42 "porque cessando o labor dos frutos do Brasil, há de perder-se também o negócio dos escravos de Angola."

43 DHAMCS, 1953, 3, 49–51; DHAMCS, 1959, 4, 3–10.

44 Hansen, 2004.

45 Suárez, 2004.

46 Mauss, 2003, 183–314.

47 Valeri, 1985; Godelier, 2001; Xavier & Hespanha, 1993; 381–393; Souza, 2006, 73–74 and 350–402.

48 "Pela razão natural / ninguém dá, o que não tem, / e pela mesma razão / ninguém pede, o que não quer." Mattos, 1968, IV, 819; Hansen, 2004, 102.

Sources and Bibliography

Cardim, Pedro, *Cortes e cultura política no Portugal do Antigo Regime*, Lisboa, Cosmos, 1998.

Fortea Pérez, José Ignacio, "Los donativos en la política fiscal de los Austrias (1625–1637: ¿servicio o beneficio?", in Luis Antonio Ribot García, Luigi de Rosa and Carlos Belloso Martín (orgs.), *Pensamiento y política económica en la Época Moderna. Actas*, Universidad de Valladolid / Istituto Italiano per gli Studi Filosofici, 2000, pp. 31–76.

Freire, Eduardo Oliveira, *Elementos para a história do município de Lisboa*, Lisboa, Typografia Universal, 1893, t. 6.

Godelier, Maurice, *O enigma do dom*, Rio de Janeiro, Civilização Brasileira, 2001.

Hansen, João Adolfo, *A sátira e o engenho. Gregório de Matos e a Bahia no século XVII*, São Paulo/Campinas, Ateliê Editorial/Editora da Unicamp, 2004.

Hanson, Carl A., *Economia e sociedade no Portugal barroco*, Lisboa, Dom Quixote, 1986.

Kantorowicz, Ernst H., *The King's Two Bodies*, Princeton, Princeton University Press, 1978.

Kishlansky, Mark, *A Monarchy Transformed: Britain 1603–1714*, London, Penguin Books, 1997.

Machado, Diogo Barbosa (org.), *Autos de cortes e levantamentos ao trono dos príncipes e reis de Portugal*, Lisboa, s. n. t., t. II.

——, *Epitalâmios de reis, rainhas e príncipes de Portugal*, Lisboa, s. n. t., t. I.

——, *Tratados de pazes de Portugal, celebradas com os soberanos da Europa*, Lisboa, s. n. t., t. I.

Mattos,. Gregório de, *Obras completas. Crônicas do viver baiano seiscentista*, Salvador, Janaína, 1968, v. IV.

Mauss, Marcel and Henri Hubert, *Sobre o sacrifício*, São Paulo, Cosacnaify, 2005.

——, "Ensaio sobre a dádiva", *Sociologia e antropologia*, São Paulo, Cosacnaify, 2003, pp. 183–314.

Mello, Evaldo Cabral de, *O negócio do Brasil. Portugal, os Países Baixos e o Nordeste, 1641–1669*, Rio de Janeiro, Topbooks, 1998.

Monteiro, Rodrigo Bentes, *O rei no espelho. A monarquia portuguesa e a colonização da América 1640–1720*, São Paulo, Hucitec, 2002.

Santarém, Visconde de, *Quadro elementar das relações políticas e diplomáticas de Portugal com as diversas potências do mundo*, Lisboa, Academia Real de Ciências, 1859, t. XVII, pp. 236–256.

Schwartz, Stuart B., "Ceremonies of public authority in a colonial capital. The king's processions and the hierarchies of power in seventeenth century Salvador", *Anais de história de além-mar*, Lisboa, 2004, v. V, pp. 7–26.

——, and Alcir Pécora (orgs.), *As excelências do governador. O panegírico fúnebre a D. Afonso*

Furtado, de Juan Lopes Sierra (Bahia, 1676), São Paulo, Companhia das Letras, 2002.

——, *Segredos internos. Engenhos e escravos na sociedade colonial*, São Paulo, Companhia das Letras, 2005.

Silva, Álvaro Ferreira da, in "Finanças públicas", Pedro Lains and Silva (orgs.), *História económica de Portugal 1700–2000*, Lisboa, Imprensa de Ciências Sociais, 2005, v. I, pp. 237–261.

Souza, Laura de Mello e, *O sol e a sombra. Política e administração na América portuguesa do século XVIII*, São Paulo, Companhia das Letras, 2006.

Suárez, Francisco, *De legibus. Da lei em geral, livro I*, Lisboa, Tribuna da História, 2004.

Troni, Joana Almeida, *Catarina de Bragança (1638–1705)*, Lisboa, Colibri, 2008.

Valeri, Valerio, *Kingship and Sacrifice: Ritual and Society in Ancient Hawaii*, Chicago / London, The University of Chicago Press, 1985.

Valladares, Rafael, *La rebelión de Portugal. Guerra, conflicto y poderes en la Monarquía Hispánica (1640–1680)*, Valladolid, Junta de Castilla y León, 1998.

Xavier, Ângela Barreto and António Manuel Hespanha, "As redes clientelares", in António Manuel Hespanha (org.), José Mattoso (dir.), *História de Portugal. O Antigo Regime*, Lisboa, Estampa, 1993, pp. 381–393.

PART II | Spaces of Circulation

Family, Bureaucracy and the Crown

5

The Wedding Market as a Form of Integration among Spanish Elites in the Early Modern Period

Enrique Soria Mesa

As the well-known genealogist José Pellicer de Tovar opportunely informed us, October 24, 1639 saw "[the passing of] doña Inés de Toledo, wife of don Juan Pacheco, Marquis of Cerralbo . . . daughter of don García de Toledo Osorio and doña Victoria Colonna, Viceroys of Naples, Marquis of Villafranca, first cousin of Francisco de Medici, the Queen's father, [and] aunt of the Mother of France, and thus a relative of all the Majesties of Europe".[1]

The words of this prolific Baroque writer[2] plunge us into one of the most fascinating peculiarities of the Spanish high nobility of the Early Modern period: its transnational character. Due to its almost infinite dimensions, the Empire projected many lineages outwards, beyond their traditional spheres of influence, to places where they entered into direct interaction with the other governing classes of Europe; or, at least with the Flemish, French, German and, above all, Italian ones.Such was the abovementioned case. When Cosme de Medici, the flamboyant Flemish governor of Florence, decided to wed, he pursued an alliance with Spain and ended up marrying doña Leonor de Toledo, a beautiful, elegant lady once painted by Broncini, daughter of Pedro de Toledo, Marquis of Villafranca and Viceroy of Naples, who was the son of the second Duke of Alba. Soon ennobled as the Dukes of Tuscany, from their union practically all the Royal Houses on the continent descended, their granddaughter being none other than Marie de Médicis, wife of Henry IV, King of France.[3]

Historians have only recently begun to study this phenomenon. The few pages that I myself devoted to it — practically a few passing references — in my recent book on the Spanish nobility in the Early Modern period, have now been complemented with by series of excellent studies by an eminent group of historians, published together in a book edited by Bartolomé Yun Casalilla,[4] who in the introduction attested that:

This study is part of the I+D+I research project, *La imagen del poder. Prácticas sociales y representaciones culturales de las élites andaluzas en la Edad Moderno* (HUM2006-12653-C04-01/HIST), funded by the Ministry of Education and Science, Spain.

> The Empire . . . represented a challenge for local elites [as] it obliged them to reformulate themselves with respect to others and in relation to that complex and diverse political and cultural space that was the Monarchy in its entirety. However, as the channel that permitted these groups to circulate through broader circles of power, thereby satisfying their need for social ascent and [settling] their internal tensions, the empire created the [foundations] of social stability and reproduction upon which it was based.[5]

Beyond the Spanish high aristocracies, however, there existed an enormous social universe, inhabited by local elites, present in every city and town, upon whose shoulders fell the responsibility for maintaining the social order, supplying grain, recruiting soldiers, and collecting taxes. The future of the Monarchy depended also upon their integration into the whole. Because the Crown was fully conscious of this reality, it foresaw incorporating such groups — or at least their highest-ranking members — through courtship. And, as below this privileged layer there were thousands of families whose collective acquiescence was also vital to the conservation of the Empire, their integration was required too. In this chapter, I focus on one form of integration, which consisted in fostering kinship bonds that would absorb all of them — if the reader would allow this exaggeration — into one immense family network; something that Jean Paul Zúñiga has recognized in the past, characterizing the Spanish Monarchy as nothing other than "a family matter".[6]

Central to this chapter is a local aristocracy that was remarkably endogamic in its behavior and that used marriage ties in order to break out of its narrow sphere of influence and expand its field of action broadly. The following pages present a first attempt to approach this topic, that is, a tentative entrance into a new research area that few have probed up to now. For practical reasons, I will focus on the Crown of Castile including the kingdoms of the West Indies, which, despite appearances, included a series of homogeneous territories both institutionally and socially.[7]

1. The King's Magistrates

The sector easiest to study are the *corregidores*, that is, Crown-appointed magistrates who, together with their delegates — the *alcaldes mayores* — constituted an extensive administrative network that by the late Middle Ages covered the entire territory of Castile. As is well- known, these magistrates formed part of a chain of transmission for superior orders, and they both issued and received vitally important information. *Corregidores* were also charged with the task of controlling, insofar as that was possible, the municipal councils (*cabildos*).[8]

For members of the local elites, who could be a more desirable son-in-law than a middle-aged *corregidor*, recently arrived in the area but very well connected with the central power? Usually noble by birth, or at least in appearance, and member of the urban oligarchy of some other city or town, *corregidores* tended to marry homogamously, or only slightly hypergamously, any difference in status being easily compensated by a generous dowry. Out of hundreds of available cases, let us examine one, in which don Alonso de Álamos Morejón, an early seventeenth-century *corregidor* of the city of Toro, played the leading role. Capitalizing on his position, Álamos married a prized local bride, doña Constanza de Quiñones from the town of Alcuetas who, "while still quite young, upon the death of her parents [and] as their only heir, was placed by her guardians in a convent, where she remained until she wed".[9] This arrangement turned out particularly well, as late in the century, the couple's grandson would acquire the Marquisate of Villasinda.[10]

But opposite cases also existed, that is, *corregidores* who took advantage of their residence in a city to marry their daughters to members of the local elites, normally at a low economic cost. In my previous work, I discussed the case of don Pedro de Porres Maraver y Silva, *corregidor* of Carmona, who became the father-in-law of two of his colleagues on the council, don Diego de Rueda y Mendoza and don Miguel Laso de la Vega y Barba, sons of two of the most locally prominent families.[11] Another variant of the same behavior involved middle-aged or elderly *corregidores,* who sought to marry their sons into the local patriarchy. This was the case of don Luis de Bañuelos y Velasco, a member of the military order of Calatrava and of a noble Cordovan family, whose father, don Antonio de Bañuelos, was *corregidor* in Jaén. Luis wed doña María de Peñalosa y Vivero, daughter of doña Mariana de Vivero y Tassis and the Segovian don Jerónimo de Mercado y Pañalosa, of the military order of Santiago. Because of her daughter's wedding, doña Mariana, by then a widow, left Jaén, eventually remarrying don Rodrigo Ponce de León, a cadet member of the noble House of La Guardia.[12]

There were yet additional variations: *corregidores* who sought not only to procure wealthy local heiresses for their own sons, but also served as bridges uniting a local oligarch with a friend, client or relative from their place of origin. This happened, for example, in the case of don Andrés de Melgosa, of the military order of Santiago and *corregidor* in Chinchilla. He took advantage of his position to arrange the marriage of an attractive local candidate to his compatriot, don Vicente de Cañas y Silva. The bride was doña María de Reina, the only daughter of a rich farmer named don Jacinto de Reina Núñez Cortés. The couple wed in 1669.[13] To the countrified landowner who would become his father-in-law, don Vicente, the second-born son of his House, brought (or, perhaps better, represented) crests of nobility and family connections that were above suspicion. His father was don Julián de Cañas Frías Ramírez y Silva, *regidor* (an alderman) in perpetuity of Burgos and judge of the Royal Chancellery of Granada; while his paternal grandfather was don Juan de Cañas Frías y Salamanca, also a *regidor* of Burgos and of the military order of Santiago, who was wed to doña Catalina de Silva, a descendent of the Houses of the Marquis de Villena and the Count of Cifuentes. To the Cañas' family ties, which placed it squarely within a powerful, extended network of high-level bureaucrats, one should add its connections to the highest blood nobility: the groom's sister was the wife of don Francisco Bernardo de Villavicencio, Marquis of Alcántara del Cuervo, one of the richest and most prestigious oligarchs in Jerez de la Frontera. In addition, the first-born brother of both, who also wore the habit of Santiago and was a *regidor* in perpetuity of Guadalajara, had married the heiress of the Marquis of Vallecerrato, doña María Juana de Acuña Altamirano, who carried with her not only the ancient blood of the Counts of Buendía, but came from a lineage of high ranking officials of the Monarchy, the Altamiranos, who served as judges in Lima. Moreover, upon the death of her husband, the mother of the Marquise, doña Mariana de Acuña y Figueroa, wed don Alonso Carnero y López de Zárate, Secretary of State and of the *Despacho Universal* of Charles II, and of the Council and the *Cámara de Indias*.[14]

The foregoing portrait of the way *Corregidores* behaved can be extended to include another similarly itinerant population, military officers, who formed a social group that became increasingly professionalized during the Early Modern Period and whose influence expanded in the eighteenth century in both Spain and the Indies.[15] Without going into too much detail, suffice to say that the higher social status acquired by military officers during that period and their growing ability to gain entrance into the highest administrative levels of the Monarchy, made them increasingly more attractive as spouses for the marriageable daughters of local elites and provincial nobilities. Better said, the progenitors of the latter were eager to encounter young, ambitious sons-in-law, who could connect their families to the Court. As they rarely had the economic means that would have enabled them to aspire to a marriage with judges, *corregidores* or *intendentes* (Intendants), for many belonging to the intermediate-level peripheral governing groups, military officers became a prime solution for establishing connections with Madrid and other Peninsular centers. Gloria Franco Rubio explores several such examples, focusing on officials belonging to the Secretary of War in the second half of the seventeenth century. In her work, she reveals the way the marriage of daughters of local oligarchs to noblemen and young lieutenants and captains, enabled these oligarchs to cultivate connections between elites of diverse social and geographic origin.[16] At the tender age of 18, Captain José de Cáceres from Madrid was stationed in Catalonia, where he wed María Francisca Portell Bru, daughter of Gaspar Portell Mata, an "honorable citizen", a *regidor* in perpetuity of Mataró, and a member of an important, ancient local family.[17] Upon the premature death of his wife (when the captain was but 22), he married doña María Ignacia Picó Bru, a cousin of his deceased spouse, who brought to the wedding a dowry of 20,000 *reales*.[18]

While relatively much is known regarding the marriage patterns of *corregidores* and military officers, much less is known regarding the participation of ecclesiastics in marriage arrangements. During this period, an immense network of clergymen crisscrossed the entire planet, supported by the territorial possessions of a Catholic prince who was lord of half of the universe. From the humblest parishes to the richest archbishoprics, thousands of ecclesiastics monitored the observance of commands, both pontifical and royal, controlled consciences and dominated bodies and souls. These individuals traveled widely from one place to another building a *cursus honorum* that rewarded not only personal ability, but also luck and, above all, the influence of relatives, allies and friends.

In terms of their activities in the marriage market, most important were the Inquisition, the Diocese and the Cathedral Chapters (*cabildos catedralicios*). The creation of the Holy Office in 1478, divided the Spanish territory into a dozen district tribunals, each staffed by a small group of officials led by Inquisitors. Usually an outsider, the Inquisitor was often accompanied by one or more of his relatives, whom he was obliged to accommodate. Such was the case, for example, of don Alonso de Herrera y Quirós, husband of doña Antonia Daza y Villalobos. Why would in the late seventeenth century a Cantabrian noble of impeccable lineage but scanty fortune,[19] marry on the other side of the Iberian Peninsula, where he had no prior connections? Not doubt, he was living in the south because his brother was don Manuel de Herrera, the Inquisitor of Granada, who procured for his kinsman the highly respectable position of *alguacil mayor* of the Holy Office. Thanks to his office and the relations established through his brother, don Alonso won the hand of the aforementioned doña Antonia, daughter and heiress of a rich local oligarch named don diego Daza Villalobos, who was not only the *caballero veinticuatro* (alderman) of Granada, but also the general collector of taxes (*alcabalas*) and other contributions, including those levied on sugar supplies for the city and its surrounding jurisdiction.[20]

A similar itinerant lifestyle also characterized certain members of Spain's Cathedral Chapters, who obtained their offices through competition (*oposición*). They formed a minority — though a significant one — as most canons and prebendaries (*racioneros*) were locals who belonged to the mesocracy and the elite of the city, which was also the seat of a Bishopric. What other cause would lead a niece of Dean Dionisio Esquivel of León[21] to marry advantageously in Murcia? Why else would doña Isabel Maldonado, a member of one of the most powerful local families in Granada, have traveled an even greater distance to wed the Asturian Álvaro Flores Meléndez, of the middling nobility of that Principality? Might the fact that her brother, Doctor don Diego Maldonado de Salazar, had attained the post of Dean of the Cathedral at Oviedo had something to do with that particular arrangement?[22]

If we would raise our eyes to the higher echelons of prelatures, we would find that the situation remains unchanged. Because Bishops and Archbishops were usually from outside the Dioceses to which they were assigned, they always arrived with a large entourage of relatives, including servants of different ilk, many kinsmen such as nephews twice- or thrice-removed, cousins, and other more-or-less close kin, all of whom were more than willing to extract whatever personal benefit they could from their relative's advantageous appointment. Because new Bishops often availed themselves of the opportunity to place their relatives in vacant canonries and prebendaries, the arrival of these prelates to town usually involved frequent confrontations between then and local Chapters. Whereby such external intervention led local power groups to fear their displacement, on many such occasions they responded by forming marriages alliances between their daughters and sons and the members of the prelate's Episcopal clientele. In exchange for money, certain ambitious families were thus able to forge direct links to important representatives of the king, men who had access to the nucleus of the central power and even to the Monarch himself. How else could we explain that a man with no fortune or position like don Alonso Carrión y Morcillo wed doña María Josefa de Tagle, the sister of two judges of Lima and the daughter of the Marquis of Torre Tagle, an affluent merchant, who had an enormous dowry of 80,000 pesos? Clearly, this union becomes comprehensible only when we discover that don Alonso was a nephew of don Diego Morcillo Rubio de Auñón, Archbishop of Charcas and Lima, and Viceroy of Peru on two occasions.[23] In a similar case, don Gaspar de Ortega Torquemada, a lawyer residing in Santiago de Compostela and a descendent of some of the principal families of the middling nobility of Galicia, married doña Isabel Pacheco Silva y Saavedra of Extremadura. In addition to being a grand-niece of the Archbishop, don Juan Beltrán de Guevara, doña Isabel also held in her hand the concession of Judge in la Quintana, one that the prelate was free to nominate.[24]

Probing even deeper, one could include in the analysis all the other members of Spain's ever growing administration. As the monarchy converted from a peripheral kingdom into a global Empire, it required thousands of educated men. The families that opted to place one or more of their sons in royal service not only achieved upwards social mobility, but also often saw themselves integrated into wider family circuits that included kinsmen posted hither and yon throughout the monarchy's immense territories. While detailed histories of the principal lineages of administrators serving the empire are scanty, the information included in studies of this particular social group, often link its members to local elites. Thus, as in the case of the *corregidores*, most administrators seemed to belong to local power groups that were (to some degree) on the move. The successful outcome of family links among urban judges and patriarchs demonstrates the vitality and strength of these processes, for marriages occurred on a massive scale.

Examples of judges and other magistrates marrying women from the local patri- archies that were under their jurisdiction are not wanting. This was especially true in the Americas, where in addition to repeating references we also have several studies, in which historians have examined these practices, among other things, as a key to understanding Creolism and the coming of Independence. "In issues concerning justice, the judges of this Court (*Audiencia*) are so burdened with dependents and relatives, their own marriages, and those of their sons and kinsmen, that it is often impossible for them to fulfill their obligations". It was in these terms that the Count de Alba de Liste, Viceroy of Peru, wrote a missive to Philip IV recommending that magistrates be moved from one *Audiencia* to another so to ensure that they would be unable to establish deep roots in any particular place.[25] This was not an isolated case. A century earlier, in 1565 to be exact, a Mexican lawyer surnamed Valderrama wrote to Philip II denouncing, among other undesirable practices, the extensive parentages that the judges of that tribunal were contracting.[26] Although there were dozens such accusations, the point here is not whether local marriage was good or bad, but that such unions existed despite the Crown's — at least in theory — pro- hibiting it.

The prohibition of local marriage by officers was established in Law 82, Title 16 of the Second Volume of the *Recopilación de Leyes de Indias* (*Collection of the Laws of the Indies*), which stated:

> We prohibit and establish that without our explicit permission, as is the custom in these our kingdoms, the viceroys, presidents and judges, *alcaldes del crimen* and attorneys of our *Audiencias* in the Indies may not marry in their districts, nor shall they do so, and prohibit their sons and daughters from doing the same while their fathers are serving us in the said posts, under the penalty that for such acts their posts shall be made vacant and shall thus be declared, in order to appoint other persons according to our will.[27]

To demonstrate the degree of non-compliance with this prohibition, suffice to say that it was reiterated time and time again for decades, and was still an issue in the final years of the Ancient Regime. In was also a topic of theoretical reflection and discus- sion by the interested parties, as evidenced by the *Tratado analítico sobre la Cédula Real de 10 de febrero de 1575 y otras semejantes que estrechísimamente prohiben el matrimonio de los oidores y otros ministros de las Indias*, by don Bernardino Figueroa de la Cerda, a judge of Lima.[28]

Some historians have posited that the prohibition was effective, or was at least a highly restrictive measure that impeded or seriously hindered such union. In my own view, anyone examining the existing bibliography and archival sources could not seri- ously defend such a position, at least with regard to the period up to the mid-eighteenth century. Thus, and as Pilar Gonzalbo had observed, " . . . despite reiterated prohibi- tions on marriage with residents of the same jurisdiction, the functionaries of the *Real Audiencia* became relatives of the local aristocracy."[29] The same could be said of the *Audiencia* of Granada in Spain.[30] Indeed, I would posit that the intention of the Crown was not so much to *prevent* such unions — a pretension that would have been impossible to achieve — but, rather, to *control* them, that is, to act as the arbiter of marriages between judges and members of local power groups by granting, or not, the required permission in accordance with the circumstances of each case.

The archives contain countless permissions, but many more petitions, a very great number of which were denied, often on the grounds of their manifest effrontery that the Crown considered unacceptable. To give but one example: in 1769, an *alcalde del crimen* in Mexico, don Francisco Leandro de Viana, requested the King's permission to wed "in the event that the occasion to marry [in that district] were to arise in the future." Charles II's response was clear: "I shall not grant such a general permission. Include in your request information on the circumstances of the woman, when you have obtained it".[31] Nonetheless, permissions to wed were usually granted with a certain liberality. In exchange for a genuine fortune (13,000 ducats), Pedro de Tapia, a lawyer and judge of the *Real Chancillería* of Granada wed doña Clara de Alarcón, a resident of the city of Loja and daughter of the powerful Del Rosal family. Although immensely rich, the family had difficulties establishing the purity of its bloodline.[32] In their condition as converts from Judaism and thus plebeians, Del Rosal searched for means to support their pretension for noble status. Clearly, their flamboyant son-in-law was anxious to help. Not surprisingly, soon after the union was accomplished the *Audiencia* ruled in favor of their petition and declared the family members legitimate nobles. As the judge's mother-in-law explained while waiting for royal permission to wed her daughter to de Tapia, the license should be granted "because it is a matter that Your Majesty has always conceded with great facility."[33]

The motives that led local power groups to seek such marriages were clear: first, to obtain support in ongoing disputes or ones that might arise in the future; second, to foster and cement connections with higher instances of authority and whatever might derive from them. For the administrators the motive was clear and can be summarized in a single word: money. In 1588, for example, don Nuño de Villavicencio, the judge of Nueva Galicia who was about to wed the daughter of Juan Bautista de Lomas, a resident of Nieves in that jurisdiction, observed that his future father-in-law "has given me his youngest daughter and with her thirty-five thousand pesos".[34]

Regardless of the specific circumstances of each case, almost anyone who wished to marry locally and had the opportunity to do so, was able to fulfill his desire; or so at least happened with those who had the good sense to first request the necessary permission. Many others went ahead with their marriages without the king's license, at times suffering, as a consequence, exemplary punishments. That royal prohibition exercised little effect is clear: during the viceroyalty of Montesclaros in Peru, six of the seven judges of the *Audiencia* were related through marriage to the principal, local Creole families.[35] As Javier Ortiz de la Tabla had observed: "through these marriages, the family of the magistrate became linked to the old families of the *conquistadors*, *encomenderos* and *hacendados* that made up the local elites, thus restoring and strengthening their influence, power and, in some cases, nobility".[36]

But judges were not the only ones to foster ties with the local society. The Viceroys, who were the King's *alter egos* in the Americas, constituted not only the highest ranked administrators in these far-off lands, but also shared the royal charisma and formed part of the Monarch's mystic body. Viceroys who arrived in New Spain or Peru and, in the eighteenth century, also in Nueva Granada and La Plata, were surrounded by swarms of servants, relatives, clients, friends and attendants of all sorts, many of whom later entered into marriage unions with urban patriarchs, especially those in their respective capital cities. Because Viceroys held prestigious local position, often competing with powerful local figures, they obtained huge economic benefits and enjoyed direct relations with the court, that is, the very nucleus of decision-making. It is thus easy to understand why so many native oligarchs yearned to form alliances with those representatives of the Crown.[37] This power game, perhaps struggle, involved not only the Viceroy as the epicenter of all movement, but also his wife (the *virreina*), who often became a source of appointments, mainly for the husbands and fathers of her ladies-in-waiting.[38]

Local unions were not free of conflict. The arrival of a new Viceroy often displaced local candidates who watched their opportunities slip away because of their inability to compete with the newcomer's entourage, whose members were considered 'prime catches'. This process of displacement was often bitterly denounced. It is thus not surprising that in 1649 don Luis Enríquez de Guzmán, elected Viceroy of New Spain, was informed of the "limited freedom that *encomenderos* have in marrying, because when [marriageable daughters] accede to a profitable rent, the Viceroys marry them to their servants, or procure them and ask for their hand, such that with the means at their disposal and especially with the Viceroy's favor bestowed upon them, these unions [succeed]."[39]

To end this long list, I would like to mention yet another social group, which was hardly studied: the Queen consort's ladies, an entourage that included all women of the middle and high nobility that served the Spanish sovereigns' wives in different palace activities (housecleaners, companions, ladies-in-waiting, and so forth). Usually members of important families, many of these young women achieved excellent marriages partners, either due to the affection that the sovereign felt for them, or because caring for them was considered the king's moral obligation. Some such unions were hypergamic, brought about by the lure of a palace appointment, the uniform of a military order, a bureaucratic post, or perhaps a title of nobility, all of which could form part of their dowry.

2. How Were Marriages Arranged?

It is thus clear that marriages tying local power groups to the court or to the members of similar groups elsewhere in the Monarchy happened constantly. The question is how were these ties forged or, to be more exact, what networks, individuals and occasions brought the members of different groups into a contact that would enabled some of them to later marry. Who did the groundwork? How were such matters negotiated? Because the search for an heiress was a universal phenomenon, certain cases may allow us to understand how the process played out.

Take for example the union of don Diego Antonio Manso de Velasco, the second son of a rather affluent noble family from La Rioja, whose personal qualities earned him the affection of his uncle, the well-known Viceroy of Peru, Count Superunda. So strong was their relationship that the Count decided to bestow upon Diego not only the ownership of an enormous entailed estate (*mayorazgo*) though he was not his first-born, but also to procure for him an excellent bride. After several trials, he finally found the ideal candidate, the Marquise of Bermudo, a young woman who lived on the outskirts of Ciudad Rodrigo under the tutelage of her father, the Marquis of Espeja.

Rarely do we have the opportunity to glimpse at the crude nature of such marriage negotiations. The Marquis was in no hurry to marry off his daughter who was a minor and assured him an income of 8,000 ducats. When it came to selling her hand, the price was dear. Among their ample assets, the Manso de Velascos had not only the personal fortune of the Viceroy of Peru but — especially — the firm friendship of the Count of Superunda with his compatriot, the all-powerful Marquis de Ensenada, at that time, the dominant political figure in Madrid. Forming part of the extended clientele of de Ensenada was thus no mere trifle and convinced the father to agree to the union.[40]

Similar information can be drawn from other cases. The protagonists of the following history were two persons of some importance in eighteenth-century Spain. The first was don Fernando José de Velasco and Cevallos, member of the *Cámara de Castilla* and one of the most cultivated men of his time, indeed, the owner of what was perhaps the largest private library in Spain.[41] The second was the Bishop of Cordova, don Martín de Barcia, born in Zamora and a childhood friend of Velasco's.[42] Among the letters they exchanged one is of especial relevance to the topic in question.[43] Sent by Velasco on January 16, 1767, it wasted no words:

> My dear Sir and friend. The confidence in which I share through your Lordship's honors, friendship and generous character bring me to take up pen to make an earnest imploration concerning a matter of the greatest interest that could ever occur to me.
>
> The issue is that as I ponder how to honorably place my firstborn son, José María de Velasco, I have received news of a young lady, the niece of the Vicar of Espejo, which would seem to be a most attractive union for all its circumstances, and your Lordship may have the strongest influence upon achieving it if you would be willing to become involved directly [sic] or through the offices of your *Provisor* . . .
>
> Thus, I appeal to your Lordship from the bottom of my heart, in hopes of receiving your great favor. And, in the happy event that you condescend to attend my request I could not but put to your Lordship's consideration that we are legitimate male descendants of the House of the *Condestables* of Castile, Dukes of Frías, as the current Duke has openly recognized, and as shown by the authentic instruments of the work *Asturias Ilustrada*, edited in Madrid in the year 1760, volume two, second part, folios 157 to 172. Moreover, the lad is of fair appearance and talent and docile . . . lovely character, disposed to live in Espejo or any other place with no objection whatsoever, as his inclinations are most innocent and his age 23 years, quite hale and hearty, as the Count de Torres Cabrera can well attest.
>
> With respect to conveniences, I admit that those of my son do not correspond to such a union, as he only possesses from his deceased mother, doña Nicolasa de Montoya, a *mayorazgo de segundos* [i.e., an entailed estate for second sons] from the lords of San Cebrián and Zurita in Palencia and its periphery that pays a rent of ten thousand *reales*, and various free and quite decent haciendas in Santander and other areas of the Mountain that his mother had chosen to bestow on him . . .

The wealthy heiress in question was doña Manuela Antonia Moro Dávalos de la Concha y Lucena, daughter of the second Viscounts of la Montesina, a prosperous and influential clan based in the town of Espejo, near the capital city of Cordoba. The extent of the family's fortune is reflected in the dowries the mother and maternal grandmother of the young lady received when they married: no fewer than 10,000 ducats each. But especially significant was the inheritance that the lady's grand-uncle, don Fernando de Lucena Castroviejo, the Vicar mentioned in the above letter, had left her: a property valued in at least 880,000 *reales*.

Unfortunately for the President of the *Audiencia* of Granada, his proposal arrived too late. As a later missive — penned by Bishop Barcia — tells us, the young lady had already been promised in marriage to her second cousin, don Antonio Melgarejo y Ortiz Rojano, Marquis of Lendínez.[44]

3. The Effects of Such Marriages

I know not for what reason your grace never writes about the kinsmen we share and who they are, which I wish to know. I ask your grace to inform me at length of all this and of what kinship we have with don Luis de Padilla y Meneses, now the judge of the Council of the [military] Orders, and with don Diego López de Ayala, of the Royal Council, [and] whatever other relatives there may be, as in this kingdom it is valuable indeed to have a relative on the Councils.[45]

It was in these terms that in 1610 don Pablo de Meneses y Toledo of Lima wrote to his aunt, doña María de Ayala, Abbess of the Convent of San Miguel de los Ángeles in Toledo. Well aware of the returns for having relatives who were judges, councilors or bishops, Menses y Toledo understood that in his society the power of kinship was enormous and it conditioned one's advancement to a much greater degree than did individual ability.[46]

Although the belief in kinship was general, measuring the effect of marriage choices on individual and collective careers would require an exhaustive analysis of hundreds — perhaps thousands — of families, tracing their descendants and relatives and measuring their success. As no such study has even been conducted, our ability to answer the question how successful were such unions in achieving the desired goals is practically nil. Furthermore, even if we traced all descendents and relatives, it would be impossible to evaluate whether success was attained due to the new kinsmen and their relatives or whether it depended on other reasons. As a result, all we can do is to follow a few concrete examples.

We begin our survey in 1630 with the union in Seville of two individuals of distinct social extraction, though both members of prominent families that had for some time pursued ambitious and ascending careers. The bride, doña Mencía de Lara, was the daughter of Francisco de Lara, a *veinticuatro* (alderman) of Seville, and doña Ana de Vitoria Bobeo, granddaughter of a wealthy merchant.[47] Don Francisco had been a merchant in the city since 1592[48] and, over time, succeeded achieving membership in the principal organs of the city, having been named lieutenant to the *caballero veinticuatro* in the Admiralty of Castile.[49] He then integrated into this new socio-professional group by wedding doña Ana, the daughter of a mercantile family that, having originated in Burgos, later settled on the promising banks of the Guadalquivir. The groom was don Alonso de Baeza Manrique de Luna, a native of Valladolid now living in Seville. His family was a large, well-connected family of high social ranking. His mother doña Ana María Manrique, was of Jewish extraction. Alonso's maternal grandfather was the fourth lord of the towns of Estepar and Frandovinez, a title acquired during the reign of Charles V by his great-grandfather, and served as *alcalde mayor* of Burgos and *corregidor* in Medina del Campo. Alonso's father, Luis de Baeza y

Mendoza, was judge of the Seville's *Almojarifazgos* (customs). He was a member of the military order of Santiago and had previously been *corregidor* in Carrión, Palencia, Zamora and Cordoba. His paternal line — equally consisting of many converts — led back to a series of aldermen of Valladolid,[50] among them the Treasurer of the Catholic Kings, Gonzalo de Baeza, and to Kings Peter I and Charles III of Navarre. His mother was the illegitimate daughter of the second Marquis of Montesclaros, that headed the secondary line of the House of the Dukes of Infantado, his father don Rodrigo de Mendoza, having been the first Marquis and the son of the third Duke.

The network of relatives accumulated by the bride and groom was therefore overwhelming: the Duchess- consort of Infantado was first cousin to the groom's father, while the bride's father, the duchess' grandmother's brother, served as Viceroy of New Spain (1603–1606) and Peru (1607–1615). There were many other important relatives, many by affinity, who belonged to the clan of the Montesclaros, who descended from the favorite Lerma (among others the Duke of Osuna and the Admiral of Castile), as well as included the entire House of the Counts of Palma. Given this background, it is hardly surprising that don Luis de Baeza and Lara, who was procreated in this marriage, received the *Marquisate* of Castromonte in 1663, a title to which in 1698 he added that of *Grande de España*, the highest social rank to which a mortal not of royal lineage could aspire within the Spanish Monarchy.

Perhaps this network of close relatives (close according to the canons of the Ancient Regime) at the Court explained the continuous social ascent of the Laras thereafter. In just a few years, the family of the bride rose from membership in the wealthy mesocracy of Seville to become fully integrated in the municipal council and cathedral chapter, earn full honors of nobility and marry splendidly. One could dare say that if the family would have produced a male heir (which it did not), it would have certainly continued its trajectory by obtaining the title of Count or Marquis. That is to say, while before the wedding the maximum the Laras could aspire to was to secure a nomination to the Holy Inquisition, after the union was celebrated the sky was the limit. Doña Mencía's three brothers demonstrated this ascent. The youngest, don Pedro de Lara, became canon of the Cathedral of Seville, as did don Jerónimo, the second-born who also became the precentor of that institution and the *Sumiller de Cortina del Rey*. But the aspirations of the family concentrated on the first-born, don Juan de Lara. In addition to his nomination to the Holy Inquisition, don Juan also obtained a *veinticuatría* (aldermenship) on the city Council. His most important promotion however occurred when he was named 'gentleman of Seville'. Throughout his life, don Juan never suspended his commercial dealings with the Americas, although he now conducted it from the more prestigious and privileged platform offered by membership in the Merchant guild (*consulado*), an institution that brought together the local nobility dedicated to such tasks.[51] Eventually, he married doña Guiomar de la Cueva y Monsalve, who on her father's side was related to some of the principal families of Jerez and, on her mother's side, descended from the Marrufos of Cádiz, a family of wealthy patricians of Genoese origin who earned nobility titles such as Marquis of the Royal House and Count of Río Molino.[52] Doña Guiomar bore Juan a son, don Francisco de Lara Monsalve, who was last of their line. In 1652 we find his exercising an ecclesiastical benefice (*medio racionero*) in the Cathedral of Seville. Thereafter the Laras disappear from the documentation or, at least, from the extensive records I could examine.

In other cases, the consequences of marriages between royal ministers and members of local elites can be traced more easily, as they revealed themselves almost immediately. An excellent example of such quick preeminence was the family of the Marquis of Escalona, surnamed Acuña. This clan knew well how to maximize its investments in the Indies in order to obtain enormous economic benefits that it than transformed into honors and offices that eventually allowed its members to become nobles or associate with ones. A lesser branch of Counts of Buendía, when the Acuñas settled in Burgos they were not particularly wealthy, nor did their fortune attain the levels they desired and that was congruent with their distant relationship to the Castilian aristocracy. Family ambition, however, was fueled by the commercial opportunities available in the Americas. Investing there augured prosperity, but it also entailed hypogamous marriages with wealthy Creole families whose pockets were as full of gold as their offices were bereft of parchments of nobility.

Don Juan Vázquez de Acuña, by then a widower, journeyed to the New World in 1635 to take up his position as *corregidor* of Quito. After performing his functions there (and later in La Plata), he became *corregidor* in Potosí, a highly coveted position that allowed controlling this important mining center and thus implied great opportunities for enrichment. Using that position to his advantage, in 1643 don Juan wed doña Margarita Bejarano de Marquina, a wealthy heiress whose dowry was no less than 140,000 pesos. Don Juan's first-born son with doña Margarita (who was his second wife), was named Íñigo. This young man followed in his father's footsteps by marrying — in Lima in 1656 — a young Creole woman whose lineage was as modest as that of his own mother, but which had a similar fortune, as she was a daughter of Juan de Figueroa, alderman in perpetuity of Lima, Treasurer, Minter and First Assayer of the *Casa de la Moneda* (Mint) of Potosí, positions that were valued in over 170,000 pesos.

Meanwhile on the Iberian Peninsula, this wealth accumulated in the Americas provided for a certain social promotion. Don Juan's son by his third wife was named Marquis of Casafuerte, while the aforementioned Íñigo, his half-brother, surpassed him in 1679, when he purchased the seigneury of the village of Escalona for 80,000 *reales* from the Marquis of Ladrada and obtained the title of Marquis of Escalona in the same year.[53]

4. By Way of Conclusion

Composite Monarchy, multinational empire, diverse states bonded only by dynastic union, these and other appellatives were used in the sixteenth, seventeenth and eighteenth centuries to classify the complex institutional reality that the Spanish Monarchy was. Whatever the case may have been, clearly, the Monarchy was a structure made of a plethora of units that desperately needed to generate webs of solidarity among its different ruling elites. In the process, provincial nobilities — as we may call them — were fluidly interrelated to the fascinating social microcosm that the Court represented. Local elites had many means of interconnecting with the Court. Among them was the re-orientation and modification of traditional marriage markets. The nascent imperial edifice required a host of new servants in the form of royal ministers who would spread out and cover the enormous geographical expanse bounded by Mexico and Lima, on the one hand, Brussels and Messina, on the other, and that included each and every one of the peninsular territories.

The hypertrophy of the royal bureaucracy, which was so essential to satisfying the needs of the Early Modern State, propitiated an additional effect: the interrelation through marriage of local power groups. Pre-existing family networks were upset and broadened as *corregidores* and judges, bishops' nephews and army captains wed the daughters of urban aldermen. But such arrangements were a two-way street: while, on the one hand, the King's ministers obtained patrimony in the form of dowries and/or inheritances and, in some cases, one or more entailed estates (*mayorazgos*); on the other, local patricians acquired ambitious sons- or brothers-in-law, with close ties to the *polysynodia* or to an important patron at Court, which allowed them to integrate into an extensive clientelist fabric that could earn them, or their male progeny, a military habit, the title of gentleman, or an appointment as *corregidor*. Through these mechanisms the different elites throughout these widespread realms were incorporated into a more global social and political universe that in some periods, at least, covered several continents. The links that made the empire possible were thus formalized before the altar. They were aimed at involving as many groups as possible in the maintenance of the imperial edifice, a construction that despite its thick walls and weak foundations succeeded in preserving itself intact for centuries.

Abbreviations

ADG   Archivo de la Diputación de Granada.
AGI   Archivo General de Indias.
AGS   Archivo General de Simancas.
AHN   Archivo Histórico Nacional.
AHN-SN   Sección Nobleza del Archivo Histórico Nacional.
APG   Archivo de Protocolos de Granada.
BNE   Biblioteca Nacional de España.
OM   Órdenes Militares.
RAH   Real Academia de la Historia.

Notes

1 Pellicer de Tovar, 1790, 90.
2 As there is no definitive biography of this author, his grandson's extensive biographical sketch, Pellicer y Saforcada 1778, 101–112, and the words of the prince of genealogists, (Soria Mesa, 1997, 93–98), are useful.
3 The ascendants and descendants of these individuals are analyzed in greater detail in Sosa, 1676.
4 Yun Casalilla, 2009.
5 *Ibid.*, 15. Also interesting are the reflections in Yun Casalilla, 2004.
6 Zúñiga, 2000, 59.
7 On this topic, I refer the reader to my book, Soria Mesa, 2007.
8 For additional information on this institution, the exceptional, and now classic, work by González Alonso, 1970, is still essential.
9 AHN, OM, *Santiago*, exp. 403, fols. 45 and ff.
10 AHN, *Consejos*, 2752, 66.
11 Soria Mesa, 2007, 181–182.
12 AHN, OM, *Alcántara*, exp. 143 (1644).
13 Molina Puche, 2007, 221. *Capitulaciones* in AHN-SN, *Torrelaguna*, 407.
14 To the data mentioned by Molina Puche, 2007, I would add those in AHN, *Órdenes Militares, Santiago*, exp. 1487, AHN, *Estado, Carlos III*, exp. 353, and various other genealogical sources.
15 There is an extended bibliography on the topic, most recently by Francisco Andújar Castillo, among many others.

16 Franco Rubio, 1997.

17 Here, I complete the data provided by Dr. Franco with the inserts in the file on that Caballero de Charles III (1814), AHN, *Estado, Carlos III*, exp. 511.

18 Franco Rubio, 1997, 81. Molas Ribalta, 1993, analyzes the Portell family.

19 Don Alonso was the son of don Fernando de Herrera y Velarde, lord of the House of Herrera in Miengo, Caballero de Santiago (1661). On his ascendancy, see Escagedo Salmón, 1932, 51.

20 APG, *Granada*, no. 1010. Juan Félix Martínez. 1705–6, fol. 279, and ADG, 5455, piece 7 discuss don Diego Daza. Domínguez Ortiz, 1989, 242–243, and Sanz Ayán, 1989, 521.

21 Irigoyen López, 2000, 238.

22 APG, *Granada*, no. 222, f. 873. In a genealogical manuscript owed to Blas de Salazar, Álvaro Flores is called the "Lord of the House of Abia in Cangas", BNE, Ms. 11.453, f. 107.

23 Turiso Sebastián, 2002, 272.

24 BNE, Ms. 20693.

25 Puente Brunke, 2006, 144. On this topic see 2004 by the same author.

26 García Marín 2005, 125.

27 For context, see Konetzke, 1969, 105–120.

28 Muñoz García, 2003, 191.

29 Gonzalbo Aizpuru, 1998, 119.

30 Gómez González, 2000, 96.

31 Konetzke, 1969, 108.

32 On this family, see Soria Mesa, 2008.

33 AGS, *Cámara de Castilla*, leg. 2724, f. 1658. On the judge and his trajectory, see Soria Mesa, 2005, 2008.

34 Enciso Contreras, 1996, 399.

35 Latasa Vassallo, 1997, 61.

36 Ortiz de la Tabla Ducasse, 1996.

37 See Torres Arancivia, 2006.

38 See Rubial García, 2005, 123 ss.

39 *Instrucciones y memorias de los virreyes novohispanos*, 1991, 553.

40 Ochagavía Fernánez, 1961. For context, see González Caizán, 2004; Latasa Vassallo, 2003; and Gómez Urdáñez (1996).

41 For biography, see Rezábal y Ugarte, 1805, and Gan Giménez, 1988. On his splendid library, see Andrés Martínez, 1995 and Moreno Gallego, 1998.

42 On this prelate, see Gómez Bravo,1778, 812 ss, and Aranda Doncel, 1991.

43 BNE, Manuscrito 2543 is digitalized in the *Biblioteca Virtual de Andalucia*, http://www.juntadeandalucia.es/cultura/bibliotecavirtualandalucia/inicio/inicio.cmd.

44 For all references on this woman's ascendancy, see Porras de la Puente, 1993.

45 Martínez Martínez, 2007, 278.

46 During this period 'Influence peddling', as we call it today, was an everyday occurrence, which was accepted without questioning: Herzog, 1995, 157.

47 See AGI, *Contratación*, 5248, 1, 4 (1594); 5261, 2, 52 (1600); 5252, 1, 10 (1596); 5308, 2, 11 (1608); 5236, 2, 17 (1592); 945, 2, 8 (1614); 5340, 27 (1614) and 5411, 12 (1621).

48 AGI, *Contratación*, 5260, 2, 5.

49 Díaz de Noriega y Pubul, 1976, III, 7.

50 Which led the malicious Duke of Saint Simón to define this Spanish figure as "proceeding from a paternal line of *regidores* and councilors of Valladolid"; Saint-Simon, 1932, 534.

51 Domínguez Ortiz, 1976. The pages of this book discuss don Juan de Lara, who appears in the Consulate lists from 1637 to 1653. In the final year he is identified as a *veinticuatro* of Seville.

52 For interesting information on them, see RAH, *Colección Salazar y Castro*, D-29, fol. 216, M-178, fol. 133, and S-62, fols. 309–329.

53 On the above, see Bravo Lozano and Hidalgo Nuchera (1995, 140); Lohmann Villena (1983), and Fernández de Bethencourt, 2002, 51 ss.

Bibliography

Andrés Martínez, G. de, "La biblioteca manuscrita del camarista de Castilla Fernando José de Velasco en la Biblioteca Nacional", *Cuadernos de Investigación Histórica*, 16 (1995), pp. 143–166.

Andújar Castillo, F., *Consejo y consejeros de Guerra en el siglo XVIII*, Granada, Universidad de Granada, 1996.

——, *Los militares en la España del siglo XVIII. Un estudio social*, Granada Universidad de Granada, 1991.

Aranda Doncel, J., "El zamorano Martín de Barcia, obispo de Ceuta y Córdoba (1743–1771)", *I Congreso de Historia de Zamora. III. Historia Medieval y Moderna*, Zamora, 1991, pp. 681–691.

Bravo Lozano, J. e P. Hidalgo Nuchera, *De indianos y notarios*, Madrid, Colegios Notariales de España, 1995.

Díaz de Noriega y Pubul, J., *La Blanca de la Carne en Sevilla*, Madrid, Hidalguía, 1976, 4 vols.

Domínguez Ortiz, A., "Comercio y blasones. Concesiones de hábitos de Órdenes Militares a miembros del Consulado de Sevilla en el siglo XVII", *Anuario de Estudios Americanos*, 33 (1976), pp. 217–256.

——, "Miscelánea motrileña", *Revista del Centro de Estudios Históricos de Granada y su Reino*, 3, 2ª época (1989), pp. 239–252.

Enciso Contreras, José, *Epistolario de Zacatecas, 1549–1599*, Zacatecas, Ayuntamiento de Zacatecas, 1996.

Escagedo Salmón, M., *Solares montañeses*, VI, Torrelavega, 1932.

Fayard, J., *Los miembros del Consejo de Castilla (1621–1746)*, Madrid, Siglo XXI, 1982

Fernández de Bethencourt, F., *Historia genealógica y heráldica de la Monarquía española*, 10 vols, Sevilla, Fabiola de Publicaciones Hispalenses, 2002.

Fisher, J.R., "Redes de poder en el virreinato del Perú, 1776–1824: los burócratas", *Revista de Indias*, 236 (2006), pp. 149–164.

Franco Rubio, G., "¿Espada o pluma? ¿Destino militar o puesto administrativo? La incorporación de los militares a las instituciones civiles en la España del siglo XVIII", *Cuadernos de Historia Moderna*, 18 (1997), pp. 71–84.

Gan Giménez, P., "Los presidentes de la Chancillería de Granada en el siglo XVIII", *Espacio, Tiempo y Forma. Serie IV. Historia Moderna*, 1 (1988), pp. 253–256.

García Martín, J.Mª, "La Justicia del Rey en la Nueva España. Algunos aspectos. Siglos XVI–XVIII", *AHDE*, 75 (2005), pp. 85–180.

Gómez Bravo, J., *Catálogo de los obispos de Córdoba*, Córdoba, Juan Rodríguez, 1778, 2 vols.

Gómez González, I., *La justicia en almoneda. La venta de oficios en la Chancillería de Granada, 1505–1834*, Granada, Comares, 2000.

Gómez Urdáñez, J.L., *El proyecto reformista de Ensenada*, Lleida, Millenium, 1996.

Gonzalbo Aizpuru, P., *Familia y orden colonial*, Mexico, El Colegio de México, 1998.

González Alonso, B., *El corregidor castellano (1348–1808)*, Madrid, Escuela Nacional de Administración Pública, 1970.

González Caizán, C., *La red política del marqués de la Ensenada*, Madrid, Fundación Jorge Juan, 2004.

Herzog, T., *La administración como un fenómeno social: la justicia penal de la ciudad de Quito (1650–1750)*, Madrid, Centro de Estudios Constitucionales, 1995.

Instrucciones y memorias de los virreyes novohispanos, Mexico, Porrúa, 1991 (estudio preliminar y notas de Ernesto de la Torre Villar), 2 vols.

Irigoyen López, A., *Entre el cielo y la tierra, entre la familia y la institución. El cabildo de la Catedral de Murcia en el siglo XVII*, Murcia, Universidad de Murcia, 2000.

Konetzke, R., "La prohibición de casarse los oidores o sus hijos e hijas con naturales del distrito de la Audiencia", en *Homenaje a don José María de la Peña y Cámara*, Madrid, 1969, pp. 105–120.

Latasa Vasallo, P., *Administración virreinal en el Perú: gobierno del marqués de Montesclaros (1607–1615)*, Madrid, Centro de Estudios Ramón Areces, 1997.

——, "Negociar en red: familia, amistad y paisanaje. El virrey Superunda y sus agentes en Lima y Cádiz (1745–1761)", *Anuario de Estudios Americanos*, 60–2 (2003), pp. 463–492.

Lohmann Villena, G., *Los regidores perpetuos del Cabildo de Lima (1535–1821). Crónica y estudio de un grupo de gestión*, Sevilla, Diputación Provincial, 1983.

Martínez Martínez, Mª C. (edición, estudio, notas e índices), *Desde la otra orilla. Cartas de Indias en el Archivo de la Real Chancillería de Valladolid (siglos XVI–XVIII)*, León, Universidad de León, 2007.

Molas Ribalta, P., "Los regidores de Mataró. Una élite local en la Cataluña borbónica", en Lambert-Gorges, M. (comp.), *Les élites locales et l'état dans l'Espagne Moderne, XVIe–XIXe siècle*, Paris, CNRS, 1993. pp. 253–280.

Molina Puche, S., *Poder y familia. Las élites del corregimiento Chinchilla-Villena en el siglo del Barroco*, Cuenca, Universidad de Castilla-la Mancha, 2007.

Moreno Gallego, V., "Burocracia y cultura libraria en el XVIII: el Camarista Velasco y su gran biblioteca", *Trabajos de la Asociación Española de Bibliografía*, vol. 2, Madrid, 1998, pp. 351–382.

Moreyra y Paz-Soldán, M., *Estudios históricos. II. Oidores y Virreyes*, Pontificia Universidad Católica, Lima, 1994.

Muñoz García, A., *Diego de Avendaño. Filosofía, moralidad, derecho y política en el Perú colonial*, Lima, Universidad Nacional Mayor de San Marcos, 2003.

Ochagavía Fernández, D., "El I conde de Superunda", *Berceo*, 58 (1961), pp. 25–48.

Ortiz de la Tabla Ducasse, J., "Si te quieres casar, toma tu par. Matrimonio y legitimidad en los grupos encomenderos de Quito y Lima", *Cuadernos de Historia Latinoamericana*, 3 (1996), pp. 145–181.

Pellicer de Tovar, J., "Avisos históricos, que comprenden las noticias y sucesos más particulares, ocurridos en nuestra Monarquía desde el año de 1639", *Semanario Erudito*, tomo 31, Madrid, 1790.

Pellicer y Saforcada, J.A., *Ensayo de una bibliotheca de traductores españoles . . .*, Madrid, Antonio de Sancha, 1778.

Porras de la Puente, A., "Los vizcondes de la Montesina", *Espejo*, 1993, pp. 79–87.

Puente Brunke, J. de la, "Codicia y bien público: los ministros de la Audiencia en la Lima seiscentista", *Revista de Indias*, 236 (2006), pp. 133–148.

——, "Las Audiencias en Indias y sus ministros: vigencia social y aspiraciones (a propósito de un oidor del siglo XVII)", in Feliciano Barrios (coord.), *El gobierno de un mundo. Virreinatos y Audiencias en la América Hispánica*, Cuenca, Universidad de Castilla-la Mancha, 2004, pp. 587–599.

Rezábal y Ugarte, J., *Biblioteca de los escritores que han sido individuos de los seis Colegios Mayores*, Madrid, Imprenta de Sancha, 1805.

Rodríguez Crespo, P., "Parentescos de los oidores de Lima con los grupos superiores de la sociedad colonial (comienzos del siglo XVII)", in *Anales del III Congreso Nacional de Historia del Perú. Descubrimiento, Conquista, Virreinato*, Lima, Centro de Estudios Histórico-Militares del Perú, 1965, pp. 17–24.

Rubial García, A., *Monjas, cortesanos y plebeyos. La vida cotidiana en la época de Sor Juana*, Mexico, Taurus, 2005.

Ruiz Medrano, E., *Gobierno y sociedad en Nueva España: segunda Audiencia y Antonio de Mendoza*, Zamora, Estado de Michoacán, 1991.

Saint-Simon, Duque de, "Cuadro de la Corte de España en 1722", *Boletín de la Real Academia de la Historia*, 101 (1932), pp. 198–259.

Salazar Mir, A., *Los expedientes de limpieza de sangre de la Catedral de Sevilla. Genealogías*, Madrid, Hidalguía, 1995–1998, 3 vols.

Sanz Ayán, C., *Los banqueros de Carlos II*, Valladolid, Universidad de Valladolid, 1989.

Soria Mesa, E., "Burocracia y conversos. La Real Chancillería de Granada en los siglos XVI y XVII", in Francisco J. Aranda Pérez (Coord.), *Letrados, juristas y burócratas en la España Moderna*, Cuenca, Universidad de Castilla-la Mancha, 2005, pp. 107–144.

——, *La biblioteca genealógica de don Luis de Salazar y Castro*, Córdoba, Universidad de Córdoba, 1997.

——, *La nobleza en la América Española* (forthcoming).

——, *La nobleza en la España Moderna. Cambio y continuidad*, Madrid, Marcial Pons, 2007.

——, *Linajes granadinos*, Granada, Diputación Provincial de Granada, 2008.

Sosa, J. de, *Noticia de la gran Casa de los marqueses de Villafranca y su parentesco con las mayores de Europa*, Nápoles, Novelo de Boris, 1676.

Torres Arancivia, E., *Corte de Virreyes. El entorno del poder en el Perú del siglo XVII*, Lima, PUCP, 2006.

Turiso Sebastián, Jesús, *Comerciantes españoles en la Lima borbónica. Anatomía de una élite de poder (1701–1761)*, Valladolid, Universidad de Valladolid, 2002.

Yun Casalilla, Bartolomé (dir.), *Las redes del Imperio. Élites sociales en la articulación de la Monarquía Hispánica, 1492–1714*, Madrid, Marcial Pons, 2009.

——, *Marte contra Minerva. El precio del imperio español, c. 1450–1600*, Barcelona, Crítica, 2004.

Zavala, S. A., *La encomienda indiana*, Mexico, Porrúa, 1973.

Zúñiga, J.-P., "Clan, parentela, familia, individuo: métodos y niveles de análisis", *Anuario IEHS*, Tandil (Argentina), 15 (2000), pp. 51–60.

6

From Alliance to Conflict, from Finance to Justice

A Portuguese Family in Spanish Naples (1590–1660)

Gaetano Sabatini

1. Introduction

The importance and weight of international finance in the study of the Spanish monarchy at the time of Charles V and Philip II has been widely recognized in the seminal works of historians such as Karl Brandi, Fernand Braudel and Ramón Carande. Nonetheless, most of these historians centered on the sixteenth century, and almost exclusively on the role of German and Genoese bankers.[1] Only recently did researchers look to the seventeenth century, demonstrating, for example, the importance Portuguese bankers had during this period.[2] Despite these significant developments, we still know little regarding the role bankers' communities had in the monarchy's multiple territories from the 1580s and into the seventeenth century. Most particularly, we lack information not only on their activities as locally based power groups that continuously interplayed and dialogued with other local political, economic and religious powers, but also on their involvement with supporting the imperial system, including their direct relations with the sovereign and the councils at the court.[3]

Nonetheless, it is clear that after the 1627 suspension of payments and as part of the political strategy of prime-minister Count-Duke of Olivares (1587–1645), the Genoese were replaced by the Portuguese as "bankers of the crown." Although this move was only partially successful, from the end of the 1620s, the power of the Lusitanian bankers and men of business increased considerably.[4] Locally, this integration into imperial finances was marked by frequent confrontations with other powers and violent episodes, frequently motivated by the fact that the vast majority of these men were New Christians.[5] The history of the Vaaz family in Naples is a highly illustrative of these tendencies of both integration and conflict that characterized the

A first version of this text was presented at the "III Colóquio Internacional Raízes do Privilégio Hierarquia e Mobilidade Social no Mundo Ibérico do Antigo Regime" (Rio de Janeiro, 22–25 June 2009); the comments then received from Rodrigo Bentes Monteiro, Pedro Cardim, Bruno Feitler and José Javier Ruiz Ibáñez, as well as those subsequently formulated by Tamar Herzog, helped me to enrich and improve this text.

prominence of Portuguese bankers in the Spanish monarchy during the seventeenth century.

2. The Vaaz in Naples

The presence in Naples of the three brothers Bento, Eduardo and Miguel Vaaz, New Christian merchants from Lisbon, is documented from the late 1580s, when their names were frequently mentioned in connection with the wheat trade, which their family had already mastered in the Iberian Peninsula.[6] During this period, among both the Neapolitan plebeian classes and the elite rulers of the city, the memory of the popular revolt of 1585, caused by the lack of bread and culminating in the lynching the *Eletto del Popolo* Gian Vincenzo Starace, an important exponent of municipal power who was considered responsible for having consented to the export of wheat despite local famine, was still very much alive.[7] In the aftermaths of this violent episode and in order to avoid repetition or other dangerous alterations of the public order, the Spanish government in Naples dedicated the maximum possible attention to the city's provisioning. As a result, the *anona*, the municipal organization charged with supplying Naples, did not hesitate to accept the onerous conditions imposed by merchants, buying wheat at exorbitant prices and subsequently introducing it into the urban market with a more accessible price.[8]

Soon after their arrival in Naples, the Vaaz occupied an important role in that wheat trade. In partnership with bankers and merchants traditionally associated with this market, they participated in the most profitable contracts for supplying the city that were made between the end of the 1580s and the beginning of the 1590s. Although all three brothers took part in this commerce, in the last decade of the sixteenth century, Miguel Vaaz became particularly prominent. Miguel arrived in Naples around 1590 when he was approximately 35 years old, after having already gained some experience in trading with wheat in the Iberian Peninsula. His capacity for inserting himself in the Neapolitan market was astonishing.[9] With great swiftness, he quickly managed to participate in all the largest contracts for supplying the city with wheat. His skill apparently consisted, in the first place, in associating himself with other foreign merchants, mainly Flemish, Dalmatians and Genovese, who succeeded importing wheat from areas further afield and who stocked larger quantities than other groups of local businessmen.[10] Yet Miguel's ability to provide large quantities of wheat was equally due to a conduct that his contemporaries did not hesitate to qualify as unscrupulous. Alone or in company with other merchants, also in this case Dalmatians or Flemish, he fitted out and armed privateers that sailed the Tyrrhenian and Adriatic seas in search of ships loaded with merchandise.

The rapid and colossal success that Miguel obtained with the wheat trade allowed him to participate in all the financial activities that were negotiated in Naples, to the point that he was considered, at the turn of the seventeenth century, the true master of the local credit market. It is thus easy to understand why a large hostile front rapidly formed against him, including the most powerful local bankers and the families of the Neapolitan aristocracy that formed the municipal power, and that were reduced to negotiated daily with him, and under his conditions, the contracts for the city's supply. These groups publicly accused Vaaz of practicing usury and denounced him to the Neapolitan plebeian classes as a speculator who, for personal gain, deliberately provoked scarcity and high prices for bread.[11] Basing their conclusions on these contemporary accounts, in the last century various historians have considered these accusations true.[12] However, a more detailed reconstruction of the activities of Miguel in and outside Naples by studying, for example, the correspondence the Venetian Ambassador in Naples (the *residente di Venezia*) maintained with the Senate of the *Repubblica Serenissima* leads to a completely different reading.[13] The dispatches that Giovan Carlo Scaramelli, and subsequently Antón Maria Vincenti sent to Venice until the end of 1601, register in much detail the central role Miguel Vaaz played in the financial life of the kingdom of Naples and his involvement with supplying the city. Most particularly, it sheds important light on the privateers armed by Vaaz that frequently set upon Venetian ships. To give but one example, the reports of the ambassador between June and November 1601 allow us to reconstruct the events surrounding the capture of the Venetian ship *Pigna* by a privateer armed by Miguel Vaaz and captained by his partner, the Flemish Petrus Orange de Bruxelles. It also demonstrates the complicity between the Portuguese merchant and the Vicereine and, above all, the Count of Castro, son of the Viceroy, who *de facto* served as an interim Viceroy between the death of his father in October 1601 and the arrival of a new mandatory in April 1603.[14] This complicity explains why the Count virtually ignored the complaints of the Venetian ambassador in February-March 1602 that Miguel was preparing four privateers and crews using Naple's arsenal, attesting that he had strict orders not to attack Venetian ships, only English or Ottoman. In successive dispatches send in 1602 and 1603, the ambassador communicated with undisguised satisfaction that on several occasions the bad state of their ships forced Miguel Vaaz's privateers to seek safe-haven in the port of Messina, where part of the crew, unhappy with the low volume of plunder, had abandoned the vessels.[15] After these episodes, the mention of Miguel's arming of privateers became less frequent;[16] nevertheless, he continued to encourage this practice by buying merchandise captured through acts of piracy.[17]

Perhaps most emblematic of Miguel's integration into Neapolitan political power were the events of July 1602, when the Venetians rescued a French ship assaulted by privateers while it was transporting a cargo of wheat property of Miguel Vaaz to Naples. The Portuguese merchant asked Venice for immediate restitution, arguing that the privateers had not become the legitimate owners of the ship because they had possessed it for less than a day. Both the vessel and its cargo were thus his, and should be restored to him. The commander of the Venetian squadron maintained, on the contrary, that the ship had been in the possession of the privateers for four days and that, as a result, it now belonged to those who liberated it, not the original owner. The Venetian ambassador Vincenti reported to the Senate he was scandalized by the disproportionate response of the *de facto* viceroy, the Count of Castro. Because Miguel Vaaz was involved, the Count considered the episode a matter of state. He even threatened to confiscate the goods and merchandise of all Venetian residents in Naples until he obtained the return of the goods to Miguel. The conflict dragged on until the spring of 1603, with Venice claiming the right to adjudicate the question through its own law courts and the Count of Castro applying all possible pressure to obtain the liberation of the ship. A solution was reached only when, with the imminent departure from Naples of the Count and the arrival of a new Viceroy, Miguel Vaaz considered it was time for a settlement.[18] And, although no documents exist that would confirm with certainty the accusation made by the Venetian ambassadors that the Count was indeed associated with Miguel in his privateering activities, it is evident that only a very close relationship with the Spanish government in Naples could explain how Miguel remained immune, at least up to 1616, to the attacks of the many enemies his activities generated.

Miguel's links with the Spanish government revealed themselves particularly strong from1599, that is, from the arrival in Naples of Viceroy Fernando Ruiz de Castro Andrade y Portugal, the first in a succession of Counts of Lemos that would occupy this position. It was probably through the intermediary of the Portuguese belonging to the Viceroy's entourage that Miguel Vaaz first made contact with Francisco Fernández, Count of Castro, son of the new mandatory.[19] The relationship between the two men continued thereafter: Vaaz managed the Count's properties after he left Naples in 1603 to become ambassador to Venice and Rome and eventually Viceroy of Sicily (1616 to 1622).[20] However, it was with Francisco's older brother Pedro Fernández de Castro, future Count of Lemos, and Viceroy of Naples between 1610 and 1616, that Miguel reached the peak of his power.

3. The Peak of Power: the Vaz, The Count of Benavente and the (Second) Count of Lemos

Upon his arrival in Naples in 1603, Viceroy Count of Benavente, who had succeeded the first Count of Lemos, attempted to reaffirm his authority *vis-à-vis* the local economic powers. Yet, the terrible shortages that marked the central years of his government and that lasted until 1610, forced him to make pacts with many local financial figures.[21] The shortages, starting in 1604 and reaching zenith in 1606, required the importation of great amounts (one and a half million *tomoli*)[22] of wheat. The report that, at the beginning of 1607, the highest magistrate charged with supplying the city (the *Grasciero Maggiore*) sent to king Philip III, testified that Miguel Vaaz was responsible for obtaining, from all over Europe, about half of this enormous quantity. He had supplied some 550,000 *tomoli* personally and brought into the market another 120,000 *tomoli* in partnership with the Genoese merchant Cesare Zattera.[23] This episode remained recorded in the memory of contemporaries, who commented on it with great delight:

> In the years 1607 and 1608 (. . .) when all Italy was in universal penury, because of the diligence of signor Count of Benavente and through the activity of Miguel Vaaz, a Portuguese gentlemen, from all parts of the world arrived ships loaded with wheat, a thing never again seen in this port [of Naples], with universal amazement.[24]

The huge benefits Miguel had obtained in these transactions was made clear by the missive that the Grand Duke of Tuscany's agent in Naples, Cosimo Del Sera, sent to Florence on July 1606, noting that the price demanded by Vaaz and Zattera was on average 26 *carlini* per *tomolo* while, a few days before news of bad harvests had arrived to the city, the same quantity was valued at eighteen *carlini* (an increase of more than 40%!).[25] Yet, in reality, the operation described by the Toscan agent was much more complex than what met the eye as the wheat came from all over Europe and varied in prices. Vaaz had imported into Naples in partnership with Cesare Zattera 120.000 *tomoli* of wheat from the interior of the kingdom (at a cost per *tomolo* of 21 *carlini* for the soft variety and 23 for the hard), from Germany (24 *carlini*) and from the north of Italy and France (26 *carlini*); subsequently 100,000 *tomoli* of wheat came from Spain and Portugal (25 *carlini* per *tomolo*) and from Northern Italy and France (28 *carlini*); finally, Vaaz brought into Naples other 450,000 *tomoli* at the price of 28 *carlini*, but its provenance and price remain unknown. It is highly probable that it was a product of Vaaz's privateering activity.[26]

If grave shortages explained the prominence of Miguel Vaaz at the beginning of the seventeenth century, it was only with the arrival in 1610 of viceroy Pedro Fernández de Castro, second Count of Lemos to hold this office, that Miguel consolidated his central role in the financial life of the city and kingdom, rapidly reaching the coveted position of counselor to the Viceroy. As the Count of Lemos confessed on several occasions,[27] Miguel Vaaz was the real author of the various reforms he attempted, above all, in the management of income and expenses, in state accounting, in elaborating a formal budget, and in issuing public debt. All these were directed at reorganizing the kingdom's finances, which were an essential component of the ability to defend the territory and participate in the rearmament process, which took place all over the Hispanic Monarchy.[28] With the *prammatica* of 15 October 1612,[29] the Count of Lemos, wishing to reorganize the administration and having studied thoroughly its disbursements with the objective of avoiding fraud and mismanagement, established that from that date on income would be subdivided into two quotas. The first, made of some 15% of all revenues, would be integrated in the general treasury of the kingdom. The other (the remaiming 85%) would go to the military treasury (the *Cassa Militare*), charged with covering not only the cost of defense and policing, but also with the funding of the most important public works and the payment of the Viceroy and his collaborators. Gradually, the military treasury would also receive all income ceded to bankers in the payment of loans, or transferred for the payment of interest on public debt.[30] The Viceroy's intention was that these reforms would serve not only to guarantee the soldiers' regular pay, thus avoiding dangerous tensions among the troops, but also to prevent the recurring emergency situations, which continuously forced him to take loans with very onerous conditions. In parallel with his other interventions, the Count of Lemos also proceeded to order a drastic reduction in the interest rates of public debt: for non-life bonds that had yielded 9–10%, the rates were reduced to 7%; for life-bonds that had yielded 12–13%, to 10%.[31]

Only a businessman so well versed in public and private finances as Miguel Vaaz could point out to the Viceroy where and how the most concealed frauds were committed and what was the best way to limit, as much as possible, bankers' control over the king's finances. The Count of Lemos, who called Miguel the "the main instrument of my actions" (*instrumento principal de mis acciones)* and who had praised the altruism with which he had worked to revise the kingdom's accounts — "he alone undid the enchantment of the Balance, showing me its errors and adjusting the account with exquisite precision and effort *(fue solo el que ha desecho el encantamiento del Balanço, advertiendome de sus errores y ajustando la cuenta con esquisito primor y trabajo)* — never failed to stress to king Philip III that the Portuguese demonstrated a loyalty to the sovereign that transcended his own interests. In the operation of reducing the yield on the public debt, for example, Miguel himself lost around 3,000 ducats.[32] Nonetheless, records indicate that, even during these years, Miguel continued his profitable activities in the wheat trade,[33] which made his losses due to the reduction in yield on public debt, seem derisory. In addition to these, during this period he had continued acquiring fiefs in the best wheat-producing areas of the kingdom (Roscignano, Saint Nicandoro and Casamassima in the province of Terra di Bari, Belrisguardo in Principato Citra, Saint Donato in the province of Terra d'Otranto), a process that culminated in the purchase of the city of Mola.[34] In 1613, in recognition of the services rendered to the Viceroy, Philip III named Miguel Vaaz Count of Mola.[35] In 1615, in the territory of Quattro Miglia, a rural fief of San Michele which he had bought in 1608, Miguel Vaaz founded a new settlement, which he christened Casa Vaaz and populated with 460 peasants of Orthodox religion, who had escaped from the Ottomans and whom he brought by ships from the coast of Dalmatia.[36] In 1616, after Miguel fell under suspicion (see bellow), the community was re-baptized with the name of San Michele and, to its original population, were added other local inhabitants in order to to exorcise the danger of heresies that could result from the continuation of Greek Orthodox rites. This transformation was sanctioned, in 1619, through the signature of a settlement contract with the new inhabitants.[37]

The nobility title acquired by Miguel Vaaz in 1613 not only resolved the problem of his status as a foreigner (for as Count of Mola he automatically became also a citizen of the kingdom),[38] but also indicated an important change in his social status. The purchase of a palace in the elegant district of Chiaia, very near the palace of the aristocratic Spanish family of Alarcón y Mendoza, was a clear sign of this mutation.[39] The consolidation of his economic, political and social position was further confirmed by the career of Simão Vaaz, son of his brother Eduardo Vaaz and also heir to the property and title of Miguel Vaaz, who had no descendents. Simão was a doctor in both civil and cannon law. In 1611, he was appointed by the Count of Lemos commissioner for the Spanish enclave in Tuscany, the *Estado de los Presidios*. In the same year, he also entered as civil judge in the *Vicaria*, the highest civil and criminal court of Naples. In 1614, he became president of a section of the *Camera della Sommaria*, the maximum administrative court of the kingdom, a position in which he remained until 1653.[40] Still more symbolic was the trajectory of Miguel Vaaz's niece, Fiorenza Vaaz, daughter of Bento Vaaz, who in 1615 married D. Giovanni Pignatelli, second-born of the Duke of Noja, of the most important aristocratic families of Naples.[41] It is of no small importance that the marriage between the two was an exception to the strict endogamy that the Vaaz usually practiced according to a very widespread custom among all New Christians, to marry into their own family. Miguel Vaaz himself was married to his niece Ana, daughter of his brother Bento, of whom another daughter, Majora, had married her cousin, the already mentioned Simão Vaaz. In his second marriage, however, Simão took as wife Anna Brancaccio, a representative of one of the oldest families of the Neapolitan nobility. Simão's son, Eduardo, also married a second cousin, Gratia Vaaz de Andrade.[42]

4. The Fall: From the Duke of Osuna to the Inquisition and the Portuguese Uprising

Until the Count of Lemos left Naples in 1616, the social position of the Vaaz, above all Miguel, was firmly consolidated. However, this situation would completely change with the arrival to Naples of a new Viceroy, Pedro Téllez Girón, Duke of Osuna.[43] The Duke of Osuna, a radical opponent of the Count of Lemos in the Court of Philip III, unleashed a violent persecution against all the closest collaborators of his predecessor suspecting them, among other things, of obstructing his nomination.[44] The transition from success to failure was quick. Soon after the viceroy had arrived, Miguel Vaaz was accused by the Municipal Council of selling spoilt or poor quality wheat to the city.[45] Yet, it was his immediate family that suffered the first blow. In 1616, Miguel's brother Bento and his wife Beatriz were accused by the Inquisition of practicing Judaism in a process considered to have been instigated by the Viceroy himself.[46] The following year, it was Miguel's turn. On May 4, 1617, the Duke of Osuna ordered his detention and the seizure of his goods alongside a group of Neapolitans suspected of conspiring against him. Miguel was also accused of having exchanged correspondence with infidels.[47] Seeing the guards approaching as he was leaving his house to go to mass in the contiguous convent of the Celestine monks, Miguel took refuge there, protected by ecclesiastical immunity.[48] He remained shut in the convent for three years until in 1620 the Duke of Osuna was released of his office under suspicion of allegedly having committed important excesses in the government of Naples.[49] Miguel, who subsequently maintained that Saint Pedro Celestino warned him in his dreams of the imminent danger, honored his debt of gratitude to the convent by offering it a piece of land contiguous to it, upon which he offered to build a church dedicated to Saint Michael, subsidizing both the construction and the decoration, among other things, by creating an endowment of bonded goods (a *monte*) to guarantee funds for the building.[50]

While he enjoyed ecclesiastical immunity at the convent, Miguel Vaaz continued to explore business opportunities. In 1619, he appeared as the title holder of a contract for provisioning 9,000 *tomoli* in Naples, but it is probable that, in reality, he traded four times as much through Francisco Vaaz de Andrade, a nephew who had arrived from Portugal and who had married his niece Beatriz.[51] The substitution of the Duke of Osuna by Cardinal Gaspar Borja y Velasco, who held the position of interim Viceroy of Naples from June to December 1620, opened up new opportunities for Miguel. These came in the form of contacts with the private secretary of the Cardinal, who also held the important position of head of the Viceroy's secretariat and Secretary of State and War, Diego de Saavedra Fajardo. Saavedra Fajardo was closely associated with the House of Lemos. He had been secretary to the Count's agent in Rome, and himself had acted as agent to the Count of Castro when he was Viceroy of Sicily.[52] Nonetheless, Miguel did not seize on these connections, perhaps because hostility against him continued. Indeed, although Osuna was no longer present, on November 1622, one of Naples' municipal bodies publically denounced the so-called speculative activities of the Portuguese merchants, and formed a delegation to petition the incoming Viceroy (Cardinal Zapata) to intervene against the fraudulent accumulation of wheat.[53] Thereafter, the Vaaz would disappear from contracts to supply wheat, except for one occasion,[54] in which this activity was carried out by other family members after Miguel Vaaz died in 1623.

Miguel's will and the numerous other documents, with which he sought to put order into his business, allow us to gauge his vast patrimony and to evaluate at 23,000 ducats his annual income. Most important among his properties were his fiefs: his nephew Simão inherited Mola (and the respective title of Count), Casamassima, Rutigliano, San Nicando and the rural village of San Michele; the nieces Fiorenza and Beatriz, daughters of his brother Bento, inherited Belriguardo and San Donato respectively.[55] Simão and Fiorenza, as executors of his will, continued building the Church of Saint Michael, employing for that end the greatest Neapolitan architect of the time,

Cosimo Fanzago and later decorating its interior with one of the best European painters of the period, Luca Giordano.[56]

Although some Vaaz were still engaged in commercial activities after Miguel was gone,[57] the most prominent members of the family no longer did. In 1633, Francisco Vaaz de Andrade, who had married Beatriz, sister of Fiorenza Vaaz, was granted the title of Duke of San Donato.[58] In 1645, Simão, heir to Miguel, obtained for his first-born son Michele Vaaz the title of Duke of Casamassima.[59] His second-born son, Eduardo, had followed in his father's footsteps, entering the courts as magistrate in 1636 and reaching, in 1643, the position of criminal judge in the court of the *Vicaria* in Naples.[60] All the daughters of Simão married prominent nobles, all members of the *Seggi* of the city:[61] Anna married the Duke of Belcastro Orazio Sersale of the *Seggio di Nido*, Gratia married Antonio Muscettola, first-born son of the Duke of Spezzano, and Fiorenza married Geronimo Carmignano of the *Seggio di Montagna*. In addition, in 1645, Simão left the palace in the district of Chiaia that had belonged to his uncle to move to an elegant, but more sober, palace on Toledo street near the palace that had belonged to the Marquis of Belmonte, Carlos Tapia, the most eminent Neapolitan magistrate of the first half of the seventeenth century.[62]

The abandonment of economic and fiscal activities and the integration into magistracies and the highest nobility seemed to have quieted the hostility against the family. During the Napolitan revolts of 1647–1648, both Simão Vaaz, who at the time held the important position of governor of the Foggia customs,[63] and his son Michele, who had the rank of captain of militia, showed their loyalty to the Spanish crown, fighting at the side of the Count of Conversano against the mutineers.[64] However, despite these demonstrations of integration and loyalty, after Portugal declared its independence in 1640, because of their Portuguese origins, the Vaaz came under suspicion. There were rumors that connected them to the Neapolitan exiles that had found refuge with the Pope after the revolt in Naples had failed and that entered into conversations with agents of the new Portuguese king John IV, particularly the Jesuit António Vieira, in order to study the possibility of a new, this time pro-Lusitanian yet anti-Spanish, uprising in Naples.[65] Although these conversations ended in nothing, during the government of viceroy Count of Oñate in Naples (1650 and 1654), the city's Portuguese community was constantly watched. If no action was taken at this time against the Vaaz, it was mainly because of the personal prestige accumulated by Simão, who had been appointed by Philip IV to the Collateral Council in 1653, the highest political organ in the kingdom.[66] Yet after Simão died in 1655 (his first-born son, Michele, had died in 1654, leaving his brother Eduardo as heir to both titles of Count of Mola and Duke of Casamassima), hostility towards the family soon emerged. In 1657, the Viceroy Count of Castrillo ordered the arrest of Eduardo on the charge that in his capacity as president of the criminal section of the court of the *Vicaria*, he had tried to protect the son of another high magistrate accused of homicide. Incarcerated in the castle of Santelmo in Naples, Eduardo was equally affected by an accusation, made by a cousin of his, Fiorenza Vaaz, of practicing Judaism.[67]

In spite of the important precedents — the trial for Judaism of his maternal grandfather Bento Vaaz in 1616[68] and the abjuration of his uncle Francisco Vaaz de Andrade, Duke of Saint Donato, who on his deathbed in 1636, declared that he had never abandoned the Hebrew religion[69] — initially, the inquisitorial proceedings did not play a determinant role in Eduardo's prosecution. However, this situation changed in 1659, with the appointment as head of the Neapolitan Inquisition of Monsignor

Camillo Piazza, whose nomination ended a long period of interim office holders.[70] Monsignor Piazza, breaking with the tradition of moderation that had characterized the Inquisition in Naples in the last quarter of the century, intensified its activities considerably, rapidly pushing forward the processes already under way and preparing new ones.[71] Eduardo Vaaz and his family immediately attracted the attention of Monsignor Piazza. Following interrogations and confessions, his men arrested Eduardo's brother Benedetto with his wife Gratia, his sisters Gratia and Fiorenza, his aunt Beatriz Vaaz de Andrade with her son Emanuele, Duke of San Donato and daughter Fiorenza, his cousin Gratia Vaaz with her husband, Eduardo de Rivieta, and her son from a previous marriage, Eduardo Mendez, his cousin Beatrice Vaaz, her husband Enrique Suarez Colonel and his brother-in-law Antonio Suarez Colonel.[72] In September the previous year, the apostolic nuncio in Naples Monsignor Giulio Spinola, had requested and then obtained permission from the Collateral Council to allow the inquisition to have suspects of Judaism be trialed in Rome.[73] Found guilty in 1660, the Vaaz abjured publicly in January 1661 in a ceremony celebrated in the Church of Santa Maria Sopra Minerva.

In addition to some minor penalties, such as the payment of 2,000 Roman *escudos* as alms, Eduardo Vaaz was also sentenced to life imprisonment.[74] Informed of this condemnation, the Collateral Council decreed the definitive confiscation of all his properties.[75] This decision, however, provoked a violent confrontation between the council and the viceroy (who wanted the properties) on the one hand, the inquisitor (who defended the rights of the Holy Office to them) and the kingdom's aristocracy (that invoked papal briefs of 1554 that prohibited the confiscation of heretics' property in the kingdom of Naples), on the other.[76] The conflict ended with the expulsion of inquisitor Monsignor Piazza from the kingdom and the reaffirmation of the right of the Collateral Council to seize the property of heretics.[77] Nevertheless, in early 1662, the seizure of Eduardo's property was revoked, perhaps as the result of a memorandum presented to the Collateral Council by his wife,[78] who was now acting as attorney in her husband's interests. Or, more probably, as an act of clemency that was included, perhaps by the wish of other high magistrates, in the pardon that the city of Naples petitioned Philip IV on the occasion of the birth of the Prince Carlos in late 1661.[79] At that point, numerous of Eduardo's properties had already been sold, among them, the most valuable one, the duchy of Casamassima. Only after a long drawn-out litigation did the family of Eduardo manage to retain the countship of Mola.[80]

In 1666, the Collateral Council pardoned not only the property but also the offenses committed by Eduardo explaining that he had been honored by his majesty with the office of judge and the ministers that his House has had (*essere stato onorato da S. Maestà con il grado di Giudice e* [per] *i Ministri che ha tenuto la sua Casa*). The following year, Eduardo himself pleaded to the Collateral Council to intervene with the Pope to secure an equivalent pardon.[81] At the end of 1670 or the beginning of 1671, Eduardo Vaaz was finally released and returned to Naples. Significantly, he did not return to the family palace in the centre of the city, but remained at the gates of Naples in the Casale di Capodimonte, where he died in 1671.[82] But even prior to his death and in spite of the partial recovery of their properties, by that time the Vaaz had already been banished from the ruling elite of Spanish Naples and no descendants of Eduardo Vaaz would ever recover the social prestige that Miguel and Simão Vaaz had once enjoyed.

Genealogy of the Vaaz Family in Naples

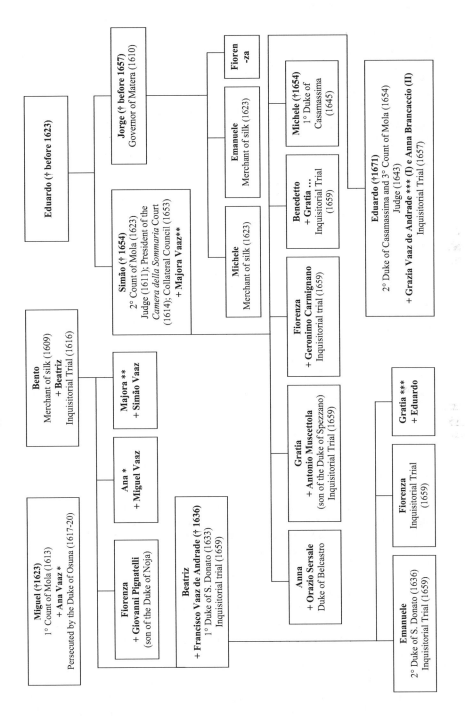

Abbreviations

AGS Archivo General de Simancas.
ASDN Archivio Storico della Diocesi di Napoli.
ASN Archivio di Stato di Napoli.
BNN Biblioteca Nazionale di Napoli.

Notes

1 See especially Carande, 1943–1949.
2 Boyajian, 1983 and 1993. Fundamental, in this context, is the study of Ruiz Martín, 1990; see also Sanz Ayán, 1989, and Álvarez Nogal, 1997.
3 As Studnicki-Gizbert, 2007, demonstrates.
4 Ruiz Martin, 1970, 1–196; Valladares, 2002; Herrero Sánchez, 2005, 115–151.
5 The case of Lima in the first half of the 1630s is exemplary because it demonstrates how the Inquisition was used against such merchants: Millar Carvacho, 1998, 129–169.
6 The most complete biographical note on the Vaaz in Naples is Belli, 1990, 7–42; see also, the somewhat inaccurate Sirago, 1987, 119–158, which studies the history of Jewish presence in Naples. On this last theme, also see Scaramella, 2003, 357–373. Among the old sources on the Vaaz, the most important is Confuorto, 1693.
7 Colapietra, 1972, 69–173; Villari, 1976, 42–52.
8 These issues, as well as the Neapolitan *anona*: Sabatini, 1998a. A synthesis of the *anona*'s activities, dated 1638, is included in Carlo Tapia, *Il trattato dell'abondanza* (Sabatini 1998b), on which see Dubuloz, Sabatini, 2003.
9 Confuorto, 1693; the chronicles of the community of which Miguel Vaaz was founder (S. Michele in the province of Terra di Bari — see below), recount how Philip II, having known Vaaz in Portugal, sent him to Naples in 1580 as his emissary (D'Addabbo, 1936); although no documentation exists that directly confirms this report, it should be noted that Miguel Vaaz appears in two lists of "*mercedes y recomandaciones*" relative to Naples, in which numerous Spaniards who fought against the Portuguese resistance in Philip II's army appear (AGS, Estado, Naples, 1.1088, years 1585–1586).
10 Coniglio, 1955, 34–39, 47, 175, 199–201, 207–213; Colapietra, *op. cit.*, 195–196.
11 Confuorto, 1693; Colapietra, 1972, 191 and 260–261.
12 In addition to the already cited Coniglio and Colapietra, see Galasso, 1959, 3–106, now partially in Galasso, 1994, 157–184.
13 Barzazi, 1991.
14 G. C. Scaramelli to the Venetian Senate, Naples, 5 June 1601 (Barzazi, 1991, 381–382): the Venetian ship *Pigna* was attacked by a boat belonging to Miguel Vaaz and his Flemish partner Petrus Orange from Bruxelles. On that occasion Vaaz is described as "*persona ricca e molto intima di tutti i signori viceré che vengono a questo governo* [of Naples]". Although the ambassador denounces the conniving with the Viceroy, the count promised to return the vessel that was encored in Palermo and arrest Orange; G. C. Scaramelli to the Venetian Senate, Naples, 12 June 1601 (383) and 19 June 1601 (385): Vaaz offered the ambassador to reach an agreement; G. C. Scaramelli to the Venetian Senate, Naples, 9 October 1601 (405): registered the restitution of the ship *Pigna* to the Venetians, but also confirmed that the privateer vessel had been armed by Vaaz in complicity with the Vicereine. During this period there were news of other cargos of wheat that arrived through Miguel Vaaz to Naples from Apulia (ASN, Camera della Sommaria, Partium, v. 1570, f. 17, 10 May 1601).
15 A. M. Vincenti to the Venetian Senate, Naples, 26 February 1602 (Barzazi, 1991, 518): Vaaz armed three privateers in partnership with captain Petrus Orange, and also, it seems, with the Vicereine. Petition of the ambassador to the Count only result in vague promises of action; A. M. Vincenti to the Venetian Senate, Naples, 2 March 1602 (435): Vaaz continued to arm ships, now as many as four, and their armament was provided by the arsenal, a clear sign of the complicity of the Count and the Vicereine; A. M. Vincenti to the

Venetian Senate, Naples, 12 March 1602 (437): to the protests of the diplomat, the Count replied that Vaaz had orders not to attack Venetian ships but only English or Ottoman and that he was doing it at the service of His Majesty; A. M. Vincenti to the Venetian Senate, Naples, 19 March 1602 (439): Vaaz's ships left Naples in the direction of the Levant; A. M. Vincenti to the Venetian Senate, Naples, 19 November 1602 (472): after practicing piracy, the ships were in Messina to undergo repairs, but the spoil was disappointing and part of the crew left to Malta in search of better fortune; A. M. Vincenti to the Venetian Senate, Naples, 31 December 1602 (478–79) and 28 January 1603 (484): Vaaz's ships returned to Messina; A. M. Vincenti to the Venetian Senate, Naples, 27 May 1603 (505): Vaaz's ships returned to Messina in very bad condition.

16 A. M. Vincenti to the Venetian Senate, Naples, 21 October 1603 (Barzazi, 1991, 524–525): after the last campaign Vaaz seemed convinced that arming privateers was no longer convenient.

17 A. M. Vincenti to the Venetian Senate, Naples, 24 August 1604 (Barzazi, 1991, 572): Vaaz was among the buyers of the merchandise of the Venetian ships, rescued from Turkish pirates and afterwards captured by the commander-general of the Neapolitan galleons, the Marquis of Santa Cruz, who did not want to recognize the provenance of the vessels and who refused to return them to Venice.

18 A. M. Vincenti to the Venetian Senate, Naples, 2 July 1602 (Barzazi, 1991, 452), A. M. Vincenti to the Venetian Senate, Naples, 20 and 23 July 1602 (455) and A. M. Vincenti to the Venetian Senate, Naples, 30 July, 6 and 13 August 1602 (456–9): Vaaz demonstrated the protection he enjoyed from the Spanish government; the Venetian Senate to A. M. Vincenti, Venice, 27 August 1602 (461): the Senate decided that the ship and its cargo should set off for Venice where the lawsuit will take place; the decision enraged the Count; A. M. Vincenti to the Venetian Senate, Naples, 22 October 1602 (461): the question was still blocked; the Venetian Senate to A. M. Vincenti, Venice, 2 November 1602 (469): the ambassador told Vaaz to send one of his agents to Venice for the suit; however, the gains resulting from the sale of some of the merchandise was deposited in a bank; A. M. Vincenti to the Venetian Senate, Naples, 12 November 1602 (470): the ambassador referred to a meeting with the Count to communicate the decision of Venice, having convinced him with some difficulty not to start anything in Naples and after having received from Vaaz confirmation that he would send an agent; A. M. Vincenti to the Venetian Senate, Naples, 19 November 1602 (472): last confirmation that Vaaz and his partners will send proxies to the process in Venice; A. M. Vincenti to the Venetian Senate, Naples, 3 and 10 December 1602 (473–5): Vaaz communicated that he aimed to prosecute in Naples. The count continued to support Vaaz and pretended that the issue should be studied by the highest political organ in Naples, the Collateral Council. A. M. Vincenti to the Venetian Senate, Naples, 7 and 14 January 1603 (479–81): the ambassador failed to convince the Count to discuss the case in Venice. The count in turn tried to persuade the ambassador to deal directly with Vaaz; the Venetian Senate to A. M. Vincenti, Venice, 21 February 1603 (488): the Senate invited all involved to present the documents of the case; A. M. Vincenti to the Venetian Senate, Naples, 11 March 1603 (490): the Ambassador had a meeting with Vaaz, who manifested against the Venice process but was disposed to arrive at a compromise.

19 On the lineage of the counts of Castro, in particular in the Neapolitan stage, see Enciso Alonso-Muñumer, 2007.

20 The functions of banker and administrator that Miguel Vaaz carried out for the Count of Castro are documented in the movements registered by the Banco della Pietà of Naples in 1612 (when the Count de Castro was ambassador of Spain in Rome) published by Nicolini, 1950, 185, and Nicolini, 1951, 239 and 299.

21 For the Benavente years in Naples, see Coniglio, 1955, 149–155, Colapietra, 1972, 195–200, De Rosa, 1987, 71–88 and 110–127.

22 The *tomolo* (plural *tomoli*) was the traditional volume unit for dry goods used in Naples

and was equivalent to 55.5 litres; it was also equivalent to the *fanega* or *henaga* used in Castille.

23 The report of the Marquis of Corleto, dated 8 January 1607, —that, in addition, estimated the population of Naples at 264,000 souls and, consequently, its minimum needs at 960,000 *tomoli* of wheat — reconstructed in detail the acquisition of wheat carried out by the *anona* in the second half of 1606 to confront the shortage (AGS, Estado, Nápoles, l. 1104, f. 12; see also Coniglio, 1955, 45–48, and Colapietra, 1972, 191 and 261). On the relations between Miguel Vaaz and Cesare Zattera see A. M.Vincenti to the Venetian Senate, Naples, 25 February 1603 and 4 March 1603: Vaaz and Zattera signed a contract for 100,000 *tomoli* of wheat to be imported from Marche and Abruzzo, in Central Italy, at a cost of 21 and 23 *carlini* per *tomolo*, respectively (Barzazi, 1991, 488–491).

24 *in questi anni 1607 and 1608,* [. . .] *essendo universale penuria per tutta Italia, per diligenza del signor Conte di Benavente et per opera di Michele Vaaz gentiluomo portughese, sono da tutte le parti del mondo concorse navi cariche di frumento, cosa mai più veduta in questo porto* [of Naples], *con stupore universale*. See, for example, Capasso, 1882 (now in De Rosa, Cestaro, 1973, 49–86, 56 for the quotation). On the author of these words, Giulio Cesare Capaccio, see Novellino, 2006. Admiration for Miguel Vaaz continued even after his luck had definitively ran out: see Parrino, 1730, v. II, 60.

25 Palermo, 1846, 264–65.

26 Vaaz's interests were not confined to the wheat trade; for example, in 1604, he had obtained the annual license for the supply of salted meat to the kingdom's galleons (ASN, Camera della Sommaria, Partium, v. 1638, c. 19 t).

27 AGS, Estado, Nápoles, l.1106, f. 133, *Relación de las rentas etc.*, memoir, dated Naples, 26 March 1611, annexed to the missive sent by the Count of Lemos to Philip III (in fact to the secretary Andrés de Prada), Naples, 28 March 1611, *idem*, f. 132.

28 For a synthetic overview on the reforms of the Count of Lemos in Naples see Enciso Alonso-Muñumer, 2007, 420–448.

29 Giustiniani, 1804, 300–333.

30 Coniglio, 1955, 207–213; Galasso, 1994, 157–158; Sabatini, 2006.

31 AGS, Estado, Nápoles, l.1106, f. 132 and 133 and Coniglio, 1955, 199. The Duke of Urbino's agent in Naples estimated that the reduction in interest rates had resulted in the saving of 400,000 ducats (Palermo, 1846, 223–224); if Miguel Vaaz was really the inspirer of this measure, it certainly did not contribute to improve his already tense relations with other Portuguese and Genoese bankers working in Naples; on this matter see Sabatini, 2011.

32 AGS, Estado, Nápoles, l.1106, f. 133; see also Muto, 1980, 93.

33 That the Count of Lemos behaved similarly to previous viceroys in wheat-provisioning is demonstrated by, among other things, the contracts signed for 1610, the year of his arrival in Naples, with Miguel Vaaz in partnership with the Genoese Giacomo Fornari (ASN, Notamenti del Collaterale, v. 3, c. 19 r); for the years following, from 1610 to 1616, see Coniglio, 1955, 34 (the source cited by Coniglio for these dates is the *Liber Conclusionum Originalium* of the *Archivio Storico del Comune di Napoli*, v. 1405 and 1406, which, however, as the author himself pointed out, was destroyed in a fire in 1946 and, accordingly, is not available for consultation). The Count of Lemos proved to be more intransigent than his predecessors in demanding from Vaaz respect for the contract clauses and in refusing imports when these were not up to the quality contracted, as occurred, for example, in 1615 (Coniglio, 1955, 200). Data for the same years on Vaaz's activities as the Count of Lemos' banker, both in his private dealings and in his functions as Viceroy, in Nicolini, 1950 and 1951.

34 ASN, Cedolari feudali, v. 44, cc. 70 v-71 r.

35 In 1612 the Count of Lemos asked Philip III for Miguel Vaaz "*por más conveniente merced que renta o ayuda de costa* [. . .] *un título de duque o marqués y plaza en el Consejo Colateral,*

que en esto segundo ganará infinito el servicio de V. Mag. [por] ser *grande su suficiencia para ocuparla en cosas publicas y de las de aquel Reyno* [of Naples], *de toda Italia y de Levante, de que tiene mucha inteligencia"* (AGS, Estado, Nápoles, l. 1107, *Consulta sobre la remuneración de las personas que estuvieron en el Parlamento general de Nápoles,* Naples, 10 September 1612, c. 1 r-4 v). For the title of Count Mola, granted by Philip III in Madrid on 4 May 1613, see AGS, Secretarias provinciales, Naples, l. 177, c. 164 v.

36 D'Addabbo, 1936, 295–96; Sirago, 1987, 130.

37 D'Addabbo, 1936, 297–298; Sirago, 1987, 130–131.

38 According to the the *prammatica De officiorum provvisione* issued on 12 March 1550 by Viceroy Pedro de Toledo and to the contemporary imperial chapters of Brussels, whoever received a feudal investiture in the kingdom of Naples *ipso facto* became *"natural del reyno"* for all effects. Villari, 1976, 20.

39 Belli, 1991, 13.

40 Toppi, 1666, 26 and 138; Intorcia, 390.

41 Confuorto, 1693.

42 *Idem.*

43 On the Duke of Osuna see Linde, 2005, and on his government in Naples see Schipa, 1911, and Colapietra, 1972, 201–208.

44 On the rivalry between the Count of Lemos and the Duke of Osuna see Galasso, 1994, 178–184. The hostility of certain sectors of Neapolitan society towards the Count of Lemos and those near him had already manifested itself from at least 1614: see Enciso Alonso-Muñumer, 2007, 383–409.

45 Zazzera, 1846, 478 and 482. The accusations made against Vaaz during the government of the Duke of Osuna find echo in numerous anonymous manuscripts that circulated in Naples during those years: BNN, ms. X B 65, *Michele Vais* [sic] *e le sue pregiudiziali invenzioni* (see Villari, 1976, 183).

46 The documents relative to the inquisitorial proceedings against Benedetto Vaaz and his wife Beatriz are in ASDN, *Fondo Sant'Uffizio*, 201 — 480 /A (Galasso, Russian, 820).

47 Comparato, 1974, 294; the persecution of Miguel Vaaz is related to the secret contacts maintained between the New Christians and the Jews exiled by the Catholic monarchy in London, Amsterdam, Leghorn and Venice, and the spy network of the Ottoman Empire (on which see Rodrigues da Silva Tavim, 2004, 273). On the contacts between the New Christians of Naples and the Hebrew communities at Leghorn and Venice see, respectively, Frattarelli Fischer, 2008, and Ruspio, 2007.

48 These events were reconstructed by Vaaz himself in the act of donation with which he subsequently rewarded the convent (see below and Belli, 1990, 13).

49 Schipa, 1911.

50 The act of donation, dated 4 May 1622, exactly five years after the failed attempt at arrest, and the act of constitution of the *monte*, dated 29 July 1623, are published in full in the appendix to Belli, 1990, 22–25 and 25–27.

51 Coniglio, 1955, 34. However, it is evident that during his internment Miguel Vaaz did not succeed in exercising full control of his business, as is demonstrated by the fact that in 1622 the payments for the supply of wheat that he had effected between 1616 and 1619 were still in suspense (AGS, Estado, Nápoles, l.1884, *Bilancio d'esatto e pagato del anno 1621 del regno di Napoli,* Naples, 25 October 1622, cc. 15 r, 20 v and 25 v.).

52 Sabatini, 2008.

53 Faraglia, 1878, 151 and 198–200.

54 In 1630, Benedetto Vaaz de Sousa, in partnership with João Mennes Eriquez (probably an error of transcription for Menezes Enriques), imported from the Levant 30,000 *tomoli* of wheat; in 1632 Simão Vaaz imported from Apulia 1,000 *tomoli* of wheat; in 1633 Benedetto Vaaz de Sousa, in partnership with Emanuel Vaaz de Andrade, imported 1,000 *tomoli* de wheat from an unspecified location; also in 1633 a group of Vaaz merchants

imported, predominantly from Apulia, 56,384 *tomoli* of wheat etc. (Coniglio, 1955, 35).

55 The will, dated 17 September 1623, and the inventory of the estate *post mortem*, dated 7 November 1623, are published in full in the appendix to Belli, 1990, respectively 27–31 and 31–42. Miguel Vaaz excluded completely from the inheritance, apart from small legacies, his nephew Jorge Vaaz, brother of Simão and governor of the city of Matera, who seemed to have become unpopular with the family because his behavior was considered an obstacle to its social rise (Jorge Vaaz, while governor of Matera, had been tried and condemned following the general inspection of his activities undertaken by Juan Beltran de Guevara from 1607, see AGS, Secretarias provinciales, Nápoles, l.235, Naples, 8 July 1617, c. 32: "*Jorge Vaaz, governador de la ciudad de Matera, ha sido condenado en quinientos ducados para el fisco por cohechos y extorsiones que ha cometido en su oficio*"; see also AGS, Secretarias provinciales, Nápoles, l.138, f. 7). The bad relations carried over into the following generation, between the children of Simão Vaaz and those of Jorge Vaaz, the latter equally being accused of having lowered the social status of the family in contracting marriages considered inappropriate and dishonorable (Confuorto, 1693). On the other hand, the accusation of a daughter of Jorge Vaaz, Fiorenza, determined the proceedings against Eduardo Vaaz for Judaism and, with his condemnation, the social ruin of the entire family (see below).

56 Belli, 1990, 13–15.

57 In 1623, the year of Miguel Vaaz's death, Jorge Vaaz's children, Michele and Emanuele Vaaz were registered as merchants in the corporation of the *Arte della Seta* of Naples (ASN, Matricole, v. 8, cc. 188 r and 216 r); previously, in 1609, Miguel's brother Bento was registered in the same corporation as a silk merchant, (*idem*, v. 7, c. 42 t).

58 Sirago, 1987, 133.

59 Confuorto, 1693.

60 Toppi, 1666, 66–71, Intorcia, 1987, 390.

61 On the Vaaz's matrimonial policy see Visceglia, 1983. The oldest families of Naples nobility were grouped into five councils, each of which designated as *Seggio*, which exercised important functions in the management of the city and kingdom (see Tutini, 1644; Galasso, 1978).

62 Belli, 1990, 14.

63 This position implied responsibility for the control of the whole administrative and fiscal machine that presided over the system of moveable seasonal pasturing in the kingdom of Naples; in this role and under suspicion of corruption, the name of Simão Vaaz was mentioned in the investigation conducted by the general inspector Juan Chacón Ponce de León from 1644 (AGS, Secretarias provinciales, Nápoles, l.227, *Instrucción al licenciado don Juan Chacón Ponce de León etc.*, Zaragoça, 9 September 1644, c. 6 v; *idem*, l. 230, *Memoria de los ministros contra quien resultan cargos de la visita general del Reyno de Nápoles etc.*, Madrid, 9 December 1651, c. 1 r).

64 Sirago, 1987, 135.

65 Cardim, Sabatini, 2011.

66 Intorcia, 1987, 390.

67 The chronicles of the time attributed Fiorenza Vaaz's accusation to the opposition that Eduardo would have shown to her marriage to the barber who apparently helped her during an epidemic the previous year (Confuorto 1693).

68 See above.

69 Francesco Vaaz de Andrade's apostasy is referred to in Capecelatro, 69–70.

70 Galasso, 1982, 62.

71 Amabile, 1892, 38–40.

72 Of the names that that appear in the records of the inquisitorial proceedings, only those of Giovanni Vargas, son of the Duchess of Cagnano, the Attorney at Law Girolamo De Rosa and his mother, aunt and nephew do not lead back directly to the family group of the Vaaz (Sirago, 1987, 138–139).

73 ASN, Collaterale, Notazioni, v. 63, cc. 142 r — t and Sirago, 1987, 139–140.

74 ASN, Collaterale, Notazioni, v. 65, c. 18 r; Confuorto, 1693; Fuidoro, 1934, 63; Sirago, 1987, 140.

75 ASN, Collaterale, Notazioni, v. 65, c. 27 r.

76 Giannone, 1865, 563 (but on 20 July 1556, the Inquisition had reintroduced in Naples the confiscation of heretics' property).

77 Amabile, 1892, 44–49; Galasso, 1982, 62–64.

78 ASN, Collaterale, Notazioni, v. 65, c. 38 (session of 2 May 1661).

79 AGS, Estado, Nápoles, l.3285, *La ciudad de Nápoles, con motivo del nacimiento del Principe Carolos, solicita [el] levantamiento del secuestro de los bienes del Conde de Mola*, Naples, 1662, unnumbered.

80 The long and complex litigation is reconstructed in Sirago, 1987, 145–148; on the condemnation of Eduardo Vaaz see Sirago, 1980.

81 ASN, Collaterale, Notazioni, v. 67, c. 123 t (session of 13 September 1666) and c. 169 r (session of 28 February 1667).

82 Confuorto, 1693.

Bibliography

Álvarez Nogal, Carlos, *El crédito de la Monarquía Hispánica en el Reinado de Felipe IV*, Valladolid, Junta de Castilla y León, 1997.

Amabile, Luigi, *Il Santo Officio della Inquisizione in Napoli: narrazione con molti documenti inediti*, Città di Castello, Lapi, 1892.

Barzazi, Antonella (ed.), *Corrispondenze diplomatiche veneziane da Napoli: dispacci*, vol. III, Rome, Istituto Italiano per gli Studi Filosofici — Istituto Poligrafico e Zecca dello Stato, 1991.

Belli, Carolina, "Michele Vaaz, hombre de negocios", *Ricerche sul '600 napoletano: saggi e documenti per la storia dell'arte*, Milan, L&T, 1990, pp. 7–42.

Boyajian, James C., *Portuguese bankers at the court of Spain (1626–1650)*, New Brunswick (NJ), Rutgers University Press, 1983.

Boyajian, James C., *Portuguese trade in Asia under the Hasbourgs (1580–1640)*, Baltimore/London, The John Hopkins University Press, 1993.

Capasso, Bartolomeo (ed.), "Napoli descritta nei principi del secolo XVII da Giulio Cesare Capaccio", *Archivio storico per le Province Napoletane*, 1882, n. 1–4.

Capecelatro, Francesco, *Degli annali della città di Napoli (1631–1640)*, vol. I, Naples, Stamperia Reale, 1849.

Carande, Ramón, *Carlos V y sus banqueros*, Madrid, Revista de Occidente — Sociedad de Estudios y Publicaciones, 1943–1949, 3 vols.

Cardim, Pedro, Sabatini, Gaetano, *António Vieira, Roma e o universalismo das Monarquias Portuguesa e Espanhola*, Lisbona, CHAM, 2011.

Colapietra, Raffaele, *Il governo spagnolo nell'Italia meridionale (Napoli dal 1580 al 1648)*, Naples, Edizioni della Storia di Napoli, 1972, pp. 69–173.

Comparato, Vitor Ivo, *Uffici e società a Napoli (1600–1647)*, Florence, Olschki, 1974.

Confuorto, Domenico, *Notizie d'alcune famiglie popolari della città e del regno di Napoli, divenute riguardevoli per causa di ricchezze, o dignitari*, Naples, 1693, in BNN, ms. X A 15 (other copy in 1. D. 5), cc. 127 r–128 t.

Coniglio, Giuseppe, *Il viceregno di Napoli nel sec. XVII: notizie sulla vita commerciale e finanziaria secondo nuove ricerche negli archivi italiani e spagnoli*, Rome, Edizioni di Storia e Letteratura, 1955.

D'Addabbo, Leonardo, "S. Michele e una colonia serba", *Iapigia*, 1936, 14, n° 3, pp. 289–301.

De Rosa, Gabriele, Cestaro, Antonio (eds.), *Territorio e società nella storia del Mezzogiorno*, Naples, Guida, 1973.

De Rosa Luigi, *Il Mezzogiorno spagnolo tra crescita e decadenza*, Milan, Il Saggiatore, 1987.

Dubuloz, Julien, Sabatini, Gaetano, "Tutto ciò confermando con autorità di leggi, dottrine et esempij. Teoria, prassi e riferimenti alla tradizione classica dell'approvvigionamento granario nel 'Trattato dell'abondanza' di Carlo Tapia", in Brigitte Marin & Cathrine Virlouvet (eds.), *Nourrir les cités de Méditerranée*, Aix en Provance, Maison Méditerranéenne des Sciences de l'Homme, 2003, pp. 539–572.

Enciso Alonso-Muñumer, Isabel, *Nobleza, poder y mecenazgo en tiempos de Felipe III: Nápoles y el Conde de Lemos*, Madrid, Actas, 2007.

Faraglia, Nunzio Federico, *Storia dei prezzi a Napoli dal 1831 al 1860*, Naples, Nobile, 1878.

Frattarelli Fischer, Lucia, *Vivere fuori dal ghetto: Ebrei a Pisa e Livorno (secoli XVI–XVIII)*, Venice, Zamorani, 2008.

Fuidoro, Innocenzo, *Giornali di Napoli dal MDCLX al MDCLXXX*, vol. I (1660–65), in Schlitzer, Franco (ed.), Naples, Società Napoletana di Storia Patria, 1934.

Galasso, Giuseppe, "Contributo alla storia delle finanze del regno di Napoli nella prima metà del Seicento", *Annuario dell'Istituto Storico per l'età moderna e contemporanea*, 1959, 9, pp. 3–106.

——, "Una ipotesi di 'blocco storico' oligarchico-borghese nella Napoli del '600: i 'Seggi' di Camillo Tutini tra politica e storiografia", *Rivista storica Italiana*, 1978, 110, pp. 507–529.

——, *Alla periferia dell'impero: il regno di Napoli nel periodo spagnolo (secoli XVI–XVII)*, Turin, Einaudi, 1994.

——, Russo, Carla (eds.), *L'Archivio storico diocesano di Napoli*, v. II, Naples, Guida, 1978.

——, *Napoli spagnola dopo Masaniello: politica, cultura, società*, vol. I, Florence, Sansoni, 1982.

Giannone, Pietro, *Dell'Istoria civile del Regno di Napoli* (original ed., Napoli, 1723), Naples, Mariano Lombardi Editore, 1865.

Giustiniani, Lorenzo, *Nuova collezione delle Prammatiche del regno di Napoli*, vol. X, Naples, Stamperia Simoniana, 1804.

Herrero Sánchez, Manuel, "La quiebra del sistema hispano-genovés (1627–1700)", *Hispania: revista española de historia*, 2005, 65, pp. 115–151.

Intorcia, Gaetana, *Magistrature del regno di Napoli: analisi prosopografica, secoli XVI–XVII*, Naples, Jovene, 1987.

Linde, Luis M., *Don Pedro Girón, Duque de Osuna, la hegemonía española en Europa a comienzos del siglo XVII*, Madrid, Ed. Encuentro, 2005.

Millar Carvacho, René, *Inquisición y sociedad en el virreinato peruano: estudios sobre el tribunal de la Inquisición de Lima*, Lima, UCP, 1998.

Nicolini Fausto (ed.), "Notizie storiche tratte dai giornali copiapolizze dell'antico Banco della Pietà", *Bollettino dell'Archivio storico del Banco di Napoli*, 1950, n° 2, pp. 97–192, 1951, n° 1, pp. 193–304.

Novellino, Pasquale "Le filigrane culturali della 'fedeltà' nella storiografia napoletana tra fine Cinquecento e inizio Seicento", in J. P. Dedieu (ed.), *Mélanges de l'Ecole Française de Rome — Italie et Méditerranée*, 2006, 118, n° 2, pp. 243–253.

Muto, Giovanni, *Le finanze pubbliche napoletane tra riforme e restaurazione (1520–1634)*, Naples, ESI, 1980.

Palermo Francesco (ed.), *Narrazioni e documenti sulla storia del regno di Napoli dall'anno 1522 al 1667*, Florence, Archivio Storico Italiano — Gio. Pietro Vieussseux Direttore-Editore, 1846.

Parrino, Domenico Antonio, *Teatro eroico e politico de'governi de' viceré del Regno di Napoli etc.* (original ed. Napoli, 1692–94), Naples, Ricciardi, 1730.

Ruiz Martín, Felipe, "La Banca en España hasta 1782", in *El Banco de España: una historia económica*, Madrid, Banco de España, 1970, pp. 1–196.

——, *Las finanzas de la monarquía hispánica en tiempos de Felipe IV (1621–1665)*, Madrid, Real Academia de la Historia, 1990.

Ruspio, Federica, *La nazione portoghese: Ebrei ponentini e nuovi cristiani a Venezia*, Venice, Zamorani, 2007.

Sabatini, Gaetano, "Il pane di Cerbero. Aspetti di politica annonaria e demografica nel regno di Napoli nell'età di Filippo II", in José Martinez Millan (ed.), *Felipe II (1598–1998): Europa y la monarquía católica*, Madrid, Parteluz, 1998a, v. I, pp. 767–776.

—— (ed.), Carlo Tapia, *Il trattato dell'abondanza* (original ed. Naples, 1638), Lanciano, Carabba, 1998b.

——, "Gastos militares y finanzas publicas en el reino de Nápoles en el siglo XVII", in García Hernán, Enrique, Maffi, Davide (eds.), *Guerra y sociedad en la monarquía hispánica: política, estrategia y cultura en la Europa moderna, 1500–1700*, Madrid, Mapfre, 2006, vol. II, pp. 257–291.

——, "Roma, Nápoles, Milán: la etapa italiana de Saavedra Fajardo en el gran teatro de la diplomacia barroca (1610–1633)", in José Javier Ruiz Ibáñez (ed.), *Pensar Europa en el siglo de hierro: el mundo en tiempos de Saavedra Fajardo*, Murcia, Ediciones del Año Saavedra Fajardo, 2008, pp. 41–74.

——, *Un mercato conteso: banchieri portoghesi alla conquista della Napoli dei genovesi (1590–1650)*, in M. Herrero Sánchez, Y.R. Ben Yassef Garfia, C. Bitossi, D. Puncuh, *Génova y la Monarquia Hispanica, 1528–1713*, vol. I, Genova, Società Ligure di Storia Patria, 2011, pp. 141–170.

Sanz Ayán, Carmen, *Los banqueros de Carlos II*, Valladolid, Universidad de Valladolid, 1989.

Scaramella, Pierroberto, "La campagna contro i giudaizzanti nel regno di Napoli (1569–1582): antecedenti e risvolti di un'azione inquisitoriale", *Le inquisizioni cristiane e gli ebrei: tavola rotonda nell'ambito della conferenza annuale della ricerca (Rome 20–21 december 2001)*, Rome, Accademia Nazionale dei Lincei, 2003, pp. 357–373.

Schipa, Michelangelo, *La pretesa fellonia del duca d'Ossuna (1619–20)*, Naples, Pierro, 1911.

Sirago, Maria, "L'Inquisizione a Napoli nel 1661", *Quaderni dell'Istituto di Scienze Politiche della Facoltà di Magistero dell'Università di Bari*, 1980, pp. 429–454.

——, "L inserimento di una famiglia ebraica portoghese nella feudalità meridionale. I Vaaz a Mola di Bari (circa 1580–1816)", *Archivio Storico Pugliese*, 1987, 40, pp. 119–158.

Studnicki-Gizbert, Daviken, *A nation upon the ocean sea: Portugal's Atlantic diaspora and the crisis of the Spanish Empire, 1492–1640*, Oxford, Oxford University Press, 2007.

Tavim Rodrigues da Silva, José Alberto, "O Aviso anónimo sobre João Micas na Colecção de S. Vicente", *Anais de história de além-mar*, Lisbon, vol. V, 2004, pp. 253–282.

Toppi, Niccolò, *De origine tribunalium urbis Neapolis*, v. III, Naples, De Bonis, 1666.

Tutini, Camillo, *Dell'origine e fundatione de' seggi di Napoli, del tempo in che furono instituiti, e della separation de'nobili dal popolo*, Naples, Ottavio Beltrano, 1644.

Valladares, Rafael, *Banqueros y vasallos*, Cuenca, Universidad de Castilla La Mancha, 2002.

Villari, Rosario, *La rivolta antispagnola a Napoli: le origini, 1585–1647*, Rome-Bari, Laterza, 1976.

Visceglia, Maria Antonietta, "Linee per uno studio unitario dei testamenti e dei contratti matrimoniali dell'aristocrazia feudale napoletana tra fine Quattrocento e Settecento", *Mélanges de l'Ecole Française de Rome — Italie et Méditerranée*, 1983, 95, n° 5, pp. 393–470.

Zazzera, Francesco, "Giornali dell'illustrissimo ed eccellentissimo signor Pietro Girone duca d'Ossuna", in Francesco Palermo (ed.), *Narrazioni e documenti sulla storia del regno di Napoli dall'anno 1522 al 1667*, Florence, Archivio Storico Italiano — Gio. Pietro Vieusseux Direttore-Editore, 1846, pp. 471-617.

7 | Trading Money and Empire Building in Spanish Milan (1570–1640)

Giuseppe De Luca

Finance played a central role in Milanese economic growth during the second half of the sixteenth century. Beginning in the 1570s, credit activities, payment systems and public bonds market in the city were gradually part of a fully integrated financial system. The supply and demand of capital came together effectively through an operational model, in which information and trust circulated in formal and informal channels, guaranteeing relatively low transaction costs. This network was alimented by both local and imperial needs. After an initial phase, in which the financial system adapted to Spain's credit requirements, fuelled by constant war, it created supply-leading innovations that drove growth in the city. As a result, the extraordinary increase in long-term public debt, contracted by both the local and imperial governments, did not crowd out private-sector borrowing for productive purposes. On the contrary, from the second half of the sixteenth century and until 1620, the new forms of long-term public debt had a pro-cyclical effect on the economy and played a key role in establishing a lively financial market, as well as guaranteeing political stability and fomenting allegiance to the Hispanic Monarchy.

The incoming and outgoing credit circuits were spread throughout the city, but also tied it to the most important economic centers of the continent and Madrid. Credit and debt relations, which criss-crossed the local society and the immediate countryside, acted as a binding agent. They were one of the leading vehicles for the social transmission of values, and the construction of individual reputation and reliability. Meanwhile, loans from private individuals to the State by way of investment in public debt, ensured involvement and integratation of investors in the strategies of the Duchy of Milan and the Hispanic Monarchy, thus guaranteeing political stability.

While consolidating its society and ties to Madrid, during this period, Milan also gradually moved from a vision, which legitimized interest on loans depending on the social standing of the parties, to a more modern approach (albeit embryonic) that regarded money as a commodity and wealth as circulating capital. This evolution was extremely suited to the establishment of financial innovations and for bolstering their refinement. Together, all these changes explained the extraordinary changes that were taking place in the city in the late sixteenth and early seventeenth century.

A Relationship-Based Financial System

After a long period of crisis, economic recovery in Milan between 1540 and 1584 was not due to changes in productive or distributive structures,[1] but to the emergence of new credit instruments and important changes in financial activities that turned the movement of capital into the keystone of local and even European economic life. During this period, the main purpose of such developments was to match supply to demand, that is, the availability of capital with the need for resources. From the simple conversion of mercantile earnings into financial trades, the new system that was structured in the second half of the sixteenth century moved on to liabilities-related transactions. In addition to their own monetary stocks, cambist-bankers in Milan began to attract and mobilize resources from other centers. The 35,000 scudi, with which Cesare Negrolo returned to Milan in 1574 after liquidating the silk and cotton cloth and arm and armour business he had run in Paris and Lyon, for example, garanteed him entry to the local financial community.[2] Yet his withering rise in Milanese society was based on his ability to match money for assets, i.e. loans, advances and bills of exchange, with capital made available in deposits or through merchants' commission and tax farming.

Two hands were held out, one giving, one receiving, but the hands rarely belonged to the same person. The passage from one hand to another, i.e. the meeting of supply and demand for money, was not a one-man operation. It was carried out by a group of people that, in Milan, comprised of "mercanti banchieri et negotianti de cambi".[3] After the 1570s, these professionals were increasingly involved in speculative dealings and began to specialize, acquiring different but related functions. The integration and linkage between those who managed small sums collected from widows and from ecclesiastical-charitable institutions, and those who invested on behalf of noblemen and Spanish officers, those who managed the capital of merchants or the proceeds from tax farming, and those who lent to sovereigns or paid bills of exchange in Europe's leading cities, represented a *de facto* financial system able to adapt to the needs of the moment and place capital wherever it was required. As a result, to restrict oneself to analyzing these financial activities 'hydraulicaly' by seeking to identify in one person or family the source of a continuous 'outflow' of money as historians have done in the past, would conceal rather than reveal the true dynamics of the system. Or, said otherwise, the search for endogenous funds, as research on late Medieval Tuscan and Lombard and German merchant-bankers at the time of Charles V has done, would lead to the conclusion that financial dealers "had such large quantities of capital that they preferred to lend rather than use them directly for commerce".[4] Yet, such a statement would be unduly simplistic not only for Milan in the last quarter of the sixteenth century, but also for the network of European cities, in which money circulated.

The peculiarity of private finance in Milan consisted of the fact that, thanks to inter-relations between and beyond the dealers themselves, supply was matched with demand. Alongside a 'hydraulic' definition of credit understood as the transfer of purchasing power, towards the end of the 1570s and in the 1580s, a new awarness emerged in the city that considered credit as the capability of bringing together diverse, even scattered, flows. In December 1581, the Governor of the Duchy asked for the release from prison of Negrolo, who he called "the best credit there is here and which served the Chamber".[5] His imprisonment on the orders of the General Inspector for connivance with the judiciary, left the State, the governor argued, "without hope of finding money and in danger, given that a soldier's rations are inexcusable".[6] The previous year, Negrolo had used his credit to make the Bonvisi family from Lyon loan to the Marquis of Ajamonte 60,000 scudi and had handled two bills of exchange for a further 100,000 scudi on behalf of the Fugger family, of which the Governor was the beneficiary.[7] Most of these large sums were not his own. His credit derived from his ability to *contratar dinero*, that is, to drain it from the various channels and redirect it to the demand, "making other people's money work for him".[8] Of the 160 creditors who presented claims at his bankruptcy hearing in 1585, 34 members of his guild and 5 foreign merchant-bankers were in direct contact with him, whilst the rest was involved with him through their relationships with third parties.[9]

Fifteen years later, the standing of Gerolamo Zavarello, exchange dealer and jewel merchant, was measured not so much by his ownership of goods and bills (with a value of 12,000 scudi), but according to his skill in moving more than 100,000 scudi and because he was well-known and respected by merchants in Milan.[10] It was now clear that the trust between dealers — their mutual dependency and reliance — was an essential element, a necessary pre-condition, for credit transactions. As a result, it is fair to say that the network of credit relations and thus the financial system itself, were held together by reputation. It is therefore not surprising that in 1578, when Cesare Negrolo made a bid for the salt tax farming, he wanted secrecy because he believed he would acquire little credit among the merchants if it were known that he had dealings with the Royal Chamber.[11] Three years later, representatives of the State of Milan at the Bisenzone exchange fair complained to Philip II that his delayed payments may lead them to lose "the credit of such honourable nations [Genoa, Florence and Lucca]" thereafter "causing of the utter ruin of their honour which they esteem above all worldly".[12]

The physical circulation of money in a variety of different channels and by numerous networks was the corollary of existing social relations. The informal obligations and commitments generated by these flows were both the result of these social links as well as a cause for new contacts. As a result, the Milanese financial system was an ensemble of relationships, in which the economic and social orders were inseparable. Friendships with neighbours, apprenticeships, marriages, meetings at charitage institutions or at the City Council, were all opportunities to make, consolidate or build upon relationships. In church pews, parish confraternities, or neighbourhood meetings, dealers spun a web of social relations and established efficient mechanisms of communication. Contacts became more numerous through assistance to baptisms, weddings, and dispensing patronage. Significantly, the correspondents of bills of exchange preferred to call themselves "exchange friends" rather than colleagues.[13] In this networks, equity, 'rational' behaviour, distributive and commutative justice coexisted and were steadily cross-fertilized. Moreover, these contacts extended beyond the city itself to other political and administrative centres, such as Madrid.[14]

The paths of money thus entwined with personal and blood relations and were strenghtened by physical and spiritual proximity. To use a Weberian terminology, actions were not 'economic' but 'economically relevant'. Together, these relations created a hierarchical structure, shaped and organized in response to the pace of the local and international markets and their financial demands.

Money-Changers, Bankers-Exchangers and *Hombres de Negocios*

What linked all these dealers together was their wish to put money to work, but the ability to use other people's money was the exclusive domain of the highest placed members of the Milanese financial system. These top ranking individuals increasingly became specialists in this financial practice and progressively ceased acting as merchants. Information was a key condition of their capacity to match financial supply and demand. The members of these upper financial stratas monitored other European centres by using a network of agents.[15] Access to data and the assessment of the 'strength' and 'weakness' of the various regional centres was usually the task of an intermediate layer of financiars. In times of plenty, capital from entrepreneurial merchants and land owners from Como, Cremona, Novara, Tortona and Lodi was brought to Milan and invested advantageously in State revenues and *asientos* with the Sovereign. In lean times, loans took the opposite route moving towards craftsmen, merchants and peasant farmers. At the base of the pyramid were direct exchanges between those who needed money and those who collected and provided it, those who wanted to keep their money safe, and those who wanted to put it to work and those who took it on deposit, and those who wanted to transfer it with money movers, those who wanted to invest in exchange fairs and those who were entitled to.

Contrary to what the literature had described, maintaining a dicothomy between, on the one hand, money-changers who converted foreign currencies and took money on deposit, and, on the other, exchange dealers, who uniquely traded bills of exchange,[16] Milanese financial dealers were highly interrelated and stratified. Banking and financial activities were characterized both by their broad extension (including many actors who were not limited to this strict dualism) and by its depth (linking leading players in different economic orders and categories).

At the base of the pyramid were money-changers ("*cambiatori-bancheri*") who, in addition to dealing with different currencies, were above all the initial source of capital for loans. These dealers (officially 18 of them in 1582 but each working with a number of unofficial colleagues) generally handled small sums, taking deposits from widows and minor religious institutions and granting loans against rural property. The capital collected by this group took one of two possible routes. It either produced interest and became a credit, often in the form of redeemable rents for landowners, or it was used to generate higher yields through the upper financial circuits and company pacts.[17] There were at least five pacts between 1580 and 1583 to "issue and to negotiate bills of exchange and to manage investments" at the Bisenzone exchange fair, each characterized by the presence, alongside numerous exchange dealers accredited in Piacenza (where the Bisezone fairs took place since 1579), of one of the eighteen money-changers of Milan, who took minority stakes but continuously supplied fresh capital coming from small deposits.[18]

At the beginning of the 1580s, there were fifteen "*banchieri-cambisti*" in Milan whose core business was centered on bills of exchange. Combining specific elements of banking with exchange letters enabled them to broaden the scope of their financial dealings.[19] The credit provided to merchants for the production of textiles and iron, to landowners or to the State, accompanied the deposits and exchanges at the fair and became an essential instrument for the circulation of resources. The ability to match supply and demand asynchronously with banking activities, allowed these traders to multiply, rapidly and fictitiously, the availability of capital, which could then be routed towards the most advantageous transactions. The time between cashing a deposit and returning or transferring it provided them with liquidity, which they could advance to merchants or to a beneficiary of a bill of exchange.

The network of correspondents of bankers-exchangers covered all the countries which, for political, military or commercial reasons, had dealings with the State of Milan. For example, Cesare Negrolo specialized in having payments made at the place of origin of Spanish soldiers or officers. He had worked out a procedure, by which those who wanted to send a certain amount to Spain paid to him and were given a receipt for the lot less 3 percent. The receipt was sent by courier to a creditor or anyone else who could cash the amount from a dealer trusted by Negrolo.[20]

When these financial cycles were used by bankers-exchangers to provide capital for *asientos* in symbiosis with exchange transactions for big amounts, to finance the Treasury or bids for tax farming, the dealers — Cesare Negrolo, Leonardo Spinola, Alberto Litta, Giuseppe Caravaggio and the Omodei family[21] — acquired the status of *hombres de negocios*, the absolute pinnacle of the financial system in Milan, that had close contacts with the social, administrative and political leadership of the city and the Crown.

Fostering and Enhancing Economic Activity

The evolution of this system, in which financial activities gradually became both more common and more complex and in which monetary flows became ever more substantial, had its origins not only in the war needs of the Spanish Monarchy but also in the rhythms and necessities of the regional economy. The structure of the financial framework, which began to take shape in the 1570s, featured an increasingly specialist group of dealers that facilitated the exchange of goods and services, supported the expansion of production and provided investment opportunities, thus allowing for an overall economic growth in the city.

The fact that Milanese merchants enjoyed the advantage of easy access to capital and financial brokerage was well known to contemporaries: "the majority of merchants in the city buy and manage their merchandise with little stock thanks to the credit they get in Milan".[22] A merchant was someone who "had capital to trade of 4,000 scudi, yet traded in one year 15 or 20 thousand using credit. Other merchants increased their capital 5 or 6 times a year".[23]

Long-distance trade was the greatest beneficiary of this financial system. Credit transactions opened in Milan and handled in Danzig allowed the Milanese merchant Fabrizio Rainoldi to supply the city with Polish wheat during the famine of 1590–1591.[24] Similarly, the grocers of Milan, using the contacts of the financiers on the Portuguese coast, were able to buy cheap pepper in Lisbon.[25] Yet, bankers-exchangers also provided support to manufacturing activities in the State of Milan, mainly the production of iron, silk and wool. Two types of transactions — loan contracts and bonds — were able to supply the iron industry with the necessary resources. To meet the considerable demand for arms in the period 1575 to 1577, Milanese entrepreneurs were encouraged to integrate vertically by opening new mines or reopening older ones. Because in this industry the quantity of fixed assets was negligeable and liquidity was necessary in order to buy raw materials or individuals parts, having a working capital in the form of a bond, was essential. When the promised financial assistance of the authorities failed to materialize, the capital required for processing the ore could be obtained from the credit circuits. Until 1577, the amount of credit provided by bonds reflected the demand for arms and military supplies almost exactly. From the early 1580s, the overall and average sums of bond loans gradually fell as it was no longer economically viable to mine iron locally for the war effort, for which demand was dwindling.[26] Furthermore, the summer of 1583 marked the beginning of a credit crunch. The Milanese financial market suffered "the greatest shortage in the Kingdom for many a year".[27] Letters between Simón Ruiz and his correspondents complained of difficulties in Milan and with its leading bankers. Tommasso D'Adda, Rinaldo Tettoni, the Triddi brothers and Cesare Foppa were all declared bankrupt in 1583. The same happened with Dario Crivelli a year later and Cesare Negrolo in 1585.[28] Added was a general economic crisis in Milan in the second half of the 1580s. What happens with credit to textile manufacturers, another leading sector of the Milanese industry, tells this story well. An analysis of credit demand by the wool sector shows how manufacturing practices reorganized and how, from the mid 1580s onwards, this industry lived through a definitive turn-down. Two main credit instruments emerged during this period: credit purchase receipts (*polizze a credenza*), a chirograph credit which became popular because it was fit to match the request for guarantees and the need to make quick loans by providing capital for manufacturers and buying the finished textiles, and bills of exchange, for the purchase abroad of raw wool. Until the early 1590s, the high volume of receipts was mainly due to the demand of wool entrepreneurs within the city walls and drapers in the capital who exported finished goods. Nonetheless, the increasing average value of credit shows that the traditional organization of the industry in craft guilds was changing into a manufacturing process controlled by the most important merchants-enterpreneurs, who handled the most delicate phases of the production cycle.[29] The weakening of the urban wool industry corresponded with the overall recession of the mid 1580s and more specifically with the crisis of the most competitive segments of the market. Rural areas were the main beneficiaries from the redistribution of production, while the capital, Milan, continued to play a key financial role.

From 1589 onwards, alongside Milanese clients in the city, credit transactions of bankers-exchangers featured wool merchants from the city and the countryside. During the early 1590s, their presence became prevalent despite the fact that credit activities had fallen sharply. Merchants from Monza and, to a lesser extent, the Gera D'Adda raised the average values of "polizze a credenza" to higher levels than ever before. They controlled large production operations through small producers and handled the exports of clothes, mostly to Naples.[30]

In view of the lengthy time before merchants received payments in the export sector, short-term loans ratified by the "polizze a credenza" soon became inadequate as the term loan was too short and payments too unreliable. With the increase in the scale of firms and the change in their supply, single credit transactions made little sense. Also contributing to the gradual obsolescence of these short-term loans was the fact that they became increasingly hard to come by. The economic crisis of the 1580s and 1590s together with the massive appetite for capital of the Imperial political and military machine had drastically reduced these loans and driven up their prices. At the same time, Milanese bankers-exchangers found themselves with too large an exposure to silk and gold cloth entrepreneurs, whose payments were frequently far from punctual. As a result, financing moved to a new instrument, the limited partnerships (società in accomandita). In Milan, although without a proper legal recognition, this type of companies came into being at around 1575. And, due to their popularity, by the end of the sixteenth century the Senate asked bankers to give them a proper basis in law.[31]

Using limited partnership agreements, merchants-enterpreneurs were given new opportunities to plan their business activities counting on the availability of working capital that would suffer no sudden credit restrictions and would be accessible during the life of the company, usually set up for five to seven years and renewable. Moreover, merchants no longer carried the considerable burden of the cost of short-term loans, which had to be paid in good and bad times alike. With this new form of financing, money was repaid out of profits. Profits thus determined whether financiers in the city would be willing to take part in a company and it often also fixed their rates.[32]

Although it is impossible to assess the exact percentage of these sorts of companies out of the total numer of companies operating in the period, notarial records demonstrate that limited partnerships played a decisive role in the Milanese silk industry at the end of the sixteenth century.[33] They spread firmly not so much because of lower management commitment, or their ability to secure assets,[34] but because they were a more efficient way of matching the needs of expanding economic sectors with the availability of capital from financiers.

Sustaining State Demands

Together with economic expansion, the other great force behind the evolution of the Milanese financial system was the extraordinary demands placed by the State and its military endevours. The public finances of the Duchy were so complex that they cannot be reconstructed here in full, but a few examples would suffice to demonstrate the interrelations between the state and the financial activities of Milanese bankers.

If before the peace of Cateau-Cambrésis, Milan was essential to Spanish Habsburgs as a means to control the Po Valley, with the ongoing Flemish revolt and with maritime routes between Spain and Flandres lacking, Lombardy became the heart of a Spanish logistical support system.[35] Because the city paid much of the military expanse and because needs were greater than the amounts locally raised by taxation, debt — city's or state's, short or long-term, became frequent. Such an extra ordinary burden fell on the city that in 1575, the Decurions had no choice but to ask for a loan, issuing a bill of exchange with Cesare Negrolo.[36] The extreme precision with which the terms of the agreement and its possible consequences were spelled out suggests that this was the beginning not only of relations between municipal finance and an individual financier, but also between municipal finances and financiers in general.[37] The importance of bankers-exchangers' circuits in Milan is also attested by their contribution to the overall city deficit. At the beginning of 1589, Milan's debt amounted to 944,000 lire, and out of it 704,000 were owed by bills of exchange.[38] Besides the specialist dealers, widows also played an important role as financiers, lending smaller amounts to the municipality.[39] Brigida Coira, for example, supplied in 1593 637 scudi, which were to be used to make the river Adda navigable.[40]

Not only municipal, but also state finances were affected by the same processes. The contribution of Milanese bankers-exchangers to the Duchy became important around the mid 1570s, as Genoese involvement with short-term loans to the governor of Milan progressively rarefied. Ottobone Giustiniani, Bernardo Gentile and Filippo Spinola were replaced by their townsmen Leonardo Spinola and Pelegro Doria, who were by now citizens of Milan, and by natives of Milan such as Cesare Foppa, Federico Cusani and Cesare Negrolo.[41] Although these contracts were extremely advantageous,[42] it was only with *asientos,* signed by the Spanish monarchy in the early 1580s, that Milanese financiers acquired a central role in short-term public debt. Asientos were a conventional way for the crown to procure cash in order to cover military expanses. They were signed in Madrid as bills of exchange in which drawees advanced money to the governors of the Netherlands or the State of Milan according to the terms and for the sums specified, in the currency used to pay the armies. The crown had various options how to repay the *asentista,* the most common among them was to assign him a portion of fiscal revenues. Before the bankruptcy of Spain in 1575, these contracts were mainly handled by the Genoese. However, from 1580 onwards, during the period in which the Genoese were banned, Milanese financiers played a major role. Two bankers at the top of the Milanese system, Cesare Negrolo and Lucio Litta, became the exclusive dealers of the bills of exchange by which the King paid the Duchy. As drawees of the letters issued by various Castilian, Tuscan, and German *hombres de negocios,* chosen by the monarch to replace the Genoese lenders, Negrolo and Litta paid into the hands of local governors vast amounts of gold coins.[43] In 1613, because of the first Mantuan war of succession, which caused havoc in Lombardy (until 1659), the Duchy of Milan began a long period of acute financial need. During this period, Emilio Omodei[44] and other Milanese *hombres de negocios* became indispensable, giving short-term credit to the State of Milan and the Spanish monarchy, also winning as a result prominence in the European private finance community.

Although short-term loans were important, it was above all in the long-term public debt (the so-called advanced sale of revenues) that the Milanese system reached its height, fostering innovations that considerably increased the collection of monies and tied financial capital to the State. Because of Spanish domination of Milan, the sale of fiscal income ceased being a compulsory subscription and became instead the keystone of a consolidated debt that took on greater dimensions starting in the mid-1570s. These types of bonds were freely subscribed, and interest was guaranteed by a fixed fiscal source. There was no set time for the return of the capital and bonds were marketable, could be inherited and were exempt from confiscation and taxes. The earmarking of future tax income for interest payment on bonds issued alongside their transferability, set up a public funded debt. The enormous growth of this new form of financing was the result of its acceptance by a large group of individuals, who found this type of investment suitable for their own needs. Returns were, in many cases, higher than those offered in the Duchy of Milan by other kinds of investments[45] and their range was in line with that of public debt in other countries.[46] However, since these annuities satisfied the need for fungible bonds in commercial and manufacturing activity, they were bought even when the yield was uncompetitive. In the process, government bonds lost their patrimonial nature and became more clearly investments, and popular investments too. Rather than restricted to the political or economic elites, or to ecclesiastical-charitable institutions (as historians have assumed in the past), in the State of Milan the sheer number and variety of subjects who, at least initially, subscribed to such bonds was striking. For revenues of 2,191,302 lire sold between 1574 and 1611 for example, there were 2,640 buyers, the average share going for 800 to 830 lire.[47]

Milanese bankers-exchangers also performed an essential role in the sale of alienated revenues: they purchased 46% of the total alienated revenues in 1579, as compared to 21% by the Genoese,[48] and in the process of farming of taxes, which functioned as a guarantee and an indemnity. Through a network of local mediators and brokers, they contributed to extending the demand for bonds to different parts of the State. Along with Genoese bankers, they were the leading players in the secondary market for Milanese alienations, which was particularly lively at that time. Technically, this was an efficient market, which offered lower transaction costs than those available in other centres as the commission of Milanese brokers (0.50% of the security) was lower than the charges levied by their Roman and Bolognese counterparts.[49] The transfer procedure provided for free registration at the Chamber registry office, while the change of ownership was not taxable (unlike in the Papal States). In addition, the norms protecting the renters and regulating their rights to collect interest were detailed and painstakingly enforced. Sources demonstrate that there was asymmetry in favour of issuer and the main bankers in term of the extent to which prices became public knowledge. Indeed, one of the main references for the smaller buyers was the behaviour of the ruling class and of the wealthiest echelons of society, enhancing official confidence in the stability and profitability of the debt.

Local financial dealers and brokers thus facilitated increasing investments in public debt, which acted as a mechanism of redistribution tying subscribers to the policies of the government. In the mid- seventeenth century, small and middle-size investors were still an important part of the Milanese securities market, especially when compared to other cases. This perhaps explains why the Duchy of Milan was the only Italian domain of the Spanish monarchy that in the mid-seventeenth century did not undergo neither political nor social insurrection, nor any significant anti-Habsburg conspiracy. Apparently, the majority of the lower and middle classes, cities, boroughs and communities, drawing yields from state bonds along with the patriciate, merchants, bankers and religious institutions, had nothing to gain from rebelling against a government from whom they claimed such advantageous credits. Public debt, therefore, may have played a crucial role in keeping Milan politically stable and politically loyal to Spain.[50]

Between the second and third decade of the seventeenth centuries, the Milanese financial system became ever more polarized. Although the total amount of credits for production and commerce did not diminish, limited partnerships were increasingly the preferred form for loans, and they were managed by a narrower group of larger lenders. In the 1570s and 1580s, Cesare Negrolo was the prominent *hombre de negocios* in Milan. He was followed by Emilio Omodei, the richest banker in Italy and an indispensable lender to the Spanish crown.[51] But it was above all Gio Giacomo Durini, Marc'Antonio Stampa, Marcellino and Cesare Airoldi, and later Giovanni Batta Crotta, who, having began as Milanese financiers in the 1630s and 1640s were promoted to the role of *factores reales*, "the cusp of financial activities" of the Austrias instead of the Genoese.[52] Durini was the first financier of the city to stipulate in January 1640 the *factoría* contract, providing 140,000 ducati in the capital to the Real Hacienda, for which he was paid a 2% comission.[53] Giovanni Battista Crotta, working at the service first of Durini and then of the Airoldi family, acted as *factor real* during the reign of Charles II. He became the first native-Milanese to be a permement member, from 1665 to 1679, of the Court of Madrid, he was appointed *contador* of the *Contaduria Mayor de Cuentas*, and subsequently Treasurer General of the Duchy.[54]

Rethinking the Use of Money

Structural changes in Milan's financial system were accompanied by a gradual rethinking of the use of money, eventually leading to the legimization of interest in more modern terms. During this period, bankers, brokers and private investors answered positively to the pressing theoretical question of the day, namely, if money should command the payment of interest. Basing his interpretation on the New Testament's parable of the talents (Matthew 25, 14–30), banker Federico Cusani argued that money should never "remain idle".[55] On the contrary, specific professional skills, such as his own and those of his collegues, were directed not to allow money any rest. As in the New Testament, inactivity was a sin. The broker Bernardo Molina motivated his request — submitted to the Judiciary — for new public bonds, by alleging that he had provided "an opportunity to buyers which do not want to leave their money idle".[56] In the early part of the 1720s, the widow Caterina Porta claimed that she had deposited the sum of 847 lire, which was not "idle but receives interest".[57] Dealers and investors, including noblemen, patricians, craftsmen, officers and women, thus agreed that money invested had to produce interest.[58]

In November 1599, the Governor of Milan also wrote to the judiciary expressing his opinion that "to all those for whom money has been idle for a lengthy time, reason and conscience dictate that they should receive interest of 8% from the day they lent the money".[59] The reason and conscience he mentioned may have been the conviction that interest should be paid to financiers whose support had become essential for the survival of the Catholic Monarchy. Nonetheless, the attitudes of the Austrias to interest payment varied by time and according to territory. In 1540, Charles V issued an ordinance for the Netherlands, in which he authorized the payment of interest on all loans on the basis of the argument of *lucrum cessans*. In 1534 and 1551, realizing that by bills of exchange and re-exchange the crown had paid interest varying between 45 and 69% when interest rate inside and outside Castile was set at 10%, orders were given to limit interests.[60]

For the monarchy, interest payment was not only a necessary tool to guarantee credit. It was also viewed as a way to reward services. Yet, while kings were willing to tolerate interest, and so did society, Milanese ecclesiastical authorities insisted on the observance of the Canon law prohibition against usury. Appointed Archbishop in 1563, Carlo Borromeo arrived to Milan in 1565, a time in which the financial sector was becoming increasingly essential for the local economy.[61] In the first and second Provincial Council of 1565 and 1568 that he held and in pastoral letters, he condemned high interest-paying loans, which could tempt and then harm the non-specialists.[62] In order to curb usury, Borromeo approved of limited partnerships, which combined aspects of a loan with a company set-up and which garanteed that profits would be shared by the capitalist and the worker according to their percentage in the company.[63] Borromeo also focused attention on transactions carried out at fairs of exchange, which could harm natives who would be burdened with too much debt. In Borromeo's opinion, the crucial distinction between trade money that produced interest, and trade money which was usurious, depended on who carried out the exchange, and who gave and received the money. Borromeo condemned the professional usures, but not the bankers-exchangers or the merchants who lent and traded in capitals in order to guarantee production, and thus were engaged in an activity that was useful for society as a whole. The productive potential of money lent, not the profit made, was, according to him, the discriminating factor between legitimate interest and usury.

A more modern theoretical grounding of interest was suggested by a Jesuit from Brindisi, Martino Fornari (1547–1612) in his *Trattato primo di cambi*. Printed in Rome in 1607 and widely read by ecclesiastics in Milan, in its final form this essay became part of the *Institutio confessariorum ea continens*.[64] Influenced by the thinking of Jesuits from Padua, where he taught moral theology for many years,[65] Fornari analyzed the legitimacy of charging interest on loans by observing the nature of money. He discarded the theological and Aristotelian notion that money was a simple measure of value, and accepted the legal opinion that money could be considered in two ways: materially as goods or metal, or formally as the proper price of certain things.[66] Money, therefore, had two uses. Just as clothing may be used to keep out the cold or be exchanged.[67]

These elaborations allowed justifying money transactions "objectively" rather than "subjectively".[68] With Sigismondo Scaccia, a jurist from Roman circles who authored in 1619 a treaty titled *De commerciis et cambio*, money as commodity was finally given a full conceptual basis that distinguished between its material aspect and its intangible function. Scaccia's work became the leading reference book both for understanding money and for explaining the evolution of financial activities. Grounding what was already happening in the markets, it may have influenced Federico Borromeo, cousin and successor to Carlo as Archbishop of Milan (from 1595 until his death in 1631). Federico Borromeo was fully aware of the reorganization of Milanese economy, whose centre of gravity gradually shifted from the city to commercial and financial flows, which were directed by important financiers (a group to which the Borromeo family belonged) towards foreign countries. He himself was skilled in using financial instruments and understood the credit markets of his day, including mortgages, deposits and bills of exchange.[69] His interest in establishing norms governing loans was less regulatory and more analytical in nature and was based on his deep understanding of economics, especially money trading. The rule-bound worries of his cousin were thus replaced with a more autonomous thinking, which had a better theoretical grounding and was more up-to-date with developments in the market. Federico's position on exchanges — now essential for the regional economy — was therefore very different from that of Carlo.

Federico's perceptions are evident in a decree of the Synod dated 1622 and dedicated to *Trenta casi risolti intorno al contratto del cambio ad nundinas per ischivare le usure*.[70] Citing the dispositions of Pope Pius V, Federico proceeded to ban all agreements similar to a "cambio secco" (dry exchange), which was fictitious.[71] According to the Commission of "wise and grave persons",[72] which he set up, exchange was legitimate when accompanied by bills facilitating the trade, removing the danger and inconvenience of transporting money and the cost of currency exchange. Exchange was nevertheless forbidden and usurous if it was only concerned with the passage of time. This was the discriminating factor in determining the difference between illegitimate usury and legitimate exchange: the former used only time to increase interest, whilst the latter used time to enable the bills of exchange to be sent and placed in circulation and thus protect all that was useful for economic life. In other words, for Federico, the art of exchange was legal when it was useful to the Republic and necessary for the needs of private individuals.[73] Exchanges by commercial and financial dealers would thus be allowed because they were a point of strength of the Milanese economy. Money, in short, was an indispensable instrument for tradesmen and a source of income for enterprising bankers and merchants.

Contemporary authors thus managed to grasp the intrinsic rules of economic phenomena, which could justify earnings.[74] Within the first three decades of the seventeenth century, a framework had been built in Milan by dealers, clergymen, theologians, experts, making the money trade a fully legitimized practice.[75] These theoretical developments mirrored the operational praxis. They emerged from the experience of the Milanese financial sector, leading —between the latter half of the sixteenth century and the 1730s — to the development of new ideas regarding financial activities. Moving away from a perspective, which legitimized interest on loans depending on the social status of the parties involved, it adopted a vision that was based on the idea that money was a commodity and wealth depended on circulation.

The new theoretical framework that emerged supported a positive interplay between trade and money. According to it, the former guided and supported the latter. Or, said otherwise, the former created a conceptual map, where the latter rooted concrete institutions, instruments and innovations enabling increased yields and enhancing the overall development of financial activities. The ideas emerging out of the Milanese environment thus provided private dealers and financiers with a 'moral' handbook with instructions supporting the creation and spread of financial technology. This, in turn, facilitating during the first half of the seventeenth century the reorganization of the markets towards a more commercial and financial core.

Abbreviations

ASMi	Archivio di Stato, Milano.
FN	fondo Notarile.
	Albinaggio p.a. = fondo Albinaggio, parte antica.
	Commercio p.a. = fondo Commercio, parte antica.
	Registri, serie XXII = fondo Registri delle Cancellerie dello Stato, serie XXII, Mandati.
ASCM	Archivio Storico Civico, Milano.
ASDMi	Archivio Storico Diocesano, Milano.
ACCMi	Archivio Storico della Camera di Commercio, Milano.
AGS	Archivo General de Simancas.
	Estado, Milán = fondo Secretaría de Estado, Milán.
SP	fondo Secretarías Provinciales.
AR	Archivo Simón Ruiz, sección del Archivo Histórico Provincial y Universitario, Valladolid.
BA	Biblioteca Ambrosiana.
BNB	Biblioteca Nazionale Braidense.

Notes

1 Aleati Cipolla, 1959; Sella, 1982; D'Amico, 1994.
2 *Protestatio societatis*, 30 October 1574, ASMi, FN, cart. 17564.
3 "Tassa fatta sopra li Mercanti Banchieri et Negocianti de cambi di Milano" dated 17 July 1582, ASCMi, *Materie*, cart. 260.
4 De Roover, 1953, 73.
5 Letter dated 2 December 1581, AGS, *Estado, Milán*, leg. 1254, f. 161.
6 *Ibidem.*
7 Letters dated 28 June 1580 and 2 August 1580, AGS, *Estado, Milán*, leg. 1251, f. 100, leg. 1252, f. 58.

8 With these words, Captain Juan de Muñatones defined the activity of Cesare Negrolo in a remainder sent to Simón Ruiz, drawee of the Milanese banker, 12 June 1580, AR, c. 62, f. 104.
9 "Ordinatione della Camera delli Mercanti di Milan sopra il Concorso de Creditori del Sig. Cesare Negrolo", ACCMi, box 24, folder 9, 10 June 1586; ASMi, *Famiglie*, cart. 148, Negroli, 10 August 1586.
10 ASMi, *Albinaggio*, p.a., cart. 29, folder 8, *Zavarello Gerolamo*.
11 "Processo del Magistrato ordinario, 1581–1584", testimony of 4 May 1584, AGS, *Visitas de Italia*, libro 308, f. 209.
12 "Supplica della Nazione milanese a Filippo II, Milan, 1581", ASMi, *Commercio* p.a., cart. 9.
13 See company agreement between Fruttuoso De Franchi and Tommaso Baudo dated 17 April 1614, ASMi, FN, cart. 23226.
14 One example will suffice: the bankers-exchangers Giuseppe Caravaggio and Alberto Litta were represented by two cousins in the General Council of Milan, while in 1577 the Court of Supply, the highest administrative body of the city, included the fathers-in-law of two of their colleagues, Dario Crivelli and Bassano Porrone. For a detailed description of these relations see De Luca, 1996, 18–20.
15 Ruiz Martín, 1973, 530.
16 De Roover, 1974; Lapeyre, 1961, 223–224.
17 "Memoriale al Governatore dei cambiatori della città", 27 October 1582, ASMi, *Commercio*, cart. 36, folder 1.
18 For example, the *Societas* of 15 September 1580, ASMi, FN, cart. 16942.
19 "Notificatione de li 10.000 scuti", August 1582, ASCMi, *Materie*, cart. 260.
20 The above-mentioned letter by Captain Juan de Muñatones, 12 June 1580, AR, c. 62, f. 104.
21 "Notificatione de li 10.000 scuti", August 1582, ASCMi, *Materie*, cart. 260.
22 "Comparitione della città di Milan contra la pubblicatione dell'Estimo del Mercimonio", 20 February 1598, ASCMi, *Materie*, cart. 263, 7r.
23 "Aggravii evidentissimi, errori, et inconvenienti", 1580, ASCMi, *Materie*, cart. 260.
24 *Confessio* dated 27 May 1592, ASMi, FN, cart. 14549.
25 De Luca, 1996, 87–101.
26 *Ivi*, 102–113, 115–120.
27 AGS, *Consejo y Juntas de Hacienda*, leg. 214, f. 17, 21 March 1584.
28 AR, c. 85, f. 162, Lyon, 26 August 1583, 14 August 1583, for Negrolo see letter by Ottaviano Cassina and Giovanni Battista Canobio from Milan, 15 January 1587, in AR, c. 122, ff. 119–127.
29 De Luca, 1996, 127–131.
30 *Ivi*, 138–141.
31 "Memoria", 31 May 1599, ACCMi, box 2, folder 17.
32 Vigo, 1979, 92.
33 For the Tuscan data see Goodman, 1994, 427, tab. 2.
34 Malanima, 1982, 131–132.
35 Parker, 1972, 139–57; Fernández Albaladejo, 1992, 185–192.
36 "Notta di tutte le gravezze straordinarie toccanti alla Magnifica Città di Milan eccetto il mensuale per li anni 1561–1583", 13 May 1584, ASCMi, *Materie*, cart. 202. The mensuale was an extraordinary tax to be paid monthly that, regardless, survived until the end of the Spanish domination.
37 "Capitolazione" dated 20 April 1575, act 8 June, notary Cesare Borsani, ASMi, FN, cart. 15505.
38 "Informatione de' cose pertinenti alla Città de Milano", 1589, ASCMi, *Materie*, cart. 202.
39 De Luca, 1996, 200.

40 BNB, manuscript AF XIII, 14, no. 40, 14 May 1593.

41 ASMi, *Registri*, serie XXII, vol. 21–23.

42 See for example dispatches dated 18 February 1575 and 21 March 1595, AGS, SP, libro 1157, 576r.–577v. and libro 1160, 100r.–107r.

43 Letter by Simón Ruiz to Cesare Negrolo from Medina del Campo dated 24 November 1580, in AR, c. 194, ff. 857–858, *Confessiones* dated 22 and 30 June 1582, notary Ottaviano Castelletti, ASMi, FN, cart. 14944.

44 AGS, *Contaduría Mayor de Cuentas*, 3ª Epoca, leg. 3519, n. 1, "Emilio Homodei, homo de Milan, 1595".

45 Prodi, 1961, 657.

46 Calabria, 1991; Pezzolo, 1999, 236 ss.

47 De Luca, 2008, 55.

48 Revenue alienation of 10 April 1579, ASMi, *Rogiti camerali*, cart. 811.

49 "Memoriale de' Mercanti di Milan", 18 January 1592, ACCMi, box 32, folder 1. In general for the Milanese brokers see De Luca, 2010, 239–257.

50 De Luca, 2008, 61–66.

51 Trevor Roper, 1969, 60.

52 Sanz Ayán, 1989, 34, Decyphered letter of Count Sirvela to Philip IV, 16 February 1638, AGS, *Estado, Milán*, leg. 3347, f. 28and Letter of Sirvela to the Duke, 21 January 1639, AGS, *Estado, Milán*, leg. 3349, f. 156.

53 ASMi, *Registri*, serie XXII, Mandati, vol. 60, 221r.–222v., Vercelli, 18 May 1640.

54 For the activities and career of Crotta — considered Genoese by Sanz Ayán, 1989, 231–322 — cf. for example AGS, *Contaduría Mayor de Cuentas, 3ª Epoca*, leg. 2456 n. 4, leg. 2656 n. 6.

55 AGS, *Secretarías Provinciales*, libro 1222, 84r.–86r., 29 March 1592.

56 Memorandum of Bernardo Molina dated 24 May 1572, ASMi, *Finanze reddituari*, cart. 3

57 Cf. the acts of 14 and 15 July 1623, notary Francesco Girolamo Giusti, ASMi, FN, file 25522.

58 Cf. *Confessio* by Cesare Negrolo dated 26 January 1581, notary by Giovanni Paolo Pellizzari, ASMi, FN, cart. 17577.

59 Letter dated 19 November 1559, ASMi, *Finanze reddituari*, cart. 1.

60 ACCMi, Box 2, folder 8, "disposizione" of 7 July 1570.

61 The Bisenzone fairs took place in Piacenza four times a year, from 1579 onwards having been transfered at the wishes of the Genoese (and Milanese) from Besançon, their location from 1535, cf. Marsilio, 2008. Via bills of exchange, it was possible to buy in Milan, or elsewhere, the "scudi di marche", the (imaginary) money of these fairs. The purpose of the meetings was to make profits from the difference between the "prezzi di andata" (going prices) at the fair and the "prezzi di ritorno" (return prices) of these scudi di marche, which were the *res* of exchange, the object of the transaction. The Exchange cycle lasted three months, but was often extended by "ricorsa" (recourse) which postponed the transaction from one fair to the next, continuously updating the price of the scudo di marche, and capitalizing any increase, in the event of the debt not being settled. Therefore, thanks to the permanent superiority of what was certain over what was not, anyone with money willing to accept the risk of a diminishing price could make profits in the region of 10–14% per annum. In terms of the demand for money, the fairs carried out an important credit function and were used by the crown, the city and merchants.

62 *De Usuris, Concilium Provinciale I*, in *Acta Ecclesiae Mediolanensis a Sancto Carolo, Cardinalis S. Praxedis Archiepiscopo . . . Gaisruck*, Milan 1843, volume I, 46.

63 *Ibidem*.

64 Sommervogel, 1998, 889–890.

65 M. Fornari, *Trattato primo di cambi*, s.d., BA, S 95 sup, f. 388 r.

66 Savelli, 2007, 110–111.

67 M. Fornari, *Trattato primo di cambi*, cit., f. 388 r. e v.
68 *Ivi*, f. 399 v.
69 Letter from Rome dated 11 July 1587, in *Lettere del cardinale Federico Borromeo ai familiari (1579–1599)*, 2 vol., Milan 1971, vol. 1.
70 *Trenta casi risolti intorno al contratto del cambio ad nundinas per ischivare le usure*, in BA, Misc. SBS IV, 31 (also SIG V 26). See also Barbieri, 1940, 76–80, who, however, gives the title *Sulle usure del Cambio delle monete*, e Mandich, 1953, 148–149.
71 *Ivi*, 16.
72 *Ivi*, 2.
73 *Ivi*, 23.
74 *Ivi*, 168–170. The three authors/essays were Giovanni Battista Cavazza, *Tractatus, disputationes, et commentaria*, Mediolani, apud Io. Iacobum Comum, 1612; *Trattato della ricorsa e continuazioni de cambii, fatta a se stesso, e di quei si fanno da fiera a fiera, del m.r.p.d. Antonio di San Salvatore*, Milan, apud Gio. Batta Bidelli, 1623 that is in fact a reprinting of the book published in Lucca in 1623; and Basilio Alemanni, *Discorso e parere d'un theologo intorno al cambio della ricorsa a se stesso*, Milan, apud Gio. Battista Bidelli, 1623.
75 Savelli, 1994, 66–67, Del Vigo, 1997, 216 ss.

Bibliography

Accolti, Girolamo, *Ragguaglio della morte di Marco Sciarra, famosissimo bandito, et del successo de' suoi seguaci*, Vicenza, Giorgio Greco, 1593.

Aleati, Giuseppe, Cipolla, Carlo. M., *Aspetti e problemi dell'economia milanese nei secoli XVI e XVII*, in *Storia di Milano*, vol. XI, Milan, Fondazione Treccani degli Alfieri, 1959.

Álvarez Nogal, Carlos, *El crédito de la Monarquía Hispánica en el Reinado de Felipe IV*, Valladolid, Junta de Castilla y León, 1997.

Arese, Franco, "Le supreme cariche del Ducato di Milano", *Archivio Storico Lombardo*, 1970, IX, pp. 1–100.

Barbieri, Gino, "Norme di morale economica dettate da S. Carlo Borromeo", in *Studi economico-giuridici pubblicati dell'Università di Cagliari*, 1938, XXVI, pp. 261–281.

Barbieri, Gino, *Ideali economici degli italiani all'inizio dell'età moderna*, Milan, Giuffrè, 1940.

Buzzi, Franco, "Il lavoro tra XVI e XVIII secolo. Alcune linee di riflessione teologica e spirituale", in D. Zardin (ed.), *Corpi, fraternità, mestieri nella storia della società europea*, Rome, Bulzoni, 1998, pp. 161–186.

Calabria, Antonio, *The Cost of Empire. The Finances of the Kingdom of Naples in the Time of Spanish Rule*, New York, Cambridge University Press, 1991.

Cipolla, Carlo M., *Mouvement Monétaires dans l'Etat de Milan (1580–1700)*, Paris, A. Colin, 1952.

Colzi, Francesco, "'Per maggiore facilità del commercio'. I sensali e la mediazione mercantile e finanziaria a Roma nei secoli XVI–XIX", *Roma*, 1998, 6:3, pp. 397–425.

D'Amico, Stefano, *Le contrade e la città. Sistema produttivo e spazio urbano a Milano fra Cinque e Seicento*, Milan, Franco Angeli, 1994.

De Carlos Morales, Carlos Javier, "Credito e coscienza religiosa. Le prammatiche per la regolazione dei tassi di cambio del 1551–1557", in F. Cantù, M.A. Visceglia (eds.), *L'Italia di Carlo V. Guerra, religione e politica nel primo Cinquecento*, Rome, Viella, 2003, pp. 187–215.

De Luca, Giuseppe, *Commercio del denaro e crescita economica a Milano fra Cinquecento e Seicento*, Milan, Il Polifilo, 1996.

——, "Government Debt and Financial Markets: Exploring Pro-cycle Effects in Northern Italy during the Sixteenth and the Seventeenth Centuries", in F. Piola Caselli (ed.), *Government Debts and Financial Markets in Europe*, London, Pickering & Chatto, 2008, pp. 45–66.

——, "Sensali e mercato del credito a Milano tra XVI e XVII secolo", in G. De Luca, E. M. García Guerra (eds.), *Il mercato del credito in età moderna. Reti e operatori finanziari nello spazio europeo*, Milan, Franco Angeli, 2010, pp. 239–257.

De Maddalena, Aldo, "Osservazioni sulle realtà socio-economiche milanesi in età borromaica", in *S. Carlo e il suo tempo. Atti del Convegno Internazionale nel IV Centenario della morte*, Rome, Edizioni di Storia e Letteratura, 1986, pp. 785–803.

——, "Tra seta, oro e argento a Milano a mezzo il Cinquecento", in A. De Maddalena, *Dalla città al Borgo. Avvio di una metamorfosi economia e sociale nella Lombardia spagnola*, Milan, Franco Angeli, 1982, pp. 46–64.

De Roover, Raymond, *L'évolution de la lettre de change (XIVᵉ–XVIIIᵉ siècles)*, Paris, S.E.V.P.E.N., 1953.

——, "New interpretations of the History of Banking", in Julius Kirshner (ed.), *Business, Banking, and Economic Thought in Late Medieval and Early Modern Europe*, Chicago & London, The University of Chicago Press, 1974, 200–238.

Del Vigo, Abelardo, *Cambistas, mercaderes y banqueros en el Siglo de Oro Español*, Madrid, Biblioteca de autores cristianos, 1997.

Delumeau, Jean, *Vie économique et sociale de Rome dans la seconde moitié du XVI siècle*, Paris, De Boccard, 1959.

Farolfi, Bernardino, "Brokers and Brokerage in Bologna from the Sixteenth to the Nineteenth Century" in A. Guenzi, P. Massa and F. Piola Caselli (eds.), *Guilds, Markets and Work Regulations in Italy, 16th–19th Centuries*, Aldershot, Ashgate, 1998, pp. 306–22.

Fernández Albaladejo, Pablo, *De «llave de Italia» a «corazón de la monarquía»: Milán y la monarquía catolica en el reinado de Felipe III*, in P. Fernández Albaladejo (ed.), *Fragmentos de Monarquía. Trabajos de historia política*, Madrid, Alianza, 1992, 185–237.

Goodman, J., "Financing Pre-Modern European Industry: an Example from Florence", *The Journal of European Economic History*, 1994, XXIII, 3, pp. 415–435.

Gorla, Carlo, "Il padre Francesco Adorno S. J.", in *San Carlo nel terzo centenario della canonizzazione*, Milan, A. Bertarelli, 1910, 529–531.

Lapeyre, Henri, "La banque, les changes et le credit en Italie du XVII au XVIIIe siècle", *Revue d'histoire moderne et contemporaine*, 1961, VIII, 3.

——, *Simón Ruiz et les "asientos" de Philippe II*, Paris, A. Colin, 1953.

Malanima, Paolo, *La decadenza di un'economia cittadina. L'industria di Firenze nei secoli XVI–XVII*, Bologna, Il Mulino, 1982.

Mandich, Giulio, *Le Pacte de Ricorsa et le marché italien des changes au XVIIe siècle*, Paris, A. Colin, 1953.

Marcora, Carlo (ed.), *Lettere del cardinale Federico Borromeo ai familiari 1579–1599*, 2 vols., Milan, L'ariete, 1971.

Marsilio, Claudio, *Dove il denaro fa denaro: gli operatori finanziari genovesi nelle fiere di cambio del 17 secolo*, Novi Ligure, Città del silenzio, 2008.

Moioli, Angelo, *La gelsi bachicoltura nelle campagne lombarde dal Seicento alla prima metà dell'Ottocento. I: La diffusione del gelso e la crescita produttiva della sericoltura*, Trento, Libera università degli studi di Trento, 1981.

Muldrew, Craig, "Interpreting the Market: the Ethics of Credit and Community Relations in Early Modern England", *Social History*, 1993, 18, pp. 163–183.

Nuccio, Oscar, *Il pensiero economico italiano*, II, 2, *Le fonti, 1450–1750. Dall'umanesimo economico all'economia galileiana*, Sassari, Gallizzi, 1992.

Parker, Geoffrey, *The Army of Flanders and the Spanish Road (1567–1659). The logistics of Spanish Victory and Defeat in the Low Countries' War*, London, Cambridge University Press, 1972.

Petronio, Ugo, *Il denaro è una merce. Il prestito ad interesse tra fisiocrazia e codificazione*, in *A Ennio Cortese*, Rome, Il Cigno Edizioni, 2001, v. III, pp. 98–126.

Pezzolo, Luciano, "Government Debt and Trust. French Kings and Roman Popes as Borrowers, 1520–1660", *Rivista di storia economica*, 1999, 15:3, pp. 233–263.

Prodi, Paolo, "Operazioni finanziarie presso la corte romana di un uomo d'affari milanese nel 1562–63", *Rivista storica italiana*, 1961, 73:3, pp. 641–659.

Ripa, Cesare, *Iconologia*, a cura di P. Buscaroli, Milan, Editori Associati, 1992.

Romani, Marzio Achille, *La finanza pubblica dei Ducati padani in tempo di carestia (1590–1630)* in A. Di Vittorio (ed.), *La finanza pubblica in età di crisi*, Bari, Cacucci Editore, 1993.

Ruiz Martín, Felipe, *Demanda y oferta banacarias (1450–1660)* in *Histoire économique du monde Méditerranéen*, 1450–1650, Toulouse, Privat, 1973, pp. 521–536.

Salomoni, Angelo (ed.), *Memorie storico-diplomatiche degli ambasciatori, incaricati d'affari, corrispondenti, e delegati, che la città di Milano inviò a diversi suoi principi dal 1500 al 1796*, Milan, Dalla tipografia Pulini al Bocchetto, 1806.

Sanz Ayán, Carmen, *Los banqueros de Carlos II*, Valladolid, Universidad de Valladolid, 1989.

Savelli, Rodolfo, "Giuristi, denari e monti. Percorsi di lettura tra '500 e '700", in G. Adani, P. Prodi (eds.), *Il Santo Monte di Pietà e la Cassa di Risparmio in Reggio Emilia. Cinque secoli di vita e di promozione economica e civile*, Reggio Emilia, Cassa di Risparmio, 1994, pp. 65–89.

——, "In tema di storia della cultura giuridica moderna: 'strade maestre' e 'sentieri dimenticati'", in L. Garofalo (ed.), *Scopi e metodi della storia del diritto e formazione del giurista europeo*, Naples, Jovene, 2007, pp. 95–160.

Sella, Domenico, *L'economia della Lombardia spagnola*, Bologna, Il Mulino, 1982.

Sommervogel, Carlos (ed.), *Bibliothèque de la Compagnie de Jésus*, vol. III, *Bibliographie*, Mansfield, Martino, 1998 [1890–1909].

Trevor Roper, Hugh Redwald, *Protestantesimo e trasformazione sociale*, Bari, Laterza, 1969.

Vigo, Giovanni, *Finanza pubblica e pressione fiscale nello Stato di Milano durante il secolo XVI*, Milan, Banca Commerciale Italiana, 1979.

Visible Signs of Belonging

8

The Spanish Empire and the Rise of Racial Logics in the Early Modern Period

Jean-Paul Zúñiga

In 1696, the President of the Royal Court (Real Audiencia) of Guadalajara in New Galicia (present-day Mexico) complied with a pressing request it had received from the monarch. Concerned with a case that had gone to trial sometime around 1688, it involved an individual described as "*morisco de nación*," who had acted as a witness. When reports regarding this trial reached Madrid, the officials of the council of Indies demonstrated their amazement: how had a man described as a Christian of Muslim origin been able to travel to the Indies despite all royal provisions, which sought to safeguard the Americas from the kinds of heresy that these sorts of men were likely to transmit? The King immediately ordered that this witness be located and that, once the circumstances surrounding his presence in America were elucidated, he should immediately be banished from the New World.

Obviously embarrassed, the royal judges of Guadalajara answered that there had been an unfortunate misunderstanding: Contrary to Spain, in New Galicia, the term *Morisco* had nothing to do with Muslims. It designated "*vulgarly and in an unsuitable [and] abusive way*" a child who was born "*to a Spaniard and a white mulatto*".[1]

The conversation taking place between Madrid and Guadalajara illustrated divergent semantic developments of local forms of Spanish, but it also provides a metaphorical short-cut into the internal organisational complexities of the gigantic Spanish empire. Like the documents produced by the local legal administrations, men who travelled the length and breadth of the empire also had to face constantly this kind of incomprehension. Despite these difficulties, men did travel. Though it was probably not common to circumnavigate the world twice as the Franciscan friar Martin de Loyola did at the end of the sixteenth century, by that time crossing the Ocean had become a relatively trivial endeavour. "One more jump", as one colonist in New Spain explained in 1566, comparing his Atlantic journey to the road trip from Arjona to Seville.[2]

Mobility of men was the very condition for the existence of the Hispanic monarchy as a body politic. Individual circulation was simultaneously a vector of imperial construction, and a guarantor of its permanence. This was all the more crucial given that the so-called "territorial power" of the Spanish Empire was largely an "insular" reality, which consisted of a reticular complex of cities, each constituting a dense yet isolated core responsible for controlling a vast hinterland. These urban centres were linked to one another by land and maritime routes, which traversed immense spaces where the power of the monarch and his viceroys was only virtual.

This atomised structure enabled relatively few persons to plausibly act as agents of an intercontinental sovereignty.[3] Yet it also led to some paradoxical effects. For if atomisation entailed certain forms of segmentation,[4] human mobility on this scale had broadly homogenising consequences. This relative uniformity, however, did not in any way correspond to a centralised vision of the Empire. If on the one hand the restricted number of individuals in circulation guaranteed a certain homogeneity in administrative and juridical practices, as well as in cultural representations, on the other, these same individuals simultaneously functioned as vectors that could disseminate local variations of more general practices on a continental, or even an imperial, scale.

From one end of the realm to another, the specific experiences of each of the various components interacted and thus informed the shape and structure of the whole concerning administrative culture, agricultural[5] and alimentary practices,[6] people's *imaginaires*,[7] and erudite debates. As a result, local and imperial levels were intrinsically interlocked. The same was true at the level of the empire itself, for the empire did not establish itself as a purely self-referring political structure, but was, on the contrary, determined and over-determined by multiple superimposed layers of interaction, both convergent and polarising, between the different geographical and political spaces among which it existed.[8]

How can we give a successful account of this generalised entanglement? Connected history, with its insistence on circulation (of ideas, notions, models . . .), certainly constitutes a plausible answer, making it possible to challenge the perception that treats cultural and political bodies as discrete entities.[9] Yet, the epistemological move to include circulatory movement in historical analysis leaves many problems unresolved. One is the need for the social contextualisation of any historical event, and thus also of any circulation of any kind (demographic, intellectual, commercial . . .). For no circulation is ever random. On the contrary, it is always determined by a series of cultural, geographical and/or economic circumstances, as well as by specific power relations. All these parameters serve to qualify the various types of *circulation*, while their frequency translates what we might call its "density".[10] Among all the possible and actual connections, the direction, the quantity and the density of existing links determines which zones would be interconnected, and these, in turn, reveal the existence of areas of negotiation and exchange, which are likely to constitute a suitable historical field of study.

This present contribution, which is only the outline of a more substantial work currently in progress, aims to combine an interest in circulatory movements with a concern for their contextualisation. We will consider these questions by examining the emergence of a particular iconographic genre in New Spain, the *"castas"* paintings. These iconographical representations of *"castas"* — or *mixed-blood individuals* — appeared in a specific area, namely the central Mexican highlands, during the first third of the eighteenth century. Rather than observing the "imperial" Hispanic space, the Hispanic-American space, or New Spain as a whole, I will therefore center my attention at a singular aspect of the socio-cultural reality of New-Spain. This approach, albeit "narrowly" situated, will allow me to reconcile the necessity of considering the multiple connections in which any social phenomenon is entangled, with the inescapable contextualisation that understanding it requires.

Phenotype and Representation: New-Spain in the Eighteenth Century

The Audiencia of Guadalajara case, cited above, constitutes a kind of *a posteriori* marker of a lexicographical phenomenon, which accompanied the appearance of a number of new human phenotypes in the Indies. This prolific lexicon provided a more specific content to the generic designation *"castas"*, which was simultaneously spreading in parochial documentation and notarial acts all over Spanish America, and which remained in usage until the beginning of the nineteenth century. The term *casta* initially referred to lineage or extraction.[11] Yet, if in the beginning it was used to indicate the origin of the non-European — *a black 'de casta Angola'*, for example — it quickly came to be used as a blanket term designating all non-Europeans, and more particularly the "new generations of men" that were to be found in the Americas and that very soon invaded not only the colonies but also the colonial documentary record.[12] In addition to European settlers, more than 36,000 African slaves may have been introduced into New Spain between 1521 and 1594, of which 8,000 were destined for Mexico City alone.[13] As early as 1605 in the opinion of one cleric, the capital of New Spain counted no less than twelve thousand slaves and four thousand free blacks.[14] It is out of the sexual relations, forced or voluntary, in which women and men of various origins were engaged, that a number of new American phenotypes were produced and were given specific names.

Juarez, Juan Rodriguez (1675–1728), *Mulatto and Mestiza produce a Mulatto Return-Backwards,* c.1715 (oil on canvas), Breamore House, Hampshire, UK / The Bridgeman Art Library.

Around 1711 (that is, almost twenty years after the "morisco" episode reported above happened), viceroy Fernando de Alencastre, duke of Linares, commissioned a series of sixteen paintings from Juan Rodriguez Juárez. The paintings were meant to show the king of Spain the diversity of the physical types found in New Spain.[15] They inaugurated what thereafter became the canonical form of this pictorial genre: each painting presented side by side a man and a woman of different complexion, with their child standing between them. Legends supplemented the paintings, specifying the precise designations reserved for each of the represented phenotypes.[16]

Other series followed, including some, such as the one painted by Luis Berrueco, in which a single panel was divided into 16 sub-panels (a formal disposition known as a *lienzo de cuadretes*), each presenting a phenotype and the term corresponding to it.[18] Although other well-known painters of New Spain, such as Miguel Cabrera (in 1763), Jose Joaquin Magón (in 1770),[19] or Andrés de Islas (in 1774), also produced comparable works, the genre also boasted a plethora of anonymous paintings, all displaying quite similar iconographic and textual arguments. This relative homogeneity was probably linked to the proximity between their places of production, which were concentrated in the Mexico City–Puebla region. Indeed, out of more than one hundred *casta* painting-series that have been catalogued to date,[20] all but one came from this region of New-Spain. The exception is an anonymous set painted in Peru in 1770 and commissioned by the viceroy Juan de Amat y Junyent, who wished to send it to Spain to enrich the prince of Asturias' natural history cabinet.[21]

These series of paintings included a rather wide range of classificatory categories (between 16 and twenty types of "mixture" were listed). As was noted more than thirty years ago by Isidoro Moreno and Juan Comas, none was identical to the other, all varying from region to region and artist to artist. [22]

Since the beginning of the 1980s,[26] *casta* images became a constant focus of scholarly interest.[27] One of the most striking features of this in-depth, even erudite production is that while it never extends its range of reference beyond the examples found in New Spain — in itself a logical and legitimate methodology, given the nature of the corpus — it nevertheless generalises its conclusions to the whole "Hispanic colonial world" — a move which is much less clearly justified. This bias on the part of contemporary scholars may well be the result of an equivalent bias in the vision of the painters themselves (or those who commissioned their work). Didn't José Joaquin Magón entitle the first painting of his series *Calidades que de la mescla de Españoles, Negros & Yndias, proceden en la América, y son como se siguen por los numeros*, thus confidently extending the classificatory system he wanted to display to the whole of the continent?[28] To this pre-existing bias, recent historiography often added another, namely translating the perception that 18th-century people had of the phenotypical differences between human beings into "race".[29] Yet, the supposed equivalence between "race" and skin colour is postulated rather than demonstrated. Furthermore, using this apparently simple and "obvious" grid to read *casta* iconography prevents us from understanding what exactly was at stake in the production of this type of representations.[30]

Both formal and conceptual elements link *casta* imagery to several wider debates. For if the notion of *casta* was deeply rooted in New Spain's colonial milieu, the conceptual tools that it deployed in order to give an account of that context were the result of the sedimentation of multiple layers of reference. Thus, as shown by the use of the term *morisco*, *castas'* vocabulary mixed nobiliary ideas of blood with botanical lexicon

New Spain *Castas* , Joaquin Magon (1770) series[23]	Anonymous panel « *a cuadretes* », Museo del Virreinato (18th century)[24]	Peruvian *Castas,* anonymous « viceroy Amat » series (1770)[25]
1. De Español e Yndia nace Mestiza	1. Español con India, Mestizo	1 Yndios Infieles de Montaña
2. Español y Mestiza producen Castiza	2. Mestizo con Española, Castizo	2. Yndios Serranos Tributarios Civilizados
3. De Español y Castiza torna a Español	3. Castizo con Española, Española	3. Español, Yndia Serrana o Civilizada produce Mestiso
4. De Español y Negra sale Mulato	4. Español con Mora, Mulato	4. Mestizo, Mestiza, Mestiza
5. De Español y Mulata sale Morisca	5. Mulato con Española, Morisco	5. Español, Mestiza producen Quarterona de Mestizo
6. De Morisco y Española sale Albina	6. Morisco con Española, Chino	6. Quarterona de Mestizo, Español producen Quinterona de Mestizo
7. De Albino y Española lo que nace Tornaatrás	7. Chino con India, Salta atrás	7. Español con Quinterona de Mestizo producen Español o Requinteron de Mestizo
8. Mulato e Yndia engendran Calpamulato	8. Salta atrás con Mulata, Lobo	8. Negros bozales de Guinea, Ydem
9. De Calpamulato e Yndia sale Givaro	9. Lobo con China, Gíbaro	9. Negra de Guinea o criolla, Español Producen Mulatos
10. De Negro e Yndia sale Lobo	10. Gíbaro con Mulata, Albarazado	10. Mulata y Mulato producen Mulato
11. De Lobo e Yndia sale Cambuja	11. Albarazado con Negra, Canbujo	11. Mulata con Español Produsen Quarteron de Mulato
12. De Yndio y Cambuja sale Sambahiga	12. Cambujo con India, Sanbaigo	12. Español, Quarterona de Mulato produce Quinterona de Mulato
13. De Mulato y Mestiza nace Cuarteron	13. Sanbaigo con Loba, Calpamulato	13. Quinterona de Mulato, Español, Requinterona de Mulato
14. De Cuarteron y Mestiza, Coyote	14. Calpamulato con Canbuja, Tente en el aire	14. Español, Requinterona de Mulato, Produce Gente blanca
15. De Coyote y Morisca naze Albarazado	15. Tente en el aire con Mulata, No te entiendo	15. Español Gente blanca Quasi limpios desu Origen
16. De Albarazado y Salta atrás, sale Tente en el Aire	16. Noteentiendo con India, Torna atrás	16. Mestizo con Yndia Producen Cholo
		17. Yndia con Mulato Producen Chinos
		18. Español, China produce Quarteron de Chino
		19. Negro com Yndia produsen Sambo de Yndio
		20. Negro con Mulata Produce Sambo

regarding the hybridisation of stocks, theological considerations, and phenotypical observations. *Casta* ideology was thus located at the centre of a genuine maelstrom of circulations (of men, of models, and of ideas), which in themselves already raise a great many epistemological issues. For this genre was only one among many ways of apprehending reality and producing knowledge. The task of analysing the environment in which such situated knowledge was produced, and the mental tools that characterised the societies which gave birth to it, still remains to be done.[31] The present essay seeks to suggest, albeit briefly, some of the ways in which this larger task might be pursued usefully.

Social Circulations: from Trade Categories to Learned Opinions?

The importance of Mesoamerican cultural legacy has often led scholars to neglect the weight of African deportees' experience in New Spain's historical and cultural development. Yet, both the geographical location of the Mexican plateau and the lexicographical characteristics of *casta* designations clearly indicated a close relationship between slavery and the phenotypical nomenclature of *casta* imagery. This link was, in the first place, a human connection, as demonstrated by the early presence of slaves of African descent in Mexico City. Since the European Middle Ages, enslaved persons were generally identified in slave markets by their physical appearance and, primarily, their skin colour.[32] A series of chromatic terms were used to designate such individuals in both Iberian and Italian legal documents. *Negro, blanco, olivastro, loro, color de membrillo cocido* (or *cocho*) were some of the most common terms.[33]

This method for describing slaves coexisted with another frame of reference, which pointed to genealogy. Its goal was to assert the *quality* of individuals, making full use of the aristocratic vocabulary of lineage and blood. This language, in full development since the end of the fourteenth century, has been studied by Roberto Bizzochi for Italy and Arlette Jouanna for France.[34] According to its logic, lineage, expressed in terms of genealogical quarters or degrees, determined the quality of individuals. The imprint of this conception in the Americas was clearly expressed by such neologisms as *cuarterón*, which was used by both Inca Garcilaso and in the anonymous Peruvian series. Indeed, genealogical designations were widely held and deployed: the Jesuit priest José Gumilla correctly pointed out that since the seventeenth century, the Church itself had required clerics to classify their congregations in the Americas according to them in order to determine who could benefit from canonical exemptions, which Amerindian neophytes enjoyed.[35] As a result, genealogical reasoning was used in order to establish the group to which individuals belonged.[36]

Complexion and ascent were thus both present in *casta* nomenclature and, in fact, the genealogical criterion merged and became confused with the phenotypical appraisal of the individual, producing an intimate fusion, of which *casta* imagery was a good example. In other words, in common practice, each label functioned as a way of providing a genealogical explanation for the *observed phenotype*: each label, thus, strictly speaking, designated a physical appearance rather than a genealogy.[37] This was why the Jesuit priest Alonso de Sandoval could use the terms, which according to the logic of *casta* nomenclature should be reserved for specific genealogies, to describe the *skin colour* of the Fulbé of Equatorial Africa. Evoking the existence of Fulbé who were light-skinned and fair-haired, Sandoval specified that these individuals were never captured or enslaved, which was why *"solo vemos aca los Fulos negros, amulatados, o del todo mulatos, pardos, zambos, de color bazo, loro, castaño, o tostado, por que toda esta variedad, y mucha mas de colores tiene esta nacion entresi, y aun tambien todas las naciones de negros que hemos referido".*[38]

The same logic applied to Francisco Castellanos, the *"morisco"* from Guadalajara, mentioned above. He was designated as *morisco* because of his skin colour, for while he was the son of a Spaniard and a *mestizo* woman, he was of a very dark complexion. As one of the witnesses questioned by the judges of the Audiencia of Guadalajara stated:

> dixo [. . .] que en este Rno. a los hixos de español y mestisa como lo es el dho fran⁰. Castellanos llaman tres albos, no moriscos, porque este nombre se da solo a los hixos de español y Mulata blanca pero que según el color del susodho bien puede ser que en alguna ocasión se haya padesido el equi-boco de tenerle por morisco . . . [39]

Despite the rhetorical articulation of these explanations, which stressed a genealogical logic, it was clearly the physical appearance of Francisco which prevailed and explained why he was described as *"morisco"*.[40] The appraisal of skin colour was a highly subjective process that referred to individual criteria and was, by definition, relative, among other things, because it depended on the position of the person who established it.[41]

One of the most noticeable elements in this synthesis between genealogical language and physical appearance was the obvious vernacular character of all classi-fications. This was demonstrated in the great variety of labels that were in use in different regions in both New Spain (and more globally, in Spanish America).[42] It implied that each terminology was shaped and structured by a distinctive local prac-tice.[43] The very character of this lexicon –vernacular, abundant, and familiar (all classificatory terms had a pejorative, or a mocking, connotation)– probably explained its belated and timid appearance in legal and notarial documents. Indeed, the court case in which Francisco was classified as *morisco* probably took place long after that term had been coined. Moreover, the "exceptionality" of its use in a legal context was emphasised by the magistrates, who used the adjectives "vulgar", "unsuitable" and "abusive" to explain what it meant (and to clear themselves?).[44]

The misunderstandings which resulted from the use of this new vocabulary also demonstrated that classification never constituted a grid — even less a "system" — that was applied by the colonial administration. Nor was it used to establish the rights and duties of individuals and "castes".[45] In this respect, the various — and vain — attempts to impose a differentiated taxation on each *casta*,[46] which were often invoked as examples of the administrative use of colonial phenotypical categorisation, in fact revealed that the colonial administration mentioned *castas* only in a very general way, never referencing a specific one. Laws would mention the "castas" as a whole (i.e. *"negros, mulatos y mestizos"*), or would at most identify those of servile origin. From a legal point of view, in short, the internal diversity of "the plebs" was quite irrelevant.[47] The only categorisation among non-Hispanics that mattered in some ways, for eccle-siastical ends, for instance, was the one separating Indians from non-Indians and, among the latter, free from unfree individuals, regardless of their complexion.[48] The transition from vernacular to official language bumped then into the abounding character of the casta-lexicon. Indeed, another element of social circulation were attempts at adopting and organising the "disorder" implied by the existence of various local practices of categorising individuals into a whole that would be both coherent and hierarchically ordered.

A Dream of Order

These learned translations of everyday practices — which can be traced in the form of the *Lienzo de cuadretes* itself, which is reminiscent of a curiosity cabinet — testify to the constitution of a body of colonial knowledge. This lore was shared and understood by the inhabitants of the Castilian Indies, whatever their origin or social position, and whatever the specific variations of these representations in different regions and/or social contexts were.

Most authors consider *castas* paintings were intended to restore order in a society that was becoming increasingly complex, perhaps chaotic. While this traditional interpretation remains plausible, we may legitimately question whether this phenomenon can be adequately accounted for by any single explanation. As historians of art have clearly shown, *castas* iconography, like any cultural product, was prone to differentiated reception. Indeed, we may well wonder from which point of view we should approach it: from that of a well-to-do public figure who commissioned one of them, such as the bishop Lorenzana, or from that of the Zapotec painter himself, Miguel Cabrera, who came from a more modest milieu? But even different members of the Creole elites could interpret these paintings in different ways that could be complimentary or contradictory to each other. In the first place, these paintings were a way of fuelling a number of debates in which those elites were engaged, by providing them with visual and textual arguments. For example, one major question at that time was the status owed to colonial patriciates, which regularly restaked their claims to nobility. Since the sixteenth century, New Spain's upper strata had expressed its social supremacy by means of a nobiliary terminology: were they not very often the heirs of the conquerors and *encomenderos,* a claim that Creoles translated as "*señores de vasallos*"? This attitude explained the strong reference to "blood" and genealogy in the imaginary organisation of the social body proposed by *casta* iconography. The specifically colonial character of this "nobility" nevertheless resided in the fact that it tended to merge with a certain phenotype. In the absence of any estates — the figure of the *pechero* did not exist in the Indies — a "Spanish" light complexion became one of the principal criteria indicating "noble birth". This peculiarity did not fail to scandalise a Castilian *hidalgo* like Antonio de Ulloa when he visited Peru. He described this American drift as an aberration — *un abuso* — and his emotions were obviously still quite raw when he reported, with shock, how, by the sole fact of having been born in Europe, servants would be invited by high-ranking Creoles to sit at their tables, side by side with their own masters![49]

Along with this nobiliary reading, *casta* imagery can also be interpreted as a Creole radical affirmation of the primacy of the *nación* over the *patria*, that is to say, of the stock over the land of origin. If this claim — quality is transmitted by filiation — was nothing but a restatement of the core beliefs of nobiliary "innatism", stressing on people's complexion added a particular quality to it. What the alchemy of bloodlines performed by *casta* iconography ultimately defended was the belief that, whatever their native land was, descendants of a Spanish father and a Spanish mother were Spanish. This position corresponded to what Creoles claimed ever since the sixteenth century, against all those who pretended that the natural environment of the New World had transformed Creoles, making them *ontologically* different from their European ancestors as Friar Jerónimo de Mendieta in 1560, Juan López de Velasco in 1574, Friar Bernardino de Sahagún at the end of the 1570s, and Juan de la Puente in 1612, to cite only the best known examples, asserted, arguing that Spaniards born in the Indies were subject to an inevitable process of degeneration.[50]

Finally, careful observation of the various classifications that were produced using both iconographic and textual evidence allows to detect another extremely important element, which has often passed unnoticed or been interpreted in an univocal way.[51] This was the iconographic "demonstration" that the "mixture of bloods" could be "washed". Thus, in a certain number of series of paintings, repeated contributions made by Spanish spouses eventually lead to the lineage reverting to the label "Spaniard". This assertion seemed to respond to the scorn of Creoles, expressed by certain "Peninsulars", who were just as much imbued with genealogical spirit as their compatriots overseas, calling them *champurros* ("adulterated"!).[52]

These questions, although local because referencing certain issues specific to New Spain's Creoles, whose genealogies often went back to an Amerindian past, was at the same time entangled in a number of much more wide-ranging discussions. Preoccupation with "mixture of bloods", for example, was also found in the French Antilles, where it constituted a leitmotiv and a grid of analysis used to account for the various human types that could be observed there. If, as early as 1658, father Jean Baptiste du Tertre had described the Antilles' population as composed of *Indiens, françoys, noirs* and *mulâtres*,[53] the most eloquent observer was probably Médéric Moreau de Saint Méry who, at the end of the eighteenth century argued that that the various colonial "combinations" or "mixtures" existing on the island constituted a set of thirteen "shades", each with a specific name: *Blanc, Noir, mulâtre, quarteron, Métif, mamelouc, quarteronné, sang-mêlé, sacatra, griffe, marabou, Indiens caraïbes ou occidentaux, Indiens Orientaux*.[54]

One of the questions raised by both Moreau de Saint Méry and the *Castas* imagery was whether the "mixture of bloods" could be "undone" by means of successive "blood contributions", thus guaranteeing the return to one of its original stocks. This issue was probably what motivated these representations, and was far more important than any preoccupation with determining precisely the name that should be applied to each phenotype, which was, by Moreau's own admission, an impossible goal.[55] Other contemporaries, dealing with the same subject, systematically ended up discussing these very same issues. When around 1720 the Royal Academy of Sciences in Paris requested its correspondent in Martinique, Laurenceau de Hauterive, for information about the names of various phenotypes involving offspring of European and African parents, Hauterive, who was a local Creole demonstrated more interest in the issue of the possible reversion of these lineages to "white" or "black" stock, than in any of the linguistic subtleties used to designate them.[56] His remarks were in this respect very close to those of Father Labat.[57] This was also at the core of the genealogical hierarchies proposed by the Spanish Jesuit José Gumilla in the 1740s, and of the *Peruano's* remarks in the *Description* of Lima of 1770, quoted above. In the latter, the *Peruano* explained this "returning mechanism" by using the image of a glass of red wine into which clear water was steadily poured. The liquid gradually became more and more transparent and limpid, until it looked as if the glass had never contained anything other than water! [58]

This "continuum mechanism" was directly linked to the problem raised by the apparent contradiction between the Christian dogma of the common origin of all mankind and the evidence of human physical diversity. The passage (*"transfiguración,"* using *Peruano*'s own terms) from one appearance to the other over the course of generations was indeed one way of surmounting what some liked to present as a fundamental and insuperable difference.[59] It was within the context of this discussion — on the origin of the various colours characterising men and, in particular, black men — that Moreau de Saint Méry took care to situate his remarks.[60] Yet, behind their apparent banality, these arguments were the reflection of deep changes in the way in which individuals' place in society and in the world was understood. They were thus part of a greater debate which engaged people far beyond Creole circles in the Antilles and New Spain.

From Image to Text and from Text to Image

Contrary to what is often advanced concerning the *castas* representations, the question they raised were not specific to the eighteenth century. If the *Novohispano* pictorial genre as I have described it did date from that period, its underlying theoretical basis derived from a huge set of texts and images reciprocally connected to and informing one another which could be traced back as far as the early sixteenth century. Far from being anecdotal, the recourse to textual inscriptions in all of *castas* paintings indicated the strong dependency between image and text that characterised its iconographic program.[61] This fact justifies reading *casta* imagery in the light of contemporary texts dealing with such notions as caste, nation, colour or quality, often in the same terms redeployed by artists.

From the first third of the sixteenth century onwards, the Portuguese in India and in Brazil had made common use of the terms *mestiço*, *mameluco* and *mulato*, and had also written about these concepts at some length. Proofs therefore points to the fact that these terms first appeared in the Portuguese world, and then spread outwards, moving from one language to another.[62] If, as early as 1524, Cristovão Vieira mentioned *mulatos*,[63] Hispanic documentation soon followed suit, mentioning them from the 1530s on. In 1544, Jean Alfonse used this term in French, and so did Filippo Sassetti in Italian (1580) followed by Francesco Carletti and Filippo Pigafetta in the 1590s.[64]

In addition to the use of this term in accounts, which were not published at the time, a great number of published narratives in Castilian, Portuguese, French, Dutch, and English, which were widely influential, also referred to it. By the middle of the seventeenth century there was a considerable mass of such texts; when Melchisédech Thévenot published his collection in 1663, he had accumulated a list of more than 290 manuscripts, a feat which exemplified the wide dissemination and intense interest aroused by this literature.[65] In all these narratives, and in those dealing with Spanish America in particular, the chapter on "cross-breeding" became an obligatory passage. Thomas Gage's *Relation*, which bore this subject in its very title, was but one late example of this persistent interest.[66]

These texts were usually accompanied by images, which were intended to express in visual terms the many wonders and curiosities which they contained. The very nature of this broad textual and iconographic field, and of its supports — books, paintings, and engravings — meant that it was highly mobile. From one continent to another, from one support to another, it constituted a distinct corpus, which can be considered as a whole, whatever the particular origin of its individual elements were. For this prolific intertextuality cared little for the linguistic and political borders of the time. Thus, if the words *white, black, mulatto, mongrel* or *pardo* first appeared in texts referring to Africa and India and then in texts about America, from the seventeenth century onwards, the Brazilian term *cafuz* or *cafuzo* can be found in narratives about Angola.[67] Not to mention such labels as *cabra* or *mamelouc*, whose geography was truly intercontinental.[68]

Iconographic representations followed similar patterns of circulation. The engravings illustrating Willem Lodewiccz's *Premier livre de l'histoire de la navigation* (1598)[69] (on India), or those in Pieter de Marées' *Description et récit historial du riche royaume de Guinea* of 1605, describing the fauna, the flora and the people inhabiting these regions,[70] were therefore a necessary precedent to understand later paintings, like those of Albert Eckhout in 17th-century Dutch Brazil. In his work (1637), Eckhout strove to make Brazilian nature visible.[71] Alongside the descriptions he gave of fruits, trees and cities, Eckhout devoted a series of paintings to the black slaves, the Tapuya Indians, and the "specific [human] characters" of the New World, such as the *mulâtre* and the *"cabocla"*.[72] This juxtaposition of Brazil's tropical nature, its people and its crafts, both African and local, within the same compositions, irresistibly evoked certain characteristics that would distinguish New Spain *castas* imagery more than a century later.

Texts and images generated throughout the sixteenth and seventeenth centuries thus firmly established both an analytical grid and a semantic and semiological field to which eighteenth century *castas* paintings were heirs. By the last third of the eighteenth century, at the moment when Miguel Cabrera, Jose Joaquin Magón and Andrés de Islas were painting their series of New Spain *castas*, the iconographic and textual corpus about human "crossbreeds" had reached a certain chronological and conceptual density.[73] The work of Father Taillandier, William Betagh, Frézier and Ulloa were some examples of the long series of texts and engravings, which repeatedly returned to this subject.[74] But perhaps the best example of this multi-layered richness could be found in Carlos Julião's work in Brazil. Julião's watercolours of 1779 expressed the diversity of the Portuguese empire as seen in the different costumes and various "qualities" of the subjects of the Portuguese monarch. Black, mulattoes, Indians, *mestiços*, *fidalgos* and commoners of Lisbon, Rio, Macau and Goa appeared assembled, but not mingled, within the same images.[75] These representations invoked a number of common referents and suggest interesting conceptual bridges linking dress, complexion and "national" assignation. It is no surprise then, that when the contemporaneous Spanish engraver Juan de la Cruz published in Madrid his costume book *Colección de trajes de España*, the images devoted to America were *castas* representations, reinterpreted for that occasion. The *coleccion* mixed the canonical *novohispano* model with representations of Lima's Creoles and Indian women who recalled the illustrations in Ulloa's *Relacion*,[76] Moreover, as was usually the case, these engravings were sold by the unit at a moderate price,[77] and seemed to have enjoyed great success, to the point that illegal copies were promptly being circulated in both Germany and France.[78] In 1796, it was the turn of the Franco-Canadian author Jacques Grasset de

Saint-Sauveur to merge West-Indian, Canadian and Spanish-American *casta* terminology and imagery in the relevant engravings of his *Encyclopédie des voyages*.[79]

These examples show the broad dissemination of a common *imaginaire*. *Casta*
notions were thus amply mobilised in a range of different pieces of literature, and in
scientific works in particular. Moreover, an important qualitative change had occurred
during the eighteenth century, in which *casta* imagery had also evolved from the status
of a *lieu commun* to the dignity of an evidence to issues such as the origin of Africans'
skin colour, or the inheritance of human physical features. By that time, the Italian
scientist Leopoldo M. A. Caldani mobilised everything he knew about American *castas*
as providing *proof* for the theories he advanced.[80]

The reference to "blood mixture" thus helped fuel the young biological sciences
and reflections on the concept of "generation" in particular.[81] The question of how
new beings were conceived had been an uninterrupted ground of polemics in Western
Europe since the Middle Ages. So was what should be considered as the determining
basis for generation: the paternal blood or seed, or the maternal "cup"? If the idea of
a double "paternal and maternal seed" acting in consort existed at least since
Hippocrates, it constituted only one way of responding to the enigma of reproduction, and it was far from being shared by all. In the eighteenth century, this controversy
opposed in particular the defenders of epigenesis to those maintaining preformationist
views, and among the latter, divided the ovists from the spermists. These controver-
sies, and the stature of the scientists involved,[82] show that a whole range of alternative
explanations existed. Thus, when Frézier and Labat wrote their travel accounts, they
naturally situated their remarks on the New World's *métis* and *mulâtres* in relation to
these debates regarding what an individual owed to each of his maternal and paternal
lines.[83]

Alongside this debate, the influence of the context and/or milieu on the individuals' physical appearance and character, in particular, was also constantly discussed
throughout the early-modern times. The strength of the sun, in particular, was the
most common reason advanced to justify the skin colour of Africans,[84] and although
this argument was increasingly being questioned, it continued to be mobilised
throughout the eighteenth century. Since the sixteenth century, many Spanish authors
held that the constellations prevailing in the American continent and more broadly-
speaking, the climate, were responsible for the qualities and character of its
inhabitants, whatever their origin was.[85] The ideas formulated by López de Velasco
in 16th-century Castile, and taken up by anonymous travellers and missionaries in the
Indies,[86] had their equivalent in other territories, where European sovereignty raised
similar ethnological questions. In James Axtell's terms, the problem of the American
milieu was related to a fear of "backsliding" that was common to all colonial societies.[87]
It constituted the central issue in narratives relating to the captivity of Europeans or
Creoles among non-Europeans.[88]

Seeds, blood, and the environment, were therefore only some of the many arguments that were advanced as plausible explanations for the problem of human
diversity. It must finally be pointed out that since the sixteenth century, the growth of
botany as an intellectual pursuit accompanied the burgeoning study of mankind.
Acclimatisation, species, and "degeneration", were notions familiar to both farmers[89]
and botanists, and were used to think about human nature as well. Far from being
accidental or academic, the presence of botanical diversity in the paintings of Eckhout,
Vicente Alban and Cabrera was thus quite logical.[90] Recourse to botany as a way of

understanding human phenomena could be justified by the fact that botany allowed to carry out experiments that were impossible to conduct on human beings.[91] Yet, in reality, it was often the opposite: for the colonial worlds supplied scientists and scholars of the late seventeenth and eighteenth centuries with a vast open-air laboratory for human experimentation.

Faced with the doubts of certain scientists and philosophers as to whether both male and female stock had a role to play in the production of new individuals, the inhabitants of the Indies could assert that their *experience* proved the fundamental importance of both genders. As J. B. Labat stated:

> Qu'après cela les Medecins nous disent tant qu'ils voudront que les deux sexes ne concourent pas également à la production de l'enfant, & que les femmes sont comme les poules qui naturellement ont des œufs dans le corps, & que l'homme comme le cocq ne fait autre chose que les détacher & perfectionner le germe. Car si cela étoit une Negresse feroit toujours des enfans noirs, de telle couleur que pût être le mâle, ce qui est tout-à-fait contraire à l'expérience que nous avons, puisque nous voyons qu'elle fait des noirs avec un noir, & des Mulâtres avec un blanc.[92]

For the people of New Spain, too, the answer was clear: an individual's nature was not determined by his environment, but by his stock. Spaniards did not become Indian by living in the Indies, nor did Africans become white by living in Europe. Something characterised each "sort" of people in an intrinsic way, and the vocabulary of the time expressed this "something" using the words "blood" or "nation". This conviction contributed to the broad controversy on milieu vs. stock, which preoccupied scientific circles on both shores of the Atlantic during this period. Out of this particular circulation of images and ideas, a specific space of knowledge arose.[93] It is therefore revealing that when Immanuel Kant determined for the first time in 1785 the difference between "species" and "race", he did by synthesising different ideas, which circulated at the time, among which the *casta* ideology held a crucial place.[94] Each "*class*" (race) of mankind was, in Kant's view, determined by a "germ" or a specific stock. The capacity to procreate together was what characterised the members of the same species. If the offspring of two parents belonging to the same *class* (race) did not inevitably reproduce their progenitors' physical features (thus, two brown-haired parents could have a fair-haired child), on the contrary, the children of parents who belonged to different groups would necessarily constitute a compromise, as was shown by the *métis* and *mulâtres* of the New World, who inherited half of their character from each of their two parents. According to Kant, it was this "infallible heredity", made manifest in these American hybrids, which both characterised and *revealed* the borders between the races. The Kantian law of "necessarily mixed generation"[95] was thus largely dependent on a detour through the colonial imagination, without which it would have been incomprehensible.

New Spain Casta ideology and imagery are often presented as a "proof" of the existence of racist prejudice well before the appearance of a biological meaning to "race", or as an evidence of the Spanish American cradle of race.[96] I hope to have shown through these lines how misleading and narrow those approaches might be. But beyond the quarrels on "race before race" or the debates on the American or European origin of contemporary racism, in this essay I strove to uncover the background to a major and fascinating development that in the first half of the nineteenth century saw the emergence of a hegemonic paradigm explaining human diversity which, in the space of a few decades, totally submerged the multiplicity of explanations that had preceded it, throughout an area that came to cover the whole of the Western hemisphere. The rapid victory of this new paradigm in both the Catholic and Protestant worlds, in Western Europe and in the New World, indicates that racial thought established itself on an extremely favourable and fertile ground, penetrating like rain into a ground that was already wet. This was perhaps possible because this new ideology was, after all, a new way of expressing an old practice that based on nature cultural and social differences[97] and that was particularly alive in Conquest societies. That there was nothing "genealogical" about these differences did not prevent the constant recourse to extraction, origin and "blood" as a language in which to *express* them, make them understandable and, at the same time, justify them.[98] The re-signification of such old, powerful and largely shared notions as lineage, family, extraction or quality by the new contexts in which they were now used, could therefore account for the rapidly-established hegemony of a racialised vision of history and society on an intercontinental scale. Thus, if *casta* nomenclature demonstrated the strong interconnections that existed across a Caribbean space that extended from the Gulf of Mexico to the Antilles, racial thought, for its part, attested to the high level of integration of another space — one in which erudite elites speaking dissimilar languages and living on different continents shared a common imaginary, largely impregnated by the colonial experience.

Notes

1   AGI Guadalajara, 27, R.1, N° 8. Unnumbered pages.
2   Luis de Córdoba, Puebla (Mexico) settler, to his wife, Isabel Carrera, Feb. 5, 1566. Published in Otte, 1966, 34.
3   On the importance of networks in imperial configurations, see Lester, 2001 and Glaisyer, 2004. On a transnational Chinese community, Wilson, 2004.
4   At the beginning of the 18th Century, Antonio de Ulloa noted the importance of local peculiarities within Spanish America. See Ulloa, 1748, 2e partie, Livre I, chap. V, § 121.
5   As appears from the *De Historia Stirpium* de Leonhardt Fuchs in 1542 and in *Rerum Medicarum Novae Hispaniae* of Francisco Hernandez, written in 1570.
6   On the dissemination of American plants in Spain and its impact on agricultural cycles and alimentary practices see Eiras Roel, 1991; Anes, 1999; Bilbao, Fernandez de Pinedo, 1982; Andrews, 1993 and Zúñiga (forthcoming).
7   Urquizar Herrera, 2009.
8   A matter of "global consciousness", in the words of Chartier, 2001, 119–123.
9   Subrahmanyam, 2005; *idem*, 2007.
10 Zúñiga, 2007.
11 Zúñiga, 1999, 436.
12 The term was then close to the South-African adjective, "coloured". On " *Generaciones* " see Inca Garcilaso [1616], II, chap. 31; Antonio de Bafaras *Origen, costumbres y estado presente de mexicanos y phillipinos* (1763), quoted by Katzew, 1996; and Gregorio de Cangas in his *Descripción*, ff. 42v et 43r. (N.B.: we could examine only the AGI truncated manuscript). The manuscript was published in 1997 on the basis of a full text dating from 1770 that had been discovered in Peru. See Vicente, Lenci, 1997.
13 Cope, 1994, 13–14.
14 AGI, Mexico 294, quoted by Bernand, Gruzinski, 1993, 262.
15 Quoted by Castro Morales, 1983, 679–680.
16 The same year, a member of the Arellano family painted two portraits entitled "*Diceño de mulata yja de negra y español*" and "*Diceño de mulato yjo de negra y español*", but their formal

representation was quite different, as Arellano's paintings each represent a single person, and not a group. See Katzew, 2004, 10 and 11.

17 Reproduction provided in Carrera, 2003, 60.
18 Luis Berrueco's work had been commissioned by Puebla Bishop (1743–1746) Juan Francisco de Loaiza. A reproduction is provided in García Saiz, 1992.
19 Commissioned by Mexico Bishop, Francisco Antonio Lorenzana.
20 María Concepción Garcia Saiz counted 90, but Ilona Katzew's work attested more than 100. García Saiz, 1989; Katzew, 2004.
21 Romero de Tejada (coord.), 2003.
22 Moreno Navarro, 1973; Comas, 1974, 126–130.
23 National Anthropology Museum, Madrid, series by Juan Joaquín Magón, commissioned by Bishop Lorenzana.
24 Reproduced in Gracia, De Greiff, 2000, 53.
25 *Frutas y castas ilustradas*, 2003, 96–135 (Peruvian series); 138–169 (Mexican series).
26 There are studies dating from the first half of the 20th century, in particular Blanchard, 1908; León, 1924; Barras de Aragon, 1929 and 1930; Pérez de Barradas, 1948.
27 Morales, 1983, García Saiz, 1989, Carrera, 2003 and 2009, Katzew, 1996 and 2004, Deans-Smith, 2005, Katzew, Deans-Smith, 2009.
28 My emphasis. See *Frutas y castas ilustradas* (2003), 139.
29 Regarding this conceptual shortcut, Carrera, 2003, chap. I, on "race", lineage and quality.
30 On the undefined character of this notion and the typical recourse to "common sense", Loveman, 1999.
31 In this respect it is worth noting the remarkable contribution of López Beltrán on medical knowledge in early modern New Spain, 2008, 289–342.
32 See for example, though his argument is very different, Forbes, 1988.
33 See Guillén (forthcoming).
34 Bizzochi, 2009 [1995]; Jouanna, 1981. On the emergence of this rhetoric of blood, see also Oschema, 2008.
35 Gumilla, 1791 [1741], 2 vols. The reference is to the papal bull *Animarum saluti*, issued by Innocent XII (March 1690) on the matrimonial privileges granted to the Indians of the Americas.
36 See Lizana, 1919, doc. n° 195, 423; Gumilla, 1791, 74; Guilij, 1784.
37 The words of the *chapetón* in the manuscript fragment "*Descripción*", a dialogue between a "Peruvian" and a "chapetón" (a Spaniard who had just arrived in the Indies), concur: " . . . *veo en [la ciudad de los Reyes] muchos negros, mulatos* y otros colores . . . ", f. 40r. My emphasis.
38 Sandoval de, 1647, volume 1, page 12. My emphasis. See Frankin, 1973, 349–360.
39 AGI Guadalajara, 27, R.1, n° 8. ff. Unnumbered pages.
40 Gregorio de Cangas' *Peruano* clearly states that the commonest way of classifying people was on the basis of their phenotype: "*Muchos hay que, llebados del tratamiento comun de estas gentes, sin consideracion a sus origenes, los reconozen, y nombran negro, Mulato, sambo etc. agrabiando en esto la Justicia de su tal y qual merito . . . *", ff. 43r. On castes as "Clasificacion colorida" based essentially on individuals' skin colour, see Beltrán, 1946, 163, 168–169.
41 On the prevalence of chaos, contradiction and approximation in the attempts by individuals to identify both themselves and others, see in particular Cope, 1994, 51. On the relativity of classifications, see Bonniol, 1990, 410–41.
42 For Venezuelan *llanos* see Gumilla, 1791, 73; for Upper Peru, Caldani, 1799, 48.
43 See for instance the specific use of the term *Tres albos* in the Peruvian context, in Garcilaso, 1617, Book IX, chap. XXXI.
44 On castas as "a product of folklore", see the too rapid but relevant interpretation of Muller-Wuller-Wille & Rheinberger, 2007, 11, note 43.
45 And yet, the expression "casta system" is currently used by anthropologists, art historians

and even by historians as if it was self-evident. See for instance, Cañizares Esguerra, 1999, 33–68; Katzew, 2004, chap. 2 et passim; Voss, 2005, Mazzolini, 2007.

46 Ramos Gómez, Ruigomez Gómez, 1999.

47 See in this connection Cope, 1994. Talking about casta diversity Ulloa states "*ni ellos[casta people] saben discernirlas . . .* ", and the manuscript of the *Descripcion,* for its part, refers to a " *. . . miscelanea quasi inhaveriguable . . .* ". See Ulloa, 1748, livre I, chap. IV, §66; *Descripcion,* ff. 41r.

48 Lima Concile of 1613 ranked *cuarteron, mestizo* and free mulattos in the same category, thus distinguishing them from both black and mulatto slaves, and from free Indians. Del Pino, 2003, 47–48.

49 Ulloa, 1826, Parte II, chap. VI, 420 and ss.

50 Letter of friar Jerónimo de Mendieta [1562], *Cartas de religiosos de la Nueva España,* 1941; López de Velasco 1971 [1574], 19–20; Sahagún, [1570–1582], published by Garibay 1992 [1956], Livre X; De la Puente, 1612, volume 1, 263.

51 Katzew, 2004, 51.

52 Quoted by Castro Morales, 1983, 679–680. Ulloa had the same attitude towards Peruvian creoles. Ulloa, 1826, Parte II, chap. VI, 421.

53 Du Tertre 1667, T.2, Traité VIII, chap. 2, §5, 511.

54 Moreau de Saint Méry, 1875, [1797–98], 93.

55 For Moreau, such distinctions could only be arbitrated on the basis of local practice based on a social consensus, Moreau de Saint Méry, 1875,100.

56 *Histoire de l'Académie Royale des Sciences,* 1724, 17–19.

57 Labat, 1724, 2nd part, in particular chap. VI.

58 Cangas de, f. 43v.

59 Moreau de Saint Méry in particular mentions this demarcation line which, according to some, could be extended "until infinity". Moreau de Saint Méry, 1875, 100.

60 Moreau de Saint Méry, 1875, 103. The nomenclature of both the Spanish American *castas* and the mixed bloods of the French Antilles (with explicit reference to the questions posed by the Paris Academy of Sciences) also constituted an important chapter in the 1777 polemic that opposed Buffon and Cornelius de Pauw. See Buffon, 1777, 502 et seq., as well as the classic study by Gerbi, 1955.

61 See in this connection the comments by Del Pino, 2003, 55.

62 In Spanish, the word *mestizo* appears as early as 1533 in a legal text, but was probably present very much earlier in the spoken language. See Recopilación, book VII, title IV, law IV, f. 284 v. The term "métis" existed in medieval French, but its meaning became more specific under the influence of its Portuguese and Spanish sense in the 16th century.

63 Ferguson, 1902, 69; Cortesão, 1990 [1944], XX et seq. See also Cunha de, 1982.

64 Fonteneau, 1904 [1544], 330; Sasetti, 1855 [1580], 280; Boutier, 1994, 157–166; Pigafetta, 1591, chap. III, 9; Carletti, 1701, 5.

65 Thévenot, 1663.

66 Gage, 1699 [1684]

67 Even if its signified could vary. See Barbeitos, 2008, 67 & ss. The word *Pardo* was also common to Spanish and Portuguese America and to Angola. See De Oliveira de Cadornega, 1972, volume III, 30.

68 The word *cabra/kabla/câpre* was common to Brazil, São Tomé and the French Antilles, with the same meaning (light mulatto or goat). See Rougé, 2004. In Guinea, Casamance and Santiago, *Kabra* was also used to refer to prostitutes. The name *mamelouc,* with changing meanings, but always related to the "mixed-blood" label, was in turn common to both the French Antilles and Brazil.

69 [Lodewicksz], 1598, chap. 30, "*pourtraict des Portuguez Mestiços ou Mulatos demourans en Iava & à Bantam*".

70 De Marees, 1605. The engraving of a " *melato* " women in page 13.

71 See Buvelot, 2004; Parker Brienen, 2006. It's worth noting that Cadornega's *Histoire* used engravings of Angolan warriors *and fruits* as the frontispieces of each of its volumes. See De Oliveira de Cadornega, [1680] 1972.

72 Euro-Amerindian girl. For an excellent catalogue of his work, see Buvelot, 2003.

73 And a strong intertextuality, permitting to wonder if the issue has not become a *topos* inseparable from the genre. See Taillandier, 1715; Pernety, 1769, volume 1, page 150–151, Frezier, 1716, 63.

74 Taillandier [1711], in *Lettres édifiantes*, 1715, p. 119, Betagh, 1728, Frezier, 1716, 55 et 63 in particular; Juan & De Ulloa, 1748, Volume 1, plate 18 and 24.

75 On the Turin-born Carlos Julião, see Hunolf Lara, 2002.

76 De la Cruz Cano y Olmedilla, 1777.

77 "Dos estampas nuevas, ó números 63 y 64 en continuacion del 6° quaderno de castas de América, y coleccion de los trages de España y sus dominios, grabada por D. Juan de la Cruz, Geógrafo de S.M. [. . .] Se hallarán á los precios de 2 y 4 rs. Iluminadas y sin iluminar en casa de Copin carrera de S. Gerónimo." *Gaceta de Madrid*, n° 93, 19.11.1784, 964.

78 As early as 1788, Juan de la Cruz was obliged to add, at the bottom of one of his plates: "*en Francia y Alemania estan copiando esta Colecn sin Gcia alguna vendiendola en nros puertos de mar; esperamos para poder continuarla q. la peninsula q la ha protegido no preferira las contra-hechas*", quoted by Larriba, 2005, note 32.

79 Grasset de Saint Sauver, 1796.

80 Mazzolini, 2007; Caldani, 1799, volume 8, 445–457.

81 Muller-Wille and Rheinberger, 2007.

82 Among others: Malebranche, Von Haller, Spallanzani (ovists), Van Leeuwenhoek, Boerhaave, d'Agoty (spermists), Wolff, Blumenbach (epigenesists).

83 Frezier, 1716. 63, Labat, 1724. chap. VI.

84 François Bernier was clearly opposed to this conception, cf. [Bernier], 1684, 135.

85 Lopez de Velasco, 1574.

86 Father José Lopez to Francisco Borgia [1569], 328–329.

87 Thus Increase Mather complained in 1679: "*Christians in this land, had become too like unto the Indians*". In 1724, his son, Cotton Mather, addressed a letter to a group of physicians who were interested in the climate's influence on people, stating that New Englanders had changed "*as if the climate had taught us to Indianize*", quoted by Axtell, 2001, 310–314.

88 Bauer, vol. 69, n° 4, 1997, 665–695. Linda Cowley also deals, less convincingly, with the same issue. See Cowley 2002.

89 See, for instance, Etienne, 1564, Livre III page 187, (species) and De Serres, 1651 [1600], 601–602 (kinship, decay).

90 Martin Teixeira, De Vries, 2004, 64–107; Carrera, 2003, 88; Santiago Sebastián, 1991, 38.

91 Muller-Wille, 2007, chap. 1.

92 Labat, 1724, chap. VI, 35.

93 Muller-Wille, Rheinberger, 2007, 13.

94 Kant, "Définition du concept de race humaine", [1785] 1981

95 Kant, "Définition du concept de race humaine", [1785] 1981, 94.

96 *Castas* ideology is often considered, in this respect, as the first expression of this racism. On different approaches on this issues, see Sweet, 1997; Cañizares, 1999; Kidd, 2006, Mazzolini, 2007.

97 On Cham's curse as a way of legitimizing the serf's status in medieval times, see Freedman, 1992.

98 On genealogical discourse as "autonomous" language describing social hierarchies (i.e. independent of any plausibility of actual ascent or descent), see Bizzocchi, 2009 [1995].

Bibliography

[Bernier, François], *Nouvelle Division De La Terre, pour les differente Especes ou Races d'hommes qui l'habitent, envoyée par un fameux voyageur à M. l'Abbé de la *****, Journal des Sçavans, XII, 24 avril 1684.

[Lodewicksz Willem] G.M.A.W.L., *Premier livre de l'histoire de la navigation*, Amsterdam, Cornille Nicolas, 1598.

Aguirre Beltrán, Gonzalo, *La población Negra de México*, Mexico, Fondo de Cultura Económica, 1946.

Alvar, Manuel, *Léxico del mestizaje en Hispanoamérica*, Madrid, Ed. Cultura hispánica/Instituto de cooperación iberoamericana, 1987.

Anes, Gonzalo, *Cultivos, cosechas y pastoreo en la España Moderna*, Madrid, Real Academia de la Historia , 1999.

Axtell, James, *Natives and Newcomers. The Cultural Origins of North America*, New York, Oxford University Press, 2001.

Barbeitos, Arlindo, *Angola/Portugal : des identités coloniales équivoques. Historicité des représentations de soi et d'autrui*, Paris, L'Harmattan, 2008.

Barras de Aragón, Francisco de las, «Documentos referentes al envío de cuadros representando mestizajes y varios productos naturales del Perú, hallados en el Archivo de Indias de Sevilla». *Actas y Memorias de la Sociedad Española de Antropología, Etnografía y Prehistoria.* IX/2–3 (1930), pp. 78–81.

——, «Noticias de varios cuadros pintados en el siglo XVIII representando mestizajes y tipos de razas indígenas y algunos casos anormales». *Memorias de la Real Sociedad Española de Historia Natural.* XV/1 (1929), pp. 155–168.

Bauer, Ralph, « Creole identities in Colonial Space : the Narratives of Mary White Rowlandson and Francisco Núñez de Pineda y Bascuñán", *American Literature*, vol. 69, n°4, 1997.

Bernand, Carmen and Serge Gruzinki, *Histoire du Nouveau Monde. Les métissages*, Paris, Fayard, 1993.

Betagh, William, *A Voyage round the world, being an account of a remarkable enterprize begun in the year 1719, chiefly to cruise on the Spaniards in the great South Ocean . . . by William Betagh, captain of marines in that expedition*, London : T. Combes, J. Lacy and J. Clarke, 1728.

Bilbao, Luís María and Emiliano Fernández de Pinedo, "Evolución del producto agrícola bruto en el País Vasco peninsular, 1537–1850. Primera aproximación a través de los diezmos y de la primicia" in Joseph Goy and Emmanuel Le Roy Ladurie, *Prestations paysannes, dîmes, rente foncière et mouvement de la production agricole à l'époque préindustrielle*, Paris, Mouton, V. 1 (1982), pp. 313–327.

Bizzochi, Roberto, *Genealogie incredibili : scritti di storia nell'Europa moderna*, Bologne, Il Mulino, 2009 [1995].

Blanchard, Raphaël, "Les tableaux de métissage au Mexique", *Journal de la Société des Américanistes*, vol. V (1908), pp. 59–66.

Bonniol, Jean-Luc, "La couleur des hommes, principe d'organisation sociale. Le cas antillais", *Ethnologie française*, 1990, T. 20, pp. 410–418.

Boutier, Jean, "Les habits de l'Indiatico'. Filippo Sassetti entre Cochin et Goa (1583–1588)", *Découvertes et explorations. Actes du colloque international* (Bordeaux, June 12–14, 1992), Paris, L'Harmattan, 1994, pp. 157–166.

Buffon, *Histoire naturelle, générale et particulière*, supplément, T.IV, Paris, Imprimerie royale, 1777.

Buvelot, Quentin (ed.), *Albert Eckhout. A Dutch Artist in Brazil*, La Haye-Zwolle, Royal Cabinet of Paintings Mauritshuis/Waanders Publishers, 2004.

Caldani, Leopoldo M. A, "Congetture intorno alle cagioni del vario colore degli Africani, e di altri popoli; e sulla prima origine du questi", in *Memorie di Matematica e Fisica della Societa Italiana*, vol. 8, (1st. part) (1799), pp. 445–457.

Cangas, Gregorio de, ["El Pretendiente"], *Descripcion de los pueblos del Peru*, AGI, Indiferente General, 1528.

Cañizares Esguerra, Jorge, "New World, New Stars: Patriotic Astrology and the Invention of Indian and Creole Bodies in Colonial Spanish America, 1600–1650", *The American Historical Review*, Vol. 104, No. 1 (Feb., 1999), pp. 33–68.

Carletti, Francesco, *Ragionamenti di Francesco Carletti Fiorentino sopra le cose da lui vedute ne' suoi viaggi si dell'Indie Occidentali, e Orientali come d'altri Paesi*, Florence, Giuseppe Mani, 1701.

Carrera, Magali, *Imagining Identity in New Spain*, Austin, University of Texas Press, 2003.

Castro Morales, Efraín, "Los cuadros de castas de la Nueva España", *Jahrbuch für Geschichte von Staat, Wirtschaft und Gesellschaft Lateinamerikas*, no. 20, 1983, pp. 671–690.

Comas, Juan, *Antropología de los pueblos iberoamericanos*, Barcelona, Labor, 1974.

Cope, Douglas R. *The limits of racial domination. Plebeian society in Mexico City, 1660–1720*, Madison, The University of Wisconsin Press, 1994.

Cortesão, Armando (ed.), *The Suma Oriental of Tomé Pires: an account of the East, from the Red Sea to China written in Malacca and India in 1512–1515*, New Delhi, AES, 1990 [1944].

Cruz Cano y Olmedilla, Juan de la, *Coleccion de Trajes de España tanto antiguos como modernos que comprehende todos los de sus dominios*, Madrid, Casa de M. Copin, 1777.

Chartier, Roger "La conscience de la globalité", *Annales HSS*, 56-1 (2001), pp. 119–123.

Cunha da, Antônio, *Dicionário Etimológico da Língua Portuguesa*, Rio de Janeiro, Nova Fronteira, c. 1982.

De Marees, Pieter, *Description et récit historial du riche royaume de Guinea, aultremenet nommé la Coste d'Or de Mina . . .*, Amsterdam ; C. Claesson, 1605.

Deans-Smith, Susan, "Creating the colonial subject : Casta paintings, Collectors and Critics in Eighteenth century Mexico and Spain", *Colonial Latin American Historical Review*, vol. 14, n°2 (Dec 2005), pp. 169–204.

Du Tertre, Jean-Baptiste, *Histoire générale des Antilles habitées par les françois*, Paris, Thomas Jolly, 1667.

Eiras Roel, Antonio (ed.): *La emigración española a Ultramar*, Madrid, Tabapres, 1991.

Etienne, Charles, *Agriculture et maison rustique*, Paris, Jacques Dupuy, 1564.

Faits et idées sur Saint-Domingue, relativement à la révolution actuelle, Paris, Impr. De Seguy-Thiboust, 1789.

Ferguson, Donald (ed.), *Letters from Portuguese Captives in Canton Written in 1534 & 1536*, Byculla, Education Society's Steam Press, 1902.

Fonteneau Jean (dit Alfonse de Saintonge), *La Cosmographie avec l'espère et régime du soleil et du Nord*, Paris, E. Leroux, 1904 [1544].

Forbes, Jack D., *Africans and Native Americans. The Language of Race and the Evolution of Red-Black peoples*, Oxford and New York, Blackwell, 1988.

Franklin, Vincent P., "Bibliographical essay: Alonso de Sandoval and the Jesuit Conception of the Negro", *Journal of Negro History*, vol. 58, n°3 (1973), pp. 349–360.

Freedman, Paul, « Sainteté et sauvagerie. Deux images du paysan au Moyen Âge », Annales ESC, vol. 47, n° 3 (1992), pp. 539–560.

Frezier, Amédée, *Relation du voyage de la mer sud aux côtes du Chili et du Pérou fait pendant les années 1712 , 1713, et 1714*, Paris, J.-G. Nyon, E. Ganeau, J. Quillau, 1716.

Gage, Thomas, *Nouvelle Relation contenant les voyages de Thomas Gage dans la Nouvelle Espagne, ses diverses avantures; & son retour par la province de Nicaragua, jusques à la Havane avec la description de la ville de Mexique telle qu'elle estoit autrefois, & comme elle est à présent. Ensemble une description exacte des Terres & Provinces que possèdent les Espagnols en tout l'Amérique, de la forme de leur gouvernement ecclésiastique & politique, de leur commerce, de leurs Mœurs, & de celles des Criolles, des Metifs, des Mulatres des Indiens et des Negres*, Amsterdam, Paul Marret, 1699 [1684].

García Saiz, María Concepción, *Las castas mexicanas. Un género pictórico americano*, Milan, Olivetti, 1989.

Gerbi, Antonello, *La disputa del Nuovo mondo: storia di una polemica, 1750–1900*, Milan-Naples, Ricciardi, 1955.

Glaisyer, Natasha, "Networking: Trade and exchange in the eighteenth-century British empire", *Historical Journal*, 47, 2 (2004), pp. 441–476.

Gracia Jorge J. E and Pablo de Greiff (ed.), *Hispanics/Latinos in the United States. Ethnicity, Race and Rights*, New York, Routledge, 2000.

Grasset de Saint Sauver, Jacques, *Encyclopédie des voyages, contenant l'abrégé historique des mœurs, usages, habitudes domestiques, religions, fêtes [. . .] sciences, arts et commerce de tous les peuples et la collection complette de leurs habillemens* [Paris], chez l'auteur, 1796.

Groebner, Valentin, "Complexio/complexion : Categorizing individual natures, 1250–1600", in Lorraine Daston and Fernando Vidal, *The moral authority of Nature*, Chicago, University of Chicago Press, 2004, pp. 361–383.

Guilij, Felipe Salvador, *Ensayo de Historia Americana*, 1784.

Gumilla, Joseph, *Historia natural, civil y geografica de las naciones situadas en las riveras del Rio Orinoco*, 2nd edition, Barcelona, Imprenta de Carlos Gibert y Tuto, 1791.

Hudson, Nicholas, "From Nation to Race: The Origin of Racial Classification in Eighteenth Century Thought", *Eighteenth Century Studies*, vol. 29–3 (1996), pp. 247–264.

Hunold Lara, Silvia, "Customs and Costumes: Carlos Julião and the image of Black Slaves in late Eighteenth-Century Brazil", *Slavery and* Abolition, vol. 23, n°2 (2002), pp. 123–146.

Johnson, Henry, *A true and particular relation of the dreadful earthquake, which happen'd at Lima,[on the 28th of october 1746: [. . .] translated from the original Spanish, by a gentleman who resided many years in those countries; To which is added a description of Callao and Lima before their destruction, and the kingdom of Peru in general, with its inhabitants . . . Interspersed with passages of natural history and physiological disquisitions, particularly an enquiry into the cause of earthquakes*, London, printed for T. Osborne in Gray's Inn, 1748.

Jouanna, Arlette, *L'Idée de race en France au XVIe siècle et au début du XVIIe*, [Montpellier], without editor, 1981.

Juan, Jorge and Antonio de Ulloa, *Relación histórica del viaje a la América meridional*, Madrid, A. Marín, 1748.

Kant, Emmanuel, *La philosophie de l'histoire (opuscules)*, Paris, Denoël/Gonthier, 1981[1785].

Katzew, Ilona, *Casta Painting. Images of Race in Eighteenth-Century Mexico*, New Haven, Yale University Press, 2004.

—— and Susan Deans-Smith (eds.), *Race and Classification. The Case of Mexican America*, Stanford, Stanford University Press, 2009.

——, *New World Orders : Casta Painting and Colonial Latin America*, exhibition catalog by the American Society Art Gallery, 1996.

Kidd, Colin, *The forging of races: Race and scripture in the Protestant Atlantic world, 1600–2000*, Cambridge, Cambridge University Press, 2006.

Labat, Jean-Baptiste, *Nouveau voyage aux isles d'Amérique, contenant l'histoire naturelle de ces pays, l'origine, les mœurs, la religion et le gouvernement des habitants anciens et modernes . . .* La Haye, Husson, Van Duren, et al., 1724.

Larriba, Elisabel, "L'art au service de la divulgation scientifique: le rôle des gravures dans le 'Semanario de Agricultura y Artes dirigido a los Parrocos' (1797–1808)", *El Argonauta Español*, n°2, (2005) http://argonauta.imageson.org/document57.html.

León, Nicolás, *Las Castas del México colonial o Nueva España*, Mexico, publicaciones del Depto. de Antropología Anatómica, n°1, 1924.

Lester, Alan, *Imperial networks: Creating identities in nineteenth-century South Africa and Britain*, London, Routledge, 2001.

Lettres édifiantes et curieuses écrites des missions étrangères, par quelques missionnaires de la Compagnie de Jésus, XI Recueil, Paris, Nicolas Le Clerc, 1715.

Lizana, Elías, *Colección de documentos históricos recopilados del Archivo del Arzobispado de Santiago. Cartas de obispos el rey, 1564–1810*, Santiago, Impr. San José, 1919.

López Beltrán, Carlos, "Sangre y temperamento. Pureza y mestizajes en las sociedades de castas americanas", in Frida Gorbach and Carlos López Beltrán (dir.), *Saberes locales. Ensayos sobre historia de las ciencias en America latina*, Zamora, El Colegio de Michoacán, 2008, pp. 289–342.

López de Velasco, Juan, *Geografía y descripción universal de las Indias* [1574], Madrid, Ediciones Atlas, 1971.

Loveman, Mara, "Is 'race' essential?", *American Sociological Review*, Vol. 64, No. 6, (Dec., 1999), pp. 891–898.

Martín Teixeira, Dante and Elli de Vries, "Exotic novelties from overseas", in Quentin Buvelot (ed.), *Albert Eckhout. A Dutch Artist in Brazil*, La Haye-Zwolle, Royal Cabinet of Paintings Mauritshuis/Waanders Publishers, 2004, pp. 64–107.

Mazzolini, Renato, "Las Castas: interracial crossing and social structure, 1770–1835", in Stäffan Muller-Wille and Hans-Jorg Rheinberger (eds.), *Heredity produced. At the Crossrads of Biology, Politics and Culture, 1500–1870*, Cambridge, Mass., MIT, 2007, pp. 349–373.

Moreau de Saint Méry, Médéric. L.-É , *Description topographique, physique, civile, politique et historique de la partie française de l'isle Saint-Domingue avec des observations générales sur sa population, sur le caractère et les mœurs de ses . . . habitans, sur son climat, sa culture . . . accompagnées des détails les plus propres à faire connaître l'état de cette colonie à l'époque du 18 octobre 1789 et d'une nouvelle carte*, Paris, Guérin et Cie., 1875, [1797–98].

Moreno Navarro, Isidoro, *Los cuadros del Mestizaje americano. Estudio antropológico del mestizaje*, Madrid, Ediciones José Porrúa Turanzas, "Colección Chimalistac de libros acerca de la Nueva España" — 34, 1973.

Morner, Magnus, *Race mixture in the History of Latin America*, Boston, Little, Brown and Co., 1967.

Muller-Wille Stäffan and Rheinberger Hans-Jorg (eds.), *Heredity produced. At the Crossrads of Biology, Politics and Culture, 1500–1870*, Cambridge, Mass., MIT, 2007.

Nenna di Bari, Giavanbattista, *Il Nennio. Nel quale si ragiona nobiltà*, Venise, A. Vavassore, 1542.

Oliveira di Cadornega, Antonio de, *Historia Geral das Guerras angolanas*, Lisbon, Agência-Geral do Ultramar, 1972 [1680].

Oschema, Klaus, "Maison, noblesse et légitimité. Aspects de la notion d'"hérédité' dans le milieu de la cour bourguignonne, XVe siècle", in Maaike van der Lugt and Charles de Miramon (eds.), *L'hérédité entre Moyen Age et époque moderne. Perspectives historiques*, Florence, SISMEL, 2008, pp. 211–244.

Parker Brienen, Rebecca, *Visions of a Savage Paradise. Albert Eckhout, Court Painter in Colonial Dutch Brazil*, Amsterdam; Amsterdam UP, 2006.

Pérez de Barradas, José, *Los mestizos de América*, Madrid, Cultura Clásica Moderna — XV, 1948.

Pernety, Dom, *Journal historique d'un voyage fait aux Iles Malouines en 1763 & 1764 pour le reconnaître et y former un établissement*, Berlin, Etienne de Bourdeaux, 1769.

Pigafetta, Filippo, *Relatione del reame di Congo et delle Circonvicine contrade*, Rome, Bartolomeo Grassi [1591].

Pino Díaz, Fermín del, "Historia natural y razas humanas en los 'cuadros de castas' hispano-americanos", in Romero de Tejada, Pilar (coord.), *Frutas y castas ilustradas*: Exhibition catalogue, Madrid, Museo Nacional de Antropología/Ministerio de Educación, Cultura y Deporte , 2003, pp. 47–66.

Porter, Martin, *Windows of the Soul : The Art of Physiognomy in European Culture, 1470–1780*, Oxford, Clarendon Press, 2005.

Puente, Juan de la, *Conveniencia de las dos monarquías católicas, la de la Iglesia romana y la del Imperio Español*, Madrid, Juan Flamenco, 1612.

Ramos Gómez, Luís and Carmen Ruigómez Gómez, "Una propuesta a la corona para extender la mita y el tributo a negros, mestizos y mulatos (Ecuador 1735–1748)", *Revista complutense de historia de América*, n° 25, 1999, pp. 99–110.

Romero de Tejada, Pilar, (coord.), *Frutas y castas ilustradas* : Exhibition catalogue, Madrid, Museo Nacional de Antropología/Ministerio de Educación, Cultura y Deporte , 2003.

Rougé, Jean-Louis, *Dictionnaire étymologique des créoles portugais d'Afrique*, Paris, Karthala, 2004.

Sahagún, Bernardino de (Fray) *Historia general de las cosas de la Nueva España,* edition by Angel Maria Garibay, Mexico, Ed. Porrua, "Colección sepan cuantos — 300", 1992 (1st.ed 1956), [1570–1582].

Sandoval, Alonso de, *De instauranda Aethiopum Salute*, Madrid, Alonso Paredes, 1647.

Sassetti, Filippo, *Lettere edite e inedite di Filippo Sassetti*, Ettore Marcucci (ed.), Florence, Felice Le Monnier, 1855.

Serres, Olivier de, *Le théâtre de l'Agriculture et mesnage des champs*, Geneva, Samuel Chouet, 1651 [1ere édition Paris, Jamet Mettayer,1600].

Subrahmanyam, Sanjay, "Par delà l'incommensurabilité: pour une histoire connectée des empires aux temps modernes", *Revue d'Histoire moderne et contemporaine*, 54-4 bis (2007), pp. 34–53.

——, *Explorations in connected history. From the Tagus to the Ganges*, Delhi, Oxford University Press, 2005.

Sweet, James, "The Iberian Roots of American Racist Thought", *William and Mary Quarterly*, vol. LIV, n° 1, (1997), pp. 143–166.

Thevenot, Melchisédech, *Relations de divers voyages curieux qui n'ont pas esté publiées, et qu'on a traduit ou tirées des originaux des voyageurs français, espagnols, allemands, portugais, anglois, hollandois, persans, arabes & autres orientaux [. . .]*, Paris, Jacques Langlois, 1663.

Ulloa, Antonio de, *Noticias secretas de América*, Edition de David Barry, Londres, R. Taylor, 1826.

——, *Relación historica del viaje a la America meridional*, Madrid, 1748.

Urquizar Herrera, Antonio "Imaginando América: objetos indígenas en las casas nobles del Renacimiento andaluz", in Enrique Soria Mesa (ed.), *La imagen del poder. Prácticas sociales y representaciones culturales de las élites andaluzas en la Edad Moderna*, Jaen, Universidad de Jaén, 2009.

Vicente, Camilo G, and L. Lenci (eds.), *Descripcion en dialogo de la ciudad de Lima entre un peruano practico y un bisoño chapeton*, Lima, Fondo del Banco Central de Reserva, 1997.

Voss, Barbara L., "From Casta to Californio : Social Identity and the Archaeology of Culture Contact", *American Anthropologist*, Vol. 107, n°. 3 (Sept. 2005), pp. 461–474.

Wilson, Andrew R., *Ambition and Identity: Chinese Merchant Elites in Colonial Manila, 1880–1916*, Honolulu, University of Hawaii Press, 2004.

Zúñiga, Jean-Paul, « Frontière et frontières dans le 'Cautiverio feliz' de Francisco de Pineda y Bascuñán », in Bertrand Michel and Natividad Planas (eds.), *Las sociedades fronterizas del Mediterráneo al Atlántico (ss. XVI–XVII)*, Madrid, Casa de Velázquez, 2011, pp. 43–58.

——, "L'histoire impériale à l'heure de l''histoire globale'. Une perspective atlantique", *Revue d'Histoire moderne et contemporaine*, 54-4 bis (2007), pp. 54–68.

——. "La voix du sang. Du métis à l'idée de métissage en Amérique espagnole", *Annales. Histoire, Sciences Sociales*, 54e année, n°. 2 (1999), pp. 425–452.

9 | Can You Tell a Spaniard When You See One?

"Us" and "Them" in the Early Modern Iberian Atlantic

Tamar Herzog

I

In recent years, historians of the European expansion and post-colonial scholars have concluded that what we identify as "European" was formed during, and because of, the engagement with overseas domains. Arguing against the perception that relegated colonial undertaking to a marginal, even eccentric place, within European history, they affirmed its centrality to both state and nation formation. Citing the work of Gauri Viswanathan, Edward Said sustained in 1994 that the canon of English-ness was defined in the colonies in order to educate the colonial population. It was than imported to England and used to edify the British youth.[1] Somewhat similarly, in 1992 and 1998 Linda Coley and Nicholas Canny proposed that the conversion of the English, Scottish, and Irish into Britons first happened in the colonies.[2] It was not until 1707 (the Act of Union between England and Scotland) that such unification was seriously (although not necessarily successfully) attempted at home. In the case of Spain and Spanish America, in 1998 and 2003 M.J. Rodríguez-Salgado and Henry Kamen argued that Spaniards originating from different Iberian kingdoms assumed a single collective identity and a single *patria* in the Americas because there they were "surrounded by diverse indigenous groups and constantly challenged by enemies such as French and English."[3] Last but not least, in 2004 Irene Silverblatt pointed out that the intellectual and political invention of Spain coincided with the conquest and colonization of the Americas.[4] Investigations into Spanishness, she argued, were necessarily influenced by the colonial experience, in which colonizers were calling themselves Spanish in order to distinguish themselves, among other things, from Indians.

This growing consensus regarding the importance of the colonies in the shaping of European identities assumed that meeting the "other" (and trying to change it) was essential to the formation of self. Whether this "other" included native-Americans, Africans or competing Europeans, the encounter allowed the formation of a unity and an identity still lacking at home. In what follows, I would like to suggest that what the above cited scholars identified as national or proto-national was in reality a discourse about civilization.[5] In the case of Spain, at least, the identification of people as

Spaniards indeed became central to the colonial enterprise. However, this identification was not concerned with nations or states. Rather than designating a political community or a community defined by origin or descent, because of Spain's particular history, during the colonial period Spanishness came to be identified with membership in a religious and a civic community. This, I would argue, was the particular contribution of empire. While discussions in Peninsular Spain were centered on the inclusion (or exclusion) of people from a political community (such as a particular Spanish kingdom), in Spanish America these debates defined a civilization.

Because scholars who identified the birth of nations in the colonies usually pointed to the importance of competition with the native population on the one hand, other Europeans, on the other, I will follow the same route in order to demonstrate the contrary. My examination will center on processes of identification.[6] For the sake of brevity and conciseness, the relationship between these processes and self-identity will not be explored. A first part, examining the classification of individuals as Spanish or Indian will be followed by a second part, explaining the way Spaniards distinguished themselves from other Europeans.

II

It is generally agreed that, in the Americas, Spaniards defined themselves first and foremost in opposition to native inhabitants. According to the bibliography, colonial society was divided into two Republics, Spanish and Indian, each having its own members, authorities, and laws.[7] Indians and Spaniards were thus considered different from one another, and were meant to remain differentiated.

Although there is no doubt that as newcomers to the New World Spaniards often benefited from rights not allowed to most Indians, nonetheless, there is plenty of evidence that during the colonial period the status of Indians and their distinction from Spaniards was a matter of debate. Besides the seminal question (mainly resolved in the sixteenth century) whether Indians were or were not human, until the early nineteenth century disagreement persisted whether the distinction between Spaniards and Indians was temporary or permanent.[8] To many holding the first view, over time Indians and Spaniards would become a "single church" and a "single republic." Explaining that there was no better political rule than forcing conquered people to become part of the conquering nation, they expressed the hope that Indians would "grow of age." [9] According to their view, this was possible because differences between Indians and Spaniards were not innate, but instead represented a distinct degree of civility.[10]

This vision of the Indians, that encored their particularity in a developmental stage not their nature, was espoused by many laws, institutions, and practices implemented in the Americas during the mid-sixteenth and most of the seventeenth century. These either stated (or implied) that after the Indians finished their religious, political, cultural, and linguistic conversion, the two republics would melt into one.[11] The Indians — now treated as minors in need of protection — would come of age and would convert from "miserable" vassals into full-fledged Spaniards.

Because by the late sixteenth century many perceived the differences between Spaniards and native-Americans as transitory, public and private discussions no longer centered on the innate character of Indians, but were focused instead on choosing the right method that would allow their conversion. At different moments and places, some proposed that indoctrination would be best achieved by separating the Indians from Spaniards.[12] Others argued that the clergy was better fit to guide the Indians than "ordinary" Spaniards. Disappointment was often expressed at the lack of serious efforts by authorities and individuals to bring about a complete conversion. In some instances, writers lamented Indian reluctance to cooperate. Whether individuals took one position or another, during the late sixteenth and the seventeenth century Indians' humanity and rationality, as well as their ability to convert into Spaniards — if the right method would be applied — were rarely questioned.[13]

III

Although the initial understanding was that Spaniards originated in Spain, Indians in Spanish America; Spaniards were Christian and civilized, Indians were not, as the colonial period advanced, these perceptions came under attack. Local birth, miscegenation and cultural mixing, as well as a general lack of information regarding where people were born and who their parents were, led to a growing difficulty to catalogue individuals into one group or the other. In practice, during the seventeenth and the eighteenth century many resorted to judging others according to their behavior. That is to say, regardless of their origin and descent, individuals and family groups who behaved like Spaniards, using Spanish cloths, speaking Spanish, and associating with non-Indians, were generally considered either Spanish or at least non-Indian.[14] The contrary was also true. While Indians who were judged sufficiently Christian and sufficiently civilized could be considered Spanish, Spaniards who were considered insufficiently Christian and insufficiently civilized could be treated as Indians.[15] In fact, "just as the category of Spaniards included acculturated persons of Indian and African ancestry, so too, did the category of savage include Hispanics and Africans and their descendents who lived among natives or behaved like natives".[16]

From as early as the seventeenth century, the classification of people as Spanish or Indian was thus determined according to performance: how individuals behaved and how this behavior was perceived, evaluated and validated by those observing them. Results depended on who was looking, when, and for which reason. No certificates existed that would determine once and for all who was whom, and individuals identified as Indians or Spaniards on one occasion could be classified differently on another. Proof of a previous classification could be helpful, but was never definitive. At stake was not what one's image was in the past, but what contemporaries were willing to acknowledge him or her in the present.

Because being classified in one way or the other produced tangible results (there were certain things you could do as an Indian that you could not do as a Spaniard and vice versa[17]), both those classifying and those being classified had powerful motives to want to influence the way classification happened. As a result, classification was often functional rather than logical, pragmatic rather than theoretically sound. Spanishness, if it had any meaning in this setting at all, equaled a way of being, not a place of origin or a national, racial or ethnic belonging. It was meant to designate those Hispanized and distinguish them from those who were not.

IV

There is reason to believe that this interpretation — that in practice, although not always in theory, viewed the differences between Spaniards and Indians as mainly embodying civilizational traits — was also shared by some Indians. In an article published in 1987 Jan Szeminski argued that during the Tupac Amaru revolt (eighteenth-century Peru) insurgents identified as Spaniards all those "Spaniards from Spain;" members of the "republic of Spaniards" in the Americas; Indian upper caste; Indian nobility; Indian local notables; any persons of Spanish culture; and, in general, all members of the upper classes".[18] According to the rebels, all these people, as well as people dressed as Spaniards, or anyone else who functioned well within the Spanish colonial system, could be grouped together and be killed because contrary to the Indians they were heretics and, consequentially, had lost their humanity and merited death. Although researchers have been unable to identify all those who were actually killed during the revolt because they were classified as Spaniards, Szeminski did mention that among them were many Mestizos and Indians. Similar remarks — linking civilizational traits with what we would identify today as ethnicity — were also made by Irene Silverblatt. According to her, by the seventeenth century some native Peruvians identified themselves as Indians precisely because they rejected Spanish way of life, as embodied in Spanish religion, food, and dress and because they feared being contaminated by Spaniards not only biologically, but also culturally.[19]

V

The placing of Spaniards and Indians on a single scale leading from Indianness to Spanishness (and, according to some, from paganism to Christianity, barbarism to civilization) had powerful affects. Besides the promise (perhaps illusion) of equality, in both Europe and the Americas it allowed to draw new boundaries. One such boundary was the growing identification between European peasants and Indians on the one hand, and their distinction from other peoples and groups, on the other. If in the early sixteenth century European peasants were a means to understand the Indians — in 1517 the governor of Hispaniola asked the colonists if the Indians were comparable to European peasants and, in 1537, Francisco de Vitoria made this comparison in order to conclude that, like peasants, Indians were also (partially) rational human beings[20] — by mid century the contrary was also true. By that time, the Indies became a metaphor of the ignorance of all populations that have not yet adopted the correct religious and civic code.[21] Writing in Spain in 1568, some people asserted that "there is no Indies that have such a necessity of priests as the kingdom of Asturias."[22] During the same period, Jesuits working in Southern Italy and Germany also complained that the people they wished to indoctrinate were similar to the Indians: they were just as pagan, savage, and uncultured. Like the Indians, even worse than some Indians, these Europeans lacked all social and political organization.[23] The Indies, these friars said, were everywhere, Europe included. French Jesuits expressed similar opinions, comparing American "savages" to villagers in Europe and maintaining that the ignorance in some areas of France was as bad as the ignorance of native-Americans.[24] Similar borrowing also happened in Ireland, where — using Spanish debates regarding native-Americans — late sixteenth-century English colonists classified local peasants as both pagan and uncivil.[25] This classification qualified these peasants as barbarians and explained the need to dominate them in order to ensure their conversion into true Christians and truly civilized human beings

In many of these cases, the comparison between European peasants and Indians was a means to argue that missionary work in Europe was equally important, perhaps even more important, than the conversion of native-Americans. Nonetheless, the comparison between peasants and Indians also sought to justify domination over a rural population that, albeit domestic, was considered alien because it failed to comply with the behavioral norms of Christians and civilized men. Thereafter, religion and civilization became a measure to define also membership in the community.[26] Whether they were "European" or not, whether they lived in the Old or the New World, those who resided outside the reach of religious and secular law were presented as the ultimate barbarians, the true outsiders.[27]

Colonialism also allowed redrawing the map in other ways. During the sixteenth century it fueled a constant preoccupation with a more general European barbarism, equal or worse to the barbarism of native-Americans. In his "Short Essays on the Destruction of the Indies" (1542) Las Casas presented the encounter between Indians and Spaniards as one between innocent, delicate people and ravening wolves led by greed and ambition.[28] Rather than worrying about the faith of Indians (as most people have assumed), Las Casas was mainly preoccupied with the effects of colonialism on Europeans. The atrocities Spaniards committed not only harmed the Indians, they also transformed their captives. The conquerors became so anaesthetized to human suffering that they ceased to be men in the meaningful sense of the term. This degradation of Europeans, Las Casas feared, could bring about the collapse of civilization and the end of the world.

Contemporary concern with a generalized European barbarism perhaps found its outmost expression in Michel de Montaigne's essay "On Cannibals" (1589).[29] Having witnessed the wars of religion in France, Montaigne questioned the assumption that the Indians were barbarians while Europeans were not. Eye witness accounts confirmed that the Indians are not barbaric, he said. Recent experiences in Europe demonstrated, on the contrary, that we were.

These concerns produced a variety of results in both Europe and abroad. In Europe, it led some authors to re-consider Indian savagery. In the late seventeenth and eighteenth centuries, Chateaubriand and Rousseau, revisiting themes already invoked by Montaigne and Jean de Léry, re-interpreted Indian barbarism as benign, even preferable, when compared to European corrupt civilization. Informing debates on the social contract, which gave rise to human societies, native Indians were now used in order to imagine what the European pre-social man may have looked like, and this pre-social man was judged either preferable to today's man or inferior to him.[30]

While this was happening in Europe, in the colonies the gradual realization that not all Indians were savages and that perhaps not all Europeans were necessarily civilized, also led to important transformations. By the mid to late seventeenth century in Spanish America, at least, the distinction between Indians (as prototyped barbarians) and Spaniards (as prototyped civilized men) metamorphosed into a new classification that differentiated "reasonable" from "non-reasonable" people (*gente de razón*). This classification sustained that, independently of their origin, either people were civilized or they were part of an indistinguishable plebs, equally consisting of Indians, individuals of mixed ancestry, African, and Spaniards.[31] This situation produced two contradictory reactions. For some, it demonstrated the need to grant complete equality to Indians. Only equality, or the promise of equality, would enable Indians to (finally) terminate both their civil and religious conversion.[32] Other people on the contrary, fearing the consequences of equality, insisted on the need to maintain a permanent distinction between Indians and Spaniards. Some even re-interpreted this distinction, claiming that it identified genetic and thus immutable differences. This reaction was justified by prejudice, but it was mainly motivated by the competition for resources. The nearer Indians were to Spanishness and the more claims they made, the greater the effort was, at least by some people, to exclude them; and, as differences between Indians and Spaniards were actually fading away, the claim that these differences existed, and were meaningful, grew in force.[33] During this period, people who were once classified as non-Indians, or even Spanish, were re-classified as Indians or mestizos. *Casta* paintings were elaborated in Mexico, and a classificatory system, distinguishing people according to their ancestry (and percentage thereof), was invented (although never truly implemented).[34]

VI

In what remains of this essay, I would like to address the second issue at stake, that is, the conclusion that confrontation with other Europeans led Iberians to adopt a common homeland. This conclusion is usually based on the following observations: (1) In Spain most people identified themselves as natives of a particular kingdom (Castile, Aragon, Catalonia, and so forth) yet, in the Americas, they identified themselves also as "Spaniards." (2) In Spain, the privileges and obligations of natives of different Iberian kingdoms were distinct; in Spanish America they were common. (3) Although in Spain local parliaments (the parliament of Castile, the parliament of Valencia, and so forth) insisted on maintaining monopolies that benefited their natives (only natives of Castile could hold offices in Castile, only natives of Aragon could hold offices in Aragon, and so forth); from as early as the late sixteenth century the Castilian parliament agreed to a colonial monopoly on immigration and trade in the New World — allegedly a Castilian territory — shared by natives of all kingdoms. In the aftermaths of these developments, a new social, legal and administrative category including "natives of Spain," also called "Spaniards," made its appearance.[35]

Despite intuitive claims that these developments must have represented a move towards the construction of a Spanish nation, there is practically no research as to why they happened, for example, why the Castilian parliament that insisted on a monopoly on office holding that excluded all other natives of Spain from holding offices in Castile — agreed to a colonial monopoly in a Castilian territory that included all Spaniards.[36] We do know that in the early sixteenth century both questions were closely related — Queen Isabel, for example, tied them together in her testament (1504) by indicating that because the New World was Castilian, both ecclesiastical benefices AND commerce should be reserved to natives of Castile.[37] We do not know what happened next.

Most historians have assumed that the inclusion of natives of other Iberian kingdoms in the colonial monopoly was a royal decision that (1) the kings could take and (2) that "made sense" given (a) royal hopes to unify Spain and (b) the growth of Spanish nationalism.[38] Yet, even if this was true — the kings acting, perhaps, at the request of the *Cortes* de Aragon that met in Monzón in 1528 and 1595 to debate, inter alia, the privileges of Aragonese in the Americas — the question remains the same: Why did the Castilian parliament agree? Why did it insist on a narrow monopoly on offices while allowing a wider, pan-Spanish monopoly in the colonies? Since existing documentation is silent on this point — the *actas* of the *Cortes* of Castile never refer to this question, limiting the discussion to the request (each time taxation is debated) to exclude foreigners, but never debating whether among foreigners were natives of other Iberian kingdoms or not, we must look for the answer elsewhere. I would like to suggest that although the inclusion of all Spaniards in the colonial monopoly and the exclusion of all foreingners, as well as the construction of a Spanish community in the Americas may sound "national" to us, it was based not on a national identification, but on religious and civilizational criteria. Let me explain.

Contemporaries insisted that the colonial enterprise was justified by the need to religiously and civically convert the Indians.[39] These claims were usually rejected by historians, who placed economic and political motivations at the center of the debate. But what happens if we take the religious consideration seriously? Is it possible that — as happened with other social sectors, such as Gypsies, heretics, and individuals of Jewish or Moorish descent — foreigners were barred from immigrating to the New World because as non-believers or as Catholics who were nevertheless "suspicious in matters of faith," they could undermine the conversion of natives?[40]

This possibility is supported by historical record. Already in 1492, Columbus suggested that because Spanish presence in the New World was meant "to enlarge and bring glory to the Christian religion," the kings should not allow foreigners to immigrate or trade in the Indies without ascertaining first that despite their foreign-ness they were "good Christians."[41] Writing in Peru in the middle of the seventeenth century, Solórzano Pereira agreed. Although he argued that according to the law of nations (*derecho de las gentes*) all foreigners should be allowed to trade in the Americas, he nevertheless suggested that foreign merchants could be expelled if there was reason to believe that their presence would cause upheaval, reveal secrets, or entail "perver-sion or corruption in faith, religion, and good customs."[42] Citing a Portuguese source that confirmed that the kings could prohibit foreigners from dealing in "lands of infi-dels" (*tierras de infieles*) whose conversion and conquest is under their responsibility, Solórzano concluded that (contrary to foreigners) "the faithful (*fieles*) can have commercial dealings with the infidels and walk among them." Even as late as 1809, Francisco Bruno de Rivarola still argued for a connection between infidelity and the restrictions placed on foreigners in Spanish America.[43] Explaining that royal decrees prohibiting the immigration and trade of aliens were meant to guarantee the purity of faith, he commended the kings for having taken measures to ensure that the advan-tages of the "religious Spanish society" would be preserved. Rivarola also insisted that, although these considerations were applicable in general, they were particularly important in the New World where it has taken a "great effort" to implement the Christian faith and the Christian way of life.

The association between foreignness and infidelity was long in the making. Already in the Middle Ages, the Spanish crown instituted the protection of the "true faith" as a social ideal, as expressed by the reconquest and the military orders.[44] In the decades following, the importance of Christianity to the construction of Spain justified the persecution of religious minorities and the rejection of heretics. During the early modern period, Spaniards often argued that they alone carried the weight of the struggle to affirm Christian superiority. Increasingly, the confrontation in the Mediterranean with Muslim powers was presented by them as a holy war that only Spaniards were willing to undertake.[45] Success in the conquest of the vast territories of the Americas (and the failure of other Europeans to do so) only intensified these beliefs. With the coming of the Reformation and the wars of religion, the relationship between Spanishnness and orthodoxy, foreignness and infidelity, intensified. Champions of the counterreformation, during this period Spaniards refashioned themselves as THE most Christian and THE most civilized, indeed the sole authentic Christians in Europe.[46] Because they identified Spanishness with orthodoxy and with membership in a superior social and political order, heretics, even when born and raised in Spain, were portrayed as foreigners. With the same token, those sufficiently faithful, even if born and living abroad, were considered Spanish or worthy of treatment as such.

These perceptions were accompanied and propagated by a literature that insisted that true civility could be found only among the very orthodox members of the Roman Church. Sixteenth-century Spanish authors such as Bartolomé de Las Casas and José de Acosta thus argued that Protestants, Jews, and Muslims were all equally barbarians.[47] Las Casas was most insistent on this point, enumerating among barbarians all those who "lacked the true religion and Christian faith, even if otherwise they were wise and prudent philosophers and politicians."[48] Specifically mentioning the case of heretics, Las Casas explained that their fault was greatest because, having once been totally rational and thus totally human and civilized, they willfully decided to cease being both. People who were nominally Christians, but who were not good Christians, committed the same offense. In summary, because of their incorrect religious belief, other European could easily be classified as barbarians. Their civility was apparent, rather than real. They were not part of the *oikumene*, a superior world and the only world in which it was possible to be totally human and totally civilized.[49] As such, they were somewhat similar to Indians.

Ironically, the fact that Spaniards may have treated their European counterparts of the late sixteenth century and early seventeenth century as Indians was captured by the proponents of the Black Legend. These proponents insisted that Spanish cruelty was equally applied against the Indians, the Dutch, and French Protestants.[50] This cruelty was based on the conviction that Spaniards were superior to all other peoples and that their way of life had to dominate.

The institution of a Spanish monopoly in the Indies that included all Spaniards and excluded all foreigners was contemporary to these developments. It is thus possible that it expressed the conviction that because non-Spaniards were insufficiently Christian and insufficiently civilized, like Gypsies or individuals of Jewish and Moorish descent, they should be barred from immigrating to (and trading in) the Americas. And, on the contrary, because all Spaniards were by definition both religious and civilized, they could all be allowed in. Said differently, although the exclusion of foreigners could be justified by contemporary economic thought, the issue here is not with the exclusion itself, but with HOW it was implemented. As happened in the case of the Indian versus the Spaniard, the question was not whether to exclude foreigners, but how foreignness would be defined. My contention is that the defining factor was religious orthodoxy, not nation or protonation.

This hypothesis is further supported by Spanish naturalization practices. These practices (which I had studied extensively in a book published in 2003[51]), allowed, even welcomed, the immigration of foreign Catholics to Spain; nonetheless, they prohibited their immigration to the colonies.[52] While in Spain, foreign Catholics could easily naturalize; in Spanish America they remained alien. The question is why. Why welcome foreign Catholics to Spain while prohibiting their immigration to the colonies? Why allow their naturalization in the Old but not the New World? The traditional response pointed to mercantilism. Yet, if we took contemporary explanations seriously we could add, perhaps replace, this response with another, suggesting that, because non-Spaniards were insufficiently Christian and insufficiently civilized and because they were somewhat similar to the Indians, they could be admitted in Spain (where religious orthodoxy and civilization reigned), but were highly dangerous in the Americas (where paganism and barbarity still dominated). In Spain, there was hope that these foreigners would learn the "right ways" and, once integrated into the community, could become equally Christian and equally civilized. In the Americas, it was unlikely this would happen.

Back to immigration and trade and the identification of Spaniards in the New World, this explanation would suggest that rather than national identity, the identification of Spaniards and foreigners was encored in religious and civilizational differences. It distinguished, as many Spaniards would say, reasonable from non-reasonable people. Precisely because the issue was not the identification of a political community, but the safe-guarding of a religion and a civilization, contrary to the situation in Spain in the Americas all Spaniards could enjoy the same status. Rather than divided by kingdoms, as was the case in Europe, in the Americas the true divide was between true Christians and unworthy Christians, civilized and barbarians. And, while in the Peninsula those constructing nativeness wanted to protect the kingdom against the king by limiting his power to appoint foreigners to local offices, in the Americas those discussing nativeness wanted to protect civilization.[53]

VII

Processes identifying Spaniards and distinguishing them from other people thus happened on both sides of the Ocean. Although the terms used were similar, what changed was meaning of Spanishness itself. In Spain, Spanishness (nativenness of the kingdoms of Spain) was located in a kingdom; in the Americas, it was founded on religion and civilization. Rather than nationalized, in the New World debates concerning nativeness universalized. It is therefore not surprising that some scholars regarded the American experience as a first move towards a theory of human rights. For some, this could happen because scholars like Vitoria considered the Indians a human group bound by the same rights and obligations as Europeans.[54] For others, it happened because alterity became internal: rather than disregarding the Indians or establishing a permanent distinction between natives and foreigners, Spaniards were willing to integrate both and, in the process, they changed the significance of what it meant to be a Spaniard. Colonialism was important, but so was the history of Europe itself. The coincidence between the discovery and the reformation was perhaps accidental, but its results were not. Internal and external colonialism coincided in the sixteenth, seventeenth, and eighteenth-centuries. They equally contributed to the creation of new formulations, new identities, and new institutions resulting in what some have described as "global colonialism."[55]

Notes

1 Said, 1994, 35 and 42.
2 Canny, 1998, 24–25 and Colley, 2005, 132–133.
3 Rodríguez Salgado, 1998, 244 and 239–240 and Kamen, 2003, 331–333.
4 Silverblatt, 2004, 19–20.
5 I use the term "civilization" despite the fact that it is anachronistic. Before the eighteenth century, the terms used were "barbarians" versus "civil", "civic," or simply "Christian:" Starbonski, 1989 and Escobar, 1984.
6 Brubaker and Cooper, 2000.
7 McAlister, 1984, 177–180.
8 Herzog, 2006b and O'Gorman, 1958, 88–99.
9 Tomás López Medel, writing in 1555, cited by Ares Quijada, 1993, 125, the viceroy of Peru Duque de la Plata in 1684, cited by Mörner, 1967, 443–444 and Solórzano Pereira, 1972 [1648], book 2, chapters 25–26.
10 These questions were debated between Bartolomé de las Casas and Sepúlveda in the 1540s: Pagden, 1982, 108–145 and Castañeda Salamanca, 2002.
11 The Laws of Burgos (1512–13), article 4 of the amendment dated July 28, 1513, stated "whereas it may so happen that in the course of time, with their indoctrination and association with Christians, the Indians will become so apt and ready to become Christians, and so civilized and educated, that they will be capable of governing themselves and leading the kind of life that the said Christians lead there, we declare and command and say that it is our will that those Indians . . . shall be allowed to live by themselves and shall be obliged to serve [only] in those things in which our vassals in Spain are accustomed to serve." In this quotation, I used the translation included in Gibson, 1968, 81.
12 The distinction most authors make between a "policy of segregation" and a "policy of assimilation" is misleading because, although choosing different methods, both policies targeted integration.
13 Llaguno, 1977 and García Gallo, 1977.
14 Mörner, 1994, 305, Minchom, 1994, 158–159, 167, 177 and 189–191, Cope, 1994, 49–55 and Weber, 2005, 15–17, 97 and 255.
15 Many Spaniards living in colonial Chile experienced this faith. According to local priests writing in the eighteenth century, they were religiously and politically as ignorant as the Indians and merited the same treatment. Like the Indians, these Chileans should be supervised and educated, tutored by priests and forced to settle in organized communities (*reducciones*). The Spaniards of Chile were treated in numerous documents, some of which are summarized in a *cédula* of May 5, 1716, Archivo General de Indias (hereafter AGI), Chile 137, fols. 240r–242v. They were also mentioned in Schiaffino and Urbina Burgos, 1978 and Schiaffino, 1983. The Chilean case was not exceptional. In most places and times Spaniards could be considered Indian if they use Indian dress, held typically indigenous occupations, were poor, and so forth: Minchom, 1994, 159, 169 and 177 and Milton, 2005, 604 and 609. On these issues also see Herzog, 2007.
16 Weber, 2005, 16–17.
17 Being classified as an Indian, for example, forced you to pay certain taxes (*tributo*), but allowed you to reside in Indian communities, receive free legal services, and so forth. On this point see Cope, 1994, 57.
18 Szeminski, 1987, 166 and 191.
19 Silverblatt, 2004, 26–27, 189 and 196–197.
20 Pagden, 1982, 200, note 236 and "Vitoria on the Justice of the Conquest," as reproduced in Parry, 1984, v. I, 290–323, point 22.
21 Nuzzo, 2004, 214–215.
22 Pagden, 1982, 97–98.

23 Prosperi, 1999, 65–87, Selwyn, 2004, 17, 95–96, 127, and 131 and Deslandres, 1992, 1, 6 and 9–11.
24 Deslandres, 1999, 258–273, 258, 261 and 266.
25 Canny, 1973 and Muldoon, 1975.
26 Lupoi, 2000, 51 and Zea, 1988, 36.
27 Jaenen, 1983, 46.
28 Las Casas, 1992 [1552], 3–25 and 127–130.
29 Montaigne, "On Cannibals" in Montaigne, 1902 [ca.1577], chapter XXX.
30 Jaenen, 1983, Lupoi, 2000, 49 and Arneil, 1996, 21, 30–43.
31 Cope, 1994, 22–26 and Lutz, 1994, 109.
32 "Extracto del informe que . . . hizo el padre Villareal en el año de 1752 para contener y sujetar los indios del reino de Chile," in Archivo General de la Nación-Buenos Aires, Fondo Biblioteca Nacional, legajo 289, expediente 4389.
33 Milton, 2005 and Minchom, 1994, 196–198. Most of the literature sustains, on the contrary, that the emergence of racial categories was linked to the failure, rather than the success, of Indian integration. See, for example, MacCormack, 1991 and Cañizares-Esguerra, 2006, 93–95.
34 Katzew, 2004 and Carrera, 2003.
35 *Recopilación de Indias* law 28, title 27, book 9 refers to "natives of our kingdoms of Castile, Leon, Aragon, Valencia, Catalonia, Navarra, Mallorca and Menorca." Nevertheless, administrative and judicial records identified this group as including "natives of the kingdoms of Spain." The Spanish monopoly was studied by many, among which are Haring, 1918, Hernández Ruíz de Villa, 1965, García-Baquero González, 1976, Bordejé Morencos, 1992 and Ruiz Rivera and García Bernal, 1992. It is unclear whether during the sixteenth century natives of the Aragon were allowed to immigrate and trade in the New World: Rumeu de Armas, 1944, 494–510, Ramos Pérez, 1976, Piña Homs, 1992 and Martínez Shaw, 1995. According to Batista i Roca, 1951, 11, the expression *naturales de estos reinos* normally referred to Castilians alone, while the term "*naturales de los reinos (o las coronas) de España*" included both Castile and Aragon.
36 These issues are treated in greater length in Herzog, 2003, 64–118.
37 Isabel's testament, dated October 12, 1504, cited in Ramos Pérez, 1976, 21.
38 Morales Álvarez, 1980, 51 and González Díez, 2003.
39 García Añoveros, 1990, 29–39 and Rivera, 1992, 200–216 and 310–313.
40 *Recopilación de Indias* law 20, title 26, book 9 and law 5, title 4, book 7; AGI, Indiferente General, 427, libro 30, fol.2v-3v and 424, libro 22, fols.239v-241r. I owe the last two references to Ana Díaz Serrano. On these issues also see Veitia Linaje, 1945 [1672], 300 and Nunn, 1979, 47.
41 Columbus on November 27, 1492, cited in Ramos Pérez, 1976, 12.
42 Solórzano Pereira, 1972 [1648], 65–66.
43 Rivarola, 1983 [1809], 99–108.
44 Linehan, 1982, 161–199, Koenigsberger, 1975 and 1986, Payne, 1984, 3–70 and Continisio and Mozzarelli, 1995.
45 Rodríguez-Salgado, 1998, 241 and 246.
46 Marco Antonio de Camos in his *Microcosmia o gobierno universal del hombre cristiano* (Barcelona, 1592), cited in Clark, 1985, 4, Herrero García, 1966, 15–31, Nunn, 1979, 51–52, Elliott, 1989, 9, Armas Asin, 1997, 359, Rodríguez-Salgado, 1998, 250 and Pudo, 2000, 10–11 and 63–107.
47 Acosta, 1987 [1588], I, 55 and Selwyn, 2004, 95–96, 120, 127 and 131.
48 Castañeda Salamanca, 2002, 18–20 and 23.
49 Pagden, 1982, 16. Also see Morán García, 2004, 124–125 and 135–136.
50 Lestringant, 2004, 265–266 and Schmidt, 2001, xvii–xxiii.

158 | Tamar Herzog

51 Herzog, 2003. Although this book is centered on Castile, a brief survey of other Iberian kingdoms is included in Herzog, 2006a, 16–17.
52 Non Catholics were prohibited from immigrating and settling in Spain, unless they were protected by special "international" agreements.
53 There were two reasons why the kingdom needed protection against the king: (1) the growing complexity of the Spanish monarchy, now composed of many kingdoms, allowed foreign vassals to access local offices. The monopoly pretended to limits such access. And (2) the monopoly was part also of a more generalized opposition to what was perceived as a growing royal absolutism.
54 Cassi, 2004, 429–436.
55 Herzfeld, 2002, 169, citing Nadel-Klein.

Bibliography

Acosta, José de, *De procuranda Indorum Salute*, Luciano Pereña Vicente, ed., Madrid, CSIC, 1987 [1588].
Ares Queija, Berta, *Tomás López Medel. Trayectoria de un clérigo-oidor ante el Nuevo Mundo*, Guadalajara, Institución Provincial de Cultura "Marqués de Santillana", 1993.
Armas Asin, Fernando, "Herejes, marginales e infectos: Extranjeros y mentalidad excluyente en la sociedad colonial (siglos XVI y XVII)", *Revista Andina*, 1997, 15 no. 2, pp. 355–386.
Arneil, Barbara, *John Locke and America: The Defense of English Colonialism*, Oxford, Clarendon Press, 1996.
Batista i Roca, J.M., "Foreword", in Helmut Koenigsberger, *The Government of Sicily Under Philip II of Spain*, London, Staples Press, 1951, pp. 9–35.
Bordejé Morencos, Fernando de, *Tráfico de Indias y política oceánica*, Madrid, Mapfre, 1992.
Brubaker, Rogers and Frederick Cooper, "Beyond 'Identity'," *Theory and Society*, 2000, 29 no. 1, pp. 1–47.
Cañizares-Esguerra, Jorge, *Nature, Empire and Nation: Explorations of the History of Science in the Iberian World*, Stanford, Stanford University Press, 2006.
Canny, Nicholas P. "The Ideology of English Colonization: From Ireland to America", *The William and Mary Quarterly* 1973, 30 no. 4, pp. 575–598.
——, "The Origins of Empire: An Introduction," in Nicholas Canny, ed., *The Origins of Empire: British Overseas Enterprise to the Close of the Seventeenth Century*, Oxford, Oxford University Press, 1998, pp. 1–33.
Carrera, Magali Marie, *Imagining Identity in New Spain: Race, Lineage, and the Colonial Body in Portraiture and Casta Painting*, Austin, University of Texas Press, 2003.
Casas, Bartolomé de las, *A Short Account of the Destruction of the Indies*, London, Penguin, 1992 [1552].
Cassi, Aldo Andrea, *Ius commune. Tra vecchio e nuevo mondo. Mari, terre, oro nel diritto della conquista (1492–1680)*, Milan, Giuffré, 2004.
Castañeda Salamanca, Felipe, *El indio: entre el bárbaro y el cristiano. Ensayos sobre filosofía de la conquista en Las Casas, Sepúlveda y Acosta*, Bogotá, Universidad de los Andes, 2002.
Clark, Peter, "Introduction", in Peter Clark, ed., *The European Crisis of the 1590s: Essays in Comparative History*, London, Allen and Unwin, 1985, pp. 3–22.
Colley, Linda, *Britons: Forging the Nation, 1707–1837*, New Haven, Yale University Press, 2005 [1992].
Continisio, Chiara and Cesare Mozzarelli eds., *Repubblica e virtú. Pensiero politico e Monarchia Cattolica fra XVI e XVII secolo*, Rome, Bulzoni, 1995.
Cope, R. Douglas, *The Limits of Racial Domination. Plebeian Society in Colonial Mexico City, 1660–1720*, Madison, The University of Wisconsin Press, 1994.
Deslandres, Dominique, "Mission et altérité. Les missionnaires français et la définition de l'autre au XVIIe siècle", in *Proceedings of the French Colonial Historical Society* 1992, 18, pp. 1–13.

——, *"Exemplo aeque ut verbo:* The French Jesuit's Missionary World", in John W. O'Mally, Gauvin Alexander Bailey, Steven J. Harris and T. Frank Kennedy, eds., *The Jesuits: Cultures, Sciences, and the Arts, 1540–1777,* Toronto, University of Toronto Press, 1999.

Elliott, J.H., *Spain and its World 1500–1700: Selected Essays,* New Haven and London, Yale University Press, 1989.

Escobar, José, "Más sobre los orígenes de *civilizar* y *civilización* en la España del siglo XVIII", *Nueva revista de filología hispánica,* 1984, 33 no.1, pp. 88–114.

Estado general de las fundaciones hechas por José Escandón en la colonia del Nuevo Santander, Mexico, Archivo General de la Nación, 1930.

Fernández Albaladejo, Pablo, "Católicos antes que ciudadanos: Gestación de una "política española" en los comienzos de la edad moderna", in José Ignacio Fortea Pérez, ed., *La imágen de la diversidad. El mundo urbano en la corona de Castilla (siglos XVI–XVIII),* Santander, Universidad de Cantabria, 1997, pp. 103–127.

——, "El problema de la "composite monarchy" en España", in Isabel Burdiel and James Casey, eds., *Identities. Nations, Provinces and Regions 1550–1900. Proceedings of the III Anglo-Spanish Historical Studies Seminar 25–26 October 1996,* Norwich, University of East Anglia, 1999, pp. 185–201.

García Añoveros, Jesús María, *La monarquía y la iglesia en América,* Valencia, Asociación Francisco López de Gómara, 1990.

García-Baquero González, Antonio, *Cádiz y el Atlántico, 1717–1778. El comercio colonial español bajo el monopolio gaditano,* Seville, Escuela de Estudios Hispanoamericanos, 1976.

García Gallo, Alfonso, "La condición jurídica del indio", in Miguel Rivera Dorado, ed., *Antropología de España y América,* Madrid, Dosbe, 1977, pp. 281–292.

Gibson, Charles, *The Spanish Tradition in America,* New York, Harper and Row, 1968.

González Díez, Emiliano, "De la naturalización y extranjería en Indias (Sólo una notación)," in Ángel B. Espina Barrio, ed., *Emigración e integración cultural. Antropología en Castilla y León e Iberoamérica,* Salamanca, Universidad de Salamanca, 2003, pp. 53–63.

Haring, Clarence H, *Trade and Navigation between Spain and the Indies in the Time of the Habsburgs,* Cambridge, MA, Harvard University Press, 1918.

Hernández Ruíz de Villa, Rafael, *Emigración a Indias: leyes reguladoras,* Segovia, Instituto Andrés Laguna, 1965.

Herrero García, Miguel, *Ideas de los españoles del siglo XVII,* Madrid, Gredos, 1966.

Herzfeld, Michael, "The European Self: Rethinking an Attitude", in Anthony Pagden ed., *The Idea of Europe from Antiquity to the European Union,* Cambridge, Cambridge University Press, 2002, pp. 139–170.

Herzog, Tamar, *Defining Nations: Immigrants and Citizens in Early Modern Spain and Spanish America,* New Haven, Yale University Press, 2003.

——, *Vecinos y extranjeros. Hacerse español en la edad moderna.* Madrid, Alianza Editorial, 2006a.

——, "Indiani e cowboys: il ruolo dell'indigeno nel diritto e nell'immaginario ispano-coloniale", in Aldo Mazzacane, ed., *Oltremare. Diritto e istituzione dal colonialismo all'età postcolniale,* Naples, Cuen, 2006b, pp. 9–44.

——, "Terres et déserts, société et sauvagerie. De la communauté en Amérique et en Castille à l'époque moderne", *Annales HSS* 2007, 62 no.3, pp. 507–538.

Jaenen, Cornellius J., "'Les Sauvages Americains': Persistence into the Eighteenth Century of Traditional French Concepts and Constructs for Comprehending Amerindians", *Ethnohistory* 1983, 29 no.1, pp. 43–56.

Kamen, Henry, *Empire. How Spain Became a World Power, 1492–1763,* New York, Harper Collins, 2003.

Katzew, Ilona, *Casta Painting: Images of Race in Eighteenth-Century Mexico,* New Haven, Yale University Press, 2004.

Koenigsberger, Helmut, "Spain", in Orest Ranum, ed. *National Consciousness, History and*

Political Culture in Early Modern Europe, Baltimore, Johns Hopkins University Press, 1975, pp. 144–172.

——, "National Consciousness in early Modern Spain", in Helmut Koenigsberger, *Politicians and Virtuosi: Essays in Early Modern History*, London, Hambledon Press, 1986, pp. 121–147.

Lestringant, Frank, *Le huguenot et le sauvage: L'Amérique et la controverse coloniale, en France, au temps des guerres de religion, 1555–1589*, Geneva, Droz, 2004.

Linehan, Peter, "Religion, Nationalism and National Identity in Medieval Spain and Portugal", in *Religion and National Identity. Papers Read at the 19th Summer Meeting and 20th Winter Meeting of the Ecclesiastical History Society*, Oxford, Basil Blackwell, 1982.

Llaguno, José A., *La personalidad jurídica del indio y el III concilio provincial mexicano (1585)*, México, Porrúa, 1963.

Lupoi, Maurizio, *The Origins of the European Legal Order*, transl. Adrian Belton, Cambridge, Cambridge University Press, 2000.

Lutz, Christopher H., *Santiago de Guatemala, 1541–1773: City, Caste and the Colonial Experience*, Norman, Oklahoma University Press, 1994.

MacCormack, Sabine, *Religion in the Andes: Vision and Imagination in Early Colonial Peru*, Princeton, Princeton University Press, 1991.

Martínez Shaw, Carlos, "El mito que no cesa. La doble exclusión de la Corona de Aragón", in *El tratado de Tordesillas y su época. Congreso Internacional de Historia*, Valladolid, Junta de Castilla y León, 1995, pp. 849–862.

McAlister, Lyle N., *Spain and Portugal in the New World, 1492–1700*, Minneapolis, University of Minnesota Press, 1984.

Milton, Cynthia E., "Poverty and the Politics of Colonialism: 'Poor Spaniards,' their Petitions and the Erosion of Privilege in Late Colonial Quito", *Hispanic American Historical Review* 2005, 85 no. 4, pp. 595–626.

Minchom, Martin, *The People of Quito 1690–1810: Change and Unrest in the Underclass*, Boulder, Westview Press, 1994.

Montaigne, Michel de, "On Cannibals", in Michel de Montaigne, *The Essays of Michel de Montaigne*, translated by Charles Cotton and edited by William Carew Hazlitt, London, Reeves and Turner, 1902 [ca.1577].

Morales Álvarez, Juan M., *Los extranjeros con carta de naturaleza de las Indias durante la segunda mitad del siglo XVIII*, Caracas, Academia Nacional de la Historia, 1980.

Morán García, Gloria M., "Los grupos sociales de religión no cristiana en el ámbito del derecho canónico", in José-Manuel Pérez-Prendes Muñoz-Arraco ed., *La violencia y los enfrentamientos de las culturas*, Madrid, Fundación Ricardo Delgado Vizcaíno, 2004, pp. 121–163.

Mörner, Magnus, "La difusión del castellano y el aislamiento de los indios. Dos aspiraciones contradictorias de la corona española", in *Homenaje a Jaime Vicens Vives*, Barcelona, Universidad de Barcelona, 1967, pp. 435–446.

——, "Ethnicity, Social Mobility and *Mestizaje* in Spanish American Colonial History", in Felix Becker, Holger M. Meding, Barbara Potthast-Jutkeit and Karin Schüller, eds., *Iberische Welten. Festschrift zum 65. Geburtstag von Günter Kahle*, Cologne, Böhlau Verlag, 1994, pp. 301–314.

Muldoon, James, "The Indians as Irishmen", *Essex Institute Historical Collections* 1975, 111 (4), pp. 267–289.

Nunn, Charles F., *Foreign Immigrants in Early Bourbon Mexico, 1700–1760*, Cambridge, Cambridge University Press, 1979.

Nuzzo, Luigi, *Il linguaggio giuridico della conquista. Strategie di controllo nelle Indie Spagnole*, Naples, Jovene Editore, 2004.

O'Gorman, Edmundo, *La invención de América. El universalismo de la cultura de Occidente*, México, Fondo de Cultura Económica, 1958.

Pagden, Anthony, *The Fall of Natural Man: The American Indian and the Origins of Comparative Ethnology*, Cambridge, Cambridge University Press, 1982.

Parry, John H. and Robert G. Keith, eds., *New Iberian World: A Documentary History of the Discovery and Settlement of Latin America to the Early 17th Century*, New York, Times Books, 1984.

Payne, Stanley G., *Spanish Catholicism: An Historical Overview*, Madison, University of Wisconsin Press, 1984.

Piña Homs, R., *La debatida exclusión catalano-aragonesa de la conquista d'América*, Barcelona, Generalitat de Catalunya, 1992.

Prosperi, Adriano, "'Otras Indias': missionari della contrarriforma tra contadini e selvaggi", in Adriano Prosperi, *America e apocalisse e altri saggi*, Pisa-Roma, Istituti editoriali e poligrafici internazionali, 1999, pp. 65–87.

Pudo, Raffaele, *I nemici del re. Il racconto della Guerra nella Spagna di Filippo II*, Rome, Carocci Editore, 2000.

Ramos Pérez, Demetrio, "La aparente exclusión de los aragoneses de las Indias: Una medida de alta política de don Fernando el Católico", *Estudios del departamento de historia — Universidad de Zaragoza*, 1976, pp. 7–40.

Rivarola, Francisco Bruno de, *Religión y fidelidad argentina (1809)*, José María Mariluz Urquijo, ed., Buenos Aires, Instituto de Investigaciones de Historia del Derecho, 1983.

Rivera, Luis N., *A Violent Evangelism: The Political and Religious Conquest of the Americas*, Louisville, Westminster/John Knox Press, 1992.

Rodríguez-Salgado, J.M., "Christians, Civilised and Spanish: Multiple Identities in Sixteenth-Century Spain," *Transactions of the Royal Historical Society*, 1998, 6th Ser. 8, pp. 233–251.

Ruiz Rivera, Julián B. and Manuela García Bernal, *Cargadores a Indias*, Madrid, Mapfre, 1992.

Rumeu de Armas, Antonio, "Colón en Barcelona. Las bulas de Alejandro VI y los problemas de la llamada exclusión aragonesa", *Anuario de estudios americanos* 1944, 1, pp. 431–510.

Said, Edward W., *Culture and Imperialism*, New York, Vintage Books, 1994.

Schiaffino, Santiago Lorenzo, *Origen de las ciudades chilenas. Las fundaciones del siglo XVIII*, Santiago de Chile, Editorial Andrés Bello, 1983.

—— and Rodolfo Urbina Burgos, *La política de poblaciones en Chile durante el siglo XVIII*, Quillota, Editorial el Observador, 1978.

Schmidt, Benjamin, *Innocence Abroad: The Dutch Imagination and the New World, 1570–1670*, Cambridge, Cambridge University Press, 2001.

Selwyn, Jennifer D., *A Paradise Inhabited by Devils: The Jesuit's Civilizing Mission in Early Modern Naples*, Aldershot, Ashgate Publishing, 2004.

Silverblatt, Irene, *Modern Inquisitions: Peru and the Colonial Origins of the Civilized World*, Durham and London, Duke University Press, 2004.

Solórzano Pereira, Juan, *Política Indiana*, Madrid, Compañía Iberoamericana de Publicaciones, 1972 [1648].

Starobinski, Jean, *Le remède dans le mal. Critique et légitimation de l'artifice à l'âge des Lumières*, Paris, Gallimard, 1989.

Szeminski, Jan, "Why kill the Spaniard? New Perspectives on Andean Insurrectionary Ideology in the Eighteenth Century World", in Steve Stern, ed., *Resistance, Rebellion and Consciousness in the Andean Peasant World, 18–20 Centuries*, Madison, University of Wisconsin Press, 1987, pp. 166–192.

Veitia Linaje, Joseph de, *Norte de la contratación de las Indias occidentales*, Buenos Aires, Comisión Argentina de Fomento Interamericano, 1945 [1672].

Weber, David J., *Bárbaros: Spaniards and Their Savages in the Age of Enlightenment*, New Haven, Yale University Press, 2005.

Zea, Leopoldo, *Discurso desde la marginación y la barbarie*, Mexico, Fondo de Cultura Económica, 1988.

10

Comprehend, Discuss and Negotiate

Doing Politics in the Kingdom of Valencia in the Sixteenth Century

Juan-Francisco Pardo Molero

Reconstructing the working of a political entity with a universal vocation — as was the Spanish Monarchy in the early modern period— presents historians with many challenges. One of the most important among them is understanding the way belonging to a greater structure may have influenced local goverment. Can local affairs be comprehended without reference to the larger tendencies that affected the entire structure? Can the different units be analyzed independently, without constantly referring to the other parts, or to what was common to many of them?

In order to answer these questions, I propose to examine the activities of the estates represented in the parliament of the kingdom of Valencia and the crown of Aragon. My aim is twofold: on the one hand, to study the language, culture, and practices that allowed the estates to play an important political role. On the other, to ask whether their actions were particular to that crown, or had important similarities with what was happening elsewhere within the Monarchy.

Existing literature had insisted that in both Aragon and Catalonia the estates claimed the preeminence of the kingdom *vis-à-vis* the king by asserting its priority or antiquity. In numerous accounts impregnated with legends, they sought to prove the preexistence of the nobility and its rights as a means of assuring royal subjection to it.[1] While this happened in Aragon and Catalonia, in the other kingdoms of the crown of Aragon (Valencia, Mallorca, and Sardinia), where elites were conscious of the foundational role of the Crown, the estates justified their participation in the political life as the king's indispensable interlocutors. A mythical past, history, law and intellectual elaborations all conjured to defend this idea, in which the concept of "representation" occupied a primary location. Yet, what representation meant, who represented what, and how and what were the relations between representation and access to the king, were all matters of debate. After Ferdinand was crowned (1479), the king's continuous absence from his hereditary kingdoms became both an abnormality and a structural feature. If, on the one hand, the eccentric nature of a headless

This study was conducted as part of a broader research project entitled "El gobierno, la guerra y sus protagonistas en los reinos mediterráneos de la Monarquía Hispánica", Código HAR2008-00512 Ministry of Science & Innovation, Spain.

political body was palliated by several ministers who represented the monarch locally, on the other, members of that political body developed assemblies or delegations through which they sought to channel their concerns to the Crown. How this happened depended on legal ordinances, the socioeconomic strength or weakness of different actors, and their respective degrees of articulation. Other codes also operated to make this complex system work; for example, intellectual habits and ways of understanding both privileges and liberties that took concrete expression in a set of practices, such as attempts to reach unanimity, electing representatives, delegating power to commissions, receiving information, and preparing embassies. Together, these practices allowed the representatives of the kingdom of Valencia to establish themselves as partners of the king. And, over time, what began as an exceptional modus operandi became the most habitual form to "make politics" in Valencia and perhaps elsewhere.

Corporation, Procuration, Jurisdiction

In his dictionary (1611), Sebastián de Covarrubias had good reason to bewail the subtleties and complexities of the concept of representation, directing readers to jurists for greater precision.[2] By the time he was writing, civil practice was saturated with legal representation by procurators and delegates. The same was true of government, the Spanish Monarchy securing its expansion by investing royal powers in representatives operating in the territories under its control. The universalization of the office of viceroy in the sixteenth century also allowed resolving many of the difficulties arising from the king's absence.[3] But fictitious presence through representation was not similarly received in all places. In the kingdom of Aragon, for example, the presence of a viceroy caused continuous disputes and challenges.[4] As problematic was also the question who of many possible local interlocutors best represented the kingdom *vis-à-vis* the monarch.

In the Early Modern Age, kingdoms were defined according to corporative and organic models. These defined the essence of the social and political order by utilizing concepts and rationales used by natural philosophy and by adopting a scholastic-Aristotelian scheme.[5] These models, which were widespread in the Spanish Monarchy, assimilated the natural world to a body, whose members were organized in accordance to a final end. An order bestowed by God upon his creation, it logically constituted the model also for organizing society, which was often defined — in imitation of the Church — as a mystical body.[6] Under this guise, kingdoms acquired the form and nature of a living organism, oriented towards some meaning or aim, a trait that was also attributed to their members, which were to perform assigned functions and were organized hierarchically so to contribute to the common good. Naturally, the king was the head, while the estates were identified with the extremities.

During the Early Modern period, political writers took these principles for granted. In the introduction to his first political treatise, the most celebrated sixteenth-century Valencian jurist, Tomás Cerdán de Tallada, waxed eloquent on a deeply-rooted "organicist conception of political society", as Teresa Canet has pointed out.[7] He reasoned that "all things depend on some cause and principle, by which they are governed and destroyed". The Supreme Creator had "ordered the movement of the heavens, the Sun, the Moon and the stars, and endowed them with natural influences and inclinations". Similarly, he gave man the "moral precepts" derived from the love for one's neighbor that, in turn, blossomed from the love of God. "In imitation of this", Cerdán proposed, "the cause and principle of the universal government of this Monarchy is to maintain the peace in order to assure the conservation of all things".[8]

This reasoning explains the enormous importance European monarchies attributed to estates assemblies over which the king presided and that visibly reconstituted the body of the kingdom, with its head and extremities duly joined. If any component went missing, the corporation was by definition incomplete, especially if the absent element was the head, the only one endowed with the power to call a general meeting of the estates in parliament (*Cortes*). While completeness was the social and political ideal, in the Crown of Aragon, at least, the question who would represent the estates when the parliament was not in session was under constant debate. Most disagreement focused on the power of *diputaciones* (deputations) formed by commission of the estates, to do so. The competencies of deputations varied from one kingdom to the other and their capacity as a representative body was often challenged by other institutions, for example, the councils of the estates. In the case of the *Diputación de General* of the kingdom of Valencia, also called *Generalitat*, this controversy was apparently resolved against that institution: in the fifteenth century, and parallel to its consolidation as an entity independent of the *Cortes*, Valencia's *Diputación* gradually lost its political weight. In the sixteenth and seventeenth centuries, its functions were limited to managing its income, while estate councils did take care of many political issues.[9] In both Catalonia and Aragon, in contrast, the protagonism of the *Diputación* was beyond doubt as, in addition to its juridical and financial responsibilities, it served as the Crown's most frequent interlocutor and channeled local demands to royal bodies, its representative character never truly threatened by the estates councils.[10] The same happened in other territories of the Monarchy, such as Castile and the Low-Countries, where similar entities, theoretically provisional, gradually incremented their power and intervention in fiscal matters.

In Valencia, disagreement over the powers of the *Diputación* was great. According to the celebrated chronicler Gaspar Escolano (1610), the *Diputación* or *Generalitat* of Valencia was "a government of the three estates, ecclesiastical, noble and commoners (town representatives) of the whole kingdom", endowed with specific income in order to "conserve local privileges and constitutions (*fueros*), and defend the realm". In his view, "the authority of this ministry is great" and its jurisdiction "so independent and absolute" that neither the king nor his officials could interfere with it.[11] On the contrary, jurist Lorenzo Matheu y Sanz (mid-seventeenth century) minimized the *Diputación*'s political capacity in favor of the estates assemblies. While emphasizing the capacity of the *Diputaciones* of Aragon and Catalonia not only in judicial and financial matters "but also to enforce observance of the laws" as representatives of the realm, he argued that Valencia's deputies, instead, "have never been granted jurisdiction or power over other matters" others than "collecting and managing" their incomes.[12] This reasoning identified jurisdiction with the power to represent. According to Matheu, when the parliament was not in session and whenever it was deemed necessary, "the kingdom met through the estates", who represented "the honors and preeminence" that pertained to it. Yet, the meetings of the estates had not the "same solemnity" as the meeting of parliament. Clearer still was his affirmation that "the true and legitimate representation of the entire kingdom is not found in other parts but in the general parliament (*Cortes*)."[13] This affirmation further reduced the degree of representativeness of the estates' meetings. Matheu did not ignore the fact that in Roman law the origin of power resided in the people.[14] For him, the organicist model of the Monarchy implied that only when the body of the kingdom was recon- structed in parliament with both the extremities (the estates, whom he insisted on identifying as *brazos* that is, literally "arms"), and the head (the king), one could speak of a complete representation. Thus, while the estates could "discuss" any matter that was not prohibited by the *Cortes*, it is probable that they could exercise decision- making power and full jurisdiction only when the parliament explicitly granted them such authority by delegating a council or a commission as happened, in Valencia, with the Councils of Defense (*Juntas de Defensa*) after 1529, and the Councils of Service and Jurisdictional Excesses (*Juntas de Servicio* and *Contrafueros*) after 1645.[15]

The power thus delegated by parliament to the estates was understood in similar ways in the other kingdoms of the Crown of Aragon. In Sardinia, for example, the elected estate bodies that emerged from vice-regal parliaments enjoyed jurisdiction only as required by the tasks they were commissioned to perform. Thus, in 1495, when the parliament elected a commission of twelve representatives to implement the taxa- tion and defensive measures adopted by the assembly, the three estates requested to give it broad jurisdiction so that it could have "authority and jurisdiction to examine, discern, define, declare and interpret all and each one of the questions or doubts that will emerge . . . regarding the dispatching of all these affairs."[16] In short, contempo- raries understood "representation" as the capacity to act under the authorization of the ultimate repository of power, the kingdom itself, and with the sanction of the Crown.

What remained unclear was whether the estates, acting outside parliament, repre- sented the kingdom. In Valencia, no one except the Crown or its representatives (and these, not without controversy, only after taking the proper oaths) could call the three estates to assemble and, as was noted on certain occasions, a separate meeting of each estate only brought together one part of the whole.[17] It was also the case that conclu- sions reached by each estate on its own could be communicated to the other estates or to other interested bodies only by formal elected representatives. Often, such dele- gates not only communicated the decision taken but also attended the meetings of the persons or corporations with whom the matter was to be discussed, fulfilling the axiom that all decisions had to be debated and approved by all interested parties.[18] Representation as a result was fragmented between one legislature and another and between the councils of each estate and the commissionaires they named. The same happened with the *Diputación* that, although a permanent body not delegated by the *Cortes*, had a limited jurisdiction, only embracing fiscal issues. Although he recognized that greater power was granted to the Catalonians, Matheu nevertheless held that Valencian deputies acted "with no little jurisdiction and power" and with a privative competence, in which not even the king could interfere. He therefore considered them "almost secular magistrates of the realm".[19]

These deliberations underlined that the key attribute of estate-assemblies was juri- sdiction. In Valencia, both the city council and the cathedral chapter had privative jurisdiction over certain affairs, but it was unclear whether they acted also as magi- strates when they represented their estate as commoners (the council) and as ecclesiastics (the chapter). Nor was it evident whether nobles as individuals could represent their estate. The corporations of course could constitute themselves as holders of jurisdiction (in a particular field of action) and they could transfer it through election to delegates named to negotiate with other institutions. But in Roman law, however, those elected had to be confirmed by their superiors — in this case the prince — before they could exercise jurisdiction.[20] This restriction became especially acute when it came to settling jurisdictional excesses (*contrafueros*), in which the estates could only deliberate (not decide) and only petition royal officials, the Council of Aragon, or the king for their intervention; or in which they insisted upon initiating new litigation or acting as interested parties in existing ones. Valencia's nobles often accused the Viceroy, the royal court (*Audiencia*) and the Inquisition of committing jurisdictional excesses. These trespasses, they argued, affected not only themselves but also the other estates. The normal practice in these cases consisted in creating a special commission that would deliberate on the matter, seek advice from the estate's attorney, and then initiate (alone or with delegates of the other estates) the procedures that may repair the wrongdoing. The delegates' limited faculties to resolve such cases were embedded in the vague nature of their powers. Though habitually these were broad and encompassed everything that the estate as a whole could do, they did not include necessarily anything that, in and of itself, could guarantee that the remedy demanded would be obtained.[21]

Deliberation, Truth and Experience

Recently, historians have insisted that in order to construct their political dominance, early modern monarchies used institutions inherited from the Middle Age, to which they gave new social, political and juridical interpretations. Despite its exceptionality, in some regards, this may have also been the case in the crown of Aragon. An analysis of the political discourse employed during this period may serve as an example. The work that Valencia's estates carried out separately when the parliament was not in session is not very well known, in part because of its institutional ambiguity. While the ecclesiastical and commoners' meetings could be confused easily with the meetings of Valencia's city council and metropolitan chapter, only assemblies of nobles had an identity that was sufficiently clear and distinguishable from other institutions and meetings. Despite these differences, all three estates shared the same predominant mode of political operation, which consisted of deliberation. The aim was to debate pending issues until an agreement was reached, also including measures for concrete actions. Topics were introduced into the debates in response to specific petitions or popular clamor as conveyed by the representative (*síndico*) of the estate involved, who could cede the floor to whoever was familiar with the specific matter at stake. The *síndico*'s proposal usually served to focus the debate that followed, in which the assistants elaborated arguments and introduced certain reasoning as a method to reach an agreement. Group and personal affinities, outside pressures, petitions and threats, also influenced decision making.[22] What ensured the freedom of members, especially nobles, was the requirement that all agreements would be adopted unanimously. As some historians have already pointed out, this prerequisite clearly privileged negotiating, as it allowed a solitary member or a minority faction to push the debate in certain directions and gain advantages by voicing its opposition to the majority. In reality, however, assemblies did not seek total unanimity, but instead a broad, qualified consensus that would be accepted by the more powerful and prestigious members who tended to pull the others along with them, at times using patronage or clientelist ties. Despite the risk that discussions would drag out into long sessions and the need for frequent adjournments, unanimity guaranteed that final agreements would be endorsed by the entire assembly and thus would carry greater authority.[23] Nevertheless, however important they may have been, these agreements did not have the weight of a judicial sentence or a governmental provision. Lacking jurisdiction, the estates could not conclude their discussions with declarations on law or resolutions endowed with executive authority, or that could affect those who were not part of the deliberations. Moreover, although their lawyers and legal advisers usually added their opinions to these decisions and cited the relevant legal texts — interpreted at their convenience — discussions did not necessarily unfold as juridical debates. To the contrary, estates' assemblies were settings *par excellence* for political debates regarding general versus private interests, the intentions of the Crown or other institutions, or the possible practical implications of certain royal or vice regal orders. Furthermore, the resolutions that these assemblies reached often gave rise to new meetings, in which debate continued, such as small commissions or organs of representation.

Frequently, and most particularly when financial support was required, discussions were moved from the estates to the *Diputación* or *Generalitat*. Such transfers were justified by the argument that the problems discussed also affected the revenues of the *Generalitat*. Thereafter, any issue that could affect even remotely the income of the *Generalitat* was considered "the *Generalitat's* affair". Yet, in meetings held to discuss the estates' demands, *Generalitat's* officials strove to fit these into existing regulations, mainly consisting in dispositions previously approved at the parliament.[24] This policy allowed lawyers working for the *Diputación* (usually prominent jurists) to intervene in the debate decisively. And, rather than seeking consensus, such joint meetings were mainly dedicated to searching for the best formula that could be employed in the petition that would be sent to the Crown, so that the justice of the request would be evident.

The jurisdiction of the *Generalitat* played a significant role in such dynamics. In order to certify the authenticity of an event, deputies — on their own initiative or in response to petitions from the estates — could request to collect declarations from witnesses. Because it was a court, the *Diputación* could request information in the form of a formal testimony (*informació de testimonis*) and could carry out this procedure with sufficient solemnity without external help. However, as in other civil cases, the reliability of the declarations collected did not rest solely upon procedure. It also had to fit the prevailing norms of reasoning derived from moral and natural scholastic philosophy. Thus, affirming facts on the basis of witnesses' statements also entailed resorting to experience and inferring "truth" through philosophical discussions. In an Aristotelian sense, experience was not based on concrete, isolated acts, whether provoked (like the experiments of seventeenth-century empiricists) or not, but on that which was observed in common by everyone, and which constituted a universal experience, molded through everyday acts that gave rise to universal truths. Experience was thus collective. It was constructed in community and through communal eyes, making a system of syllogistic reasoning possible. As a result, "truth" relied more on the authority of the source than on the verisimilitude of the facts to such a degree that experience and social credit became united.[25]

This logic guided the ways declarations were collected. Witnesses may have responded individually to a questionnaire, yet the opinions they expressed were rarely their own. Rather, they were those of *vox populi*. Expressions like "it is common knowledge" and "it has been widely heard" were repeated by trustworthy and reputable people, who reproduced collective meanings as their own. Similar statements were repeated in one declaration after the other, revealing the guiding hand of judges and scribes and the existence of pre-established agreements regarding the "facts" to be proven. The content of declarations, in short, concurred with the deliberations and debates at the estates or the *Generalitat*, and constituted a political, not necessarily a juridical, truth. As a result, factors such as common experience and moral authority became decisive to channeling the discussions and taking decisions.[26]

The petitions of the estates and the *Generalitat*, alongside the negotiations among their representatives, often resulted in the formation of an embassy. In the Spanish Monarchy, city councils and other institutions frequently sent emissaries to the Court, or even appointed permanent agents there, whose role was to insure that proper attention would be given to their petitions and a favorable result would be obtained.[27] The Crown usually attempted to impede such embassies from presenting themselves at the Court, arguing that they caused unnecessary expenses and that the Viceroy had full authority to resolve all pending issues. This reasoning potentially strengthened the jurisdiction and preeminence of Viceroys, who were to act as filters between the local community and the king. It also led to the proliferation of juridical arguments that would support such a role. In his treatise on the government of the Monarchy, for example, Cerdán de Tallada included a brief colophon based on Romanist sources concerning how the Viceroy should conduct himself. Reproducing Justinian's *Corpus*, which instructed officials to hear litigants thus preventing them from approaching the emperor directly "because of their negligence", according to Cerdán, the goal of this precept was to ensure that the emperor would not be disturbed.[28] Because Cerdán reproduced an instruction that could be applied to any appeal — not necessarily juridical — sent from any territory to the king, he could thereafter conclude that "those coming from the provinces should not be permitted to access his Majesty if they had not first adressed his lieutenant."[29]

Estates' institutions looked unfavorably on these arguments. Acknowledging their existence, they strove even harder to have their voices heard directly by the king and his immediate advisers. To this end, they argued that in both law and reason the vassals of the kingdom of Valencia, and especially the estates, had every right to approach their king whenever they felt it was advisable, and state in his presence their pretensions, or request a remedy when one was needed. At stake were not the particular privileges of the kingdom of Valencia or the crown of Aragon. All the territories belonging to the Monarchy should enjoy it.[30] The result was a collision between two distinct discourses: one royal, based on written principles of Roman law; the other invoked by the estates and founded on a supposed natural law not bereft of feudal connotations. Although the two were not necessarily contradictory to one another because Roman law was also considered an order based on natural reason, the latter rather than the former, however, meshed better with certain practices of negotiation. Besides procurators and attorneys, extraordinary agents, messengers and emissaries also approached the king, attempting to negotiate with him directly matters of great political importance. All used whichever resources at hand to carry favor with influential councilors but, in the case of ambassadors, this was particularly explicit, as they usually arrived armed with numerous credentials. Their nominators counted on their personal qualities and ability to achieve their goals. And, while procurators who wanted to pressure the judges or councilors could find their hands tied by the powers they received that usually restricted their activity to one concrete grievance and instructed them how they should proceed, an ambassador, in contrast, was normally free to interpret his instructions and maneuver as he saw fit.[31]

Those sent to carry out embassies needed broad-based support, as well as enjoy of large personal prestige. Frequently, emissaries were nobles from the city or canons of its cathedral chapter, but among them were also royal officials, especially if the demands to be voiced already had the support of the Crown's ministers in the kingdom. One such case transpired in 1509, when the interests of royal, as well as urban treasury, and the *Generalitat*, were all affected by a tax that King Ferdinand had imposed on Genoese commerce. After long negotiations, the person sent to the Court was the royal minister Joan Escrivà, whose experience and access to the king's closest councilors were highly valued. With the aid of royal secretary Juan Ruiz de Calcena, vice-chancellor of Aragon Antonio Agustín and the regent of the Council of Aragon Pere Alpont, all of whom received a handsome recompense from the *Generalitat* for their efforts, Escrivà convinced the king to remove the tax in exchange for a "voluntary" donation.[32] During the reign of Charles V, numerous delegations left Valencia for the Court, where they played a significant role in the genesis of the popular revolt known as the *Germania*.[33] A few years later, royal policy towards Valencia's Muslims moved the estates and the *Generalitat* to organize embassies to discuss this issue with the Monarch.[34] Nonetheless, both Charles V and Philip II strove to strengthen the buffering functions of the Viceroy, especially in matters that were framed as grievances or jurisdictional excesses. Thus, in 1540, when the estates openly challenged the Inquisition on its intention to persecute certain crimes committed by *Moriscos* (Muslims converted to Christianity and their descendants), emperor Charles V made it clear that protests must be directed first to the Viceroy, who would remit them to the Council of Aragon if he saw fit. The estates, however, maintained that in disputes over jurisdictional excesses custom mandated deliberation by delegates who, if they found a just cause, could take the issue before the tribunal or official involved, not necessarily the Viceroy.[35] Ten years later, after the death of Viceroy Duke of Calabria and fearing uncertainty, the estates planned to send an embassy to the imperial Court. When Maria of Austria, the emperor's daughter and regent in Spain, attempted to block their maneuvers, the estates, and especially the nobles, issued an angry protest that stoutly defended their right to access the Monarch.[36]

During this period, estates' embassies increasingly came to focus on negotiation as a strategy for presenting their vision of the *Morisco* problem to the king. But by no means did they neglect the use of personal resources in the pursuit of jurisdictional questions. For example, in late 1561, Cardinal of Sant'Angelo filed suit claiming the right to receive pension from the estate of the Order of Malta in Torrent, near the city of Valencia. The courts of the kingdom have already ruled against his request, upholding the rule that foreigners were not eligible to such benefices or income. When the Cardinal took his grievance to the Court, the three estates of Valencia followed him, immediately informing the Viceroy of their intention.[37] As much as they may have been interested in obtaining a favorable result, in this case, the estates were also motivated by their wish to consolidate embassies as ordinary procedures. Embassies, they argued, demonstrated both their loyalty and royal magnanimity. Rather than resorting to justice — that could be granted by the courts — they appealed to grace, the exclusive competence of the Monarch.[38]

Negotiating and petitioning on the margins of the law was again the mechanism chosen in late 1561, when the estates faced yet another conflict with the Inquisition. The incident began when the Inquisitor, Francisco Ramírez, forced the first Archdeacon of Valencia's Cathedral, Frederic de Borja, to cede him his seat in the choir. As both parties quarreled, Archbishop Francisco de Navarra looked the other way, thus disqualifying him from acting as a potential arbiter. Forced to intervene as representative of the ecclesiastical estate, the chapter sent emissaries to the other estates, and all of them together drafted a response that was to be taken to the Court by an ambassador. The estates also appealed to the *Generalitat* and, at a meeting with officials from that institution, an experienced canon named Miquel de Vich delivered an eloquent speech. Though he recognized that great scandal was avoided thanks to the patience, benignity and prudence that the archbishop had demonstrated, Vich also censured him, suggesting that he was more concerned with extinguishing the scandal than with defending his jurisdiction. The *Generalitat* approved sending an ambassador, naming Gaspar Joan to the mission.[39] The king was far from pleased when he heard the news. He gave strict orders that the delegation be detained, but this measure met with the protest of the estates, which alleged that the royal order was flawed because it had not been ratified by the Council of Aragon or, at least, bore no evidence of such ratification and that, at any rate, they had full right to send embassies to the Monarch.[40]

A few months later, Philip II's decision to build a fort in the sierra of Bernia and rumors that he planned to revive the Inquisition and have it act rigorously against the *Moriscos*, once again upset the estates in Valencia. In a session held on April 12, 1562, the noble estate resolved that the matter should be treated and maturely negotiated with great authority. In addition to electing delegates, it considered the possibility of sending an embassy to the Court. The members of the estate approached the *Diputación* with the hope of receiving economic and jurisdictional support. The estates asked the deputies to collect information from witnesses who would unanimously, and echoing the general opinion, manifest the gravity of the situation and the serious consequences that such 'novelties' may cause. Having gathered these reports, the estates named Baltasar Mascó, the *síndico* of the *Generalitat*, as their ambassador and entrusted him with explaining the stakes to the king. They also drew detailed instructions that, in the opinion of Dr. Rafael Benítez, summarized the "traditional position" of the estates regarding the *Morisco* question, including "simplifications that served their interests".[41] Apparently, Mascó encountered no difficulties in presenting their points of view at the Court and, sometime later, he reported back to Valencia on his efforts.[42]

On yet another occasion, questions of jurisdictional and ecclesiastical importance brought up the estates against Philip II. The problem began on July 9, 1562, during a meeting of the assembly of the nobility called to discuss threats against the ecclesiastical jurisdiction. Though during this session the members evaluated the convenience of maintaining one of their own at the Court permanently in order to procure reparations for grievances and solutions to jurisdictional disputes, the matter was ultimately left at the hands of a delegation that was to negotiate with the other estates. Eventually, a decision was taken to send ambassadors to the king. But the monarch quickly issued orders that all preparations must stop. Affronted, the noble estate argued that Philip II's predecessors had always allowed the estates to send embassies and that nothing should interfere in their right to "see the face of their king," a privilege which they held to be one of their most fundamental freedoms, on which all other freedoms depended.[43]

The estates also insisted upon their right to hold assemblies that met, they affirmed, to serve God, king and the wellbeing of the realm. Concerned mainly with questions of justice and defense, such assemblies, they argued, gathered prestigious individuals and their actions were limited to informing the king of what had transpired and procuring timely remedies. The mere notion that such assemblies met to plot against the Crown was preposterous.[44] Furthermore, these meetings were an obligation. The estates were required to ensure their integrity, and this responsibility entailed sending emissaries to the Court from time to time.[45] The king could not take away this right, because it was founded upon both justice and law. In their earnest attempts to convince the monarch not to deprive them of "royal presence" that constituted the "true solution" to the kingdom's needs, the estates stressed their loyalty to the Crown and listed the services they had already rendered, and would continue to offer in the future.[46] This rhetoric, stressing the loyalty of vassals and the theoretical exceptionality inherent to a polycentric monarchy, in which the king was constantly absent became, by the mid-sixteenth century, the universal tool that most territories belonging to the Hispanic Monarchy used (including Portugal since 1583). A method allowing justifying political negotiations, it was also an efficient mechanism to protest against the scarcity of royal grace that was only partially mended by the existence of viceroys and vice-regal courts.[47]

The disarming of *Moriscos*, decreed by Philip II in early 1563, set off renewed protests by the estates, which emphasized the benefits this minority provided to the empire, as well as denounced the exaggerated nature of these measures. The canon Miquel de Vich and the nobleman Francesc de Vilarig carried their objections to Madrid, but their protests were rejected.[48] Because the king reiterated his instructions, the estates moved to take action. All three estates presented to the Cortes of 1563–1564 a petition to approve measures that would finance the expenses incurred in the embassies. The king consented but with one condition: that visits by such delegations would be limited to cases judged "unavoidable" and that they would generate as few expanses as possible.[49] This response triggered discussion regarding what "unavoidable" meant. As a result, in the ensuing years, embassies that the estates considered sufficiently justified were blocked by Madrid, that did not consider them thus. In the Cortes of 1585, the estates once again insisted on their right in "law and reason" to send agents to the king. Once again, the Monarch recognized the right, but decreed that in their search to resolve their grievances the estates first needed to address the Viceroy.[50] Though this response was in agreement with common law, it was surely not to the pleasantness of the estates. More than applying a strictly juridical reasoning, the estates had always emphasized the virtues of the bonds of affection that united king and vassals, thus situating their claims squarely in the terrain of grace, not law.[51] Their insistence on this type of argumentation was no accident, as it reproduced with greater fidelity than jurisdictional contentions the negotiations taking place in Valencia. Nor was it by mere chance that in 1581, Cerdán de Tallada distinguished among government, justice and grace: three prerogatives that alluded to different ways to practice public activity.[52] He also suggested the benefits for conserving negotiations in the realm of grace. Thus, although the estates felt that their grievances were firmly grounded in law, their emissaries' efforts to persuade the Crown to act outside the normal procedural order, together with the estates' insistence upon receiving royal grace and establishing their right to send embassies, helped consolidate their appeal to grace, not law. By the seventeenth century, this appeal was clearly included in Court rituals and had become one of the most conspicuous forms of "doing politics" in the kingdom of Valencia and all over the Spanish Monarchy.[53]

In a passage from *Diana enamorada*, a novel published by Gaspar Gil Polo in Valencia in 1564, upon learning of the protagonist's desire to leave them, the two shepherds Taurisio and Berardo begged her to stay a little longer. When Diana insisted on departing, a third person, called Marcelio, also shepherd, interceded on their behalf, arguing that their "firm faith and true love" to her were obvious and, therefore, "it is right that their just demand be conceded". Finally, "all being of the same mind, Diana no longer wished to contradict them".[54] Gil Polo, who managed to have his novel published to coincide with Philip II's first visit to the territory as king of Valencia, was a royal official quite familiar with contemporary political practices.[55] As in the debate between Diana and the shepherds, the grounds upon which the estates based their petitions to the king were those of social unanimity and the authority of reason. These were endorsed by bonds of loyalty to, and love for, the Crown and represented ordinary channels to obtain (and give) royal grace. During this period both the political and legal idea of representation and the intellectual concepts of truth and experience were key elements in the definition of politics, shaping the discussions, organizing the arguments and providing the structure of the allegations of the kingdom of Valencia to the Crown. Nevertheless all were covered by the affective ties between lord and vassal that were typical of an organic corporation, as were the kingdom of Valencia and the Spanish Monarchy at that time. It was in this search for mutual convenience that political deliberation took place and their conclusions were presented to the king by representatives whose performance, though conditioned by the ceremonials of the Court, also depended on flexible practices and the ability of negotiators.

In sixteenth-century monarchies, the tripartite structure of Crown, corps of officials, and estates, thus constituted the setting for both negotiations, as well as the construction of authority. In Valencia, as in all the other territories of the crown of Aragon and the Spanish Monarchy, this setting offered sufficient channels for the development of an intense political activity. Variations in rights, laws and constitutions were not an impediment for the sharing of mechanism, criteria and values among the different units of the Monarchy. All units of the Monarchy were convinced that the king was accessible, that qualified representatives could negotiate with him, basing their arguments on a shared experience and on a certain moral discourse that would enable them to obtain what they wished if not by invoking law, at least by resorting to grace. In this way, similar if not identical images of the Monarchy were reproduced all over, facilitating a dialogue not only between the king and the parts, but also inside and between the parts themselves.

Notes

1 For Catalonia, Villanueva, 2004; Palos Peñarroya, 1997, 139–163. On Aragon, see Gascón Pérez, 1999.
2 Covarrubias, 1611, voz *Representar*. "This matter is very subtle and delicate according to the jurisconsuls, to whom I refer [the reader]".

3 Lalinde Abadía, 1964; Hernando Sánchez, 1999; Cañeque, 2004; Rivero Rodríguez, 2011.

4 Colás Latorre — Salas Ausens, 1982, 624–631; Gascón Pérez, 2010, 94–96, 107–111.

5 On the relations between science, society and the moral order, Shapin, 2000, 160–161 and 205–206.

6 Kantorowicz, 1957; Maravall Casesnoves, 1973; Redondo, 1992.

7 Canet Aparisi, 2009, 122; this work is fundamental for understanding the work of Cerdán de Tallada.

8 Cerdán de Tallada, 1581, ff. 7v–8r.

9 Muñoz Pomer, 1987, 1994; Castillo del Carpio, 1993, 1994; Guia Marín, 1984, 142–143; Giménez Chornet, 1992; Salvador Esteban, 1995; Lorite Martínez, 1999, 2000.

10 For Catalonia, see Ferro, 1987, 271–279 and Pérez Latre, 2004, 42–43, 161, 193. On Aragon, see Gil Pujol, 1992. In contrast, these polemics were not posited in Mallorca and Sardinia, where the territorial assemblies, though of a distinct nature, had full representativity: Juan Vidal, 2008, Guia Marín, 2008.

11 Escolano, 1610, Book IV, cols. 856–857, and Book V, cols. 1.088–1.089.

12 Matheu y Sanz, 1677, 118.

13 Matheu y Sanz, 1704, 68 b (*Totius regni vera et legitima representatio alibi non reperitur, nisi in Comitiis generalibus, vulgo Corts generals*).

14 McIlwain, 1947, 46; Vallejo, 1992, 56–60.

15 Guia Marín, 1975, 1992; Pardo Molero, 2001b.

16 Oliva — Schena, 1998, 185–194, quotation on page 192.

17 Canet Aparisi, 2002, 211–212; Bernabé Gil, 2007, 10.

18 See, for example, ARV, *Generalitat, Provisiones*, 2.971, f. 298v. On the maxim *quod omnes tangit*, Post, 1943, 1946.

19 Matheu y Sanz, 1704, 82 a: *cum jurisdictione atque potestate non exigua (. . .) quasi regni ipsius temporales magistratus.*

20 Vallejo, 1992, 61–63; on the charges brought by the military estate, see Lorite Martínez, 1999, 10–23.

21 Numerous examples are found in ARV, *Real Cancillería, Deliberaciones del Brazo Militar*, 523, 524.

22 On Valencia's noble estate, see Lorite Martínez, 1999.

23 Gil Pujol, 1991, 107–111; Serra i Puig, 2001–2002; Guia Marín, 1984, 62–63, 2003, 907.

24 Mora de Almenar, 1625.

25 Dear, 1997, 19–23, 44–45; Shapin, 2000, 109–113.

26 Valencia was not the only case where this was practiced. An analysis of negotiations in other territories is included in Merluzzi, 2008.

27 Gil Pujol, 1997, 237–238; Álvarez-Ossorio Alvariño, 2000.

28 *Corpus Iuris Civilis, Novellae Constitutiones*, Constitutio XVII, ch. III: *Alioquin etiam gratis lites audire et non permittere ex neglegentia de provincia cui praesides ad hanc currere felicissimam civitatem et nobis molestum esse.* (I cite here the version of *The Roman Law Library*, http://webu2.upmf-grenoble.fr/Haiti/Cours/Ak/).

29 Cerdán de Tallada, 1581, f. 178r: *Nec debent permittere quod provinciales ad Suam Maiestatem aditionem faciant quin prius dicto Locumtenenti adierint.* On this issue see Canet Aparisi, 2009, 88.

30 Gil Pujol, 1997, 237–238; Álvarez-Ossorio Alvariño, 2001, 204–221; Mazín Gómez, 2007; Díaz Serrano, 2010.

31 In the case of the city of Orihuela, Bernabé Gil distinguishes between the allegations in law used in juridical procedures and the less formal *memorias* that functioned through negotiations and advocated not justice, but grace. Gil also insists on the importance of personal qualities to the negotiation (2007, 235–236 and 247–272).

32 ARV, *Generalitat, Protocolos*, 2.730, 123v–125r, May 5 1509; especially the issue, ff.

18v–20v, 35r–38r, 74v–79v, 113r–117v, 119r–v, 121r–123v. On the petitions of the Sardinian parliament to eliminate this tax, see Oliva — Schena, 1998, 669.

33 Vallés Borràs, 2000, 143–177.
34 Castillo del Carpio, 1993, 157–159; Benítez Sánchez-Blanco, 2001, 99.
35 Pardo Molero, 2001a, 375–377.
36 Canet Aparisi, 2002, 206–214.
37 ARV, *Real Cancillería, Deliberaciones del Brazo Militar*, 524, ff. 6v–8v, acts of December 10 and 11, 1561.
38 Gil Pujol, 1997, 235–236. On the values implicit in royal grace, see Hespanha, 1992, 151–176; Bernabé Gil has accurately situated in this way the negotiations by the agents of the city of Orihuela, *passim*.
39 ARV, *Real Cancillería, Deliberaciones del Brazo Militar*, 524, ff. 5r–6v, act of December 9 1561; *Generalitat, Provisiones*, 3.024, ff. 168r–v, 171v–173r and 178r, acts of December 17, 19, 24, 1561. On this issue, see García Cárcel, 1980, 41–42 and Haliczer, 1993, 79–80.
40 ARV, *Real Cancillería, Deliberaciones del Brazo Militar*, 524, ff. 11r–12r, January 3 1562: a similar declaration was made in 1550: Canet Aparisi, 2002, 211.
41 Benítez Sánchez-Blanco, 1978, 186. The agreement of the noble estate and the instructions are in ARV, *Real Cancillería, Deliberaciones del Brazo Militar*, 524, ff. 32v–34v and 36r–39v; the *Generalitat's* provisions and information from witnesses are in ARV, *Generalitat, Provisiones*, 3.026, ff. 150v, 153r–157r and 159r–161v.
42 ARV, *Real Cancillería, Deliberaciones del Brazo Militar*, 524, ff. 39v–40v.
43 ARV, *Real Cancillería, Deliberaciones del Brazo Militar*, 524, ff. 43r–v and 53v–54r (July 9, August 28 1562). The *Diputación* of Catalonia in 1576 and the Congragation of the State of Milan in 1671 employed similar terms (Pérez Latre, 2004, 158; Álvarez-Ossorio Alvariño, 2001, 211–212).
44 "The liberty that the estates have to meet when they wish was given to them by the King and his predecessors as it is convenient to the service of God and the King and to the benefit and peace of the kingdom and its inhabitants, because in these meetings the only thing that is discussed are matters related to the good administration of justice and the defense of the kingdom (. . .). What is decided in these meetings is meant only to give notice to his Majesty and his officials of the necessities that exist so that they can be resolved (. . . .). In these meetings never was anything discussed or imagined that would be of prejudice to his Majesty or against his orders:" Instructions of the delegates of the three estates for Bernardino Gómez de Miedes and Pere Benavent; Ocober 27, 1562: ARV, *Real Cancillería, Deliberaciones del Brazo Militar*, 524, ff. 59r–61v.
45 "By law of the kingdom it is ordered that the estates are obliged to defend the rights and privileges, and that orders given against these rights and privileges would not be executed. As a result, the estates must notify his Majesty (of such violations) and procure remedy through the customary means: through embassy or messengers so that the King would know the necessities that exist and must be remedied." (*ibidem*).
46 "The main relief and pleasure of the estates is that always when some necessities have occured in the said kingdom they had had the liberty to come to his Majesty and see his royal person, because in this way they found reparation for all their needs. And this resort and refuge in his Majesty should not be taken away or denied because by justice and law and privileges it is permitted and because the fidelity that these estates have had and have for his Majesty and his royal Crown and the services that they have rendered and are ready to render, must incline his Majesty not to deny them the refuge of his royal presence, which is the true remedy against all the necessities of the said kingdom, as his Majesty until now has not taken away anything from these estates, on the contrary, he favored them, amplifying the grace, favors and grants that they received from the kings his predecessors and this because his Majesty knows well that these estates have been, are and will be very good subjects and very faithful vassals and loyal to the royal Crown, and that in them never

was it and will it be seen anything that may include infidelity or disrespect" (*ibidem*).

47 Pérez Samper, 1997; Gil Pujol, 1997, 234–236; Hernando Sánchez, 1999; Cañeque, 2004, 157–183; Rivero Rodríguez, 2011, 97–116, 133–173.
48 ARV, *Real Cancillería, Deliberaciones del Brazo Militar*, 524, ff. 72v–77r, instructions for the ambassadors, given February 25 1563; 77r–v, credential for the king, February 27; and ff. 83v–84r, response by the king, Madrid, April 2, 1563. Salvador Esteban, 1973, XXVIII–XXX, and Benítez Sánchez-Blanco, 1978, 188–189.
49 Salvador Esteban, 1973, 34–35.
50 If the Viceroy did not resolve the issue within ten days, they could send the embassy to the court: Salvador Esteban, 1973, 96–97; see also Guia Marín, 1984, 139–140.
51 Hespanha, 1992; Bernabé Gil, 2007, 10–11, 113–114; regarding affective bonds and their role in politics, Cardim, 1999.
52 Cerdán de Tallada, 1581, ff. 11v–12r.
53 Álvarez-Ossorio Alvariño, 2000.
54 Gil Polo, 1564, f. 77r (Book III).
55 López Estrada, 1988, 14–18.

Bibliography

Álvarez-Ossorio Alvariño, Antonio, "Ceremonial de palacio y constitución de monarquía: las embajadas de las provincias en la Corte de Carlos II", *Annali di Storia Moderna e Contemporanea*, 6 (2000), pp. 227–358.

Álvarez-Ossorio Alvariño, Antonio, *Milán y el legado de Felipe II. Gobernadores y corte provincial en la Lombardía de los Austrias*, Madrid, Sociedad Estatal para la Conmemoración de los Centenarios de Felipe II y Carlos V, 2001.

Benítez-Sánchez Blanco, Rafael, "Felipe II y los moriscos valencianos: el intento decisivo de asimilación", *Estudios de historia de Valencia*, Valencia, Publicacions de la Universitat de València, 1978, pp. 183–201.

Benítez-Sánchez Blanco, Rafael, *Heroicas decisiones. La Monarquía Católica y los moriscos valencianos*, Valencia, Institució Alfons el Magnànim, 2001.

Bernabé Gil, David, *El municipio en la Corte de los Austrias. Síndicos y embajadores de la ciudad de Orihuela en el siglo XVII*, Valencia, Institució Alfons el Magnànim, 2007.

Canet Aparisi, Teresa, *Vivir y pensar la política en una monarquía plural. Tomás Cerdán de Tallada, Valencia*, Valencia, Publicacions de la Universitat de València, 2009.

Canet Aparisi, Teresa, "Entre la visita y la sucesión. La resistencia a la virreinalización adminsitrativa en Valencia entre Carlos V y Felipe II", *Estudis. Revista de Historia Moderna*, 28 (2002), pp. 205–240.

Cañeque, Alejandro, *The King's Living Image. The Culture and Politics of Viceregal Power in Colonial Mexico*, New York-London, Routledge, 2004.

Cardim, Pedro, "Amor e amizade na cultura política dos séculos XVI e XVII", *Lusitania Sacra*, 11 (1999), pp. 21–57.

Castillo del Carpio, José María, *La Diputación de la Generalidad valenciana en un período de crisis (1510–1527)*, tesis de licenciatura (BA dissertation), Universitat de València, 1993.

Castillo del Carpio, José María, "Una institución valenciana en el umbral de la modernidad: la Diputación del General durante el primer cuarto del siglo XVI", *Estudis. Revista de Historia Moderna*, 20 (1994), pp. 311–316.

Cerdán de Tallada, Tomás, *Verdadero govierno desta Monarchía, tomado por su proprio subiecto, la conservación de la paz*, Valencia, Pedro de Huete, 1581.

Colás Latorre, Gregorio and Salas Ausens, José Antonio, *Aragón en el siglo XVI. Alteraciones sociales y conflictos políticos*, Zaragoza, Publicaciones de la Universidad de Zaragoza, 1982.

Covarrubias Orozco, Sebastián de, *Tesoro de la lengua castellana o española*, Madrid, 1611.

Dear, Peter, *Discipline and Experience. The Mathematical Way in the Scientific Revolution*, Chicago, The University of Chicago Press, 1995.

Díaz Serrano, Ana, "Repúblicas de indios en los reinos de Castilla: (re)presentación de las periferias americanas en el siglo XVI", in Sabatini, Gaetano, (ed.), *Comprendere le monarchie iberiche. Risorse materiali e rappresentazione del potere*, Roma, Viella, 2010, pp. 343–364.

Escolano, Gaspar, *Década primera de la historia de Valen*cia, Valencia, 1611 (facsímile edition, Valencia, Publicacions de la Universitat de València, 1972).

Ferro, Víctor, *El dret públic català*, Vic, Eumo, 1987.

García Cárcel, Ricardo, *Herejía y sociedad en el siglo XVI. La Inquisición en Valencia, 1530–1609*, Barcelona, Península, 1980.

Gascón Pérez, Jesús, *Alzar banderas contra su rey. La rebelión aragonesa de 1591 contra Felipe II*, Zaragoza, Prensas Universitarias de Zaragoza — Institución Fernando el Católico, 2010.

Gascón Pérez, Jesús, "Los fundamentos del constitucionalismo aragonés", *Manuscrits. Revista d'Història Moderna*, 17 (1999), pp. 253–275.

Gil Polo, Gaspar, *Diana enamorada*, Valencia, Juan de Mey, 1564.

Gil Pujol, Xavier, *De las alteraciones a la estabilidad. Corona, fueros y política en el reino de Aragón, 1585–1648* (dissertation PhD), edition in microfilm, Universitat de Barcelona, 1992.

Gil Pujol, Xavier, "Las Cortes de Aragón en la Edad Moderna: compración y reevaluación", *Revista de las Cortes Generales*, 22 (1991), pp. 79–119.

Gil Pujol, Xavier, "Una cultura cortesana provincial. Patria, comunicación y lenguaje en la Monarquía Hispánica de los Austrias", in Fernández Albaladejo, Pablo, (ed.), *Monarquía, imperio y pueblos en la España moderna*, Alicante, Caja de Ahorros del Mediterráneo, Universidad de Alicante, Asociación Española de Historia Moderna, 1997, pp. 225–257.

Giménez Chornet, Vicente, "La representatividad política en la Valencia foral", *Estudis. Revista de Historia Moderna*, 18 (1992), pp. 7–28.

Guia Marín, Lluís-J., *Cortes del reinado de Felipe IV. Cortes valencianas de 1645*, Valencia, Publicacions de la Universitat de València, 1984.

——, "El regne de València. Pràctica i estil parlamentaris (L. Mateu i Sanz, *Tratado de la celebración de cortes generales del reino de Valencia*)", *Ius Fugit. Revista Interdisciplinar de Estudios Histórico-Jurídicos*, 10–11 (2003), pp. 889–933.

——, "La Junta de Contrafurs. Uns inicis conflictius", *Saitabi. Revista de la Facultat de Geografia i Història*, 42 (1992), pp. 33–45.

——, "Los estamentos valencianos y el duque de Montalto", *Estudis. Revista de Historia Moderna*, 4 (1975), pp. 129–145.

——, "Més enllà de les Corts: els estaments sards i valencians a les acaballes de la Monarquia Hispànica", in Remedios Ferrero Micó and Lluís-J Guia Marín, eds., *Corts i Parlaments de la Corona d'Aragó. Unes institucions emblemàtiques en una monarquia composta*, Valencia, Publicacions de la Universitat de València, 2008, pp. 517–532.

Haliczer, Stephen, *Inquisición y sociedad en el reino de Valencia (1478–1834)*, Valencia, Institució Alfons el Magnànim, 1993.

Hernando Sánchez, Carlos José, "Estar en nuestro lugar, representando nuestra persona. El gobierno virreinal en Italia y la Corona de Aragón bajo Felipe II", in Belenguer, Ernest, *Felipe II y el Mediterráneo*, 5 vols., Madrid, Sociedad Estatal para la Conmemoración de los Centenarios de Felipe II y Carlos V, 1999, vol. III, pp. 215–338

Hespanha, Antonio Manuel, *La gracia del derecho. Economía de la cultura en la Edad Moderna*, Madrid, Centro de Estudios Constitucionales, 1993.

Juan Vidal, Josep, "Les reformes de Felip III en el Gran I General Consell de Mallorca", in Remedios Ferrero Micó — Lluís-J Guia Marín, eds., *Corts i Parlaments de la Corona d'Aragó. Unes institucions emblemàtiques en una monarquia composta*, Valencia, Publicacions de la Universitat de València, 2008, pp. 395–411.

Kantorowicz, *The King's two Bodies. A Study in Medieval Political Theology*, Princeton, Princeton University Press, 1957.

Lalinde Abadía, Jesús, *La institución virreinal en Cataluña (1471–1716)*, Barcelona, Instituto Español de Estudios Mediterráneos, 1964.

López Estrada, Francisco, "Introducción biográfica y crítica" a Gil Polo, Gaspar, *Diana enamorada*, Madrid, Castalia, 1988, pp. 9–50.

Lorite Martínez, Mª Isabel, "La presencia de las Cortes en las Juntas Estamentales valencianas durante el reinado de Fernando el Católico", *Saitabi. Revista de la Facultat de Geografia i Història*, 50 (2000) pp. 29–44.

Lorite Martínez, Mª Isabel, *Las deliberaciones del estamento militar valenciano (1488–1510)*, tesis de licenciatura (G.A. dissertation), Universitat de València, 1999.

Maravall, José Antonio, "La idea del cuerpo místico en España antes de Erasmo", en *Estudios de historia del pensamiento español. Edad Media*, Madrid, Cultura Hispánica, 1973.

Matheu y Sanz, Lorenzo, *Tractatus de regimine regni Valentiae, sive selectarum interpretationum ad principaliores foros eiusdem tribus libris contentus et explicatus*, Lyon, Sumptibus Anisson et Joannis Posuel, 1704.

Matheu y Sanz, Lorenzo, *Tratado de la celebración de Cortes generales del reino de Valencia*, Madrid, Julián de Paredes, 1677.

Mazín Gómez, Óscar, *Gestores de la real justicia. Procuradores y agentes de las catedrales hispanas nuevas en la Corte de Madrid*, Mexico, El Colegio de México, 2007.

McIlwain, Charles Howard, *Constitutionalism Ancient and Modern*, Ithaca and London, Cornell University Press, 1947.

Merluzzi, Manfredi, *La pacificazione del regno. Negoziazione e creazione del consenso in Perù (1533–1581)*, Rome, Viella, 2010.

Mora de Almenar, Guillem Ramon, *Volum e recopilació de tots los furs e actes de cort que tracten dels negocis y affers respectants a la casa de la Deputació y Generalitat de la ciutat e regne de València*, Valencia, Felipe Mey, 1625.

Muñoz Pomer, Rosa María, *Orígenes de la Generalidad valenciana*, Valencia, Generalitat Valenciana, 1987.

Muñoz Pomer, Rosa María, "La Generalidad valenciana en el siglo XV. Entre la representación y los mecanismos de control", *El poder real en la Corona de Aragón*, vol. IV, Zaragoza, Gobierno de Aragón, 1994, pp. 203–218.

Oliva, Anna Maria — Schena, Olivetta, *I Parlamenti dei viceré Giovanni Dusay e Ferdinando Giron de Rebolledo (1495, 1497, 1500, 1504–1511). Acta Curiarum Regni Sardiniae*, vol. 5, Sassari, Consiglio Regionale della Sardegna, 1998.

Palos Peñarroya, Joan Lluís, *Els juristes i la defensa de les Constitucions: Joan Pere Fontanella (1575–1649)*, Vic, Eumo, 1997.

Pardo Molero, Juan Francisco, "Imperio y cruzada. La política mediterránea de Carlos V vista desde Valencia", in Castellano Castellano, Juan Luis and Sánchez Montes González, Francisco (eds.), *Carlos V. Europeísmo y universalidad*, 5 vols., Madrid, Sociedad Estatal para la Conmemoración de los Centenarios de Felipe II y Carlos V, 2001 a, vol. III, pp. 359–378.

Pardo Molero, Juan Francisco, *La defensa del imperio. Carlos V, Valencia y el Mediterráneo*, Madrid, Sociedad Estatal para la Conmemoración de los Centenarios de Felipe II y Carlos V, 2001 b.

Pérez Latre, Miquel, *Entre el rei i la terra. El poder polític a Catalunya al segle XVI*, Vic, Eumo, 2004.

Pérez Samper, María de los Ángeles, "El rey ausente", in Fernández Albaladejo, Pablo (ed.), *Monarquía, imperio y pueblos en la España moderna*, Alicante, Caja de Ahorros del Mediterráneo, Universidad de Alicante, Asociación Española de Historia Moderna, 1997, pp. 379–393.

Post, Gaines, "Plena Potestas and Consent in Medieval Assemblies. A Study in Romano-Canonical Procedures and The Rise of Representation", *Traditio. Studies in Ancient and Medieval History*, 1 (1943), pp. 355–408.

——, "A Romano-Canonical Maxim, 'Quod Omnes Tangit', in Bracton", *Traditio. Studies in Ancient and Medieval History*, 4 (1946), pp. 197–251.

Redondo, Augustin, (ed.), *Le corps comme métaphore dans l'Espagne des XVIe et XVIIe siècles*, Paris, Publications de la Sorbonne, 1992.

Rivero Rodríguez, Manuel, *La edad de oro de los virreyes. El virreinato en la Monarquía Hispánica durante los siglos XVI y XVII*, Madrid, Akal, 2011.

Salvador Esteban, Emilia, *Cortes valencianas del reinado de Felipe II*, Valencia, Publicacions de la Universitat de València, 1973.

——, "Un ejemplo de pluralismo institucional en la España moderna. Los estamentos valencianos", *Homenaje a Antonio de Béthencourt Massieu*, Las Palmas de Gran Canaria, 1995, vol. III, pp. 347–365.

Serra i Puig, Eva, "Els dissentiments del braç reial. El cas de Barcelona a la Cort General de Montsó de 1547", *Ius Fugit. Revista Interdisciplinar de Estudios Histórico-Jurídicos de la Corona de Aragón*, 10–11 (2001–2002), pp. 685–719.

Shapin, Steven, *La Revolución Científica. Una interpretación alternativa*, Barcelona, Paidós, 2000.

Vallejo, Jesús, *Ruda equidad, ley consumada. Concepción de la potestad normativa (1250–1350)*, Madrid, Centro de Estudios Constitucionales, 1992.

Vallés Borràs, Vicent, *La Germania*, Valencia, Institució Alfons el Magnànim, 2000.

Villanueva, J. *Política y discurso histórico en la España del siglo XVII. Las polémicas sobre los orígenes medievales de Cataluña*, Alicante, Publicaciones de la Universidad de Alicante, 2004.

PART III | External Projections

11 | Republican Monarchies, Patrimonial Republics

The Catholic Monarchy and the Mercantile Republics of Genoa and the United Provinces

Manuel Herrero Sánchez

I. Introduction: Republics *versus* Monarchies?

This chapter argues that to assure its continued existence and projection, the Spanish Monarchy relied not only on its multiple decision-making centers spread around the globe, but also on its relations with foreign powers such as Genoa and the United Provinces that, according to their own conjunctures and chronologies, performed an indispensable function as satellites or allies. It further sustains that despite their importance, these questions have rarely been examined because the complex political realities of the Early Modern state and its polyhedral character were obscured by a state-centered historiographical tradition, which was often reinforced by national myths. Nonetheless, although existing bibliography tends to present the Monarchy and the Republic as contradictory, indeed rival, models, both Genoa and the United Provinces shared the same corporative and patrimonial social structure as the dynastic systems with which they collaborated and they became strongly attached to monarchies, in which the sovereign's power was circumscribed by numerous privileges and prerogatives. Thus, rather than analyzing each republic separately, much less present them as an alternative, homogeneous model, to the Spanish Monarchy, we must study them comparatively also including in our analysis their relations with the various other powers that existed in Europe at the time. Such a study would demonstrate their relative symbiosis with Europe's dominant imperial structures in the sixteenth and seventeenth centuries, as well as allow us to elaborate a less anomalistic view of the characteristics, scope and transformations of republican thought in the Early Modern Era. It would also suggest a new perspective on the functioning of certain dynastic aggregates that depended, at least until the early eighteenth century, on a range of financial, naval and logistical services, and on the circulation of news and products

This chapter forms part of a research project supported by the Spanish Ministerio de Ciencia e Innovación titled *El papel de las repúblicas europeas en la conformación del Estado Moderno:¿Alternativa modernizadora o motor del sistema?* ("The Role of the European Republics in the Formation of the Modern State: An Alternative for Modernization or the Motor of the System?"), HAR 2010–19686.

that the emerging family-based and mercantile networks in Genoa and the United Provinces came to offer in incomparable conditions. Last but not least, it would demonstrate that this close interrelationship of cooperation and confrontation had affected these republics and their institutions as much as it had brought substantial changes to the monarchies too, monitoring the balance of power in Europe and effectively moderating incipient tendencies towards absolutism.

Recent years have experienced the proliferation of studies that expounded an unconcealed exaltation of the principles of republican ideology. These works, which focused on the republics of Early Modern Europe,[1] searched for the imprint that the model of Italian Renaissance city-states may have left by upon the republican tradition, first in Britain, later in America.[2] In the process, Venice, Genoa, the Swiss Confederation and, especially, the United Provinces, have all been described as the last bastions of urban particularism in the struggle against the centralizing tendencies of the state. They were portrayed as the only possible alternative to the might of monarchical structures, and as systems best adapted to develop mercantile capitalism.[3] Analysts had thus stressed their characteristic modest degree of state intervention and their support for individualistic values, which was derived from a cultural milieu that spurred innovation and economic development.[4] These views affirmed, as well as accentuated, the exclusivity of these republics as anomalous entities. Small but prosperous, they had risen as the modernizing exception in a world dominated by dynastic-seigniorial systems, mercantilism and religious intolerance. Extracting them from their historical context, historians imagined a centralizing, homogenizing and *dirigiste* states such as the one characteristic of French absolutism in order to compare them to the republics. These were portrayed as an alternative: an innovative path that blended a curious mixture of British parliamentarianism and republicanism that, in the words of Hans Blom, rested upon the right to resist tyranny and formed one of the bases for a pacifist, federal Europe, founded upon the principals of tolerance and political participation.[5]

One of the most problematic aspects of this approach is that in the 16th and 17th centuries, precisely at the time of their greatest splendor, these republics' theoretical alternative coexisted not only with the French absolutist model (revised by recent historiography[6]), but also maintained close relations of confrontation and collaboration with a monarchy that, like the Spanish one, owed much of its stability to a negotiated respect for the juridical, cultural and institutional systems of the territories that joined it through inheritance or conquest.[7] Together, these territories made up a dense network of cities, each a zealous defender of its own privileges and freedoms, but each playing a fundamental role in maintaining the imperial system. The result was that a Spanish Monarchy based on the association of "urban republics," which even in the lands where the king exercised greatest authority such as Castile, allowed the persistence of a certain republicanism with providential hues and a pronounced anti-Machiavellian tradition, constituting a powerful barrier to the application of *raison d'etat*.[8] This was, in short, a composite monarchy[9] that, as Grubb put it so eloquently in his study of Venice, like many other republics, including the Swiss Confederation or the United Provinces, was plurijurisdictional in nature.[10] What were the relations between this monarchy and the republics?

2. The Monarchy and "its" Republics

Recent political history has portrayed the Spanish Monarchy as a structure articulated through a powerful network of cities, territories, seigniorial domains and court nuclei that secured and conserved broad spaces of autonomy. The mechanisms that lend cohesion to such disparate dominions were jurisdictional diversity, profession of the Catholic faith as the primary identitary element, and obedience to the same sovereign. The Crown was also skilled in implementing measures that facilitated the circulation of elites among the separate territories to the point that these came to form complex transnational aristocratic, mercantile and religious networks, all of them with vested interests in preserving the imperial structures.[11] Despite the existence of policies that supported protecting domestic markets from external competition, the very multiterritorial character of the Monarchy made it impossible to instrument economic programs of a mercantilist ilk like those that France and England were putting into play by the mid-seventeenth century. Economic warfare and commercial embargoes were of course employed, but they were viable only during military confrontations. Moreover, such measures achieved nothing more than granting certain advantages to some communities of businessmen to the detriment of others. They therefore did little to indicate that the Crown was autonomous or self sufficient when it came to controlling supply.[12] Quite to the contrary, the Monarchy strove to strengthen its ties of collaboration with the republics that were capable of providing it with the solvency it required and the naval resources it needed to maintain communications among its farflung lands. Businessmen in these oligarchic republics were best positioned to supply the Castilian, Neapolitan or American elites with a wide range of products that allowed them to preserve their social status, optimize the distribution of their agricultural surpluses and recreate behaviors that characterized a hybrid cultural model with a strong cosmopolitan slant.

Because of this close collaboration, the teleologically shaded historiography that linked republics to modernity and liberalism, selected not France, but the Spanish Monarchy, as the parameter that acted as a their counterpoint. It gave protagonism to areas that proved capable of maintaining full autonomy with respect to Madrid (Venice, the United Provinces and, perhaps, some Swiss cantons), underestimating those other republics that, like Genoa and the Hanseatic cities, collaborated closely with the Spanish Monarchy. Even a rigorous historian as Wim Blockmans opted to emphasize the insurmountable difficulties that arose in integrating the Low Countries — territories jealous of their autonomy and with the highest indices of urban and economic development in Europe — into the bosom of the most powerful and highly militarized monarchy of the period, which made the eventual revolutionary rupture virtually inevitable.[13] The defense of urban privileges against the standardizing policies of the Crown became, in Secretan's words,[14] the basis of a new concept of individual liberty that, together with the promotion of religious tolerance as the best means of facilitating mercantile exchanges, would transform the Dutch republic into a unique and isolated case. Following Huizinga's traditional thesis, the so-called 'Dutch miracle' is still judged in relation to the anomalous character that the republic adopted with respect to the countries around it.[15] The imposing economic development of the Dutch emporium analyzed by Israel, Van der Woude and De Vries[16] was thus intertwined with the existence of a society of bourgeois hues in which an urban elite of anti-aristocratic bent laid the foundations of a spectacular process of development. In this vein, following Wallerstein's approach, which described Holland as the first center of a world capitalist economy, Price pointed out that it was the Netherlands' decentralized and only marginally cohesive political structure that eventually fostered the promotion of individual initiative.[17] Prak, in turn, highlighted the uniqueness of the Dutch case that, when compared to the creation of the imposing bureaucratic structures and massive centralized institutions of the Modern State, succeeded in shaping a space that fostered economic development thanks to its maintenance of local institutions that prioritized the defense of urban privileges associated with medieval traditions. As Prak stated it, "The Golden Age was the product of its own past".[18]

The case of Genoa demonstrated the same prejudices on the inverse. A clear lack of interest in the model of the Genovese state was closely related to that republic's modest political autonomy and the strong financial ties of dependency that linked it to the Spanish Monarchy. Following this path, present day historians perpetuated the disdain that nineteenth-century liberal-romantic historiographical tradition held for an allegedly subjected Genoa, a sentiment that contrasted sharply with the exalted vision associated with the myth of Venice.[19] According to these postures, the *condotta* agreement signed in 1528 by Andrea Doria and Charles V not only constituted one of the most palpable expressions of the onset of foreign domination of Italy, but also fostered the formation in Genoa of an oligarchy made up of dynamic mercantile groups.[20] As Pacini and Kirk pointed out,[21] the idealization of a medieval past and the criticism of an Early Modern period, were already visible in the works of contemporary political writers who were highly critical of the alley contractors (*asentistas*) and prosperous bankers who served the Catholic King, whom they also accused of causing a crisis in Genovese manufacturing and of maintaining an aristocratic lifestyle far removed from republican sobriety and virtue.[22]

Although the differences between the various republics of the *Ancien Regime*, their relative degrees of autonomy, and their capacity to absorb the costs of protection without having to depend for their defense on militarized dynastic apparatuses, are clearly matters that deserve attention, a more fruitful approach would consist in studying comparatively those republics that integrated into an imperial system. This perspective by no means entails an approach that would view the republics as a common block that was antagonistic to the monarchical systems. As Durand rightly warned some time ago, these were aristocratic republics in which a closed, inflexible group of urban patricians imposed its criteria and patrimonial interests upon the rest of the community thanks to its numerous corporative and monopolistic privileges.[23] This was done in the framework of a political structure that, far from innovative, emerged as a perfected continuation of an iron-fisted urban particularism with medieval roots.[24] In short, the republics had an ankylosed governmental and social model that continued unmodified into the late eighteenth century and that, despite its seeming singularity, maintained tight bonds with the dynastic systems that dominated Europe. As Adams stated recently, far from fulfilling the Weberian parameters of an impersonal bureaucracy, these republics must be defined — like the dynastic systems of the period — as familial states.[25] We must therefore approach their study from an actor-oriented perspective that would take into account individuals, family networks and a plethora of different pressure groups.[26]

3. Economic Dependency and Political Articulation

The close collaboration between the Spanish Monarchy and the mercantile republics, as well as the dynamic nature of these relations during the sixteenth and seventeenth centuries, gains in perspective once we contrast the substantial differences that existed between the agreement reached by Genoa and the Catholic King in 1528 and the process of Spanish–Dutch *approchement* that followed the peace of Westphalia in 1648. This comparison provides valuable information on the decline of the Spanish imperial system and as well as serves as a platform from which to study comparatively the two republics that, to cite Haistma Mulier, still constitute uncharted territory.[27]

The Spanish Monarchy's growing dependence on foreign businessmen was not only a reflection of the Crown's urgent need for credits besieged, as it was, by the high costs of its imperial policies. Indeed, it would be a grievous error to lose sight of the fact that the debilitating war effort had not only supported the dynastic interests of the Hapsburgs, but also allowed the aristocracy to recover its military, administrative and diplomatic functions, such that any reduction of commitments abroad would have brought about a significant limitation of royal patronage (*patronazgo*) and the creation of new paths for promotion to, and accumulation of, offices.[28] For their part, despite their veiled criticisms of foreign contractors, Castile's urban oligarchies succeeded in turning the Crown's fiscal policies in their favor, and soon became a *rentier* class that also had vested interests in maintaining and consolidating the system.

In this setting, Genoese businessmen, attracted by the liquidity that came with the enormous shipments of silver from America and by Madrid's excellent political relations with the republic, became the Crown's primary moneylenders, carrying out with great efficiency their function as the capitalist component of the ensemble. In return, the Spanish Monarchy agreed to provide the Ligurian republic with the military protection it required and, despite a series of bankruptcies, offered members of the Genoese elite attractive means of joining the ranks of the governing class by, for example, purchasing lands or public offices, accepting titles of nobility, or taking advantage of their access to other types of royal patronage offered as recompense for the services they provided.[29]

The integration of the United Provinces took place somewhat later, but by the 1620s the crisis in Italy's exchange markets, the Monarchy's intensified military commitments in northern Europe, and the need to assure the continued support of financial networks operating out of Amsterdam (the new center of international capital), all forced Madrid to seek alternative sources of financing. At that point, the Genoese providers were joined by converted Jewish businessmen of Portuguese origin who, however, were unable to supply the Crown with wheat, munitions and naval equipment from Baltic markets without eroding the policies of commercial embargoes that Madrid had implemented in the hope of forcing the United Provinces to the negotiating table. When in 1635 France entered the war, Philip IV had no choice but to accept a compromise with a mercantile power that commanded sufficient naval force to move troops and money through the Monarchy's dispersed territories.[30] The limited effectiveness of the agreements signed with Denmark and the Hanseatic seats, the difficulties in which English businessmen found themselves after the outbreak of civil war there and, finally, the uprising in Portugal that facilitated the resolution of colonial tensions with The Hague, all led to the organization of peace talks with the United Provinces, which resented French advances in the

Low Countries and, therefore, were quite pleased by the substantial mercantile benefits that might accrue from an advantageous understanding with Madrid. With the signing of the peace of Munster in 1648, the Spanish Crown finally found a business partner with sufficient resources to satisfy — in very attractive conditions — its mercantile and logistical necessities. Together with the unrest in France (the *Fronde*), these developments allowed the Monarchy to achieve a significant recovery of its international position in the first half of the 1650's.

Under these circumstances, and in contrast to the situation of the Genoese financiers and Jewish converts, businessmen from the United Provinces secured the support of a republic with sufficient defensive autonomy to impose its criteria upon its former sovereign. In return for their services, the Dutch extracted an increasing number of prerogatives that made it rather easy for them to enforce their will upon their remaining adversaries in some extremely lucrative markets and to strengthen their position as the continent's principal mercantile emporium.[31] The "desire to avoid any occasion of trouble with the Dutch", on which the Spanish State Council tended to insist, gave virtually free reign to contraband activities and ended up seriously depleting the fiscal resources of a Crown that, because it needed the collaboration of these traffickers, refrained from prosecuting their illegal activities. Moreover, in contrast to their Genoese counterparts, the merchants from the United Provinces — with very few exceptions — were not attracted by the lucrative benefits that the Crown offered and, moreover, showed a complete disinterest in the financial negotiations of a bankrupt Monarchy.[32]

Lack of solvency forced the Crown to entrust the defense of its widespread territorial possessions to allies that, in return, demanded additional advantages and exemptions, especially the elimination of all attempts to impose controls on their commercial activities. Such measures were, of course, supported by local elites in the Monarchy's peripheral areas that, given the weakness of the central power, were able to increase their autonomy quite significantly. Contrary to what one might think, this development did not lead to a reduction of their loyalty to the Spanish monarch because, truth be told, by that time it constituted much less of a threat to their interests than did, for example, the French. The members of Castile's high aristocracy, meanwhile, opted to make up for the palpable diminution of royal patronage that came with the crisis in Spain's imperial structure by substantially increasing their own participation in fraudulent activities, taking full advantage of the protection provided by the concessions that the Crown had granted foreign merchants. The active participation of noblemen in illicit commerce was equally evident in Naples, as demonstrated by the fact that in 1652 the Viceroy, Conde de Oñate, attempted to force that kingdom's leading barons to settle in the capital as a measure barring them from involvement in smuggling.[33]

These beneficial diplomatic and commercial ties between the mercantile republics and the Spanish Monarchy also spurred a process that fortified the position of elites in both entities. The United Provinces' understanding with Madrid was sponsored from its beginning by the wealthiest of its regents, men who continued to identify their interests with large-scale international commerce while constantly guarding against a move to a dynastic order, which the presence of the populist Orange party could imply.[34] The situation in Genoa was similar. Although its gradual distancing from Madrid after the 1630s had fostered the appearance of a *repubblichista* party desirous of strengthening the republic's political autonomy through a program designed to reactivate its navy and bring about an *approchement* with France, the governing elite remained steadfastly loyal to the Catholic King.[35]

Given that Genoa was linked to the Spanish Monarchy by a chain of gold, it is hardly surprising that in 1651 Brasset, France's ambassador to The Hague, warned Dutch leaders of the danger of allowing themselves to be lured by the attractive mercantile privileges that Madrid offered in exchange for an alliance against France because, as he pointed out, they might suffer the same fate as the Genoese, whom, he said, " . . . [Madrid] abused and maintained in severe dependence by extracting all its effects under the broad pretext of commerce".[36] Despite this appeal, by the mid-seventeenth century, far from constituting a threat, Spain's weak military presence in the Low Countries became nothing more than a defensive security barrier against France's expansionist policies.

Their understanding with Madrid stipulated a series of strategic advantages and commercial concessions that clearly strengthened the position of merchants from the United Provinces in world markets. Their privileged access to shipments of silver from the Americas allowed these merchants to make up the losses they had suffered with the contraction of trade with the Baltics, and gave a renewed impulse to Dutch advances in Asian markets and the Ottoman Levantine, where exchanges involved mainly precious metals. The distribution of heavy products, like wheat and naval gear that required a large mercantile fleet but minimal armed protection, gradually ceded space to the commercialization of luxury products that, because of their high commercial value, were handled by a group of wealthy businessmen that had ever fewer members, but held enough political ascendancy to deploy an efficient system of convoys that, whenever it was deemed necessary, enjoyed the full military support of the republic.[37]

The increasing demand for sumptuary products that emerged in Spanish markets and the control of shipments of Castilian Merino wool sustained a process of industrial reconversion in manufacturing centers like Leiden, where production of low-quality fabrics was abandoned in favor of specialization in the elaboration of luxury items. Though the influence of guild corporations in the United Provinces has often been minimized because of their marginalized position in relation to local government structures and their pronounced localism, total decentralization led to inter-urban rivalries that translated into a strict regulation of industrial activity and tight protectionist policies on the part of those municipalities that were able to secure supplies of raw materials in particularly advantageous terms and had the ability to avoid potential competition.[38] Despite the decided support of local authorities, Dutch industry experienced growing difficulties in competing with external production.

Contrary to what historians have often concluded, high wages were not a reflection of the elevated standard of living of the popular sectors in the republics. Rather, Dutch and Genoese governing groups confronted the imposing burden of public debt and the need to raise funds to protect and promote their mercantile interests against the advances of numerous rivals by significantly increasing fiscal pressures through the imposition of indirect taxes that severely affected consumption of items of basic necessity such as wheat, meat, salt, wood, soap and butter. This was a reality that hardly seemed to jibe with the idealized image of Dutch society that Arnauld de Pomponne offered in 1671.[39] Shortly before that, Spinoza's mentor, Franciscus Van den Enden, had denounced the grievous conditions of the republic's working class and the disdain with which it was treated by the regents who, as can be seen in the writings of the La Court brothers, warily observed the subversive tendencies of the masses and their scarcely concealed attachment to the Prince of Orange.[40] Indeed, as Dekker has emphasized, the apparent stability of the United Provinces was bespattered with frequent revolts, plots and popular altercations that, on some occasions, appeared to threaten the monopoly of power that a small group of urban patriarchs held, and whose members had no qualms about harshly repressing any and all uprisings that challenged their authority.[41] Testifying to this reality were revealing testimonies, such as that of Vincent Richard, Secretary of the Spanish embassy in The Hague, who on the occasion of the publication of the Act of Seclusion of the Orange Family from the office of Stadtholder, wrote to Madrid alarmed by the negative consequences that rejection of the measure by the populace might provoke coming, as it did, on top of their miserable living conditions.[42]

The situation in Genoa was governed by the same canons. The misery of the popular sectors and the poor living conditions of the artisan class could serve as a basis for a revolt that could be used by certain discontented sectors to propel a transformation of the aristocratic constitution of 1576.[43] It is therefore not surprising that Spain's diplomatic delegates collaborated resolutely with Genoese authorities to stifle a series of plots that, in general, were supported by the Monarchy's enemies with the objective of cutting the links that tied that republic's elite to the Crown. The Vachero conspiracy, financed by the Duke of Savoy in 1628, which was based on a program of populist hue, manifested the danger that the intense factional conflicts that were boiling in the very heart of the governing class posed for the stability of that regime.[44] Gian Pablo Balbi's failed conspiracy in 1648 — supported by Paris–[45] was followed two years later by a plot orchestrated by Stefano Raggio and Ottaviano Sauli that, in the opinion of Secretary of the Spanish embassy, Diego de Laura, found its main sustenance in the misery of the rabble: "which in Genoa is very populous and poor".[46]

4. Scope and Limits of the Republican Model in a Europe Made of Monarchies

The question how under these circumstances the republics survived is difficult to answer. The claim to defend the common good, central to republican ideals, functioned extremely well as a mechanism of ideological hegemony for the patrician group that considered itself best qualified to guarantee respect for the rights and privileges of the urban population. Moreover, its sponsorship of celebrations and iconographic programs that exalted a glorious shared past allowed its members to muffle the protests of popular sectors through the construction of a collective identification that embraced all the social segments residing in the city.[47] Together, these mechanisms identified the interests of the republic with the aspirations of oligarchies that, thanks to their complete control of public offices, nepotistic and endogamic family ties, eventually transformed into aristocratic groups that gradually tended to lose some of their entrepreneurial spirit.[48] Other mercantile and republican virtues, such as frugality and moderation in one's habits, also began to recede with the wave of luxury consumption and ostentation that became visible in Genoa in the sixteenth century and would become palpable in the United Provinces in the second half of the seventeenth, as manifested in burdensome investment in public debt and the high costs of building palaces sumptuously decorated in the French style, which were well underway by the 1660s.

The markedly aristocratic character of these republican regimes explained why it was more difficult to achieve social mobility in Genoa or the United Provinces than in the dynastic systems, where the grace of the prince was a permanent source of advancement. Nonetheless, these republican aristocracies did guarantee some measure of freedom because control of the organs of government rested in the hands of a select group of *ottimati* (*optimates*), which was fully capable of assuring the survival of a series of privileges and franchises the defense of which constituted the primary guarantee of autonomy from both desires to centralize administrative functions and tendencies towards absolutism. Just like the Genoese *repubblichiste* Raffaele della Torre, who went to great lengths to demonstrate that "the Republic had achieved freedom before the world came to know the glorious name of Austria";[49] the grand tradition of uprisings, which Blockmans described in the case of the cities of Flanders and Brabant,[50] would be perpetuated in the United Provinces through the adoption of a discourse focused on the defense of urban privileges and self-government against a tyranny, whose antecedents began, it was argued, as far back as the Batavian revolt against the Roman Empire.[51]

This ability to moderate the possible evolution of European entities towards absolutism, however, should not lead us to assume the existence of some kind of coherent program that could expand republicanism into foreign lands. There is no question that the examples of Venice, Genoa and the United Provinces fascinated other territories that wished to preserve their autonomy, freedoms and privileges despite the interference of their respective sovereigns, as occurred in Catalonia in 1640, in Naples during the 1647 uprising, and in France with the *Fronde*.[52] The publication of a series of pocketbooks known as the *petites républiques* by Abraham and Bonaventura Elzevier between 1626 and 1649, which examined several examples of republics that dated from antiquity to the recently created Dutch regimen, was an additional indication of such interest. However, none justified positing the existence of an international republicanism as an alternative to the monarchical system.[53]

The rejection of the proposal to establish a confederation of the two mercantile republics of England and the United Provinces, formulated by Cromwell in 1651 and subsequently presented to The Hague, suffices to establish that, more than viewing each other as allies, both republics tended to behave as direct, and quite fierce, competitors. It would appear that their respective commercial interests, competing for ascendancy over the same markets, took priority over any prospect for solidarity. Indeed, Genoa's attempts to earn independence from Madrid's tutelage in the 1640s and 1650s by implementing a program that would revitalize its naval capacity and stimulate colonial expansion were undermined, at least partially, by the posture adopted by the United Provinces.[54] Businessmen from the latter not only replaced their Genoese counterparts in Spanish markets by operating with greater efficiency and thus diminishing the effect of the reprisals directed against Madrid, but also enjoyed the support of its government in launching punitive acts against these rivals who lacked the military means necessary to put up resistance. Thus, in 1648, the recently formed Genoeve *Compagnia Genovese delle Indie Orientali* looked on with great dismay as the ships it had purchased in the dockyards of Amsterdam were confiscated in the harbor of Batavia by the *Dutch East India Company*, which was not about to cede one iota of its mercantile monopoly in Asian waters.[55]

While they competed with one another, the Spanish Monarchy, pressured by France and harassed by England's eagerness to divest it of its colonial possessions, showed a keen interest in tightening its diplomatic ties with both republics, which guaranteed the safety of its sea routes and the supplies of many products, and provided the financial resources the Crown so badly needed. It is therefore easy to understand why in 1672, when the Ligurian republic was invaded by the duchy of Savoy, and Holland by France, Spain's ambassador to The Hague wrote to his counterpart in Genoa to express the following wish: "May God help you get out of this storm and, despite what had happened in this country, this year would not become one of accused decline of the republics, as our health and conservation depend, to a large extent, on them".[56] Eventually, thanks to the military support it provided to the Genoese, the Monarchy was able to strengthen its traditional function as the principal protector of that republic's freedom from any and all external threats.[57] As the Genoese representative in Madrid Giovanni Andrea Spinola pointed out, this protection also brought about the collapse of the local pro-French party, thus reinforcing Genoa's ties with the Spanish Monarchy that, at least, represented no threat to its territorial integrity.[58] Nonetheless, although these events strengthened the relationship with the Monarchy, the intense bombardment of Genoa by the French fleet in 1684 also exposed the limits of such a protection.

More valuable still was the unconditional support that Madrid provided to the United Provinces during the tense months of the Franco-British invasion of 1672. The entry of the Spanish Monarchy into this war led to a shift in the theater of operations towards the Flemish front. This proved to be a decisive factor when time came to force England's retreat from the conflict, because fears arose that a rupture with the Catholic monarch might result in Spain closing its markets to British merchants.[59] Madrid backed the Prince of Orange as he sought to recover the reins of government, for which he was soon awarded the rank of Captain-General of the allied armies and honored with the title 'Your Highness'.[60] Still, the Crown felt rather relieved when the provincial states of Holland and Zealand impeded William III from accepting the title of Duke of Gelderland because, as Spain's ambassador in The Hague, Francisco Manuel de Lira, had warned:

> . . . I judge that our interests have escaped from a serious contretemps as popular riots had begun to break out against such initiatives and the Prince, having been convinced by the other provinces with votes based on flattery and politics, to accept this offer that entails a great risk for those of us who desire that this government would be more aristocratic than monarchical.[61]

Despite its defense of the republican model of government in the United Provinces, the neutralist position taken by the Dutch regents towards Louis XIV's expansionist policies explained the Spanish Monarchy's unconditional support of the dynastic interests of the Prince of Orange in England as the most adequate means of forcing the English to enter into the conflict with France. The success of William III's 1688 naval expedition was deemed by some contemporaries an able maneuver by the United Provinces to rid itself of the Prince of Orange and strengthen the republic's position in international markets,[62] but events soon demonstrated the falsity of these predictions. While the United Provinces took charge of the expensive war effort against France in the Low Countries, England ultimately ousted that republic from its role as the dominant naval and mercantile power, as would soon become manifest with total clarity in the Spanish War of Succession.

Conclusions

The articulation of an enormous Monarchy-market divided between two oligarchic republics may have differed in chronology and meaning, but its consequences, in contrast, were quite similar: Both the Catholic King and his republican allies sought to procure and then support the political *and* social stability of the sectors that played an indispensable role in the functioning of their respective systems of government. Given that there was no need to modify the services that these providers already rendered, the tendency veered towards immobility. In contrast, during this period, France and England — both badly shaken by acute internal conflicts in the seventeenth century (a situation that contrasts strongly with the high degree of stability that the Spanish Monarchy, Genoa and the United Provinces had enjoyed)— began emerging as two dynastic models endowed with a sufficient capacity to break Spain's bonds of dependence with both mercantile republics. In spite of the important divergences in their respective political systems, both France and England were able to push forward a process of administrative centralization, effectively restricting local privileges, and implementing economic mercantilist programs that defended their national businessmen. This process translated, in the eighteenth century, into the gradual loss of political influence by republics that up to then had played a fundamental role in maintaining a balance among Europe's powers. By that time, any comparative advantage that they could have accrued from associating with a composite Monarchy, whose logic they ultimately shared, had vanished. Before long, they would vanish too, just like the Monarchy with which they had allied, deteriorating into nothing other than relics of a great past.

Abbreviations

AGS   Archivo General de Simancas.
       E   Estado.
AHN   Archivo Histórico Nacional.
       E   Estado.
ASF   Archivio di Stato di Firenze.
MdP   Mediceo del Principato.

Notes

1 Pettit, 1999; Q. Skinner, 1998, 82; Ovejero, 2003.
2 Pocock, 1975; G. Bock, Q. Skinner Y. M. Viroli, 1990; Kossmann, 1985.
3 Blockmans, 1998, 52.
4 Burke, 1994.
5 Blom, 2002, 91–115.
6 Beick, 1985; Schaub, 1993; Consanday and Decimon, 2002.
7 Ruiz Ibáñez and Sabatini, 2009.
8 Centenero de Arce, 2010; Aranda Pérez, 2006; Gil Pujol, 2008; Iñurritegui, 1998; Fernández Albaladejo, 1996.
9 Gil Pujol, 1996.
10 Grubb, 1988.

11 Yun Casalilla, 2009.

12 Herrero Sánchez, 2006; Alloza, 2006.

13 Blockmans, 1999, p. 112; Echevarría Bacigalupe, 1998; Rodríguez Salgado, 2008, 181–183.

14 Secretan, 1990; Van Gelderen, 1992.

15 Huizinga's thesis of exception, which reveals the pronounced nationalist tendency that colored Dutch historiography from 1941, appeared in Huizinga, 1981. On the so-called *Dutch miracle*, see Swart's work, 1969; and a comparative perspective that seeks to place the republic in European context, but that gradually accentuates differences, Davids and Lucassen, 1995.

16 Israel, 1995; De Vries and Van Der Woude, 1992.

17 Price, 1998.

18 Prak, 2005, 4.

19 De Sismondi, 1996.

20 Pacini, 1999, 9–14; Braudel, 1979, 140; see also Grendi, 1987.

21 Pacini, 2005; Kirk, 2005.

22 Bitossi, 1990; Costantini, 1992.

23 Durand, 1973.

24 Herrero Sánchez, 1999 and 2005.

25 Adams, 2005.

26 Grendi, 1997; Herrero Sánchez, 2009.

27 Haitsma Mulier, 1983.

28 Yun Casalilla, 2002.

29 Herrero Sánchéz, 2007.

30 Alcalá Zamora, 2001.

31 Herrero Sánchez, 2000.

32 Sanz Ayanz, 1992.

33 ASF MdP leg. 4116, 23 April 1652, Naples, Vincenzo Medici to the Grand Duke.

34 Israel, 1982.

35 As expressed in a letter to Antonio Ronquillo by Philip IV in the midst of the Monarchical crisis; see ASG E leg. 3603, Genoa, 28 April 1648.

36 AGS E. leg. 2076, 19 April 1651, Madrid, Memorial elevado a los Estados Generales por el enviado francés en la Haya, incluido en una consulta del Consejo de Estado.

37 Israel, 1990, 197–291.

38 Noordegraaf, 1992, 20.

39 Rowen, 1955, 46.

40 Bedjaï, 1993.

41 Dekker, 1996.

42 AGS, E., leg. 2083, 15 April 1654, La Haya, Vincent Richard to Philip IV. Roorda, 1969.

43 Costantini, 1978, 119.

44 Venturi, 2001, 39.

45 AGS E 3604, 26 March 1649, Genoa, Antonio Ronquillo to Philip IV. Bitossi, 1986.

46 AGS E 3605, 10 July 1650, Naples, letter from Diego de Laura. For a similar interpretation, see Braudel, 1997, 480.

47 Blockmans, 1998, 64; Adams, 1993, 331.

48 Roorda, 1964; Bitossi, 1990; Pacini, 1999; Grendi, 1987.

49 AGS E 3608 f 222, 1655, Genoa, Memorial de Raffaele della Torre.

50 Blockmans, 1988.

51 Van Gelderen, 1990, 215.

52 Mastellone, 1983 and 1985; Gil Pujol, 2002, 279–285.

53 Conti, 1997.

54 Kirk, 1996; Herrero Sánchez, 2000, 304–307.

55 Subrahmanyam, 1988.
56 AHN E book 146, 16 November 1672, La Haya, Manuel de Lira to Marqués de Villagarcía.
57 AGS E 3636, 22 November 1672, Consulta del Consejo de Estado sobre el conflicto entre Génova y Saboya.
58 Ciasca, 1957, Vol. V, 190.
59 Herrero Sánchez, 2000, 187–199.
60 On this issue, see Brom, 1911, Vol. II, 387.
61 AHN, E., book 146, 7 March 1675, La Haya, Manuel de Lira to Marqués de Villagarcía.
62 Brom, 1911, Vol. II, 80.

Bibliography

Adams, J., "Trading States, Trading Places: the Role of Patrimonialism in Early Modern Dutch Development", *Comparative Studies in Society and History*, 36, no. 2 (1994), pp. 319–355.

——, *The Familial State. Ruling Families and Merchants Capitalism in Early Modern Europe*, Ithaca, Cornell University press, 2005.

Alloza Aparicio, A., *Europa en el mercado español. Mercaderes, represalias y contrabando en el siglo XVII*, Salamanca, Junta de Castilla y León, 2006.

Alcalá-Zamora, J., *España, Flandes y el mar del Norte (1618–1639)*, Madrid, Planeta, 2001 (1st ed. 1975).

Aranda, F.J, "'Republicas ciudadanas'. Un entramado político oligárquico para las ciudades castellanas en los siglos XVI–XVII", *Estudis* 32 (2006), pp. 7–46.

Bedjaï, M., "Pour un État populaire ou une utopie subversive", in H. Méchoulan (ed.), *Amsterdam, XVIIe siècle. Marchands et philosophes: les bénéfices de la tolérance*, Paris, Autrement, 1993, pp. 194–213.

Beick, W., *Absolutism and Society in Seventeenth-Century France. State, Power and Provincial Aristocracy in Languedoc*, Cambridge, Cambridge University Press, 1985.

Bitossi, C., "'Mobbe' e congiure. Note sulla crisi política genovese di metà seicento", in *Miscellanea Storica Ligure*, XVIII, (1986), pp. 587–626.

——, *Il governo dei magnifici. Patriziato e politica a Genova fra Cinque e Seicento*, Genoa, Edizioni culturali internazionali Genova, 1990.

Blockmans, W., "Alternatives to Monarchical Centralization: The Great Tradition of Revolt in Flanders and Brabant", in H.G. Koenisberger (ed.), *Republiken und Republikanismus im Europa der frühen Neuzeit*, Munich, Oldenbourg Wissenschaftsverlag, 1988, pp. 145–154.

——, "Villes et états. Deux modèles de pouvoir à la fin du moyen âge", in A. Alvar, J.M. de Bernardo and P. Molas (coords.), *Espacios urbanos, mundos ciudadanos. España y Holanda (ss. XVI–XVIII)*, Cordoba, Universidad de Córdoba, 1998.

——, "The Formation of a Political Union, 1300–1600", in J.C.H. Blom and E. Lamberts, (eds.), *History of the Low Countries*, Oxford, Berghahn Books,1999, pp. 55–140.

Blom, H. W., "The Republican Mirror: The Dutch Idea of Europe", in A. Pagden (ed.), *The Idea of Europe: From Antiquity to the European Union*, Cambridge, Cambridge University Press, 2002, pp. 91–115.

Brom, G., *Archivalia in Italië. Belangrijk voor de Geschiedenis van Nederland, Vol. III. Vaticaansche Bibliotheek*, The Hague, 1911.

Bock, G., Q. Skinner and M. Viroli, *Machiavelli and Republicanism*, Cambridge, Cambridge University Press, 1990.

Braudel, F., *Civilisation matérielle, économie et capitalisme, XVe–XVIIIe siècles. III: Les Temps du monde*, Paris, Armand Colin, 1979.

——, *En torno al Mediterráneo*, Barcelona, Paidós, 1997.

Burke, P., *Venice and Amsterdam: A Study of Seventeenth-Century Elites*, Cambridge, Cambridge University Press, 1994 (1st ed. 1974).

Centenero de Arce, Domingo, *De repúblicas urbanas a ciudades nobles. La vida y el pensamiento de Ginés de Rocamora de Torrano*, Unpublished B.A. Thesis, 2010, Universidad de Murcia.

Ciasca, R., *Istruzioni e relazioni degli Ambasciatori genovesi in Spagna*, Rome, Istituto Storico Italiano per l'età moderna e contemporanea, 1957.

Conti, V., *Consociatio Civitatum. Le repubbliche nei testi elzeviriani (1625–1649)*, Florence, Centro Editoriale Toscano, 1997.

Cosandey, Fanny and Robert Decimon, *L'Absolutisme en France. Histoire et historiographie*, Paris, Seuil, 2002.

Costantini, Claudio, *La repubblica di Genova nell'età moderna*, Turin, Utet, 1978.

——, "Politica e storiografia: l'epoca dei grandi repubblichisti", in *La letteratura ligure. La Repubblica aristocratica (1528–1797)*, Genoa, Costa & Nolan, 1992, vol. II, pp. 93–135.

Davids, K. and J. Lucassen (eds.), *A Miracle Mirrored: The Dutch Republic in European Perspective*, Cambridge, Cambridge University Press, 1995.

Dekker, R., "Complots dans la république des Provinces-Unies au XVIIe siècle", in Y.M. Bercé and E. Fasano Guarini (eds.), *Complots et conjurations dans l'Europe Moderne*, Rome, Ecole Française de Rome, 1996, pp. 579–595.

Durand, Yves, *Les républiques au temps des monarchies*, Paris, PUF, 1973.

Echevarría Bacigalupe, Miguel Angel, *Flandes y la Monarquía Hispánica (1500–1713)*, Madrid, Sílex, 1998.

Fernández Albaladejo, Pablo, "Católicos antes que ciudadanos. Gestación de una 'política española' en los comienzos de la Edad Moderna", in J.I. Fortea Pérez (ed.), *Imágenes de la diversidad: el mundo urbano en la corona de Castilla XVI–XVII*, Santander, Universidad de Cantabria, 1996, pp. 103–127.

Gelderen, Martin Van and Quentin Skinner, *Republicanism: A Shared European Heritage*, 2 vols., Cambridge, Cambridge University Press, 2002.

Gelderen, Martin Van, "The Machiavellian Moment and the Dutch Revolt. The Rise of Neostoicism and Dutch Republicanism", in G. Bock, Q. Skinner and M. Viroli (eds.), *Machiavelli and republicanism*, Cambridge, Cambridge University Press, 1990, pp. 205–224.

——, *The Political Thought of the Dutch Revolt (1555–1590)*, Cambridge, Cambridge University Press, 1992.

Gil Pujol, Xavier, "Visión europea de la Monarquía española como monarquía compuesta. XV–XVII", in Conrad Russell and José Andrés Gallego (eds.), *Las Monarquías del Antiguo Régimen. ¿Monarquías compuestas?*, Madrid, Editorial Complutense, 1996, pp. 69–95.

——, "Republican Politics in Early Modern Spain: The Castilian and Catalano-Aragonese Traditions", in M. Van Gelderen and Q. Skinner, *Republicanism: A Shared European Heritage*, vol. I, Cambridge, Cambridge University Press, 2002, pp. 263–384.

——, "Concepto y práctica de república en la España moderna. Las tradiciones castellana y catalano-aragonesa", *Estudis* 34 (2008), pp. 111–148.

Grendi, Edoardo, *La repubblica aristocratica dei genovesi. Politica, carità e commercio fra Cinque e Seicento*, Bologna, Il Mulino, 1987.

——, *I Balbi. Una famiglia genovese fra Spagna e Impero*, Einaudi, Turin, 1997.

Grubb, James, *Firstborn of Venice. Vicenza in the Early Renaissance State*. Baltimore, Johns Hopkins University Press, 1988.

Haitsma Mulier, E.O.G., "Genova e L'Olanda nel Seicento: contatti mercantili e ispirazione politica", in R. Belvederi (ed.), *Rapporti Genova-Mediterraneo-Atlantico, Atti del Congresso Internazionale di studi storici*, Genoa, 1983, pp. 431–444.

Herrero Sánchez, Manuel, *Las Provincias Unidas y la Monarquía Hispánica (1588–1702)*, Madrid, Arco Libros, 1999.

——, *El acercamiento hispano-neerlandés (1648–1678)*, Madrid, CSIC, 2000.

——, "Las repúblicas mercantiles, ¿alternativa al modelo dinástico? Génova, las Provincias Unidas y la Monarquía Hispánica en la segunda mitad del siglo XVII", in A. Crespo and M. Herrero (eds.), *España y las 17 Provincias de los Países Bajos. Una revisión historiográfica (siglos XVI–XVIII)*, Cordoba, Universidad de Córdoba, 2002, pp. 189–228.

——, "La monarchie espagnole et le capital marchand. Les limites de la guerre économique et la lutte pour la suprématie dans l'espace atlantique", in Marzagalli, S. and Marnot, B. (eds.), *Guerre et économie dans l'espace atlantique du XVIe au XXe siècle*, Bordeaux, Presses universi- taires de Bordeaux, 2006, pp. 195–209.

——, "La finanza genovese e il sistema imperiale spagnolo", *Rivista di Storia Finanziaria*, 19 (luglio-agosto 2007), pp. 27–60.

——, "La red genovesa Spínola y el entramado transnacional de los marqueses de los Balbases al servicio de la Monarquía Hispánica", in Bartolomé Yun Casalilla (ed.), *Las redes del Imperio. Élites en la articulación de la Monarquía Hispánica, 1492–1714*, Madrid, Marcial Pons, 2009, pp. 97–133.

Holenstein, A., T. Maissen and M. Prak (eds.), *The Republican Alternative: The Netherlands and Switzerland Compared*, Amsterdam, Amsterdam University Press, 2008.

Huizinga, J., *Dutch Civilisation in the Seventeenth Century and Other Essays*, Fontana London, 1968.

Iñurritegui Rodríguez, J.M., *La gracia y la república. El lenguaje político de la teología católica y el 'Príncipe Cristiano' de Ribadeneira*, Madrid, UNED, 1998.

Israel, Jonathan I., "Un conflicto entre imperios: España y los Países Bajos, 1618–1648", in J. Elliott (ed.), *Poder y sociedad en la España de los Austrias*, Barcelona, Crítica, 1982, pp. 145–197.

——, *Dutch Primacy in World Trade, 1585–1740*, Oxford, Clarendon Press, 1990.

——, *The Dutch Republic. Its Rise, Greatness, and Fall, 1477–1806*, Oxford, Clarendon Press, 1995.

Kirk, Thomas A., "A Little Country in a World of Empires: Genoese Attempts to Penetrate the Maritime Trading Empires in the Seventeenth Century", *The Journal of European Economic History*, 25, 2, (1996), pp. 407–421.

——, *Genoa and the Sea. Policy and Power in an Early Modern Maritime Republic, 1559–1684*, Baltimore, The Johns Hopkins University Press, 2005.

Kossmann, E.H., "Dutch Republicanism", in *L'età dei lumi: studi storici sul Settecento europeo in onore di Franco Venturi*, vol. I, Naples, Jovene Editore, 1985, pp. 455–486.

Mastellone, S., "Holland as a Political Model in Italy in the Seventeenth Century", *Bijdragen en Mededelingen betreffende de Geschiedenis der Nederlanden*, 4, (1983), pp. 568–582.

——, "I repubblicani del Seicento ed il modello politico olandese", *Il pensiero politico*, XVII, 2, (1985), pp. 145–163.

Moatti, C. and M. Riot-Sarcey, *La République dans tous ses états: Pour une histoire intellectuelle de la république en Europe*, Paris, Payot, 2009.

Noordegraaf, L., "Domestic Trade and Domestic Trade Conflicts in the Low Countries: Autonomy, Centralism and State-formation in the Pre-industrial Era", in S. Groenveld and M. Wintle (eds.), *State and Trade. Government and the Economy in Britain and the Netherlands since the Middle Ages*, Zutphen, Walburg Pers, 1992, pp. 12–27.

Onuf, N.G., *The Republican Legacy in International Thought*, Cambridge, Cambridge University press, 1998.

Ovejero Lucas, F. *et al.*, *Nuevas ideas republicanas*, Barcelona, Paidós, 2003.

Pacini, Arturo, *La Genova di Andrea Doria nell'Impero di Carlo V*, Florence, L.S. Olschki, 1999.

——, "Grandes estrategias y pequeñas intrigas. Génova y la Monarquía Católica de Carlos V a Felipe II", *Hispania*, LXV, 219, (2005), pp. 21–44.

Pagden, Anthony, (ed.), *The Idea of Europe. From Antiquity to the European Union*, Cambridge, Cambridge University Press, 2002.

Pettit, Philippe, *Republicanismo: una teoría sobre la libertad y el gobierno*, Barcelona, Paidós, 1999 (1st English edition, 1997).

Pocock, J.C.A., *The Machiavellian Moment. Florentine Political Thought and the Atlantic Republican Tradition*, Princeton, Princeton University Press, 1975.

Prak, Maarten, *The Dutch Republic in the Seventeenth Century*, Cambridge, Cambridge University Press, 2005.

Price, J.L. *Holland and the Dutch Republic in the Seventeenth Century: The Politics of Particularism*, Oxford, Clarendon Press, 1998.

Rodríguez Salgado, María José, "Amor, menosprecio y motines: Felipe II y las ciudades de los Países Bajos antes de la revolución", in J.I. Fortea and J.E. Gelabert (eds.), *Ciudades en conflicto (siglos XVI–XVIII)*, Valladolid, Junta de Castilla y León, 2008, pp. 181–219.

Roorda, D.J., "The Ruling Classes in Holland in the Seventeenth Century", in J.S. Bromley and E.H. Kossmann (eds.), *Britain and the Netherlands, II*, Groningen, J.B. Wolters 1964, pp. 109–132.

——, "Party and Faction. The Riots of 1672 in the Towns of Holland and Zealand. A Trial of Strength between Parties and Factions", *Acta Historiae Nederlandica*, 2 (1969), pp. 188–221.

Rowen, H.H. (ed.), *Pomponne's 'Rélation de mon ambassade en Hollande', 1669–1671*, Utrecht, 1955.

Ruiz Ibáñez, José Javier and Gaetano Sabatini, "Monarchy as Conquest: Violence, Social Opportunity, and Political Stability in the Establishment of the Hispanic Monarchy", *The Journal of Modern History*, 81 (2009), pp. 501–536.

Sanz Ayán Carmen, "Negociadores y capitales holandeses en los sistemas de abastecimientos de pertrechos de la Monarquía Hispánica durante el siglo XVII", *Hispania*, LII, no. 182, (1992), pp. 915–945.

Schaub, Jean Frédéric, "El Estado en Francia en los siglos XVI y XVII. Guía de lectura para la historiografía de los años 1980–1992", *Cuadernos de Historia Moderna*, 14, (1993), pp. 225–241.

Secretan, Catherine, *Les privilèges berceau de la liberté. La Révolte des Pays-Bas: aux sources de la pensée politique moderne (1566–1619)*, Paris, Vrin, 1990.

Sismondi De, J.C.L.S., *Storia delle repubbliche italiane*, Turin, Bollati-Boringhieri 1996 (1st ed. 1807).

Skinner, Quentin, *Liberty before Liberalism*, Cambridge, Cambridge University Press, 1998.

Subrahmanyam, Sanjay, "On the Significance of Gadflies: the Genoese East India Company of the 1640s", *Journal of European Economic History*, 17, 3, (1988), pp. 559–581.

Swart, K.W., *The Miracle of the Dutch Republic as Seen in the Seventeenth Century*, London, HK Lewis, 1969.

Venturi, Franco, *Utopie e riforma nell'illuminismo*, Turin, Enaudi, 2001 (1st ed. 1970).

Vries Jan De and A. Van Der Woude, *The First Modern Economy: Success, Failure, and Perseverance of the Dutch Economy, 1500–1815*, Cambridge, Cambridge University Press, 1995.

Wooton, D. (ed.), *Republicanism and Commercial Society, 1649–1776*, Stanford, Stanford University Press, 1994.

Yun Casalilla, Bartolomé, "La aristocracia castellana en el Seiscientos: ¿Crisis, refeudalización u ofensiva política?", in Bartolomé Yun Casalilla, *La gestión del poder. Corona y economías aristocráticas en Castilla (siglos XVI–XVIII)*, Madrid, Akal, 2002, pp. 197–219.

——, (ed.), *Las redes del Imperio. Élites en la articulación de la Monarquía Hispánica, 1492–1714*, Madrid, Marcial Pons, 2009.

"A Thing Not Seen in Paris since Its Founding"

12

The Spanish Garrison of 1590 to 1594

José Javier Ruiz Ibáñez

1. The Spanish Monarchy beyond its Borders

The image is eloquent: some two hundred Spanish soldiers, banners held high, marching along the boulevards of a walled city, while spectators in the streets shout "*Long live the King of Spain*" and the legitimate prince of that town observes the parade from behind the fortifications. While such a scene could be deemed "normal" if happening in certain places, it is nothing short of extraordinary that it took place in Paris in 1590, and that the sovereign overlooking the march was Henry IV of France.[1] This event was perhaps the culminating moment of Philip II's reign; his troops were welcomed as liberators in the capital of the Monarchy that had been his father's greatest rival and would later vanquish his grandson.

Spanish military presence in Paris in 1590 was the clearest expression of the arrival of a new hegemony, one whose programmatic development was as yet incomplete, but whose leadership was centered on the Iberian Peninsula and whose mode of action surpassed the ordinary logic of a political confrontation among princes. The Catholic King, it seemed, would become a new "Father Abraham of many peoples,"[2] leading Catholics everywhere and uniting them under his guiding hand in their own Reformation and Counterreformation.

Today, more than 400 years later, we can legitimately ask whether this 'Spanish Paris' was a historical anecdote, or was it a reflection of a more enduring phenomenon that the historiography has so far largely ignored. Is it possible that the Spanish Monarchy suceeded in the sixteenth century not only because of the accumulation of resources and military might, but also due to its acceptance, indeed welcoming, by dissidents in other kingdoms who were seeking to influence or overthrow local govern-

This study was conducted as part of a broader research project entitled, "Hispanophilia: The Political Projection of the Spanish Monarchy (I): External Allies and Political Refugees (1580–1610) [HAR2008-01107] and (II): Policies of Prestige, Migrations and Representations of Hegemony (1560–1650) [HAR2011–29859-C02-01]" ["Hispanofilia, la proyección política de la Monarquía Hispánica (I): Aliados externos y refugiados políticos (1580–1610); (II) políticas de prestigio, migraciones y representación de la hegemonía (1560–1650)"]; Ministry of Science and Innovation, Spain.

ments, usually in the name of Catholicism? If this were true, it would imply that in a period of enormous political instability, brought about by the most intense phases of the religious confrontation in Europe, the Iberian Monarchy could find allies not only in England and France, but also in Switzerland, the German Empire, the Balkans, the United Provinces (the Netherlands) and even in extra-European territories such as North Africa, Japan, Georgia, the grand Chichimec and Chile's Araucania region. It would further suggest that if we have missed this point so far, it was because contemporary historiography, to a great extent the heir of national histories, was not interested in studying the global projection of the Monarchy. The Monarchy, if at all, was treated as a source of contention: instead of a constitutive part of the local scenery, its actions were reduced to a simple binary that made its agents "external" and that argued that the "national" community opposed them, or that classified those acting against the Monarchy locally as "loyal," and those collaborating with it, as "traitors." But this type of analysis obscures the contribution of extra-territorial expansion to the Monarchy's growing hegemony, and it avoids the question how commitments such an expansion entailed weigh down on imperial politics.[3] Moreover, taking this interpretative route impedes us from observing how external projection was also an opportunity to expand the Monarchy's borders by supporting allies both diplomatically and militarily, through direct interventions, many of which took place between 1588 and 1610 and were aimed at England, Ireland, France, North Africa, Southeast Asia and The Valtellina.

The interdependence between royal politics and external allies implied that on many occasions decision making that affected the Monarchy as a whole was located beyond its borders and was only partially under its control. Hence, although the resources at the Monarchy's disposal were indeed formidable, their application resulted at times, consciously or not, in policies quite different than those initially projected from Madrid. This factor influenced the ability of the Monarchy to intervene in foreign lands, and it explains its failure to convert political influence into successful territorial incorporations. To some extent, royal ability to obtain allies and pensioners was matched only by the difficulty the King encountered in controlling these individuals and groups. Wherever an external garrison, a King's ambassador, a "friendly" prince, or a rebel that swore to fight for the Catholic faith was found, what succeeded were processes of political rapprochement, alliances, dependence, support and commitment that thereafter determined the expectations, achievements and realities of imperial policy. It is high time we inquire into how such global phenomena propitiated this Hispanophilia, and determined its scope and effects.

Back to the Spanish garrison in Paris, this military presence demonstrates with particular eloquence the above mentioned processes. For contemporary observers, this was no minor event. Neither was a minor event the subsequent expulsion of the same garrison by a triumphant Henry IV in March 1594. This expulsion constitutes a critical chapter in France's grand historical narrative. Nonetheless, until the present there are no detailed studies of the garrison. It is mostly mentioned in secondary sources that serve only to corroborate its coming and going. But it is precisely this military presence in the French capital that may serve as a tool for understanding the contradictions embodied in the Monarchy's search for hegemony. For Philip II, the entry of the troops was an achievement that his father dared not even dream of: not only did he manage to convert the capital city of a rival kingdom into an allied town, but he also was able to deploy his soldiers there. This was a clear demonstration of how markedly the political scenario could change over a short period and how, in the context of a Europe replete with conflicting princes in the first half of the sixteenth century, Spain's preponderance seemed to rest upon a religious alignment that allowed it to bring former enemies under its leadership.[4] Given the scant importance that French historiography has given to the garrison, contemporary narratives that have been preserved to-date are indirect, often incomplete, and they tend to be reflected mainly in writings on diplomatic history.[5]

The objective of this chapter is to examine the garrison in order to gain a better understanding of the means that the Monarchy had at its disposal in order to project its influence beyond its borders, and of the consequences that this projection had for the political evolution of the Monarchy's allies in the late sixteenth century; in this case, the most important city in Europe[6] and the Catholic League as part of Philip II's grand political gambit of subordinating the kingdom of St. Louis to his Monarchy. During the period in which the Catholic king's soldiers were stationed in Paris, what was at stake was nothing less than France's political and dynastic destiny, as the conflict among the radical *Seize* movement (more or less pro-Spanish), the moderates and *mayennistes* (*grosso modo*, the supporters of the Duke of Mayenne, the League's Lieutenant General of France), and the *politiques* (defenders of Henry IV of France), was played out within its walls.[7] This confrontation reached its climax with the oft-postponed celebration of the General Estates of 1593, where the representatives of the Catholic king (the Duke of Feria, don Diego de Ibarra and Juan Bautista de Tassis) not only failed in their effort to have Isabel Clara Eugenia elected Queen of France, but also proved incapable of ensuring the election of the Archduke Ernest or some other French prince — preferably, the Duke of Guise –[8] as sovereign. This disappointing result does not fit the usual historical portrait that emphasized the more or less uncontested control of the city by the Spanish garrison and its fanatical allies; it is thus necessary to re-analyze this episode and determine the exact nature and extent of Spain's military presence in Paris.

2. The Garrison in Paris

The establishment of Spanish garrisons on French territory was not exclusive to the capital city. Spanish troops also collaborated militarily with the *ligueurs* in Brittany and Languedoc and would do the same at a later date in Pont-Audemer, Beauvais, Soissons, Meaux, Pontoise, Neufchâtel, Epernay, Ham, La Fère, La Cappelle and, though only momentarily, in Marseille.[9] However, as in Paris, this military presence was not a synonym of occupation. In fact, it would be incorrect to speak of true occupations until 1595, because before that date, Spanish forces — still dependent on the Catholic king's administration — were limited to supporting their French allies and were careful to leave effective control of the cities and territories in the latter's hands, mainly as a means of belying the propaganda of Henry IV's supporters who claimed that the objective of their intervention was to dismember the realm. Neither should the presence of Spanish garrisons be confused with the subsidies Spain granted to units that were under the authority of French rulers, as occurred in Paris during the siege of 1590.[10] Moreover, the presence of the garrison was testimony to the military weakness, not strength, of the League. The assassinations of the Duke of Guise and his brother, the Cardinal (December 23 and 24, 1588) in Blois, led to institutional contacts between the government of Brussels and radicals in the city of Paris who rebelled against Henry III and, after his assassination on the following first day of August, his successor, Henry IV of Navarre. Gunpowder arrived in the city from the Low Countries,[11] together with troops to support the League's army that had been destroyed at the battle of Ivry (March 14, 1590).[12] The siege of the capital that Henry IV orchestrated was the event that finally stirred the Catholic king to send troops. The news that the siege had been broken in late August 1590 reached the town in the form of two hundred Spanish soldiers sent by Alejandro Farnesio (the governor-general of the Low Countries) to deliver the first relief supplies. These were met with a euphoric reception by residents of that pauperized city. Although some of these soldiers would remain in Paris for the following months,[13] the retreat of the Spanish Army to Flanders, the proximity of Henry IV's troops, the failed attempt to conquer the town of Saint Denis, and a certain sympathy for the Bourbon king in the city, led the local *Parlement* to permit, on February 6, 1591, the entry in Paris of the foreign troops that were stationed nearby.[14] Taking advantage of the arrival of a supply convoy, on February 12th a decision was taken to leave some of the soldiers in this supply contingent in the city. The first to arrive were the Spanish,[15] followed by the rest of the troops.[16]

The size of the garrison oscillated between the original one thousand two hundred soldiers who arrived to the city initially and eight hundred men (Appendix 1) who remained, but these figures do not include the troops commanded by the Duke of Mayenne.[17] And, although both contemporary observers and modern authors tended to identify these two contingents as one unit, perhaps because they would later abandon the city together,[18] perhaps because it allowed overestimating the garrison's effective political and military weight,[19] it is nevertheless important to note that they did not form part of a single army. With the exception of the one hundred men who remained in the city,[20] the Spanish garrison participated in the rescue of Rouen in 1592, before returning to Paris on May 24.[21] Despite the concern expressed by Spanish ambassadors and the early arrival of some troops,[22] the disastrous situation in Flanders[23] impeded sending reinforcements in 1593 and 1594, except for a few hundred German soldiers. During this period, Mayenne feared losing control of the city, and thus did everything in his power to strengthen the troops under his direct command.[24] Following this rational, at one point he even sought to have the Spanish garrison expelled.[25]

Like the Flanders army,[26] the so-called Spanish garrison was organized by nationalities: in this case, Spaniards, Italians and Walloons. The Spaniards belonged to the *tercio* of Don Martín de Idiáquez or, more concretely, the Companies of Esteban de Legorreta (a veteran of the Invincible Armada who was serving as *gobernador*), Alonso de Mercado and a third Captain, as yet unidentified, and a few detachments from other units.[27] The Neapolitans were the remnants of the *tercio* of Pietro Caietano, which explains the high number of officials and gentlemen,[28] and of companies reduced to very few soldiers (some twenty units were reorganized into just eleven upon their return from the rescue of Rouen). As their Field Marshall was absent, command passed to don Alessandro del Monte, a Neapolitan aristocrat and brother of the Marquis of Corigliano. The three companies of Walloons (before the rescue of Rouen, there had been sixteen), were from the Balançon Regiment, commanded by Captain Saint Quintin.[29] The soldiers were billeted in barracks according to their country of origin: the Italians south of the Seine in the parishes of Saint Séverin, Saint Côme and Saint André des Arts, and the Spanish to the north, in Saint Germain l'Auxerrois and

Saint-Eustache "near the house of Roine," while some soldiers were lodged in colleges in the Latin Quarter that were deserted because of the war.[30] The military contingent in Paris was later complemented by the house of the Duke of Feria, the *hôtel de Longueville*, which was patrolled on a daily basis by a rotating guard of soldiers from the three nations.[31]

In theory, the garrison was to respect the authority of the Lieutenant General and, therefore, that of the city's governor, but the final word was held by the highest-ranking Spanish diplomat present. Joint military command was exercised by del Monte and Legorreta, with the former holding a certain precedence. Both these officials were well regarded by the Spanish ministers, who recommended them to the court without reserve,[32] proposed that they serve as military advisers to the Pontifical delegate during his stay in Paris[33] and, in 1593, placed Legorreta in charge of the mission that was to advocate to the authorities in Flanders the urgent need for additional resources.[34]

The garrison had no intention of controlling a city, in which the main armed force was still the militias,[35] and where the Catholic king's troops held no strongly fortified positions, such as the Bastille or the Arsenal. This weakness was confirmed on the night of March 22, 1594, when measures implemented by the Spanish ministers to control the governor, Count of Brissac, failed.[36] Having changed his allegiance, the Count had re-opened the gates of *Neuve* to Henry IV. The garrison was unable to organize an effective defense because it was physically divided, with some elements deployed at the Duke of Feria's residence and the rest distributed in the various barracks assigned to the Spanish, Neapolitan and Walloons, while the German troops belonging to it were stationed with Mayenne. Counted together, these five separated units, joined by a dozen or so gentlemen that accompanied Feria, numbered no more than 700–800 men at that time. Entrenched in their lodgings and the nearby streets they controlled, these soldiers were isolated, separated from one another by the Seine, and thus incapable of coordinating their actions or supporting those of the more militant *Seize*.[37] After a tense night of negotiations, they agreed to evacuate the city. The convoy set out from the Duke of Feria's home and gathered on their way the Spanish soldiers at their barracks. Accompanied by don Diego de Ibarra, the troops than proceeded to Saint Denis street, where they were joined by the Italians who arrived from the left bank on Feria's orders. Once assembled, the entire contingent went to Saint Denis gate, where the celebrated scene of their exodus from the city took place, accompanied by the *mayenniste* garrison and a group of *Seize* radicals. The Germans and Walloons members of the garrison joined them later, though some may have taken advantage of the situation and deserted to the Bourbon camp.[38] The troops' miserable retreat continued under incessant rain until they reached Laon and La Fère, where they joined the debilitated Spanish army that was still operating in the north of France.[39]

3. Money, Bread, Politics and Discipline

Besides its military function, the Spanish garrison in Paris had an important political role to play: it demonstrated that the Catholic king was committed to the League and was a trustworthy and loyal member of it. For this reason, the image of his soldiers had to be beyond reproach; if not, both their own presence in the city and the interests of their lord would be jeopardized. However, because often the soldiers did not receive their pay in a timely manner, they attempted to obtain a living through other means. This was a perilous situation. In the eyes of his allies, disorders championed by the troops diminished the prestige and credibility of the Catholic King, one that he so sorely needed in order to bring his political plans in France to fruition. Initially, funds destined to pay soldiers' wages were sent directly to the city's *mayennista* administration, but payment was often late and incorrect. When on June 3 and 4, 1591, the soldiers went to the French governor — the Count of Belin — to demand their pay, the only advice they received was to collect it themselves from the burgers.[40] Although no such thing happened, to avoid greater disruptions and to bypass the assistance of their French partners (whom they openly distrusted), the Spanish Ministers stipulated on July 1 that their own officials would effectuate payments.[41]

Esteban de Ibarra, the Minister in charge of finances in Flanders, expressed his surprise to Philip II when he learned how terribly expensive it was to maintain the garrison.[42] He was quite justified in feeling that way because, if payment was made in a timely fashion, the monthly cost was a little over twelve thousand *escudos*[43] for about one thousand men.[44] Certain factors seemed to make this presence in Paris so expensive: for example, the soldiers "had to pay even for water"[45] in a city where prices were particularly high due to the blockade sustained by Henry IV's troops. To assure the soldiers' sustenance, Mayenne authorized payment of elevated supplementary wages on a *per diem* basis. Though this outlay was decreased by officials after Farnesio reestablished the garrison in the aftermath of the rescue of Rouen, it still constituted an enormous sum of money that was not habitual in soldiers' normal wages.[46] An additional, but by no means trivial, consideration was the cost of rations of army bread.

Because Spanish Ministers in the city gave priority to paying the soldiers,[47] soldiers were paid to the extent that the chronically scarce reserves in the Spanish treasury in Paris allowed. That is, despite contemporary Bourbon propaganda and subsequent claims made in the historiography[48] that insisted on Spanish Embassy's unbridled largesse, Philip II's agents in Paris experienced severe problems in coming up with sufficient amounts of cash. Money had to be procured either directly in Flanders or by exchanging currency at prohibitively high prices in the French capital through financiers who received letters of exchange drawn on banks in Antwerp.[49] By November 1591, the troops were owed substantial amounts of backpay: no less than 70 days' wages for the 1,044 members of the garrison. Worse yet, the soldiers had received no bread for three months.[50] Thus, ensuring the payment of troops became increasingly urgent. Upon his return to Paris, don Diego de Ibarra perceived the severity of the situation. He described the garrison as a group of hungry soldiers who, in his view, had maintained discipline only because of the timely actions of their officials. The Minister also proposed a plan to rationalize the cost of the garrison by limiting it to Spaniards and reducing the number of officials[51]. In a measure designed to announce a change in policy, in early December two soldiers of the Spanish guard were executed in front of their comrades because they had robbed two women who were leaving the city with safe conducts in hand.[52] At that moment, through the efforts of don Diego de Ibarra, a program of more-or-less regular relief payments was instituted (every 5 to 10 days). Between July 1, 1591 and March 18, 1593, the soldiers received eleven such payments in seven ordinary installments, as well as bread and some clothing worth a total of 104,743.02 *escudos* of the accumulated debt of 250,630.00.

Although it is possible to argue that despite delays and amounts owed,[53] for the standards of that time, the garrison in Paris was reasonably well paid, nonetheless, the lack of punctuality in paying the troops had immediate political repercussions. The most difficult moment came precisely upon the return of the garrison from Rouen. Though Farnesio had arranged the transfer of a sum of money to sustain the soldiers, the cash never arrived.[54] Disobeying their officers, the troops began to make incursions on the outskirts of the city where they sacked ecclesiastical properties, threatened merchants and peasants, and extorted money and goods from them. Some went so far as to seize a house on the banks of the Seine, at two leagues' distance from the city, where they set up a kind of custom's house, boarded boats and charged duties on the products that were transported along this key waterway, ignoring safe conducts signed by Mayenne, the governor, or the local council. In the words of the latter: "The townspeople are so irritated with them that they have been tempted on several occasions to take up arms and attack them, and this would have happened had the magistrates not impeded it . . . " The city sent a delegate, M. de Chaillou, to don Diego de Ibarra — who was absent — and Farnesio to inform them that "it had been resolved that there was no need for men of war, as [the people] preferred the fate of dying at the hands of their enemies."[55] They urged Don Diego de Ibarra that they be paid "so opportunely that none of them lack bread, and that they receive their complete wages because they cannot live on less."[56] Searching for ways to send money to the troops and put an end to the disorders, Farnesio received Chaillou with his most eloquent words at Spa on August 11.[57] Disturbances outside the city walls did not cease completely, however, as witnessed by the complaint of the provost (*prévot des marchands*) against a few soldiers to the Duke of Feria when he returned to the city in 1593.[58]

The troops were paid regularly from November 1592 until the arrival in the city of Henry IV, except for a lapse from April to June 1593 that coincided with another wave of disturbances.[59] Because of the direct connection between lack of payment and misbehavior, during the negotiations for the election of France's new king, in order to prevent the Spanish administration from losing credibility, decision was taken to do everything possible to pay soldiers in full.[60] Indeed, during the final moments of Spain's presence in Paris, more money was available thanks to thirteen advances worth a total of 87,007.2 *escudos* that were sent explicitly to "succor Your Majesty's men of war . . . ," though money was also spent " . . . on other things that were needed there,"[61] including Mayenne's garrison in the city.[62]

4. The Catholic King's Soldiers and French Policy

For the local urban population, the presence of a professional garrison under the authority of a foreign prince in Paris involved a double otherness. The acceptance of that presence can be explained by the genuine prestige that the garrison itself — and its king[63] — enjoyed, which made it not only tolerable, but even opportune and necessary. The most radical Catholics in Paris could see in the soldiers both allies and a precursor of the "just government" that they hoped to restore in their land. In June 1591, the *Seize* declared that had it not been for Spanish support during the siege, "Paris would no longer be Paris," and that "having thus [put an end] to the infinite hardships that God's enemies had inflicted upon the city that in the end would have ruined it and been its perdition without [the] said Majesty's men of war, who have shown that their King's orders were to preserve our religion and our city." Because of their virtues, the soldiers "engaged in normal conversation with our people as ordinary and natural citizens, as believers in the Church, and as Caesars in combat." For the king and his advisors, Spanish presence in Paris was an experiment in the administration of the empire that Spain yearned to establish. For the *ligueurs*, who warned of the dishonesty of the French accountants who were largely responsible for ruining the kingdom, the Spanish army's model payroll system was an example to follow.[64]

Radicals in Paris would have preferred a garrison made up exclusively of Spaniards[65] and would even have been willing to cede control of the Bastille to its members.[66] They expressed their positive, almost angelical view, of the soldiers in a famous letter sent to Philip II in September 1591,[67] and in their opposition to the removal of the garrison the following year.[68] However, this persistence did not imply stagnation. While in the beginning, the garrison was an instrument radicals used to oppose the *politiques* and *navarristes*, after the *mayennista* repression of the *Seize* in November 1591, radicals hoped it would impede a definitive pogrom against the *zélés* (zealots). But even ordinary citizens may have had interest in the presence of the garrison. Because they had assumed that these soldiers would maintain public order and defend the city, the Sorbonne wrote to Farnesio asking him to bring back the men sent to Rouen as quickly as possible.[69] Nonetheless, the presence of the soldiers in a city ever more divided between radicals and moderates was a novelty. After all, the garrison was highly visible and must have generated feelings of both attraction and rejection. Despite its privations, its members enjoyed substantial purchasing power that certainly caught the attention of a circle of people that extended far beyond those who had originally proposed bringing the troops into the city. As Pierre de l'Etoile narrates in his *Journal*, his own brother-in-law, M. de Gland, was commissioned to survey del Monte's three hundred Neapolitans.[70] As it turned out, these soldiers were consumers *par excellence*, who required all sorts of services, engaging from lackeys and errand boys[71] to wheat merchants like Jacques Forchet (Fouchet or Fochet), a sergeant major from the villa of Paris, gunpowder traders like Jacques Sulli,[72] and moneylenders.[73] Moreover, the garrison itself offered a range of services; for example, its resplendent companies dignified the arrival of the ambassador Feria[74] and the visit of the General Estates,[75] and festooned celebrations[76] and religious ceremonies (e.g., at the funerals of Farnesio and the Duchess of Feria).[77] The military displays and mock battles staged during training sessions on the quays of the Seine were a welcome diversion for a populace bedeviled by political-religious tension, disease, poverty and hunger.[78] Soon, the city was rife with adventurous and comic tales of encounters between soldiers and burgers that, while narrating their mutual attempts to abuse or take advantage of one another, in reality reflected the initial stages of the establishment of normal ties of interaction between an essentially male garrison and a civilian population familiar with the lay of the land whose resources the soldiers were rapidly depleting.[79]

The religiosity of the troops was another of the features that differentiated them from their hosts. Spaniards accompanied by their own chaplains and confraternities,[80] constituted a religious microcosm, and they viewed the French as backwards pre-Tridentines.[81] This was evidenced, for example, by an incident involving the Franciscan Yves Magistri de Laval who preached to the Spanish during Lent 1591 but who shortly thereafter was the presumptive author of a virulent anti-Spanish pamphlet that he was later forced to retract. Interestingly, the outrageous behavior he attributed to the Spanish garrison — an opinion shared in *politique* circles in Paris— referred, above all, to moral issues (sodomy, zoophilia, rape and robbery), and was less concerned with the political sphere.[82]

In the summer of 1593, the radicalization of political life, the meager pay that the troops had received, and the increasing marginalization of their radical allies, triggered multiple incidents, especially in the aftermath of Henry IV's abjuration. By that time, only the Spaniards' staunchest allies still saw them as the guardians of public order — however the term may have been understood — while more generally they were considered as an obstacle to peace.[83] It is significant that frictions first emerged in disturbances involving women. While clearly reflecting a growing discontent, it also demonstrated that things had not yet reached the stage of direct confrontation.[84] The two co-existing societies watched as their relations became increasingly tense and generated a growing estrangement.

The inrush of Spanish troops into a French city propitiated two obvious subversions of the urban order. Paris was at one and the same time a bourgeois corporation and an aggregate of subjects. Allowing the entry of a foreign garrison violated both the city's freedoms and the autonomy of its bourgeoisie. For contemporaries it is clear that such a political inversion could only have been brought about by some higher power: "pure zealousness in the service of God and his Holy Faith."[85] That is to say, although the garrison was clearly a political force, what was at stake in Paris was much more than the city's security. As a result, the garrison needed to perform constant balancing acts, in order to prevent Philip II's policies from losing the support of nobles and moderates, without at the same time disillusioning too greatly the radicals. That any move by the soldiers could be seen — correctly or not — as the expression of the political decisions taken by their lord can be proved by two incidents. The first featured the incursion of one hundred and fifty Spaniards into Suresnes in 1593, seeking to divest the deputies of their valuables while they were negotiating a treaty between royalists and *ligueurs*. The response was immediate. The active forces in Paris went to see the Duke of Feria and demanded that he ordered these soldiers to return. They also reproached him for what had happened, which they interpreted as a desperate attempt to boycott the conference. Feria defended himself by claiming that he had not ordered any such action, which he attributed to the delay in paying the soldiers. He then sent his Captains to order the troops to return.[86] The second incident occurred a short time later, when Spanish envoys decided to throw their support behind the Duke of Guisa's candidacy for the French crown and provided him with an honor guard, thus allegedly revealing the Catholic king's preference for that young aristocrat.[87]

Despite their shared sympathies with the *zélés*, the extent of the garrison's collaboration with that group barely exceeded that of cordial relations. Of course, the soldiers joined radicals when it came time to block the ascent of Henry IV and his defenders. They also supported the *Seize* in their attempts to forestall the making of accords in the city,[88] but they were not particularly involved or effective in the confrontation between radicals and moderates. Because Ibarra was absent during this confrontation, despite requests on the part of the *Seize*, Legorreta and Del Monte chose to act prudently and refused to allow their troops to become involved in a Saint Barthélemy of *politiques* after the execution of President Brisson on November 25, 1591.[89] After

Mayenne's counterattack on December 4–5 that eliminated the radical leaders, don Diego, recently returned to the city, not only ordered the soldiers to their barracks, but also convinced the *Seize* not to take up arms by warning them that they could not count on Spanish support.[90] It is thus possible that the only accomplishment that can be attributed to the Spanish military presence in Paris was that it prevented the taking of even more severe retaliations against its allies.[91]

The garrison's diplomats and soldiers were well aware of the contradictory nature of the situation. Ibarra considered that the only way to secure the French cities was for the Catholic king's garrisons to take effective control of them.[92] But one of his gentlemen — and later chronicler — later argued that the only real solution would have been to provoke a rebellion by Catholics, expel the *politiques* from the city or, better still, "throw them in the river with rocks around their necks," and see that the city's gates would be patrolled by the Catholic king's forces.[93] Such actions, however, would have involved modifying the garrison's mandate by changing it from an ally and instrument of the League, into a leader of the struggle against Henry IV and the moderates. This did not happen. The garrison remained in Paris to demonstrate the Spanish king's commitment to that city, but beyond such dissuasive functions, the political actions taken by the troops were disappointingly limited, for example, the brief detention of the priest Chavagnac of Saint Sulpice by the Neapolitans.[94] As conditions worsened, in August 1593 the *zélés* asked the Neapolitans to parade, their drums booming, and drown out the proclamation of the truce signed with Henry IV.[95]

Thus, the garrison was sufficiently strong to make its presence felt, but too limited to play any decisive role in French politics. In the view of Spain's ambassadors, the only way for the garrison to exercise any real influence on the States would have been to station the Flanders army near the city.[96] However, as this did not happen, all soldiers could do was to play a testimonial role amidst the jealousies of French authorities with whom relations were crumbling rapidly. Apart from the parliament's attempts to force the garrison to leave,[97] the most serious incident involving local authorities occurred two weeks before Henry IV's entrance into the central square, when it became clear that Captain Saint Quintin had conspired with Henry IV to facilitate his return to the city, which is why he was subsequently taken prisoner. Governor Brissac, who may have been in on the plot too, attempted to free Saint Quintin from the Duke of Feria's house, but the latter's firm posture, the twelve gentlemen who accompanied him, and Alonso de Mercado's company that was on guard duty that day at the embassy, dissuaded him.[98] Retrospectively, this was the last opportunity of the garrison to lead an uprising of radicals against moderates.[99] After it was over, all that the soldier could do was to wait, weapons in hand, for an attack by the *politiques* or, alternatively, Henry IV's entrance to Paris. When the latter occurred, the only coordination with the residual *Seize* consisted in simple exchanges of information.[100]

Conclusion

The soldiers who proudly paraded out of Paris on March 23, 1594, banners on high as they passed in front of Henry IV, closed the circle that had opened in 1590 with the arrival of the first two hundred Spaniards. Never before had the Spanish Monarchy enjoyed such a capacity for projection, nor would it ever again. National histories soon catalogued the garrison's presence in Paris as a venal pathology that occurred during a time of insanity. As a result, the episode has failed to draw the interest of historians. But the history of the Spanish garrison in Paris is revealing of other fiascos that the Monarchy had suffered in its attempts to extend its hegemony, and can help us understand its global policy. In the French case and, more concretely, in that of Paris, the charisma that the Catholic king yearned to attain and that his associates attributed to him, made it unthinkable to abandon allies who sought his help and whose support promised brilliant political expectations. However, supporting allies came at an enormous financial expense and often proved insufficient, even counterproductive, as it brought to light the contradictions of local politics. The truth was that no real French ally ever existed, only various factions that were struggling to define, and capitalize on, Spain's aid, each according to its own political agenda. Committed to maintaining collaboration with all these groups, the garrison could not be used to sustain the local hegemony of the Monarchy's closest ally, the minority *Seize* (*espagnolissans*). It thus remained, in a certain sense, a hostage of global diplomacy. The Monarchy failed to find a *tertium quid* willing to contribute with its interests and the aspirations of the French nobility. Thus, its policy of hegemony became a prisoner of itself at the cost of consuming resources that were becoming ever scarcer. Furthermore, some effects of the military presence in Paris were clearly counterproductive, as the enemy was able to take advantage of the obvious argument that the *ligueurs* were not defending any legitimate project but, rather, had simply sold out to the Spanish. In the end, the effort produced nothing but frustration as, paradoxically, the resources invested in France did not lead to consolidating a friendly regime, but actually helped a government characterized by Hispanophobia to take power. This particular process played itself out in Paris, but in one way or another, and despite certain unique features in each case, can also be detected in other areas of late sixteenth-century monarchic expansion (England, Ireland, Japan, Araucania). As a result, what is presented here as a case study may in fact be just one example — perhaps the most spectacular and unknown of all — of the Monarchy's global ambitions, also reflecting its transition from an expanding power fueled by militant religious leadership to a realm that met its limits at the borders of its political rivals.

Appendices

**1. Composition of the Spanish garrison in Paris, February 16, 1593
(AGS Ek 1588, 86)**

	Captains	*Ensigns*	*Sergeants Officials*	*Minor*	*Soldiers*	*Total*
Spaniards	3	3	3	17	190	216
Italians	10	11	11	40	320	392
Walloons	3	2	9	10	320	344
Total	16	16	23	67	828	950

2. Daily relief payments authorized by the Dukes of Mayenne and Farnesio for the Paris garrison, in *escudos* of 50 *patards* (AGS Ek 1588, 86)

Relief authorized by		Military positions and amount of daily support received
Farnesio	Mayenne	
7.2	9.6	Governor
3.6	4.8	Captain Sergeant Major
1.8	2.4	Ensign Aide Auditor
0.8	1.2	Sergeant
0.3	0.4	Corporal
0.6	0.8	Quartermaster
0.4	0.6	Chaplain-Major
0.3	0.4	Drum Chaplain
0.4		Drum Major
	0.4	Doctor Lieutenant-Captain of Campaign
	0.3	Overpaid soldier[102] Musketeer
	0.2	Soldier

Abbreviations

AGS	Archivo General de Simancas.
E	Estado.
CMC	Contaduría Mayor de Cuentas.
Plº	Pliego.
AGR/AR	Archives générales du Royaume/ Algemeen Rijksarchief (Brussels).
A	Audience (Papiers d'État et de l'Audience)/Audiëntie (Raad van State en Audiëntie).
SEG	Secrétairerie d'État et de la Guerre/ Secretarie van State en Oorlog.
AGI	Archivo General de Indias.
AHN	Archivo Histórico Nacional.
BNM	Biblioteca Nacional (Madrid).

Notes

1 Armenta y Córdoba, 1596, 24v–25.
2 Descimon and Ruiz Ibáñez, 1998.
3 Space here is insufficient to mention the various analysis of dissident Catholic groups of a more or less pro-Spanish bent. Consult the bibliographies in Descimon and Ruiz Ibáñez

(2005) and Pérez Tostado (2008). Specific studies of the Spanish Monarchy's global exterior vision — of unquestioned quality — have focused more on the negative cultural construction built up against it (i.e., the so-called Black Legend [*Leyenda Negra*]) than on the political opportunities generated; see, for example, García Cárcel, 1996; Hillgarth, 2000.

4 Vincent and Ruiz Ibáñez, 2007, 199–218.

5 Mariéjol, 1983, 364, 425; Vázquez de Prada, 2004, 371, 424.

6 On Paris at the time of the League, see Salmon, 1972; Barnavi, 1980; Descimon, 1983 and 1990; Barnavi and Descimon, 1985.

7 Descimon, 1983, 67–70; Descimon and Ruiz Ibáñez, 2005, 90–91.

8 Vázquez de Prada, 2004, 394–410.

9 A study that forms part of a wider inquiry into these interventions; on Brittany, the area most thoroughly studied; see Vázquez de Prada, 1998 and Tenace, 1996.

10 AGS CMC III 2906, "Cuenta y tanteo del pan . . . de don Bernardino de Mendoça . . . para el sustento de la infantería alemana . . . de guarniçion en Paris".

11 AGR/AR 1830–2, no number, April 30, 1589, Paris, "Les gens tenans le conseil general de l'Union des catholiques" to Alejandro Farnesio.

12 AGS E 598 39, April 4, 1590, Brussels, Alejandro Farnesio to Philip II; Armenta y Córdoba, 1596, 19–20; Vázquez de Prada, 2004, 347.

13 AGS CMC II 41, "Compañía de don Matheo de Muxica", file of Manuel de Aranduça.

14 AGS Ek 1578 83, January 13, 1591, Guisa, don Bernardino de Mendoza to Philip II.

15 AGS E 600 16, February 17, 1591, Brussels, Alejandro Farnesio to Philip II.

16 Etoile, 1875–99, IV, 100–1.

17 Etoile, 1875–99, V, 8; Vázquez, 1880, III, 176. AGS E 599 187, Artel, November 1, 1591, don Diego de Ibarra to Alejandro Farnesio; AGS Ek 1588 no. 84, March 18, 1593, Paris, "Relaçion de Juan Alonso Çerezo . . . " and 86; AGS Ek 1587, 28, April 6, 1593, Paris, Juan Bautista de Tassis to Philip II; AGS Ek 1585 49, June 6, 1593, Duke of Feria to Philip II, and 81, July 10, 1593, Paris, Juan Bautista de Tassis to Philip II; AGS Ek 1590 10, January 14, 1594, Paris, Juan Bautista de Tassis to Archduke Ernesto.

18 Etoile (*Supplément*), 1875–99, V, 334; Babelon, 1982, 589–590.

19 Babelon, 1982, 521: "Paris had never spoken with such vehemence since a detachment of 4,000 Spaniards and Neapolitans took over the quarters within its walls". In his partial edition of Armenta y Córdoba's version, Cloulas also prefers, though with certain reservations, the figure of 4,000 soldiers, despite the data in the abovementioned chronicle.

20 AGS Ek 1581 33, March 1592, "papel de don Diego de Ibarra para el duque de Parma".

21 AGS Ek 1585 49, June 6, 1593, Duke of Feria to Philip II; AGS Ek 1581, 73, June 1, 1592, Château-Thierry, don Diego de Ibarra to Philip II, and 72, May 30, 1592, Château-Thierry, don Juan Bautista de Tassis to Philip II.

22 AGS E 1599 183, November 25, 1591, Montcornet, don Diego de Ibarra to Philip II; 216, November 29, 1591, Paris, don Diego de Ibarra to Alejandro Farnesio; Vázquez, 1880, III, 13–15 and 165.

23 Etoile 1875–99, V, 157, 321 and 323; AGS Ek 1590, 31, February 26, 1594, Paris, Juan Bautista de Tassis and (35, March 4, 1594) don Diego de Ibarra to Philip II.

24 AGS Ek 1588 48, February 2, 1593, Paris, don Diego de Ibarra to Philip II; AGS Ek 1585 115, Paris, October 9, 1593, Paris, Duke of Feria to Philip II. AGS E 1589, 79, September 11, 1593, Paris, don Diego de Ibarra to don Martín de Idiáquez.

25 AGS Ek 1588 46, January 25, 1593, Paris, don Diego de Ibarra to Philip II; AGS Ek 1585 102, Paris, September 10, 1593, Duke of Feria to Philip II.

26 Parker, 1972, 27–31.

27 AGS CMC II 41, "Compañía de don Matheo de Muxica", file of sergeant Juan García.

28 Armenta y Córdoba, 1596, 60v.

29 Armenta y Córdoba, 1596, 26v.

30 Etoile, 1875–99, IV, 73: Etoile (*Supplément*), 1875–99, IV, 296.

31 Armenta y Córdoba, 1596, 49.

32 AGS Ek 1585 54 y 84, June 13 and August 16, 1593, Paris, Duke of Feria to Philip II; AGS Ek 1588 33 and 34, January 15, 1593, Paris, Diego de Ibarra to don Martín de Idiáquez and don Juan de Idiáquez; AGS Ek 1589, 50, August 7, 1593, Paris, don Diego de Ibarra to don Martín de Idiáquez.

33 AGS Ek 1581, 96, June 14,1592 and AGS Ek 1582, 14, August 5, 1592, Château-Thierry, don Diego de Ibarra to Filippo Sega.

34 AGS Ek 1585 135, Paris, October 13, 1593, Paris, Duke of Feria to Philip II; AGS E 1589, 78 and 79, September 11, 1593, Paris, don Diego de Ibarra to Philip II and to don Martín de Idiáquez; AGS CMC III 942, "Contabilidad de . . . Gabriel de Santiesteban, data", 17, September 11, 1593.

35 Descimon, 1993.

36 Etoile, (*Supplément*), 1875–99, V, 331–3; Vázquez de Prada, 2004, 424.

37 AGS Ek 1590, 50, March 28, 1594, Laon, Duke of Feria to Philip II; Armenta y Córdoba, 1596, 54–56; Babelon 1982, 585–590.

38 Armenta y Córdoba, 1596, 53–59; Carnero, 1625, 304b; Vázquez de Prada, 2004, 424–425.

39 Armenta y Córdoba, 1596, 58v–61; Coloma, 1948, 90–91; Carnero, 1625, 342; Del Monte: Vázquez, 1880, III, 421; AHN E Lb 253 fo. 197v, August 28, 1596, San Lorenzo, Philip II to Archduke Alberto. Legorreta died in Madrid in 1607 while serving as Field Marshall in the *Armada del Mar Océano*; AGR/AR SEG 18 fo. 301v, December 28, 1598, Brussels; Vázquez, 1880, III, 377. Mercado was sent to Puerto Rico in 1599 as governor, *alcalde* and Captain General (AGI *Contratación* 5788 L. 1 fo. 319v–321), but drowned upon his return to the Peninsula in 1602.

40 Etoile, 1875–99, IV, 102–3.

41 On the Spanish paymaster's administration in Paris: Ruiz Ibáñez, 2006. The information cited in the following paragraphs on the cash outlays made is reconstructed from AGS CMC III 942, "Contabilidad de . . . Gabriel de Santiesteban, data", and the private accounts of San Juan de Barrundia and Alvaro Ximenez Spinaredo; AGS E 343, 105; AGS Ek 1588, 86; AGS Ek 1589, 71 and 90; and AGS CMC II 41, no number, "Compañía de Matheo de Muxica", files of soldiers in Legorreta's company in Paris between 1590 and 1594.

42 AGS E 605 169 y 178, October 5 and 6, 1593, Brussels, Esteban de Ibarra to Philip II.

43 The monetary references in the text have been unified in *escudos* of 50 *patards*, the usual currency of the Flanders army in the decade of 1590.

44 The aforementioned sample from February 1593 calculated that the monthly cost was 10,440 *escudos* and that army bread (seven and a half *septiers* per day), added another 1,350 *escudos*; AGS Ek 1588, 86.

45 AGS Ek 1585 49, June 6, 1593, Duke of Feria to Philip II.

46 AGR/AR SEG 14 fo. 61, August 12, 1592, Spa, order of Alejandro Farnesio.

47 AGS Ek 1587 no. 28, April 6, 1593, Paris, Juan Bautista de Tassis to Philip II; AGS Ek 1589, 13, Paris, June 4, 1593, don Diego de Ibarra to Philip II.

48 Descimon and Ruiz Ibáñez, 2005, 91.

49 Robert Descimon and I have undertaken a detailed study of the finances of Spanish policies in Paris from 1590 to 1594.

50 AGS E 599 187, Artel, November 1 1591, don Diego de Ibarra to Farnesio; Vázquez, 1880, III, 21–22, 99 and 128.

51 AGS E 599 185, October 28, 1591, Artil-Soissons?, and 216, November 29, 1591, Paris, don Diego de Ibarra to Alejandro Farnesio.

52 L'Etoile, 1875–99, IV, 194.

53 AGS CMC II 41, no number, "Compañía de Matheo de Muxica", files of soldiers.

AGR/AR 17, fo. 269, March 12, 1597, Brussels: on the salary owed to Captain Alonso de Mercado.

54　AGS E 602, 85, June 2, 1592, Château-Thierry, Alejandro Farnesio to Philip II.

55　AGR/AR A 1830–2, no number, July 17, 1592, Paris, the village to Alejandro Farnesio, with the "Instructions baillees au s^r Chaillou . . . ". AGS Ek 1582, 15 and 26, Château-Thierry, don Diego de Ibarra to Philip II.

56　AGS Ek 1582, 67, November 1 and 3, 1592, Paris, don Diego de Ibarra to Philip II (quotation).

57　AGS E 602 129, August 24, 1592, Spa, Alejandro Farnesio to Philip II.

58　L'Etoile, 1875–99, IV, 225.

59　AGS Ek 1585 30, April 7, 1593, Paris, Duke of Feria to don Juan de Idiáquez.

60　AGS Ek 1585 49, June 6, 1593, Paris, Duke of Feria to Philip II.

61　AGS CMC III 942, "Contabilidad de . . . . Gabriel de Santiesteban", pl° 24a.

62　Correspondence between Mayenne and Feria on this matter from January 17 to February 3, 1594, in AGS Ek 1590 17 and 19.

63　Descimon and Ruiz Ibáñez, 1998 and 2005, Ch. II.

64　AGR/AR A 1830–2, no number, July 29, 1591, Paris, Council of the *Seize* to Alejandro Farnesio.

65　AGS Ek 1579 37, June 1591, Paris, *Avis des Seize de Paris*; and 62, 1591, Friar Matheo de Aguirre to Philip II.

66　AGS E 600 16, February 17, 1591, Brussels, Alejandro Farnesio to Philip II; from Descimon and Ruiz Ibáñez, 2005, 93–94.

67　AGS Ek 1579, 73, September 1591, the *Seize* to Philip II: "Men of war chosen from among your vassals from whom we receive such a grand [performance] for their religious zeal, bravery in combat and modesty among us".

68　AGS Ek 1581, 45, April 7, 1592, Paris, the *Seize* to don Diego de Ibarra.

69　AGR/AR A 1830–2, no number, April 14, 1592.

70　Etoile, 1875–99, IV, 82.

71　Armenta y Córdoba, 1596, 56v.

72　AGS Ek 1589, 90, October 30, 1593; AGS CMC III 942, "Contabilidad de . . . Gabriel de Santiesteban", account books of San Juan de Barrundia, June 30, 1593.

73　AGS CMC II 41, no number, "Compañía de Matheo de Muxica", file of Sebastián de Morales; AGS E 602, 129, August 24, 1592, Spa, Alejandro Farnesio to Philip II.

74　Armenta y Córdoba, 1596, 38.

75　AGS Ek 1585 34, Paris, April 8, 1593, Duke of Feria to Philip II.

76　Etoile, 1875–99, V, 163.

77　Etoile, 1875–99, IV, 96; L'Etoile (*Supplément*), 1875–99, IV, 342; Armenta y Córdoba, 1596, 51. AGS Ek 1589 97, Paris, November 16, 1593, don Diego de Ibarra to don Juan de Idiáquez.

78　Etoile, 1875–99, IV, 104 and 112.

79　Etoile, 1875–99, V, 127.

80　Vázquez, 1880, II, 484.

81　Vázquez, 1880, III, 96.

82　Etoile, 1875–99, IV, 153–4; Barnavi, 1980, 188.

83　Armenta y Córdoba, 1596, 49.

84　Etoile, 1875–99, V, 56 y 69.

85　AGS E 598 142, November 19 1590, Alejandro Farnesio to Philip II.

86　AGS Ek 1585 49, June 6 1593 Paris, Feria to Philip II.

87　Armenta y Córdoba, 1596, 48v.

88　Vázquez, 1880, III, 109.

89　Etoile, 1875–99, IV, 133–4; Mariéjol, 1983, 369; Barnavi and Descimon, 1985, 210–211; Vázquez, 1880, III, 152–3 and 157–8.

90 Mariéjol, 1983, 380–1; Barnavi and Descimon, 1985, 223–234; Vázquez de Prada, 2004, 381. Etoile (*Supplément*), 1875–99, IV, 310–1; Vázquez, 1880, III, 162–3 and 174–7. AGS E 599 216, 226 and 217, November 29, December 5 and 10, 1591, Paris, don Diego de Ibarra to Alejandro Farnesio; and 219, December 10, 1591, Paris, don Diego de Ibarra to Philip II.

91 AGS E 599 224, December 20, 1591, Landresí, don Diego de Ibarra to Philip II.

92 AGS Ek 1581, 47, April 11, 1592, Formentier, don Diego de Ibarra to Philip II.

93 Armenta y Córdoba, 1596, 51v–53v.

94 Etoile, 1875–99, IV, 178.

95 Etoile, 1875–99, V, 77.

96 AGS Ek 1589, 92, November 13, 1593, Paris, don Diego de Ibarra to Philip II.

97 AGS Ek 1581, 13, January 18, 1591, don Juan Battista de Tassis to Philip II.

98 AGS Ek 1590 44, Mars 20, 1593, Paris, Duke of Feria to Philip II, and 47, Mars 21, 1593, don Diego de Ibarra to Philip II. Armenta y Córdoba, 1596, 52–53; Etoile, 1875–99, V, 175.

99 Labitte, 1971, 234–239; Armenta y Córdoba, 1596, 53.

100 Descimon and Ruiz Ibáñez, 2005, 106–107.

101 N. T.: "Soldado aventajado".

Bibliography

Armenta y Córdoba, Damián de, *Los tres libros de la Guerra de Francia . . . 1596*, (BNM, ms 2126).

Babelon, Jean-Pierre, *Henri IV*, Paris, Fayard, 1982.

——, *Paris au XVIe siècle* en *Nouvelle Histoire de Paris*, Paris, Bibliothèque Historique de la Ville de Paris/Association pour la Publication d'une Histoire de Paris (diffusion Hachette), 1986.

Barnavi, Elie, *Le parti de Dieu. Étude sociale et politique des chefs de la Ligue parisienne, 1584–1594*, Lovaina, Nauwelaerts, 1980.

—— with Descimon, Robert, *La sainte Ligue, le juge et la potence. L'assassinat du président Brisson (15 novembre 1591)*, Paris, Hachette, 1985.

Carnero, Antonio, *Historia de las Guerras Civiles que ha avido en los Estados de Flandes desde el año 1559 hasta el de 1609 y de la rebelion de dichos Estados*, Brussels, Juan de Meerbeque, 1625.

Cloulas, Ivan, "Un témoignage espagnol sur la Ligue: Los tres libros de la guerra de Francia de Damián de Armenta y Córdoba (1596)", *Mélanges de la Casa de Velázquez*, no. 2, 1966, pp. 129–162.

Coloma, Carlos, *Las guerras de los Estados-Bajos, desde el año de 1588 hasta el de 1599*, Madrid, Biblioteca de Autores Españoles, vol. XXVIII, 1948.

Descimon, Robert, *Qui étaient les seize? Mythes et réalités de la Ligue parisienne (1585–1594)*, Paris, Federation des Societes Historiques et Archeologiques de Paris, 1983.

——, "Milice bourgeoise et identité citadine à Paris au temps de la Ligue", *Annales ESC*, 48/4, 1993, pp. 885–906.

—— with Ruiz Ibáñez, José Javier, "La imagen de Felipe II en la Liga radical francesa (1589–1598)", in Rivero Rodríguez, Manuel (ed.), *Felipe II (1598–1598). Europa y la Monarquía Católica*, Madrid, Parteluz, 1998, pp. 111–136.

——, *Les ligueurs de l'exil: Le refuge catholique français après 1594*, Seissel, Champ Vallon, 2005.

Etoile, Pierre de *Mémoires-Journaux 1574–1611*, Paris, Librairie des Bibliophiles 1875–99, Paris, XI vols.

García Cárcel, Ricardo, *La Leyenda Negra: Historia y Opinión*, Madrid, Alianza, 1996.

Hillgarth, Jocelyn N., *The Mirror of Spain, 1500–1700: The Formation of a Myth*, Ann Arbor, University of Michigan Press, 2000.

Parker, Geoffrey, *The Army of Flanders and the Spanish Road, 1567–1659. The Logistics of Spanish Victory and Defeat in the Low Countries' Wars*, Cambridge, Cambridge University Press, 1972.

Pérez Tostado, Igor, *Irish Influence at the Court of Spain in the Seventeenth Century*, Bodmin, Four Court Press, 2008.

Ruiz Ibáñez, José Javier, "Alimentar a una hidra: la ayuda financiera española a la Liga Católica en el Norte de Francia (1586–1595)", in Carmen Sanz Ayanz and Bernardo José García García (eds.), *Banca, crédito y capital. La monarquía hispánica y los antiguos Países Bajos (1505–1700)*, Madrid, Fundación Carlos de Amberes, 2004, pp. 181–204.

—— and Bernard Vincent, *Historia de España. Política y sociedad, siglos XVI–XVII*, Madrid, Síntesis, 2007.

Salmon, John H. M., "The Paris Sixteen, 1584–1594: The Social Analysis of a Revolutionary Movement", *Journal of Modern History*, no. XLIV/4, 1972, pp. 540–576.

Tenace, Edward S., *The Spanish Intervention in Brittany and the Failure of Philip II's Bid for European Hegemony 1589–1598*, Ph.D. dissertation, University of Illinois, 1996.

Vázquez, Alonso de, *Los sucesos de Flandes y Francia del tiempo de Alejandro Farnesio*, Madrid, Documentos inéditos para la Historia de España, 1880, 3 vols. (LXII–LXIV).

Vázquez de Prada, Valentín, "Un episodio significativo de las relaciones de Felipe II con la Liga: la intervención en Bretaña (1589–1598)", in José Martínez Millán, (dir.), *Felipe II (1527–1598). Europa y la Monarquía Católica*, Madrid, Parteluz, 1998, vols. I-2, pp. 923–952.

——, *Felipe y Francia (1559–1598). Política, religión y razón de estado*, Pamplona, Eunsa, 2004.

Epilogue

Epilogue
Polycentric Monarchies: Understanding the Grand Multinational Organizations of the Early Modern Period

Alberto Marcos Martín

This is a generational book, the work of a group of young historians who think and work in a new historiographical context. The different nationalities and academic backgrounds of the authors and their rich and varied scientific production reveal some of their principal concerns. Having matured intellectually in the 1990s at a time in which the political history of the 16th and 17th had undergone an important renovation, they have not only contributed to this trend in an outstanding fashion, but also added to it new dimensions. Their chosen object of study here is the development of the state in early modern Europe, most particularly on the Iberian Peninsula. The world they analyze was composed of the Spanish Hapsburg and Portuguese Monarchies, the two most complex and geographically extensive political entities during that period that would persist for the longest time and would be even united from 1580 to 1640.[1]

To approach the study of these two political constructions, the authors of this book adopt a vision couched in terms of global power (even world hegemony); they think not in terms of unitary nation-states, but of conglomerates composed of distinct dominions spread across the entire planet, and they examine long-lasting temporal currents and almost unbounded spatial milieus. Doing so, they reconstitute and make their own the vision of their historical subjects, the men who governed these entities who, without doubt, also thought about them in a global way. On the many occasions in which Juan de Zúñiga, Spain's ambassador to Rome and Gregorio XIII met in 1574, they conversed not only on Philip II's financial difficulties and the Pontiff's obligation to ease them by way of a Papal grace but also of the possible reconstitution of a league for the purpose of confronting the Turks; of events in France; and, more generally because of their direct impact on the interests of both parties, of "matters of the world".[2] Similarly, in 1630, Bartolomé Spínola emphasized "the general perturbation [and] distrust that runs across the globe with respect to credit and trade" as a means of raising the price of his services as *factor general* to Philip IV at a bleak conjuncture in which he promised to provide 666,000 *escudos* to Flanders and Germany, all the while intimating through his words that the economic crisis they were experiencing was one of a planetary scale, and that the difficulties that had to be resolved before credit could begin to flow again normally spanned the entire "international republic of money."[3] And, in 1652, when the Royal Council (*Consejo Real*) delivered Philip IV the good news of the surrender of Barcelona, it attributed the rebellion of Catalonia to a "universal commotion" that every kingdom and province of Europe had suffered since 1640. It also mentioned the situation of the King of Spain, who "was close to losing Flanders; [with] similar movements afoot in Naples and Sicily [such] that those vassals were on the point of changing their loyalty; the principal *presidios* of Tuscany had been won by the very Christian king [of France] and, with them, the door had opened for the French to infest and invade all of Italy; [while] Portugal absolutely refused to show obedience to [Your Majesty] when it crowned a tyrant as its king".[4] From the historiographical perspective, therefore, the only element of surprise is the persistence for such a long period — far beyond what nineteenth-century construction of modern national states demanded — of a nationalist focus as 'the' approach to the analysis of early modern political entities that, pondered from the vantage point of their own space and time, had virtually nothing 'national' about them.

Though the road still to travel is long, there can be no doubt that the essays presented in this volume foreshadow other contributions that will similarly supersede the national perspective adopted by so many historians. Because to abandon the "national," one needs to go far beyond simply substituting certain spatial frames of reference for others; the authors that penned the different chapters of this book were moved also by an ongoing concern to broaden the range of themes and problems that should be analyzed and they inserted in the very center, as an indispensable methodological principal, the comparative perspective. With this book, in short, they aspire to demonstrate the practical crystallization of all these elements and the analytical operability and strength of a concept-paradigm, which they title "polycentric monarchies", and which the editors set out to define, with special care, in the introductory pages.[5]

The historians who participate in this volume are not satisfied with concepts such as 'center' and 'periphery,' deeming them both insufficient and simplifying with respect to the goal of attaining an understanding of the relations among the diverse territories that constituted the Iberian Monarchies. They also question a second categorization, which posits contrasts between dominant and dominated countries, as they argue that such a vision only corresponds to a colonial view of early modern history that they, in general, reject. In their view even the term 'composite monarchies', which constitutes the starting point of their argument and to which they recognize a debt in both theoretical and methodological terms, must be revised or, at the very least, nuanced.[6] Hence, they propose we adopt a new concept, 'polycentric monarchies,' in order to analyze and understand the grand multinational organizations of the early modern period not only, as has often been the case up to now, from the perspective of their political centers (defined as the site where the sovereign resided alongside the central institutions of Monarchical government), but also from that of other 'centers', ones that pertained to the distinct territories that fell under the sovereignty of that leader. Each of these centers, they argue, was endowed with its own peculiar political-institutional complexity, its own juridical and historical status, and its own local power groups.

In his chapter, J. F. Schaub defines the Spanish and Portuguese Monarchies as "polycentric political-institutional systems". Although their union lasted from 1581 to 1640, giving birth to the most extensive empire known up to that time, it also made the internal structure of its principal partner, the Spanish Monarchy, even more complicated than it was before. And, although one partner was principal and the other not, the relations between both by no means entailed the subordination of the Portuguese to Spain. Quite to the contrary, the former maintained its autonomy in all areas and Lisbon became one of the indisputable centers of imperial organization, clearly conserving its status as the capital of the Crown of Portugal. What the incorporation of the Portuguese Crown did little or nothing to resolve was how the metropolitan possessions on the continent, on the one hand, and each one of the territories that made up the imperial domains overseas, on the other, would relate in the future to the political center that was now so firmly ensconced in Madrid. Exploring this fascinating issue in the setting of the archipelago of the Azores, the last Portuguese territory to recognize Philip II as king of Portugal, Schaub argues that this case sheds light on the political dynamics followed by the two empires during their union. In spite of the fierce resistance that the archipelago's inhabitants (*naturales*) put up at first, Spain's construction of a political system on the islands led to the crystallization of a "complex institutional stratigraphy," in which the authority of the military governor and the presence of Spanish soldiers were superimposed on existing institutions without suppressing any. As a result, the preeminent position of the local power groups that dominated local institutions was sanctioned from the outset. Whenever the governors found themselves embroiled with local institutions, for example, by intervening in the composition of municipal chambers or in the process of forming Portuguese militias, their pretensions encountered firm resistance in the form of recourse to the well-known instruments of jurisdictional protection and the presentation of complaints to the authorities in both Lisbon or Madrid.

Oscar Mazín's contribution to the book compares the incorporation of the New World with that of other territories, among other things, in order to determine the place that the Americas occupied in the Spanish Monarchy. As he makes clear, because the New World possessions were incorporated into the Crown of Castile as "accessories" (that is, not through a union denominated *aeque principaliter*), they lacked their own political constitution and, for juridical purposes, were considered parts fully integrated in the empire. As a result, Spanish America held a subordinate, even secondary, position within the complex network of the Monarchy. Yet, by the second half of the seventeenth century, increasingly important groups, both Indian and Creole, reinterpreted the reality of the conquest of the Indies and their incorporation into Castile, and replaced it with a discourse that emphasized the "aggregated" (*agregado*) character of those lands and their "voluntary" adherence to the Crown. Using these means, they sought to obtain a distinct status for their territories, based on contractual foundation and justified on the basis of loyalty and consensus that could also serve as to support the autonomy they had begun to claim, with great insistence. If after their incorporation to Castile, nothing impeded the Spanish Indies from sending representatives to its parliament (the *Cortes of Castile*), it was only in 1530 that Charles V finally granted Mexico City the seat that it had petitioned from 1520 (just as Philip II would do a few years later for the city of Lima). Nonetheless, due to a series of unforeseen events, this participation failed to materialize. In contrast, after separating from the Spanish Monarchy (1640), the Portuguese Crown did call representatives of its overseas territories to Court, in an attempt to consolidate the loyalty to the new Braganza dynasty. Goa, Salvador de Bahía and São Luís de Maranhão, as well as Angra (in the Azores) and Funchal (in Madeira), indeed sent representatives. Pedro Cardim uses this fact (as well as the absence of overseas representatives in the parliaments of the Spanish Monarchy) as a starting point to analyze and compare the political condition of the overseas territories of both monarchies. He demonstrates that the status of the different parties that made up each one of these two monarchies varied substantially, as did their respective rights and obligations. For Cardim, hierarchy and asymmetry were the best way to describe the way the Iberian monarchies governed the political-territorial organization of their states.

Both Mazin and Cardim stress that, from the very beginning, the European territories of both Monarchies were granted a higher rank than overseas lands, which were relegated to a secondary position. This was of vital importance. The category of each territory depended on the existence of political institutions capable of being molded into European forms; the contribution of its inhabitants to the totality of the political body; the worthiness of the noble families that resided there; and the distance in relation to the Court. The territory's mode of entry into the Monarchy and the date of incorporation were additional factors that weighed heavily when it came to assessing the rank of a particular locality. The secondary position that the overseas dominions occupied was thus fully justified, because they were spaces that had been won by 'conquest' (that is, were neither 'assimilated' nor 'aggregated', and therefore undeserving of political rights) and were located far beyond Europe's frontiers. That in the second half of the seventeenth century the capitals of the "State of India", the "State of Brazil" and the "State of Maranhão" (but none of the African possessions) were successively granted political representation in the Portuguese parliament (*Cortes*) may seem unimportant. After all, they were only three among many more territories that could obtain such a right. Nonetheless, participation by Asian and American cities in the Portuguese assembly gave expression to some very important developments, mainly, the capacity of some overseas municipalities and their governing elites to communicate and negotiate with the political center, confirming their sense of belonging to an imperial organization and their wish to participate in projects that were broader than their own, particular goals; their identification with both the metropolis and other parts of the empire; and their defense of prerogatives and rights susceptible of configuring a particular status that they wanted to vindicate.

Cardim alludes to the petition that the city of Salvador de Bahía formulated in 1673 to have its procurator at the Portuguese parliament occupy a seat in the first row instead of being relegated to the second, as Goa had done. Among the reasons that the political leaders of Salvador de Bahía, capital of the "State of Brazil," adduced to back their pretension were the successive demonstrations of loyalty to the Portuguese Crown, in particular, its support of the house of Braganza; its meritorious performance in the recent war against the Dutch; and the fact that the title of the regent himself, don Pedro, was "Prince of Brazil". According to both he and Rodrigo Bentes Monteiro, the representatives of Bahia were not remiss in recurring to an additional argument, one that they may well have considered even more decisive because it recognized the fiscal efforts that the city had made for several years in the form of contributions to the peace treaty with the United Provinces and the dowry of Catalina de Braganza on the occasion of her marriage to Charles Stuart. In the view of its governing group, the payments made to the king were not part of the pecuniary obligations to which the latter was entitled with no obligation to reciprocate in any way. Rather, according to their logic, these services were a factor that propitiated the city's integration into the political body. They were elements of the union that bonded the subjects/contributors overseas to the Monarchy. In light of their fidelity, they could expect recompense in the form of receiving the graces and mercies they solicited.

Bentes Monteiro also stresses the role played by the celebrations organized on the occasion of the infant Catalina's wedding. Reaffirming the political unity of the distinct parts of the empire, these were also meant to generate a sense of community with the new Braganza dynasty. Yet, implicating the vassals in the destinies of the Monarchy could also be achieved by other means such as paying taxes and other fiscal contributions, as the ones he examines. Armed with concepts adopted from the 'anthropology of sacrifice' and the historiography on the 'economy of the gift', he insists that instead of seen as obligatory — as most historians have considered them in the past – unidirectional transfers of rent by subjects-vassals to their king-lord may best be understood as signs of gratitude, benefit or recognition of the Monarchy on the part of its American vassals.

Juan Francisco Pardo Molero examines a particularly intriguing topic: the "freedom of the estates" in the particular context of the kingdom of Valencia in the sixteenth century. Rather than centering on formulas of resistance or doctrinal substrate, as many historians have done before him, he analyzes the practices that molded the kingdom's political pretensions. His contribution transports us to a land where the estates enjoyed a remarkable capacity for independent operations, as often happened in the territories subjected to the Crown of Aragon. Describing a political body bereft of its leader due to the absence of the king, this shortcoming or vacuum was compensated by ministers who represented the royal person and, simultaneously, by locals who, organized in assemblies or delegations, were capable of channeling their voices through institutional circuits. Pardo Molero argues that the estates assemblies of Valencia were the setting *par excellence* for political discussions, debates on public and private interests, the intentions of the Crown and other institutions, and the consequences they might have for the royal or vice-regal order. The resolutions taken by these bodies frequently led to new instances of debate, at times in small commissions with representatives of each estate or other institutions, either royal or estate-related. Discussions, for example, were transferred to the *Generalitat*, where they would be carefully prepared before being sent to the embassies in the Court for the purpose of manifesting local pretensions directly to the king, or petitioning him to remedy a certain situation that required his intervention. However, and despite their reiterated insistence on the right to send emissaries to the king — a position based on appeals to justice and reason- on occasions the estates also adopted a different discourse that justified their petitions on the basis of their loyalty and services to the crown. They judged this last recourse to be the fastest, most expedient way to gain the king's magnanimity as, when all was said and done, grace, rather than justice, was a better way to advance their claims. The question that remains unsolved is to what extent their continual recourse to negotiations and implorations on the margins of "justice" favored their real political participation or, instead, propitiated a behavior that better served the interests of the Crown by strengthening its authority.

Investments in public debt in the short- and, especially, long-term was also an instrument of participation and integration in the Monarchy, as well as a factor contributing to political stability and peace. The emission of titles of debt entailed a commitment to the state on the part of those who acquired them who were now linked to it through personal, vested interests. According to Giuseppe De Luca, this is what happened in Milan from 1570 to 1640. Purchases were not limited to members of the economic or political elites, or to ecclesiastical institutions. Quite to the contrary, a great variety of people placed their savings in such investments, which they considered 'solid', for they were backed by established fiscal resources. Moreover, the titles could be sold, exchanged, and even transmitted through inheritance and could not be confiscated. But most striking in De Luca's study is the conclusion that the increase in the volume of such titles in circulation seemingly exercised no negative effect on Milan's flourishing economy. There is no proof that after 1570 — the period that coincided with the increase in the scale of consolidated debt — there was any significant reduction in the amount of productive investments in Lombardy, a situation that contrasts sharply, for example, with that of Castile at around the same time, where the outlandish growth of public credit seriously damaged the course of its economy. In De Luca's opinion, public debt played a crucial role in maintaining the peculiar, long-lasting political stability of the Duchy of Milan through the seventeenth century. During this period, Milan was indeed the *only* Italian domain of the Spanish Monarchy that did not experience any uprisings or insurrections against the Crown.

Another theme common to many of the authors, and one that advances their retreat from historical analysis based on contemporary nation-states, is a shared interest in issues of internal circulation. As Jean-Paul Zúñiga accurately points out, the circulation of people inside the Hispanic Monarchy constituted a vector of imperial construction and a guarantee of permanence. Indeed, it was one of the very conditions of the Monarchy's existence. A complex tapestry of mercantile, aristocratic and religious networks fostered by the Crown crisscrossed the entire structure and endowed it with consistency, thus ensuring its preservation. In addition, just as mobility as a concept should not be applied exclusively to the movement of people, merchandise, mercantile and banking activities, information and ideas, the providences of government, administrative documents, agricultural and alimentary practices, imaginaries, for example, also moved through space. Furthermore, in Zúñiga's view, the study of circulation should not be restricted to a purely geographical sphere, that is, to the analysis of flows between different territories. Instead, it should also include a social dimension. Zúñiga puts this methodological proposal into practice in his study of the *raison d'être* and multiple meanings of the particular iconographic genre known as 'casta paintings', which emerged with great force in the first third of the eighteenth century in a clearly delimited zone to the south of the sierra Mexica. The significance of this art form, he argues, cannot be reduced to its role as providing proof of something that was clearly evident, that is, the appearance of new human phenotypes in the Americas as a result of circulation and relations — forced or voluntary– between men and women of different origins. The concept of 'caste', Zúñiga indicates, was at the epicenter of an authentic whirlwind of circulation that gave rise to a great many epistemological questions and that swept up not only people but also models and ideas that we must examine as a whole. He proposes to study how all these different circulations crystallized in the space of New Spain to produce such unique items as the 'casta paintings'. The clues to follow are provided by the very language that sustained and illustrated these, one that blended the noblilty's imaginary of blood with the botanical lexicon of plant hybridization, and theological considerations with phenotypical observations. As he demonstrates, a series of very different logics merged in that language, some taken from scholasticism, others from the aristocratic culture of Western Europe, the milieu of the slave trade, and contemporary experiences of contact with Asia and Africa in that first phase of globalization.

The sociocultural aspect of circulation is also the focus of the essay by Tamar Herzog. She proposes to prove how, and to what a degree, overseas expansion and the subsequent confrontation with the "other" contributed to the formation of European identities. Paying specific attention to Spain and Spanish America, she argues that what historians have traditionally identified as "national" or "proto-national" was in reality nothing other than a discourse on religion and civilization. She concludes that the distinction between Spaniards and Indians, on the one hand, and between the former and other Europeans, on the other, was not based so much on political, national, racial or ethnic factors as on religious and civic considerations. Belonging to a religion and a civic community — regardless of the categorization of individuals as 'Spanish' or 'Indian' — was what established differences, separating people who were 'good civilized Christians' from those who were not. Hence, more than designating a political community (as was the case in the Iberian Peninsula), in the Americas and, increasingly, also in Europe, the denomination 'Spaniard' became based on (and identified with) participation in a community that shared certain beliefs and life-styles. In other words, what actually distinguished 'Spanishness', Herzog emphasizes, was Catholic religious orthodoxy and civilization, and not a division into a nation or proto-nation.

Circulation was also a characteristic feature of many merchants and businessmen as well as the financial instruments that they used in their dealings. The expansion of trade over ever longer distances, alongside the flourishing of high finances in Europe in the sixteenth century — the latter a consequence of the sudden growth in the monetary needs of the nascent states with their pressing financial concerns — accentuated the protagonism of agents, who held such occupations, moved from place to place, established companies, maintained regular contacts with correspondents in other localities and markets, and formed mercantile and financial networks that spanned dispersed territories. Yet, although the role of the large foreign bankers (Germans, Genoese, Portuguese) who provided funds to the Spanish Hapsburgs' is well known, but much less appreciated are the actions of their colleagues in other territories of the Monarchy, where they also constituted a firm element of the imperial system. To fill this void, Gaetano Sabatini offers a study of the presence of the Vaaz, a Portuguese business family of Jewish origin, in Spanish Naples. According to Sabatini, their history is representative of the integration and conflict that characterized the presence of Portuguese businessmen in the Spanish Monarchy in the seventeenth century. Although reproducing some of the experiences families of similar origin settled in Castile since the sixteenth century had, their particular story was nevertheless distinct. Chronology differed, for rather than substituting commercial activity for financial services to the crown, the culmination of Miguel Vaaz' dealings in Naples (that centered, in principal, on commerce in wheat and satisfying that city's demand for grain but included also activities as corsair in the Mediterranean) came at the same time that he acted as banker and councilor to the Viceroy. This also meant that the rise of the Portuguese as privileged businessmen and lenders to the Crown began in Spain when their religious brethren in the kingdom of Naples were in demise.

However, the roads traversed by one and the other present many similarities, not only in terms of the typology and nature of the business activities they developed, but also with respect to forms of social mobility and the strategies implemented to obtain it; similarities that can be found, as well, in some of the elements that led to their downfall that were marked, as is inevitably the case with population groups plagued by problems of blood purity, by the use of the Inquisition as a weapon, and by social and political confrontations.

Diverse works published in recent years have referred to the significant mobility of the Spanish nobility in early modern Europe, emphasizing its 'transnational' character, while also stressing its capacity to forge relations with other nobilities and governing classes, especially in Flanders, France, Germany and Italy. These circumstances facilitated the cementing of family and solidarity networks among distinct power groups that, in turn, constituted an important element in structuring the Monarchy. Maintaining the imperial edifice, however, also depended on integrating other, more numerous local groups, as Enrique Soria Mesa demonstrates. Fomenting the integration of these lower power echelons through marriage propitiated opportunities for social ascendance, integrated royal office holders natives of other regions in the locality where they served and linked locals to the court. This became a means, indeed a necessity, for allowing the incorporation of thousands of families in cities and towns across Castile into the social and political fabric of the empire. All parties stood to gain from such marriages. The king's men, most of them noble, often received a substantial patrimony in the form of a dowry and/or inheritance and, in more than a few cases, also entailed estates (*mayorazgos*). On the other side of the equation, in return for their financial support, local oligarchs entered into unions with socially superior families, thus gaining social ascendance and, no less important, an increased capacity for future prosperity, especially if the new son- or brother-in-law had direct relations with the organs of the central administration, or an influential patron at the Court.

The final two chapters of this volume focus on the Spanish Monarchy beyond its borders, that is, on its projection to the exterior. Collectively they argue that the Monarchy was not only defined from within, but also from without. External definitions varied according to the identity of the political rival and/or ally. José Javier Ruiz Ibáñez sustains that the crowning moment of the Spanish Hapsburgs' Monarchy, which came towards the end of Philip II's reign, was founded not only on the resources that the Monarch had at its disposal, but also on the fact that the monarch was recognized as a key ally by dissidents in other lands, who considered his support and aid indispensable for achieving their own, local political objectives. At this stage, the opportunities the Monarchy enjoyed to project itself beyond its frontiers and reaffirm its hegemony were multiple, and they depended not only on the availability of men and resources under its command but — just as much or perhaps even more — on its capacity to construct a hegemonic ideological discourse and generate a soft power that its potential allies could accept. During times of maximum confessional confrontation, this power was founded, above all, on the recognition other territories and communities gave the Spanish king as the universal Catholic king and the protector of the true religion. The story of the Spanish garrison deployed in Paris from 1590 to 1594 that Ruiz Ibáñez studies is revealing because, while the entrance of a small contingent of Spanish soldiers into the French capital in 1590 may well have represented the culminating moment of Philip II's policies, its departure, just four years later, could be construed as a metaphor for the end of the Spanish Monarchy's hegemonic pretensions or, at least, as an example of the many failures that it had suffered in that period. As the author points out, the Spanish military presence in Paris is thus useful not only as for understanding monarchical hegemony in the late sixteenth century, but also for identifying the internal contradictions that would ultimately lead to the demise of the Spanish Monarchy, which up to then had been grown dramatically due to its vindication of Catholic militancy in battles with political rivals on its frontiers.

Finally, the contribution of Manuel Herrero Sánchez similarly debunks some of the most widely disseminated ideological prejudices and nationalist myths surrounding the study of early modern Europe. Herrero insists that elements of interrelation and dependence existed between the two political models — republican and dynastic-monarchical— that existed in the continent during this period. These, he argues, were much stronger in practice than the traditional historiography marked by 'republicanist' tendencies, which had an *a priori* inclination to stress the supposed exceptionality and progressive character of the republics, has recognized. The different institutions of the Republics, mainly Genoa and the United Provinces, which he examines, were greatly affected by their contacts, some friendly and marked by cooperation, others unfriendly and marked by confrontation, with the continent's monarchies. By the same token, the former constantly inspired or induced substantial changes inside the monarchies, all the while striving to maintain a balance of power in Europe and blocking absolutist tendencies that were surfacing everywhere. The study of the nature and development of European monarchies in general, and of the Spanish Monarchy in particular, will therefore benefit greatly from taking into account their relations with the Republics.

This highly suggestive volume is the latest product in the rich activity that *Red Columnaria*, a network of historians working internationally, has developed in recent years. Becoming one of the most vital and forceful research networks focused on the early modern, it has already achieved many of the objectives that it had proposed in late 2004, when its members decided to construct a new space for the exchange and circulation of ideas and proposals. Among their objectives was the internationalizing not only of research but also of the objects of study themselves, the superseding of national frameworks, a dedication to a post-national historical perspective, the utilization of multiple methodologies, the search for new forms of analysis, the creation of spaces for reflection, in which historians from all over the world would be invited to participate and, above all, the irrevocable commitment to understanding the past on the basis of its own logics, escaping anachronistic prejudice. It is now up to the critical reader to judge, and testify to, the success or failure of this ambitious enterprise.

Notes

1 See, for example, Gaetano Sabatini (a cura di), *Comprendere le monarchie iberique. Risorse materiali e representation of the potere*, Rome, Viella, 2010.
2 AGS (Archivo general de Simancas), *Estado*, legs. 923 and 924.

3 AGS, *Consejo y Juntas de Hacienda*, leg. 665 (consultation 15 July 1630). Aldo De Maddalena and Hermann Kellenbenz (ed.), *La repubblica internazionale del denaro tra XV e XVII secolo*, Bologna, Il Mulino,1986.

4 AGS, *Consejo y Juntas de Hacienda*, leg. 985 (21 October 1652).

5 As had previously been done by some members of the group in earlier publications; especially José Javier Ruiz Ibáñez and Gaetano Sabatini, "Monarchy as Conquest. Violence, Social Opportunity, and Political Stability in the Establishment of the Hispanic Monarchy", *The Journal of Modern History*, 3 (2009), 501–536.

6 John H. Elliott, "A Europe of Composite Monarchies", *Past and Present*, 137 (1992), pp. 48–71. On the paternity of the concept, shared with professor Koenigsberger, see, also by Elliott, "Monarquía compuesta y Monarquía Universal en la época de Carlos V", in Juan Luis Castellano Castellano and Francisco Sánchez-Montes González (coords.), *Carlos V. Europeísmo y Universalidad*. Vol. V, *Religión, cultura y mentalidad*, Madrid, Sociedad Estatal para la Conmemoración de los Centenarios de Felipe II y Carlos V, 2001, pp. 699–710.

The Editors and Contributors

Rodrigo Bentes Monteiro, Associate Professor, Universidade Fluminense, Rio de Janeiro, Brazil. Ph.D., Universidade de São Paulo, Brazil. Bentes Monteiro is principal investigator of the Conselho Nacional de Pesquisa (CNP) and a member of the work team of Companhia das Índias (UFF). Among his publications are *O Rei no Espelho. A monarquia portuguesa e a colonização da América 1640–1720*, São Paulo, 2002 and "Aparente e essencial. Sobre a representação do poder na Época Moderna", in L. de Mello e Souza, J. Ferreira Furtado and M. F. Bicalho (eds.), *O governo dos povos*, São Paulo, 2009. He is the editor of *Espelhos deformantes. Fontes, problemas e pesquisas em História Moderna. Séculos XVI–XIX*, São Paulo, 2008 and the coeditor of *Imperio de varias faces: relaçoes de poder no mundo iberico da epoca moderna*, São Paulo, 2009.

Pedro Cardim, Associate Professor, Universidade Nova de Lisboa, Portugal. Ph.D., Universidade Nova de Lisboa and member of the board of Centro de História de Além-Mar. Among his publications are *Cortes e Cultura Política no Portugal do Antigo Regime*, Lisbon, 1998; *D. Afonso VI*, Lisbon, 2006 (with A. Barreto Xavier); "From Periphery to Centre: The Internationalization of the Historiography of Portugal," *Historisk Tidskrift*, 127, 4, 2007 (with M. Soares da Cunha); "Felipe III, la Jornada de Portugal y las Cortes de 1619," in J. Martínez Millán and M. A. Visceglia (ed.), *La corte de Felipe III y el gobierno de la Monarquía Católica (1598–1621)*, Madrid, 2008; "La jurisdicción real y su afirmación en la corona portuguesa y sus territorios ultramarinos (siglos XVI–XVIII): reflexiones sobre la historiografía," in F. Aranda Pérez and J. Damião Rodrigues (eds.), *De Re Publica Hispaniae. Una vindicación de la cultura política en los reinos ibéricos en la primera modernidad*, Madrid, 2008; "Una Restauração visual? Cambio dinástico y uso de las imágenes en el Portugal del siglo XVII," in J. L. Palos and D. Carrió-Invernizzi (ed.), *La Historia Imaginada. Construcciones visuales del pasado en la Edad Moderna*, Madrid, 2008; as well as an edited volume (with M.F. Rollo and A. I. Buescu), *O Terramoto de 1755. História e Ciência da Catástrofe*, Lisbon, 2008.

Giuseppe De Luca, Associate Professor, Università degli Studi di Milano, Italy. Ph.D., Università L. Bocconi, Milan. De Luca is also the co-editor of the Italian Financial History Bibliography online (http://www.cirsfi.it/bsfi.html), a member of the Scientific Board of the review "Studi Storici Luigi Simeoni", and sits on the Board of the Center for the Italian-Swiss History 'Bruno Caizzi'. He is the author of *Le società* *quotate alla Borsa Valori di Milano dal 1861 al 2000,* Milan, 2002; "Government Debt and Financial Markets: Exploring Pro-cycle Effects in Northern Italy during the Sixteenth and the Seventeenth Centuries," in F. Piola Caselli (ed.), *Government Debts and Financial Markets in Europe,* London, 2008; "Il potere del credito. Reti e istituzioni in Italia centro-settentrionale fra età moderna e decenni preunitari," in A. Cova, S. La Francesca, A. Moioli, C. Bermond (eds.), *Storia d'Italia — La Banca,* Turin, 2008 (with A. Moioli); and co-editor of *Il mercato del credito in età moderna,* Milan, 2010 and *Debito pubblico e mercati finanziari in Italia. Secoli XIII–XXI,* Milan, 2007.

Manuel Herrero Sánchez, Associate Professor, Universidad Pablo de Olavide, Spain. Ph.D., The European University Institute, Florence, Italy. He is the author of *Las Provincias Unidas y la Monarquía Hispánica (1588–1702),* Madrid, 1999; *El acercamiento hispano-neerlandés (1648–1678),* Madrid, 2000; "La monarchie espagnole et le capital marchand. Les limites de la guerre économique et la lutte pour la suprématie dans l'espace atlantique," in S. Marzagalli and B. Marnot (eds.), *Guerre et économie dans l'espace atlantique du XVIe au XXe siécle,* Bordeaux, 2006; the co-editor of *España y las 17 Provincias de los Países Bajos. Una revisión historiográfica (siglos XVI–XVIII),* Cordoba, 2003; and the editor of *Génova y la Monarquía Hispánica, Hispania,* 65, 220, 2005.

Tamar Herzog, Professor of History, Stanford. Ph.D., École des Hautes Études en Sciences Sociales, Paris, France. Among her publications are *Upholding Justice: State, Law and the Penal System in Quito,* Ann Arbor, 2004 (English translation of *La administración como un fenónemo social,* published in Spanish 1995 and in French 2001); *Defining Nations: Immigrants and Citizens in Early Modern Spain and Spanish America,* New Haven, 2003 (Spanish translation 2006); *Ritos de control, prácticas de negociación: Pesquisas, visitas y residencias y las relaciones entre Quito y Madrid (1650–1750),* Madrid, 2000 (French translation forthcoming); *Mediación, archivos y ejercicio: los escribanos de Quito (siglo XVII–XVIII),* Frankfurt, 1996; and *Los ministros de la Audiencia de Quito 1650–1750,* Quito, 1995. She is also the co-editor of *The Collective and the Public in Latin America: Cultural Identities and Political Order,* Brighton, 2000 and *Observation and Communication: The Construction of Realities in the Hispanic World,* Frankfurt, 1997.

Alberto Marcos Martín, Professor, Universidad de Valladolid, Spain. Ph.D, Universidad de Valladolid. Marcos Martín was director of the Instituto Universitario de Historia Simancas. Among his publications are *Auge y declive de un núcleo mercantil y financiero de Castilla la Vieja. Evolución demográfica de Medina del Campo durante los siglos XVI y XVII,* Valladolid, 1978; *Economía, Sociedad, Pobreza en Castilla: Palencia, 1500–1814,* Palencia, 1985; *De esclavos a señores. Estudios de Historia Moderna,* Valladolid, 1992; *España en los siglos XVI, XVII y XVIII. Economia y Sociedad,* Barcelona, 2000; and *Agua y sociedad en la Época Moderna,* Valladolid, 2009. He is currently in the process of writing a monograph on the financial makeup of the Crown of Castile, which is mainly focussed on the transfer of patrimony from Crown to Kingdom and vice versa.

Oscar Mazín, Professor, El Colegio de México, Mexico. Ph.D., École des Hautes Études en Sciences Sociales, Paris, France. Since 2002, Mazín is editor of the journal

Historia Mexicana. He is the author of *Entre dos majestades. El obispo y la Iglesia del gran Michoacán ante las reformas borbónicas, 1758–1772*, Zamora, 1987; *En torno a la Conquista, une anthologie*, Paris, 1995 (with C. Val Julián); *El cabildo catedral de Valladolid de Michoacán*, Zamora, 1996; *Gestores de la Real justicia. Procuradores y agentes de las catedrales hispanas en la corte de Madrid*, Mexico, 2007; and *Iberoamérica, del descubrimiento a la independencia*, Mexico, 2007.

Juan Francisco Pardo Molero, Associate Professor, Universitat de València, Spain. Ph.D., Universitat de València, Spain. Among his publications are *La defensa del imperio. Carlos V, Valencia y el Mediterráneo*, Madrid, 2001; *La guerra de Espadán (1526). Una cruzada en la Valencia del Renacimiento*, Segorbe, 2001; "Le gouvernement du royaume de Majorque et la régulation de la défense en Méditerranée occidentale (1500–1550)," in A. Brogini and M. Ghazali (eds.), *Des marges aux frontières. Les puissances et les îles en Méditerranée à l'époque moderne*, Paris, 2010; and "Obstacles à l'intégration des morisques du royaume de Valence: discrimination légale et résistance morisque," *Cahiers de la Méditerranée*, 79, (2009) (with R. Benítez Sánchez-Blanco).

José Javier Ruiz Ibáñez, Professor, Universidad de Murcia, Spain. Ph.D., Universidad de Murcia. Among his publications are *Las dos caras de Jano. Monarquía, ciudad e individuo. Murcia, 1588–1648*, Murcia, 1995; *Felipe II y Cambrai: el consenso del pueblo*, Madrid, 1998 and Rosario, 2003; *Les ligueurs de l'exil. Le refuge catholique français après 1594*, Paris, 2005 (with R. Descimon); *Historia de España, política y sociedad. Siglos XVI–XVII*, Madrid, 2007 (with B. Vincent); "Théories et pratiques de la souveraineté dans la Monarchie Hispanique: un conflit de juridictions à Cambrai," *Annales HSS*, vol. LXXXI, (2000); and "Monarchy as Conquest. Violence, Social Opportunity, and Political Stability in the Establishment of the Hispanic Monarchy," *The Journal of Modern History*, vol. LXXXI (2009) (with G. Sabatini).

Gaetano Sabatini, Professor, Università degli Studi Roma Tre, Italy. Ph.D., Istituto di Storia Economica Istituto Universitario Navale de Naples, Italy. Among his publications are *Proprietà e proprietari a L'Aquila e nel contado tra XVI e XVII secolo. Le rilevazioni catastali in età spagnola*, Naples, 1995; *Il controllo fiscale sul territorio nel Mezzogiorno spagnolo. Le province abruzzesi*, Naples, 1997; *Lo Stato feudale dei Carafa di Maddaloni. Genesi e amministrazione di un ducato nel regno di Napoli (secc. XVI–XVIII)*, Naples, 2009 (with F. Dandolo); and "Monarchy as Conquest. Violence, Social Opportunity, and Political Stability in the Establishment of the Hispanic Monarchy," *The Journal of Modern History*, vol. LXXXI (2009) (with J. J. Ruiz Ibáñez).

Jean-Frédéric Schaub, Professor, École des Hautes Études en Sciences Sociales, Paris, France. Ph.D., École des Hautes Études en Sciences Sociales, Paris, France. Among his publications are: *Le Portugal au temps du comte-duc d'Olivares (1621–1640); Le conflit de juridiction comme exercice de la politique*, Madrid, 2001; *La France espagnole. Les racines hispaniques de l'absolutisme français*, Paris, 2003 (Spanish translation Madrid, 2004); *L'Europe a-t-elle une histoire?*, Paris, 2008; "Révolutions sans révolutionnaires? Acteurs ordinaires et crises politiques sous l'Ancien Régime," *Annales*

HSS, 55-3 (2000); "Novas aproximações ao Antigo Regime português," *Pénélope*, 22 (2000); "Une histoire culturelle comme histoire politique," *Annales HSS*, 4–5 (2001); "História da Europa e histórias nacionais," *Ler História*, 50 (2006); and "La catégorie 'études coloniales' est-elle indispensable?," *Annales HSS*, 63–3 (2008).

Enrique Soria Mesa, Associate Professor, Universidad de Córdoba, Spain. Ph.D., Universidad de Granada, Spain. Among his publications are *La biblioteca genealógica de don Luis de Salazar y Castro*, Córdoba, 1997; *Señores y oligarcas. Los señoríos del reino de Granada en la Edad Moderna*, Granada, 1997; *El cambio inmóvil. Transformaciones y permanencias en una elite de poder (Córdoba, siglos XVI–XIX)*, Cordoba, 2001; *La nobleza en la España Moderna. Cambio y continuidad*, Madrid, 2007; and *Linajes granadinos*, Granada, 2008.

Jean-Paul Zúñiga, Associate Professor, École des Hautes Études en Sciences Sociales, Paris, France. Ph.D., European University Institute, Florence, Italy. Among his publications are *Espagnols d'outre-mer. Émigration, métissage et reproduction sociale à Santiago-du-Chili au 17e siècle*, Paris, 2002; "La voix du sang. Du 'métis' à l'idée de 'métissage' en Amérique espagnole", *Annales HSS*, n° 2 (1999); and "L'histoire impériale à l'heure de l'histoire globale'. Une perspective atlantique", *Revue d'Histoire Moderne et Contemporaine*, tome 54, n° 4bis (2007).

Index

Page numbers in italics refer to illustrations or tables; *n* after page numbers indicates a note.